Crop Production in Acidic Environment

Crop Production in Acidic Environment

Editor

Dharmendra Singh

Senior Scientist
Division of Genetics
Indian Agricultural Research Institute
New Delhi

CBS

CBS Publishers & Distributors Pvt Ltd

New Delhi • Bengaluru • Chennai • Kochi • Kolkata • Mumbai
Hyderabad • Nagpur • Patna • Pune • Vijayawada

Crop Production in Acidic Environment

ISBN: 978-81-239-2904-0

First Edition: 2016

Published by Satish Kumar Jain and produced by Varun Jain for

CBS Publishers & Distributors Pvt Ltd

4819/XI Prahlad Street, 24 Ansari Road, Daryaganj, New Delhi 110 002, India.

Ph: 23289259, 23266861, 23266867   Website: www.cbspd.com

Fax: 011-23243014   e-mail: delhi@cbspd.com; cbspubs@airtelmail.in.

Corporate Office: 204 FIE, Industrial Area, Patparganj, Delhi 110 092

Ph: 4934 4934   Fax: 4934 4935   e-mail: publishing@cbspd.com; publicity@cbspd.com

Branches

- **Bengaluru:** Seema House 2975, 17th Cross, K.R. Road,
  Banasankari 2rd Stage, Bengaluru 560 070, Karnataka
  Ph: +91-80-26771678/79   Fax: +91-80-26771680   e-mail: bangalore@cbspd.com
- **Chennai:** 7, Subbaraya Street, Shenoy Nagar, Chennai 600 030, Tamil Nadu
  Ph: +91-44-26680620, 26681266   Fax: +91-44-42032115   e-mail: chennai@cbspd.com
- **Kochi:** Ashana House, No. 39/1904, AM Thomas Road, Valanjambalam,
  Eranakulam 682 018, Kochi Kerala
  Ph: +91-484-4059051-65   Fax: +91-484-4059065   e-mail: kochi@cbspd.com
- **Kolkata:** 6/B, Ground Floor, Rameswar Shaw Road, Kolkata-700 014, West Bengal
  Ph: +91-33-22891126, 22891127, 22891128   e-mail: kolkata@cbspd.com
- **Mumbai:** 83-C, Dr E Moses Road, Worli, Mumbai-400018, Maharashtra
  Ph: +91-22-24902340/41   Fax: +91-22-24902342   e-mail: mumbai@cbspd.com

Representatives

- **Hyderabad** 0-9885175004   • **Nagpur** 0-9021734563   • **Patna** 0-9334159340
- **Pune** 0-9623451994   • **Vijayawada** 0-9000660880

Printed at India Binding House, Noida, UP

Contributors

Aski M
Scientist
Division of Genetics
Indian Agricultural Research Institute
New Delhi 110 012

Barua NG
Department of Soil Science
College of Agriculture
Assam Agricultural University
Jorhat 785 013, Assam

Baruah TC
Associate Dean
BNAC College of Agriculture
Assam Agricultural University
Jorhat 785 013, Assam

Bhardwaj SK
Department of Soil Science
CSK Himachal Pradesh Krishi Vishvavidyalaya
Palampur 176 062, Himachal Pradesh

Chaturvedi SK
Principal Scientist and Head
Division of Crop Improvement
Indian Institute of Pulses Research
Kanpur 208 024, Uttar Pradesh

Chauhan SK
Senior Technical Officer
Division of Horticulture
Krishi Anusandhan Bhavan II
Pusa Campus, New Delhi 110 012

Das KN
Department of Soil Science
Assam Agricultural University
Jorhat 785 013, Assam

Gautam NK
Senior Scientist
Division of Germplasm Evaluation
National Bureau of Plant Genetic Resources
New Delhi 110 012

Hazarika BN
Professor
College of Horticulture and Forestry
Central Agricultural University
Pasighat 791 102

Kalita N
Associate Professor
Department of Soil Science
College of Agriculture
Assam Agricultural University
Jorhat 785 013, Assam

Kumar A
Assistant Professor
Department of Wood Science
College of Horticulture and Forestry
Central Agricultural University
Pasighat 790 112, Arunachal Pradesh

Panwar NS
Assistant Chief Technical Officer
Division of Plant Exploration and
Germplasm Collection
National Bureau of Plant Genetic Resources
New Delhi 110 012

Patgiri DK
Department of Soil Science
Assam Agricultural University
Jorhat 785 013, Assam

Patiram
Former Head
Division of Soil Science
ICAR Research Complex for NEH Region
Umiam 793 103, Meghalaya

Raje RS
Senior Scientist
Division of Genetics
Indian Agricultural Research Institute
New Delhi 110 012

Rathore DS
Former Vice-Chancellor
CSK Himachal Pradesh Krishi Vishvavidyalaya
Palampur 176 062, Himachal Pradesh

Saharia P
Associate Professor
Department of Agronomy
BNAC College of Agriculture
Biswanath Charali, Sonitpur, Assam

Sehgal RN
Ex-Professor, Tree Improvement
College of Horticulture and Forestry
Central Agricultural University
Pasighat 791 102, Arunachal Prdaesh

Sharma Ph R
Professor
Department of Plant Breeding and Genetics
College of Agriculture
Central Agricultural University
Imphal 795 004, Manipur

Sharma VK
Senior Scientist
Department of Soil Science and Agricultural
Chemistry
Indian Agricultural Research Institute
New Delhi 110 012

Sharma SP
Director of Research
CSK Himachal Pradesh Krishi Vishvavidyalaya
Palampur 176 062, Himachal Pradesh

Singh D
Senior Scientist
Division of Genetics
Indian Agricultural Research Institute
New Delhi 110 012

Singh M
Division of Nematology
Indian Agricultural Research Institute
New Delhi 110 012

Singh NP
Director
Indian Institute of Pulses Research
Kanpur 208 024, Uttar Pradesh

Singh R
Senior Scientist
Water Technology Center
Indian Agricultural Research Institute
New Delhi 110 012

Yadav IS
Research Fellow
NRC on Plant Biotechnology
Indian Agricultural Research Institute
New Delhi 110 012

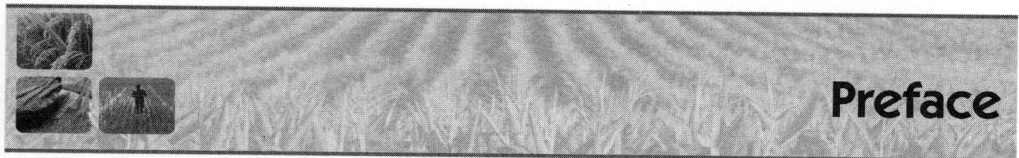

Preface

Soil acidity is one of the most prevalent problems in production of food and fibre. Approximately 30 per cent of the world's total land area consists of acid soils, and as much as 50 per cent of the world's potentially arable lands are acidic. In India, almost 25 million hectares of cultivated lands with pH less than 5.5 are critically degraded. The states occupying sizeable areas are Arunachal Pradesh, Chhattisgarh, Kerala, Assam, Manipur, Nagaland, Mizoram, Meghalaya, Uttaranchal, Odisha, West Bengal and Jharkhand, etc. The magnitude of loss in crop productivity varies with varying degree of soil acidity. The productivity of these states is very low due to aluminium, manganese and iron toxicities and nutrient deficiencies mainly phosphorus, calcium, magnesium and potassium. Although liming of acid soils can improve the productivity of acid soil, this is neither an economic option for poor farmers nor an effective strategy for alleviating soil acidity. Therefore, combining the use of acid tolerant genotypes with liming is often the most effective strategy for improving crop production on acid soil.

In this book we have attempted to review the present status and progress in the area of acidic soils which will be helpful for the scientists and students working on such aspects.

I would like to thank the authors for their outstanding and timely work in producing such fine chapters. I am also thankful to Dr SN Puri, Ex Vice-Chancellor, Central Agricultural University; and Dr DS Rathore, Former Vice-Chancellor, CSK HPKV (Himachal Pradesh Krishi Vishvavidyalaya), Palampur, Himachal Pradesh; for their advice, support, guidance, and encouragement during the development of this important book. I am also thankful to CBS Publishers & Distributors, for publishing this book.

Dharmendra Singh
Editor

Author Index

Contents

1 Crop Tolerance to Aluminium Toxicity: Current Status and Future Research Needs

Dharmendra Singh

ABSTRACT

Aluminium (Al) toxicity is the primary factor limiting crop production on acidic soils around the world. It is considered as the main abiotic stress that causes 25–80% yield losses in various crop plants grown on soils containing excessive aluminium contents. Aluminium toxicity can be reduced by application of lime. However, this is often not economically or physically feasible. An alternative is the search for genetic variability in the crop species and/or their wild relatives for Al-tolerance. This chapter discusses the effects of aluminium toxicity on plant growth, aluminium accumulation and distribution in various parts of the plant, target sites of aluminium toxicity, criteria for threshold and critical levels of aluminium toxicity, mechanisms of aluminium tolerance, physiological and biochemical parameters for aluminium tolerance, nutrient interaction with Al-toxicity and genetic and molecular bases of aluminium tolerance.

Key words: Acidic soil, Al-toxicity, crop tolerance.

INTRODUCTION

Soil acidity is one of the major problems for crop production in many parts of the world. Poor crop productivity and soil fertility in acid soils are mainly due to a combination of aluminium and manganese toxicities and nutrient deficiencies (mainly deficiencies in P, Ca, Mg and K). Among these problems, aluminium toxicity is one of the major factors limiting crop production in acidic soils. Aluminium, the third most abundant metal in the earth's crust, poses a serious threat to crop productivity in acidic soils. It covers approximately 40 per cent area of the earth's arable land (Ma *et al.* 2001). Aluminium exists in nature as mononuclear, polynuclear and also as low molecular weight complexes. However, mononuclear is considered as highly toxic as compared to other forms (Taylor 1991, Kinraide 1993). When the soil pH drops below 5.0, aluminium is solubilized as the phytotoxic Al^{3+} species from non-toxic aluminium silicates and oxides (Lindsay 1979). The mobility of aluminium increases sharply with the reduction in the availability of exchangeable cations such as Ca^{2+}, Mg^{2+} and K^+ (Parker *et al.* 1989). The high mobility of aluminium is seen in Kaolinite rich soils at pH levels as high as 5.5 (Alam and Adams 1979, Foy 1974, Roy *et al.* 1988). The toxicity will be acute at pH 4.1 in soils than at pH 4.5. However, in nutrient solutions, aluminium toxicity is more severe at pH 4.5 than at 4.0 due to the formation of $Al(OH)^{2+}$ ions, which are more toxic than Al^{3+} itself (Moore 1974).

Young seedlings are more sensitive to aluminium toxicity than older plants (Thaworuwong and Van Diest 1975, Rengel and Robinson 1989). Higher concentration of aluminium is highly toxic to plants and is detrimental to their growth (Foy and Flemming 1978, Haug 1984, Kochian 1995, Flemming and Foy 1968, Furlani and Clark 1981, Rhue and Grogan 1977, Sartain and Kamprath 1978). However, at low concentrations, aluminium in solution cultures was found to stimulate growth of sugarbeet (Keser *et al.* 1975), tea (Matsumoto *et al.* 1976), maize (Llugany *et al.* 1995), rice (Howeler and Cadavid 1976), wheat (Foy and Flemming 1978), eucalyptus (Mullette 1975) and peach (Edwards *et al.* 1976). Chenery (1955) has reported levels of Al as high as 200–500 ppm and it is considered necessary for the normal growth of the tea bush.

Some of the earlier workers (Kochian *et al.* 2004, 2005, Song 2006) have discussed mainly symptoms of aluminium toxicity, mechanism of tolerance and tolerance in plant root systems. Presently, I have discussed the recent progress and some uncovered aspects of aluminium tolerance in crop plants and have identified some critical areas that need further studies.

ALUMINIUM IN THE SOIL

In acidic soils, the total aluminium content ranges from 1 to 30 per cent (Lindsay 1979, Dragun 1988). Lietuvos and Diroozomill (1998) reported that in the neutral and lightly acidic soils, the amount of Al was lower than 10 mg kg^{-1}. At pH 4.0, the content of Al increases and may reach to 100 mg kg^{-1}. In Nagaland (India) soils, the exchangeable aluminium content was 7.1 mEq 100 g^{-1} soil with the saturation reaching up to 85 per cent (Kumar 1995). In general, in sandy loams and loamy sands of tropical areas (Oxisols, Utlisols and Alfisols) with pH values lower than 5.0, exchangeable aluminium may increase to 80 per cent saturation. In acid clay or clay loam soils at such pH values, the aluminium saturation would not be more than 20 to 25 per cent (Ariyanayagan and Griffith 1987). Kamprath (1970) reported that growth of most maize varieties was affected at the aluminium saturation of 30 per cent. Fox (1979) observed that yields of maize were reduced at aluminium saturation of 50 per cent. Aluminium concentrations up to 5 ppm in soils are not harmful but its concentration above 5 ppm becomes toxic (Singh, Unpublished results).

EFFECTS OF ALUMINIUM TOXICITY ON PLANT GROWTH

Germination

Aluminium does not inhibit seed germination but does impair the growth of new roots and seedling establishment (Nosko *et al.* 1988, De Lima and Copeland 1990, Henrickson *et al.* 1992, Singh 2001, Singh 2007). However, Klimashevskii (1972) noted that toxic effect of Al was apparent in the seed germination stage in pea.

Pollen germination is more sensitive to aluminium and it decreased significantly in the cultivars of tomato (Searcy and Mulcahy 1990).

Root Growth

The toxic effects of aluminium in plants start from the roots. The most prominent symptom of Al toxicity is the inhibition of root growth. The affected roots become short, stubby and lateral roots become peg-like or fail to develop and thus the whole root system fails to elongate (Foy *et al.* 1978, Singh *et al.* 2007, Singh *et al.* 2009) and acquire brownish coloration. Fine branches and root hairs are reduced and root system has a corraloid appearance. Root tips are the most Al-sensitive region, as have been demonstrated by exposing only certain regions of the root to Al (Ryan *et al.* 1993). Cracks can be observed in the epidermis at root apex. The yields of crops are affected as nutrient and water absorption by roots is reduced.

Inhibition of root elongation occurs due to disturbed mitosis in the apical meristem (Rhue *et al.* 1978) and it is inhibited within some minutes/hours after providing aluminium (Delhaize and Ryan 1995, Kochian 1995, Marschner 1991, Kidd *et al.* 2001, Llugany *et al.* 1995, Matsumoto 2000). Matsumoto *et al.* (1977) suggested that binding of aluminium to DNA was a potential cause for inhibition of cell division. Matsumoto and Morimura (1980) found that Al binds to phosphorus in DNA and prevents the double helix from separating to serve as the template for RNA synthesis. Both the rate of DNA synthesis (Sirover and Loeb 1976) and DNA template activity (Morimura and Matsumoto 1978) are decreased due to aluminium toxicity.

Shoot Growth

Shoot growth is often considered as a secondary visible symptom of aluminium toxicity and often similar to deficiencies of phosphorus, calcium, magnesium and iron (Foy 1984). Generally, the plant tops of aluminium affected plants appear as phosphorus deficient. This reflects aluminium induced dislocation of the plant phosphorus metabolism. Clark (1982) reported that deficiencies and toxicities may act independently or together to reduce plant growth.

Curling or rolling of young leaves and collapse of growing points of petioles are well-known symptoms of Ca deficiency induced by Al toxicity in crops (Singh *et al.* 2007). Foliar symptoms resembling phosphorus deficiency have small dark green leaves, yellowing and death of leaf tips, stunted growth, delayed maturity and chlorosis in soybean, rice and purple colour in petiole, abaxial leaf surface and stems in tomato (Wheeler *et al.* 1992, Singh *et al.* 2007).

Aluminium Uptake, Accumulation and Distribution

Aluminium tolerant plants have been classified into two groups (Watnabe and Osaki 2002), *viz.* non-accumulator (<400 ppm) and accumulator (>400 ppm). In the first group, aluminium tolerance is associated with less accumulation of aluminium in the plant shoot (Fageria and Carvalho 1982, Lidon *et al.* 2000), and such plants may entrap more aluminium in their roots as in rice, triticale, rye, wheat, barley and potato (Foy *et al.* 1978) and grass and cabbage (Huett and Menary 1980). Aluminium-sensitive cultivars generally accumulate more aluminium in the root than the aluminium-resistant cultivars in wheat (Tice *et al.* 1992), soybean (Silva *et al.* 2000), *Arabidopsis* (Larsen *et al.* 1998) and maize (Eticha *et al.* 2005).

In the second group, aluminium tolerance is associated with aluminium accumulation in plant shoot as seen in pine trees and tea (Foy *et al.* 1978), *Arnica montana, Deschampsia flexuosa* L. (Pegtel 1987), *Melastona malabathricum* (Watnabe *et al.* 1998) and *Hydrangea macrophylla* (Ma *et al.* 1997). These species are well-known aluminium accumulators and collect a large amount of aluminium in the leaves. Aluminium accumulating species detoxify the internal Al^{3+} by forming aluminium organic complexes. In tea leaves, aluminium is detoxified by catechin and phenolic compounds. In older leaves, the aluminium accumulation can be to the extent of 30,000 mg kg^{-1} against 600 mg kg^{-1} observed in young leaves (Matsumoto *et al.* 1976). *Melastoma malabathricum* L. is a woody plant that accumulates more than 10,000 mg Al kg^{-1} in its leaves in the form of monomeric Al and aluminium oxalate complexes (Watnabe *et al.* 1998). *Hydrangea macrophylla* can accumulate more than 3,000 mg kg^{-1} Al dry weight in its leaves (Ma *et al.* 1997) and it is complex with citrate. Buckwheat also accumulates (1500 mg kg^{-1}) high levels of aluminium in the leaves without showing any symptoms of toxicity (Ma *et al.* 1997).

TARGET SITES OF ALUMINIUM TOXICITY

Root Apex

The primary target of aluminium is localized in the root apex (Taylor 1995, Sivaguru *et al.* 1999, Ryan *et al.* 1993). The root apex consists of root cap, meristem and elongation zone which accumulates more aluminium and shows greater sign of physiological damage than the mature root tissue (Delhaize and Ryan 1995). The root tip accumulates more aluminium than other portions (meristem and elongation) of the root (Kochian 1995, Ciamporova 2002). Root tip is the primary region where toxic aluminium induces the inhibition of root growth and other plant parts of the root are not affected (Ryan *et al.* 1993, Kochian 1995, Delhaize and Ryan 1995). Principally aluminium accumulates in the root tips of the main root and lateral root tissues, with small quantities in the cortex and epidermal cells as shown by root staining (Matsumoto *et al.* 1976). However, Ryan *et al.* (1993) observed a greater penetration of hematoxylin stain for aluminium into the meristematic region. This indicates that highest accumulation of aluminium is observed in meristematic region.

Silva *et al.* (2000) found that aluminium enters cells of sensitive genotype and accumulates in nuclei in the meristematic region of the soybean root tips.

Cell Wall

In soil solution, aluminium first interacts with the cell wall and the outer face of the plasma membrane before passing into the cytoplasm. Several reports indicate that aluminium is localized in the cell wall (Clarkson 1967) and disrupts the function of the cell wall (Blamey and Dowling 1995, Wehr *et al.* 2004). Aluminium concentration is maximal in the cell walls and in the cell nuclei (Clarkson 1967).

Ma *et al.* (2004) found that more than 77 per cent of the total Al was in the cell wall of wheat root apices. Wang *et al.* (2004) reported that 85 per cent of the total Al accumulated in the cell wall of maize root tips. Major portion of absorbed aluminium is localized in apoplast varying from 80–90 per cent of the total tissue aluminium content (Rengel 1996).

Plasma Membrane

The plasma membrane of younger and outer cells in the roots was proposed as the primary site of aluminium toxicity (Wagatsuma *et al.* 1995, Horst *et al.* 1999, Basu *et al.* 1994) and disrupts the functions of the plasma membrane (Chen *et al.* 1991, Ishikawa and Wagatsuma 1998). Aluminium can bind to either cell membrane proteins or lipids, depending on the pH and other conditions of the surrounding cells and thus decrease the fluidity of lipids in the membrane (Foy 1983, 1984). This allows nutrient losses through plasma membrane (Ishikawa and Wagatsuma 1998) or cell walls (Blamey and Dowling 1995, Wehr *et al.* 2004), decreases nutrient uptake, *viz.* Ca, Mg, P and K resulting inhibition of plant growth (Foy 1983).

Symplasm

There is considerable evidence showing that Al may enter the symplasm quite rapidly (Lazof *et al.* 1996, Vazquez *et al.* 1999). It has been reported that 50–70 per cent of total aluminium might be present in the symplasm (Tice *et al.* 1992) and that aluminium can be present in the symplasm after only 30 minutes exposure to a solution containing Al (Lazof *et al.* 1994).

Initial target site of accumulation remains poorly understood and controversial (Kochain 1995, Matsumoto 2000, Yamamoto *et al.* 2001 Kochian *et al.* 2004) and there is a long-standing debate as to whether Al-toxicity is an apoplasmic or symplasmic phenomena. There is a need to reassess.

CRITERIA FOR THRESHOLD AND CRITICAL LEVELS OF ALUMINIUM TOXICITY IN CROP PLANTS

Root growth reduction of 50 per cent is usually considered a critical level for evaluating the relative aluminium tolerance of crops (Meda and Furlani 2005). The threshold level of the crop can be defined when root growth is not decreased significantly at particular aluminium concentration. Critical limits of different crops for aluminium tolerance at which 50 per cent reduction in root growth is observed (Table 1.1).

Table 1.1: *Relative aluminium tolerance in crop plants (Singh 2008)*

Crops	Threshold level[a] (Al, ppm)	Critical levels[b] (Al, ppm)	Category of tolerance*
Tomato	5.0	10.0	Sensitive
Pea	5.0	10.0	Sensitive
Cabbage	10.0	20.0	Moderately tolerant
Okra	5.0	10.0	Sensitive
Radish	10.0	20.0	Moderately tolerant
Onion	2.0	5.0	Highly sensitive
Chilli	5.0	10.0	Sensitive
French bean	10.0	20.0	Moderately tolerant
Rice	10.0	20.0	Moderately tolerant
Mustard	2.0	5.0	Highly sensitive
Chickpea	5.0	10.0	Sensitive
Corn	10.0	20.0	Moderately tolerant

[a] maximum aluminium concentration at which a crop has no significant root growth reduction.
[b] maximum aluminium concentration at which a crop has 50% root growth reduction.
* Categorized based on root growth in nutrient solution.
Source: Singh (2008)

MECHANISMS OF ALUMINIUM TOLERANCE

A plant is considered tolerant to aluminium toxicity when it shows improved growth and productivity under aluminium stress environments. Generally, plants have developed two types of mechanisms (external and internal) by which the plants cope up with aluminium stress (Taylor 1991, Kochian 1995, Rengel 1996). In exclusion mechanisms, the aluminium uptake is prevented by roots (Delhaize and Ryan 1995, Kochian 1995, Kochian *et al.* 2004) whereas in internal mechanism absorbed aluminium is detoxified. Several external mechanisms have been suggested of which the most important are: (i) exudation of chelating compounds such as organic acid or polypeptides (Kochian 1995), (ii) immobilization at the cell wall (Kochian 1995, Taylor 1991), (iii) Al efflux across the plasma membrane (Zhang and Taylor 1991), (iv) exudation of phosphate (Pellet *et al.* 1996, Zheng *et al.* 2005) and (v) formation of a plant induced pH barrier in the rhizosphere (Degenhardt *et al.* 1998). The exudation of organic acids by the roots such as citrate, malate and been shown to have a central role in exclusion of aluminium. Release of various di- and tricarboxylic acids form stable complexes with the aluminium present in the rhizosphere, reducing its toxic effects. Such complexes have shown that plants use this as a defense mechanisms against aluminium toxicity (Ishikawa *et al*. 2000, Kochian *et al*. 2005).

The internal resistance mechanisms are those which operate within the symplasm and are mediated at the cellular level either by detoxification or immobilization of aluminium ions that have penetrated into plant cells (Taylor 1995). The most important internal tolerance mechanisms are chelation with the organic acids in the cytosol, compartmentation in the vacuole, production of specific aluminium binding proteins and evolution of aluminium tolerant enzymes (Taylor 1991, Taylor 1988, Carver and Ownby 1995, Kochian 1995, Rengel 1996). For detailed literature, *see* reviews (Kochian, 1995; Taylor 1988, 1995).

PHYSIOLOGICAL AND BIOCHEMICAL PARAMETERS FOR ALUMINIUM TOLERANCE

Organic Acids

The release of organic acids from roots under aluminium stress has been identified as the most reliable mechanism for aluminium tolerance. Many scientists have reported that aluminium-tolerant crop genotypes release organic acids and detoxify aluminium in the rizhosphere (Miyasaka *et al*. 1991). However, it is still unknown whether the organic acid secreted is sufficient for detoxification of Al or not. Organic acid secreted from roots has varying ability to precipitate aluminium and reduce toxicity. Organic acids have been suggested to be secreted through an anion channel located on the plasma membrane (Ryan *et al*. 1995, Pineros and Kochian 2001). For detailed literature, *see* Chapter 5.

Callose

Callose (1, 3-beta-D-glucan) formation is an early, rapid, accurate and sensitive marker for screening the cultivars of wheat (Zhang *et al*. 1994), soybean (Wissemeier *et al*. 1992), maize (Llugany *et al*. 1994), rice (Meriga *et al*. 2003) and Norway spruce (Hirano *et al*. 2004) for aluminium sensitivity.

Callose accumulates in root tips after exposure to toxic levels of aluminium (Wissemeier *et al*. 1987, Zhang *et al*. 1994, Tomioka and Takenaka 2004). Aluminium-resistant cultivar produces less callose compared to aluminium-sensitive cultivar. Callose synthesis has been demonstrated to be a sensitive short-term (1–8 h) and short- and medium-term (8–24 h) indicators for aluminium injury in soybean (Wissemeier *et al*. 1992) and maize (Horst *et al*. 1997, Collet *et al*. 2002). Callose synthesis was positively correlated with internal aluminium concentration and negatively correlated with root elongation rate (Llugany *et al*. 1994, Horst *et al*. 1997). In contrast, Tomioka and Takenaka (2004) found that a positive correlation was observed between the relative root callose content and relative root length.

Mucilage

Polysaccharids are consisted of major sugar components like glucose, galactose and albinose present in plant cell wall and are excreted as mucilage by the roots. The root cap releases mucilage that binds and immobilizes the aluminium, and thus reduces the aluminium toxicity (Horst *et al.* 1982, Henderson and Ownby 1991). In cowpea, mucilage of an aluminium-tolerant cultivar bound more than one half of the total aluminium content of the apical 1 cm of root tips and its removal depressed root elongation in the presence of aluminium (Horst *et al.* 1982). Henderson and Ownby (1991) found strong correlation between root mucilage and root growth assay.

Photosynthesis and Transpiration

Photosynthesis is an important process through which plants can accumulate their own food that is carried out in all living green plants. In this process, the physical energy of light is used to convert chemical substances to a more energetic state (Salisbury and Ross 1992, Taiz and Zeiger 2002).

Suppression of the photosynthetic capacity of different plant species by aluminium toxicity has been reported in a number of studies (Haug 1984, Ohki 1986, Moustakas and Quzounidou 1994). Reduction in photosynthesis by increased aluminium toxicity could be due to partial inhibition of photosynthesis electron transport at photosystem II and closure of photosystem II reaction centers (Michael *et al.* 1995).

Aluminium stress decreases total chlorophyll concentration and photosynthetic rate in wheat, but the decline in transpiration rate is the most severe. In sorghum, photosynthesis and chlorophyll concentration were also decreased by aluminium but transpiration was increased (Ohki 1986). He also reported that reduction in growth, chlorophyll, photosynthesis and transpiration was negatively correlated with aluminium concentration in leaf blades in wheat. Loss of potassium (K) or calcium (Ca) ions from the membrane of the chloroplast envelops is associated with stomatal acidification and photosynthetic inhibition (Demming and Gimmler 1983, Moustakes and Ouzounidou 1994).

Enzyme Activities

In general, aluminium adversely affects several physiological activities producing a severe physiological stress which increases peroxidase activity (Peters *et al.* 1989). Increased peroxidase activity might be linked to a decrease in growth rate, as found in plants after treatment with aluminium (Cakmak and Horst 1991). Aluminium effectively interferes with metabolisms of cell wall polysaccharides, it may be related to the increase in peroxidase activity (Severi 1997). Subrahmanyam (1998) reported that aluminium increased lipid peroxidation activities of superoxide dismutase and peroxidase enzymes and reduced the activity of catalyse. Peroxide activities occur mostly at the cell wall where these enzymes have been suggested to module cell wall rigidity and extensibility, thus reducing the rate of aluminium diffusion through the cell wall (Hamel *et al.* 1998).

Carbohydrates

Previous reports suggest that the effects of aluminium on carbohydrates depend on plant species and aluminium concentrations. Graham (2002) reported that 1 mmol/L aluminium concentration for 8 weeks decreases glucose, sorbitol and total soluble carbohydrate content but increases the sucrose content in peach. Chen *et al.* (2005) found no difference in leaf carbohydrate content between Al-treated and control leaves but the demand for carbohydrates decreases in Al-treated leaves of citrus seedlings.

NUTRIENT INTERACTIONS

Aluminium toxicity is a complex event which may interfere with the uptake, transport and utilization efficiency of most of the mineral elements including Ca, Mg, K, N, P, Cu, Fe, Mn and Zn (Foy 1984, Roy *et al.* 1988, Taylor 1988, Simen *et al.* 1994, Foy 1988, Marschner 1991, Lazof *et al.* 1994, Ryan and Kochian 1993). Under some conditions, increasing concentrations of cations, *viz.* Ca, Mg, K, Na and Si in several plant species may alleviate aluminium toxicity (Camargo 1987, Kinaraide and Parker 1987, Alva *et al.* 1986).

Interaction with Nitrogen

In general, the nitrogen concentration in different plant parts decreased with increasing aluminium in nutrient solution. The decreases in nitrogen concentration in different plant parts is due to interference of aluminium in nitrogen metabolisms and translocation of nitrogen within the plant (Lidon *et al.* 2000). Nitrogen content of maize shoots decreases significantly with increasing aluminium concentration in nutrient solution (Pintro *et al.* 1996). Smalley *et al.* (1993) found that nitrogen content in the roots and shoots was reduced by aluminium treatments but leaf nitrogen was unaffected. Nitrogen content of longan stems increases when aluminium concentration in nutrient solution raises from 0 to 185 µmol/L, then decreases as aluminium concentration increases further (Xiao *et al.* 2005).

Interaction with Phosphorus

Aluminium toxicity has been associated with decreases in the uptake and utilization of phosphorus (Foy and Brown 1963, Pavan and Bingham 1982, Singh and Bhardwaj 2007). In some plant species, a decrease in the uptake and utilization of phosphorus is the primary symptom of aluminium toxicity (Mac Lean and Chiasson 1966, Singh and Bhardwaj 2007). Aluminium inactivates phosphorus, within the plant roots and thus renders phosphorus immobile as aluminium phosphate and unavailable to plants. The precipitation of Al-P was considered to be greater in the symplast than the apoplast (Ishikawa *et al.* 2003).

Aluminium usually increases phosphorus content of roots and decreases phosphorus content of shoots (Liang *et al.* 2001, Singh and Bhardwaj 2007). This is due to the formation of phosphorus (P) and aluminium (Al) complexes in root, which inhibit phosphorus transport from root to shoot and/or can be associated with the decrease in phosphorus active uptake due to aluminium induced decrease in the activity of ATP-dependent H^+ transport system (Liang *et al.* 2001). Fageria and Carvalho (1982) reported that phosphorus concentration and content decreased at higher levels of aluminium in the tops as well as in the roots. Lin and Myhre (1991) observed that phosphorus content of both roots and shoots of citrus rootstocks increases as the aluminium concentration in nutrient solution is increased from 4 to 178 µmol/L, then decreases as aluminium increases further. Xiao *et al.* (2005) found that phosphorus content of both roots and stems increases and decreases P content of longan leaves in aluminium toxic environments.

Some aluminium-tolerant plants have low phosphorus requirement while some cultivars absorb more phosphorus per unit root length as compared to aluminium-tolerant (Fox 1979). Sivaguru and Paliwal (1993) found that aluminium-tolerant cultivars efficiently absorbed phosphorus as compared to those that are susceptible. Howeler and Cadavid (1976) also observed that aluminium-tolerant cultivars had higher levels of phosphorus and lower levels of aluminium in their shoots than aluminium-sensitive ones.

Interaction with Potassium

In a number of plant species, aluminium toxicity interference with potassium is reported by many researchers (Sarkunnan and Bidappa 1982, Singh and Bhardwaj 2007).

Fageria and Carvalho (1982) reported that increased aluminium concentration of nutrient solution exerted on inhibitory effect on potassium concentration and content of rice. The decrease in potassium uptake due to the presence of excess aluminium in the medium was noticed in rice (Sarkunan and Bidappa 1982), pea (Wagatsuma *et al.* 1987), tomato and cabbage (Singh and Bhardwaj 2007) and cotton (Lance 1968). Lin and Myhre (1991) reported that potassium content of both roots and shoots of citrus rootstocks increases when aluminium concentration in nutrient solution increases from 4 to 178 µmol/L, then decreases as aluminium concentration increases further. However, some crops remain unaffected in this regard by aluminium (Cumming *et al.* 1985). Foy and Peterson (1994) noted that aluminium-tolerant cultivars have two to four folds more shoot potassium than sensitive lines.

Interaction with Calcium

The ability of aluminium (Al) to decrease Ca uptake and translocation in plants has been well-documented (Singh and Bhardwaj 2007, Sivaguru and Paliwal 1993, Foy and Brown 1963, Foy 1984, Lazof *et al.* 1994, Rengel and Eliott 1992, Ryan and Kochian 1993, Marschner 1995). The reduction level of Ca and other elements due to high aluminium level is the result of reduced root surface rather than a specific aluminium effect (Clarkson 1967). Huang *et al.* (1992) reported that aluminium blocks Ca transport across the root cell plasma membrane and does not act within the root cell wall to alter Ca transport. Pineros and Tester (1995) found that 70 µM aluminium completely blocked the Ca channels of plasmaless-enriched fractions from wheat roots.

Concentrations of Ca in the roots and shoots are decreased dramatically under high level of aluminium in wheat (Jones *et al.* 1978). Aluminium-tolerant cultivar is able to resist aluminium inhibition of Ca uptake from roots to shoots. Quellette and Dessureaux (1958) found that aluminium-tolerant clones contained lower concentration of aluminium and higher concentrations of Ca in their shoots. In contrast, Mac Lean and Chaissan (1966) reported that the roots of aluminium-sensitive variety accumulate more Ca than those of the tolerant variety which suggests varietal differences in Ca translocation rather than uptake.

Interaction with Iron

Decreased plant uptake of Fe in stems and leaves due to excess aluminium in nutrient solution (Smalley *et al.* 1993). Wheeler *et al.* (1992) found that increasing aluminium concentration decreased the top Fe concentration in tomato, petunia, beans and tobacco.

Interaction with Manganese

Blair and Taylor (1997) observed that concentration and content of Mn are decreased significantly with increasing aluminium concentration in the tops as well as in the roots (Mathan 1980, Alam 1983). Smalley *et al.* (1993) also found significant reduction in Mn uptake with increasing aluminium treatments.

Interaction with Boron

Aluminium toxicity has been associated with decrease in the uptake and utilization of boron. Boron content in the tops was increased with up to 10 ppm aluminium and above this level it decreased in most of the rice cultivars (Fageria and Carvalho 1982). Symptoms of boron deficiency and aluminium toxicity were very similar and generally impaired membrane function and root growth (Lukaszewski and Blevins 1996).

The supplement of boron protects against aluminium induced inhibition of root growth. Protection was apparent at primary root and lateral root lengths, primary root cell elongation, cell elongation rate, tissue organization and cell structure, primary root morphology and maturation. Protection against aluminium inhibition was also apparent for shoot growth (Le-Noble *et al.* 1996).

Interaction with Copper

Reduction in copper was observed by different researchers (Foy and Brown 1963, Pavan and Bingham 1982, Pintro *et al.* 1996). Patel *et al.* (2002) also observed that concentration and content of Cu are decreased significantly with increasing aluminium concentration in nutrient solution. Fageria and Carvalho (1982) noticed that copper concentration up to 20 ppm aluminium was not affected much but decreased at 40 to 60 ppm of aluminium in the tops and roots of most of the rice cultivars.

Interaction with Magnesium

Negative effects of aluminium on the uptake of Mg have been reported in plant species like maize (Clark 1977), rye grass (Rengel and Robinson 1989a) and wheat (Fageria and Cavarlho 1982). Concentration of magnesium reduced significantly in roots as well as in shoots of wheat at higher levels of aluminium in nutrient solution (Patel *et al.* 2002). Wagatsuma *et al.* (1987) observed that the concentration of Mg in the apical 1 cm of roots decreased more in aluminium-sensitive cultivars than in tolerant cultivars.

Interaction with Zinc

High aluminium concentration decreased zinc (Zn) content in roots and shoots (Clark 1977). He reported that aluminium resistant maize genotypes with enhanced uptake of Zn when grown in 93 µM Al nutrient solution, whereas reduced an Al-sensitive genotypes.

Interaction with Silicon

Silicon has been reported to decrease aluminium uptake in tomato (Peaslee and Frink 1969). Some aluminium tolerant varieties of rice are known to accumulate higher levels of silicon in the epidermal cells of leaves (Ota 1968). Silicon positive complexes aluminium and reduces their toxicities (Foy *et al.* 1978). Galvez *et al.* (1987) reported that silicon alleviated aluminium toxicity by an increased pH of the nutrient solution which leads to a reduced aluminium availability to the plant. However, Cocker *et al.* (1998) reported that silicon does not reduce aluminium phytotoxicity. In an aluminium-tolerant cultivar, aluminium exposed plants pretreated with Si exuded up to 15 times more phenolics than those plants not pretreated with silicon (Kidd *et al.* 2001).

RANGE AND TIME OF EXPOSURE OF ALUMINIUM

Levels of Aluminium

A range of aluminium levels in hydroponics has been used by various researchers varying from 1 to 30 ppm. Most of the work has been in the range of 5 to 10 ppm (Aniol 1981, Aniol 1985, Campbell and Lafever 1981, Fyre and Anderson 1978), while a few workers have tried in the range of 10 to 50 ppm Al (Singh *et al.* 2007, Singh and Chaturvedi 2007).

Time of Exposure

Many researchers have tried with aluminium levels in solutions used for growing plants for 14 to 21 days (Singh *et al.* 2007, Singh and Chaturvedi 2007, Singh and Sureja 2008), while a few even tried up to 70 days (Manivannan and Singh 2008). The staining and root re-growth studies were carried out for periods ranging from 17 to 72 hours. Later on, the plants were transferred to solutions free of aluminium and observed for their recovery (Singh *et al.* 2007, Singh and Chaturvedi 2007).

Sources of Aluminium Tolerance

The requirement of breeding for aluminium tolerance is to find a suitable source of tolerance. The tolerance to aluminium can be transferred from different sources. Sources of aluminium tolerance are presented in Table 1.2. Adequate level of aluminium tolerance occurs within the species. When the desired level of tolerance is not available within crop species a search for sources is made in closely related species or even in different genera.

Genetic Variability

Existence of genetic variability for aluminium tolerance within species is of great importance for crop improvement programme. Natural variation for aluminium tolerance in crops is well-documented (Foy 1988). The most common approach to

Table 1.2: *Aluminium- and acid-tolerant genotypes of various crops*

Crop	Genotype	Category	Reference
Rice	CO-37, Basmati 370	Al-resistant	Sivaguru and Paliwal 1993
Wheat	Atlas 66	Al-resistant	Tang *et al.* 2002, Rengel and Jurkick 1992
	Trigo 43, 35, EMBRAP A15, Trigo, BR, IAC5-Maringa, BH1146, K9107, PBW343	Al-resistant Acid-tolerant	Kim *et al.* 2001, Sharma and Sarkar 2005
Maize	1X1, 5A, 203 B & 4D, Agroceres-152, Yellow Carimagua, Cargill-111	Al-resistant Acid-tolerant	Gudu *et al.* 2001, Salinas 1978
Barley	Antarctica, BR-1, F4 404	Al-resistant	Minella 1989
Sorghum	G4, Real 60, SPA2 & SPAD	Al-resistant	Anas and Yoshida 2000
Groundnut	ICG 813, 1001, 1021, 1048 1056, 1064, 1355, 3606, 86644, 10271, 10465, 10964, 11183, 11954.	Al-resistant	Singh *et al.* 2006
Rapeseed	Sonmukh	Acid-tolerant	Sharma and Sarkar 2005
Mustard	Sanjukta, Pusa Bold	Acid-tolerant	Sharma and Sarkar 2005

identify sources of variability for breeding for aluminium tolerance has been to look among the primitive cultivars, landraces, wild relatives and world collections for those genotypes which exhibit characteristics for aluminium tolerance. Varietal differences to aluminium tolerance within species have been reported in crops like wheat (Foy 1988), barley (Minella and Sorrells 1992), maize (Pandey *et al.* 1994, Magnavaca *et al.* 1987, Singh and Chauhan 2008), rice (Fageria *et al.* 1988, Foy 1988, Khatiwada *et al.* 1996, Sivaguru and Paliwal 1993), rye (Foy 1988), tomato (Singh *et al.* 2007, Baumgartner *et al.* 1976), alfalfa (Devine *et al.* 1990, Mugwira and Haque 1993), cowpea (Horst 1987), common bean (Varges and Graham 1988), soybean (Campbell and Carter 1990, Foy *et al.* 1993), pea (Singh *et al.* 2009), cabbage (Singh and Bhardwaj 2007), chickpea (Singh and Raje 2011), okra (Singh 2012), lentil (Singh *et al.* 2015), *Vigna* species (Singh *et al.* 2015).

Genetics of Aluminium Tolerance

Crop production has suffered great losses due to aluminium toxicity in acidic soils. Breeding crop varieties for increased aluminium tolerance is now realized as a more promising, energy efficient, economical and socially acceptable approach than soil amelioration technique which has now gone beyond the reach of marginal farmers. An aluminium stress environment is often associated with poor plant growth. The interaction between aluminium stress and other environmental factors also influences the plant's response. It is therefore important to develop crop genotypes and lines that can withstand the aluminium toxic environments.

An understanding of genetic basis of aluminium tolerance in crop plants is a pre-requisite for a geneticist to evolve superior genotypes through either conventional breeding or biotechnological approach. The success of any breeding programme depends on the availability of the screening technique, knowledge of inheritance pattern (qualitative or quantitative), the number of genes with major effects and nature of gene action involved, and presence of a great magnitude of heritable variation for aluminium (Al) tolerance. Breeder prefers to use major genes rather than polygenic variation. Selection of traits controlled only by one gene is relatively easy. A trait is controlled by a few genes of major effect, a larger number of genes with moderate effects and many genes whose effects are too small to be individually identified. Studies on genetics of tolerance of aluminium toxicity are very limited. The inheritance and genetics of Al tolerance have been assessed mostly in cereals like wheat, maize, rice, etc. Some of the reports in crops such as wheat, maize and rice are inconclusive. However, there is an increasing awareness that Al tolerance is more likely a polygenic trait. There is also need to re-assess the number of genes, governing tolerance, which are available against aluminium toxicity.

The best method for improving aluminium tolerance is the backcross method. The tolerance expression can be first identified from the rapid solution culture screening. Al tolerance genes are easily tracked through consecutive backcross (BC) generations by hematoxylin staining (Carver and Ownby 1995). Once identified, the alleles governing aluminium tolerance may be introgressed into a genotype possessing desirable traits via a backcrossing programme using the inexpensive and less laborious hematoxylin method. Recurrent selection is a potential breeding method that increases the frequency of desirable genes. Giaveno and Miranda Filho (2002) reported that potential improvement for Al resistance was obtained through recurrent selection. Eticha *et al.* (2005) reported that aluminium resistance is mainly conditioned by additive genes and Al tolerance can be further improved through crossing among the good combiners followed by recurrent selection.

Biotechnological Approaches

The success in getting stress plants via conventional breeding has not been very encouraging, therefore researchers feel less motivated to employ this method which is also time consuming and laborious. On the other hand, improvement of stress tolerance by biotechnology can overcome the bottlenecks of plant breeding method.

DNA based marker speed up to advance in the improvement of crop for stress tolerance. Identification and integration of genes for stress tolerant into high yielding genotypes would increase crop production in toxic soils. The use of marker assisted selection technology in QTL analysis has opened new opportunities to work with the tolerance for aluminium toxicity. Molecular markers linked to aluminium tolerant gene or QTLs governing aluminium tolerance have been identified in several crop plants (Table 1.3).

Table 1.3: *Molecular mapping of some major genes and QTLs for aluminium tolerance in different field crops*

Crop	Gene/ QTLs	Designation and chromosome location	Contribution	Mapping population	Marker type	Reference
Alfalfa	QTL	–	–	–	SSR, RFLP	Sledge *et al.* 2002
Barley	Gene	*Alt* (4H)	Single major gene	Wheat–barley chromosome addition lines 67F$_2$	AFLP and SSR	Raman *et al.* 2003
	Gene	*Alp* (4H)	Single major gene	48F$_2$	RFLP	Tang *et al.* 2000
Maize	Genes	*Alm1* (10S) *Alm2* (6)	24.2 7.67	56 inbred lines	RFLP	Sibov *et al.* 1999
	QTLs	QTL1 (2) QTL2 (6) QTL3 (6) QTL4 (8) QTL5 (8)	10.9% 5.3% 15.6% 7.4% 8.6%	168F$_{3:4}$	RFLP and SSR	Ninamango Cardenas *et al.* 2003

(Contd.)

Table 1.3: *Molecular mapping of some major genes and QTLs for aluminium tolerance in different field crops (Contd.)*

Crop	Gene/ QTLs	Designation and chromosome location	Contribution	Mapping population	Marker type	Reference
Rice	QTLs	*QAlRr*1.1 (1) *QAlRr*3.1 (3) *QAlRr*7.1 (7) *QAlRr*8.1 (8) *QAlRr*9.1 (9)	9.0% 24.9% 22.5% 20.8% 9.9%	171F_6 RILs	RFLP and SSR	Nguyen *et al.* 2003
	QTLs	*qALRR*-1-1 *qALRR*-1-2 *qALRR*-2 *qALRR*-3 *qALRR*-4 *qALRR*-7 *qALRR*-8 *qALRR*-9 *qALRR*-10 *qALRR*-12	24.1% 18.5% 13.4% 12.8% 20.1% 10.3% 28.7% 19.3% 17.7% 19.7%	146 DH lines	RFLP, AFLP and SSR	Nguyen *et al.* 2002
	QTLs	QTLs 2 weeks (1) (3) (12) QTLs 4 weeks (1) (9) (12)	 19% 9% 10% 15% 9% 20%	159F_9 RILs	AFLP and RFLP	Wu *et al.* 2000
	QTLs	QTL (1) QTL (2) QTL (6)	11.1% 7.3% 8.7%	183 Backcross lines	RFLP	Ma *et al.* 2002
	QTLs	QTL (1) QTL (9) QTL (11)		71F_7 RILs		Xue *et al.* 2006
Rye	Gene	*Alt1* (6RS)	Dominant	F_2	RAPD and SCARs	Gallego *et al.* 1998
	Gene	*Alt3* (4RL)	Single	F_6 RILs	AFLP	Miftahudin *et al.* 2002

(Contd.)

Table 1.3: *Molecular mapping of some major genes and QTLs for aluminium tolerance in different field crops (Contd.)*

Crop	Gene/ QTLs	Designation and chromosome location	Contribution	Mapping population	Marker type	Reference
Soybean	QTLs	–	–	$40F_2$	SSR	Tasma *et al.* 2008
	Genes	Sali 5–4a Sali 3–2	–	–	–	Ragland and Soliman 1997
	QTLs			F_4	RFLP	Bianchi-Hall *et al.* 2000
Wheat	Gene	Alt_{BH} (4DL)	85%	$101F_5$ RILs	RFLP	Riede and Anderson 1996
	Gene	Alt_{BH} (4DL)	Single dominant	$91F_5$ RILs	RFLP, SSR and AFLP	Milla and Gustafson 2001

The generation of aluminium tolerant plants through genetic engineering has been demonstrated in various crops (Table 1.4). This is an alternative to form a part of crop management strategy to enhance agricultural production in acidic soil.

Table 1.4: *Aluminium tolerance in transgenic plants expressing gene involved in organic acid synthesis and release*

Gene	Gene product	Source plant	Target	Al-resistance	Reference
CSb	Citrate synthase	*Pseudomonas aeruginosa*	Tobacco, papaya	Increases	De la Fuente *et al.* 1997
CSb	Citrate synthase	*P. aeruginosa*	Tobacco, alfalfa	Does not change	Delhaize *et al.* 2001
neMDH	Malate dehydrogenase	Alfalfa	Alfalfa	Increased	Tesfaye *et al.* 2001
PEPC	Phosphoeno-pyruvate carboxylase	Alfalfa	Alfalfa	Does not change	Tesfaye *et al.* 2001
At-mtCS	Citrate synthase	*Arabidopsis*	Oilseed	Increases	Anoop *et al.* 2003
ALMT1	Malate channel	Wheat	Barley	Increases	Delhaize *et al.* 2004

CONCLUSION

The suppression of plant growth casn be severe in aluminium toxic soils and for this reason Al^{3+} is one of the most deleterious factors in acidic soils. Generally, the plants are more sensitive at seedling stage than at adult stage.

Some earlier workers have found that low level of aluminium may stimulate plants but the exact mechanisms and concentration needs to be assessed. Aluminium has been shown to be localized in root apex, plasma membrane, cell wall and symplast, but the primary site of aluminium toxicity, whether apoplast or symplast, remains to be confirmed. Threshold and critical values of aluminium toxicity have been worked out for many crops and these need to be determined for other crops too to enhance productivity of acidic soils. Plants have generally two strategies for aluminium tolerance, *viz.* exclusion and internal detoxification. Chelation of aluminium with organic acids is a very important adaptation for acidic soils. Aluminium-tolerant species secrete more organic acids than sensitive plants. The acids secreted are citrate, malate and oxalate or sometimes other organic acids which can vary with species. Some plant species secrete citrate and some secrete malate and oxalate or some other organic acids. There is need to identify the exact reason for secretion of specific organic acids. Chelators other than the organic acids need to be further investigated.

Breeding for aluminium tolerance through conventional approaches has resulted in a limited success to date. Very little is known about the inheritance pattern and nature of gene action. Reports on inheritance pattern in several crops are still not conclusive and there is need to undertake a more intensive effort to re-examine inheritance pattern for aluminium tolerance. Assessment of variation for aluminium tolerance by screening the available germplasm of various crops suggests that aluminium tolerance in some crops exhibits simple inheritance and in others continuous variation, i.e. the trait is under the control of a number of genes. If these polygenes are closely linked to other genes with amplified effects, then the latter can be easily used as markers to trace the inheritance of the linked polygene(s). The molecular markers which are associated with genes for aluminium tolerance have been identified in maize, rice, wheat, rye, etc., and there is need to attain such success in other crops. It is proved that there has been success in developing Al tolerant transgenic such as rice, alfalfa, papaya and tobacco, and there is dire need to introduce these success in other crops. To face aluminium stress in a better manner, collaboration among soil scientists, plant breeders, plant molecular biologists, plant physiologists, plant biochemists and plant nutritionists are needed to limit the losses in crop quality and production attributed to Al-toxicity.

REFERENCES

Alam SM. 1983. Effects of flooded and unflooded soil conditions, Fe and Mn application on growth and nutrient content in rice plants. *J. Sci. Tech.* **7:** 1–2.

Alam SM and Adams WA. 1979. Effects of aluminium on nutrient composition and yield of roots. *J. Plant Nutr.* **1:** 365–375.

Alva AK, Asher CJ and Edwards DG. 1986. Role of calcium in alleviating aluminium toxicity. *Aust. J. Agri. Res.* **37:** 375–382.

Anas and Yoshida Y. 2000. Screening of Al tolerant sorghum by hematoxylin staining and growth response. *Crop Production Sci.* **3:** 246–253.

Aniol A. 1981. Aluminium and phosphorus content in wheat varieties of different tolerance to aluminium toxicity. *Biul. Inst. Hodowli Aklim. Rosl.* **143:** 15–19.

Aniol A. 1985. Tolerancyjnosi zboa na tocksyczne dzialanie jonow glinu. *Biul. Inst. Hodowli Aklim. Rosl.* **156:** 7–11.

Anoop VM, Basu U, Mc Cammom MT, McAlister-Henn L and Taylor GJ. 2003. Modulation of citrate metabolism alters aluminium tolerance in yeast and transgenic canola over expressing a mitochondrail citrate synthase. *Plant Physiol.* **132:** 2205–2217.

Ariyanayagam RP and Grifitth SM. 1987. Soil and climatic environment in the Caribbean region: Yield reduction in pigeonpea due to drought, salinity, acidity and alkalinity. Proc. workshop, p149–158. ICRISAT, Patencheru, India.

Basu A, Basu U and Taylor GJ. 1994. Induction of microsomal membrane proteins in roots of an aluminium resistant cultivar of wheat (*Triticum aestivum* L.) under conditions of aluminium stress. *Plant Physiol.* **104:** 1007–1013

Baumgartner JG, Haag GD, De Oliveire and Perecin D. 1976. Mineral nutrition of vegetable crops. XXVIII. Tolerance of aluminium and manganese in cultivars of tomato (*Lycopersicon esculentum* Mill). *Ess Sup. Agric.* Luiz de queiro, University Sao Paulo. **33:** 513–541.

Bianchi-Hall CM, Carter Te Jr, Bailey MA, Mian MAR, Rufty TW, Asley DA, Boerma HR, Arellano C, Hussey RS and Parrot WA. 2000. Aluminium tolerance associated with quantitative trait loci derived soybean PI416937 in hydroponics. *Crop Sci.* **40:** 538–545.

Blair LM and Taylor GJ. 1997. The nature of interaction between aluminium and manganese on growth and metal accumulation in *Triticum aestivum* L. *Environ. Exp. Bot.* **37:** 25–37.

Blamey FCP and Dowling AJ. 1995. Antagonism between Al and Ca for sorption by calcium pectate. *Plant Soil.* **171:** 137–140.

Cakmak I and Horst WJ. 1991. Effect of aluminium on lipid peroxidation, superoxide dismutase, catalase, and peroxidase activities in root tips of soybean (*Glycine max* L.). *Physiol. Plant.* **83:** 463–468.

Camargo CEO. 1987. Trigo: Tolerancia ao aluminio em solucao nutriva. *Bragantia.* **46:** 183–190.

Campbell GKA and Carter Jr TE. 1990. Aluminium tolerance in soybean: Genotypic correlation and repeatability of solution culture and greenhouse screening methods. *Crop Sci.* **30:** 1049–1054.

Campbell LG and Lafever HN. 1981. Heritability of aluminium tolerance in wheat. *Cereal Res. Commun.* **9:** 281–287.

Carver BF and Ownby JD. 1995. Acid soil tolerance in wheat. *Adv. Agron.* **54:** 117–173.

Chen J, Sucoff EI and Stadelmann EJ. 1991. Aluminium and temperature alteration of cell membrane permeability of *Auerecus rubra*. *Plant Physiol.* **96:** 644–649.

Chen LS, Qi YP, Smith BR and Liu XH. 2005. Aluminium induced decrease in CO_2 assimilation in citrus seedlings is unaccompanied by decreased activities of key enzymes involved in CO_2 assimilation. *Tree Physiol.* **25:** 317–324.

Chenery EM. 1955. A preliminary study of aluminium and the tea bush. *Plant Soil.* **6:** 174–200.

Ciamporova M. 2002. Morphological and structural responses of plant roots to aluminium at organ, tissue and cellular levels. *Biol. Plant Prague.* **45:** 161–171.

Clark RB. 1977. Effect of Al on growth and mineral elements of Al tolerant and Al intolerant corn. *Plant Soil.* **47:** 653–662.

Clark RB. 1982. Plant genotype differences to uptake, transpiration, accumulation and use of mineral elements. In: Genetic specificity of mineral nutrition in plants, p41–55. Saric MR (Ed) Serbian Acad. Arts, Belgrade, Yugoslavia.

Clarkson DT. 1967. Interactions between aluminium and phosphorus on root surface and cell wall material. *Plant Soil.* **27:** 347–356.

Cocker KM, Evans DE and Hodson MJ. 1998. Amelioration of aluminium toxicity by silicon in higher plants: Solution chemistry or on in plant mechanisms. *Physiol. Plant.* **104:** 608–614.

Collet L, de Leon C, Kollmeier M, Schmohl N and Horst WJ. 2002. Assessment of aluminium sensitivity of maize cultivars using roots of intact and excised root tips. *J. Plant Nutr. Soil Sci.* **165:** 357–365.

Cumming JR, Eckert RT and Evans LS. 1985. Effect of aluminium on potassium uptake by red spruce seedlings. *Can. J. Bot.* **63:** 1099–1103.

De la Fuente-J M, Ramirej-Rodriguez V, Cabrera-Ponce J and Herrera-Estrella L. 1997. Aluminium tolerance in transgenic plants by alteration of citrate synthesis. *Sci.* **276:** 1566–1568.

De Lima ML and Copeland L. 1990. The effect of Al on the germination of wheat seed. *J. Plant Nutr.* **13:** 1489–1497.

Degenhardt J, Larsen PB, Howell SH and Kochina L. 1998. Aluminium resistance in the *Arabidopsis* mutant alr-104 is caused by an aluminium increase in rhizosphere pH. *Plant Physiol.* **117:** 19–27.

Delhaize E, Hebb DM and Ryan PR. 2001. Expression of a *Pseudomonas aeruginosa* citrate synthase gene in tobacco is not assocaited with either enhanced citrate accumulation or efflux. *Plant Physiol.* **125:** 2059–2067.

Delhaize E and Ryan PR. 1995. Aluminium toxicity and tolerance in plants. *Plant Physiol.* **107:** 315–321.

Delhaize E, Ryan PR, Hebb DM, Yamamoto Y, Sasaki T and Matsumoto H. 2004. Engineering high level aluminium tolerance in barley with the *ALMTI* gene. *Proc. Natl. Acd. Sci.* USA. **101**: 15249–15254.

Demming B and Gimmler H. 1983. Preparation of isolated intact chloroplast at cytoplasmic K^+ concentration. 1. Light induced cation uptake into intact chloroplast is driven by an electrical potential difference. *Plant Physiol.* **73**: 169–174.

Devine TE, Bouton JH and Mabrahtu T. 1990. Legume genetics and breeding for stress tolerance and nutrient efficiency. In: Crops as enhancer of nutrient use, p211–52. Baligar VC and Duncan RR (Eds), Academic Press, Diego.

Dragun J. 1988. The chemistry of Hazardous materials. Hazardous material control Research Institute, Siver Spring, MD, USA.

Edwards JH, Horton BD and Kirpatrick HC. 1976. Aluminium toxicity symptoms in peach seedlings. *J. Amer. Soc. Hort. Sci.* **101**: 139–142.

Eticha E, Carles T, Welcker T, Nano CL and Horst WJ. 2005. Aluminium induced callose formation in root apices: Inheritance and selection trait for adaptation of tropical maize to acid soil. *Field Crop Res.* **93**: 252–263.

Fageria NK and Carvalho JRP. 1982. Influence of Al in nutrient solution on chemical compositions in upland rice cultivars. *Plant Soil.* **69**: 31–44.

Fageria NK, Wright RJ and Baligar VC. 1988. Rice cultivars response to aluminium in nutrient solution. *Commun. Soil Sci. Plant Anal.* **19**: 1133–1142.

Flemming AL and Foy CD. 1968. Root structure reflects differential aluminium tolerance in wheat varieties. *Agron. J.* **60**: 172–175.

Fox RH. 1979. Soil pH, aluminium saturation and corn grain yield. *Soil Sci.* **127**: 330–334.

Foy CD. 1974. Effect of Al on plant growth. In: The plant roots and its environment, p601–642. Carson EW (Ed), University Press of Virginia, Charlottesville, Vir, USA.

Foy CD. 1983. The physiology of plant adaptation to mineral stress. *Iowa State J. Res.* **57**: 355–391.

Foy CD. 1984. Physiological effects of hydrogen, aluminium and manganese toxicities in acid soils. In: Soil Acidity and liming, p57–97. Adams F (Ed), 2nd ed. *Soil Sci. Soc., Am. Soc. Agron. and Crop Sci of Am.*, Madison, WI.

Foy CD. 1988. Plant adaptation to acid aluminium toxic soils. *Commun. Soil Sci. Plant Anal.* **19**: 959–987.

Foy CD and Brown JC. 1963. Toxic factors in acid soils. I. Characterization of aluminium toxicity in cotton. *Soil Sci. Soc. Am. Proc.* **27**: 403–407.

Foy CD, Chaney RL and White MC. 1978. The physiology of metal toxicity in plants. *Ann. Rev. Plant Physiol.* **29**: 511–566.

Foy CD and Fleming AL. 1978. The physiology of plant tolerance to excess available aluminium and manganese in acidic soils. In Crop tolerance to suboptimal land conditions, p301–328. Jung, GA (Ed), ASA Spec. ASA, CSSA and SSSA, Madison, WI.

Foy CD and Peterson CJ. 1994. Acid soil tolerance of wheat lines selected for high grain protein. *J. Plant Nut.* **17**: 377–400.

Foy CD, Shalunova L and Lee E. 1993. Acid soil tolerance of soybean *(Glycine max* L.) germplasm from the USSR. *J. Plant Nutr.* **16:** 1593–1617.

Frye SU and Anderson JC. 1978. Effects of aluminium on elongation and DNA synthesis of wheat roots. In: Agron. Abstr. p152–153. *Am. Soc. Agr.* Madison, USA.

Furlani PR and Clark RB. 1981. Screening sorghum for aluminium tolerance in nutrient solution. *Agron J.* **73:** 587–590.

Galvez L, Clark RB, Gowley LM and Maranville JW. 1987. Silicon interactions with manganese and aluminium toxicity in sorghum. *J. Plant Nutr.* **10:** 1139–1147.

Gallego F, Calles B and Benito C. 1998. Molecular markers linked to the aluminium tolerance gene Alt in rye *(Secale cereale* L.). *Theor. Appl. Genet.* **97:** 1104–1109.

Giaveno CD and de Miranda Filho JB. 2002. Selection methods for maize in greenhouse as related to aluminium tolerance. *Sci. Agric.* **59:** 807–810.

Graham CJ. 2002. Nonstructural carbohydrate and prunasin composition of peach seedlings fertilized with different nitrogen source and aluminium. *Sci. Hort.* **94:** 21–32.

Gudu S, Maine SM, Onkar AO, Ombakho G and Ligeyo DO. 2001. Screening of Kenya maize germplasm for tolerance to low pH and aluminium for use in acidic soils of Kenya. *Seventh Eastern and Southern African Regional Maize Conference.* p216–221.

Hamel F, Breton C and Houde M. 1998. Isolation and characterization of wheat aluminium-regulated genes: possible involvement of Al as a pathogenesis response elicitor. *Planta.* **205:** 531–538.

Haug A. 1984. Molecular aspects of aluminium toxicity. *Critical Rev. Plant Sci.* **1:** 345–373.

Henderson M and Ownby JO. 1991. The role of root cap mucilage secretion in aluminium tolerance in wheat. *Curr. Top. Pl. Biochem. Physiol.* **10:** 134–141.

Henrickson TM, Eldhusat TD, Stuanes AO and Langerud BR. 1992. Effects of Al and Ca on *Picea abies* seedlings. *Scand. J. Res.* **7:** 63–70.

Hirano Y, Pannatier EG, Stefan Z and Brunner I. 2004. Induction of callose in roots of Norway spruce seedlings after short-term exposure to aluminium. *Tree Physiol.* **24:** 1279–1283.

Horst WJ. 1987. Al tolerance and Ca efficiency of cowpea genotypes. *J. Plant Nutr.* **10:** 1121–1129.

Horst WJ, Puschel AK and Schmohl N. 1997. Induction of callose formation is a sensitive marker for genotypic aluminium sensitivity in maize. *Plant Soil.* **192:** 23–30.

Horst WJ, Schmohl N, Kollmeier M, Baluska F and Sivaguru M. 1999. Does Al affect root growth of maize through interaction with the cell wall plasma-membrane-cytoskeleton Continuum. *Plant Soil.* **215:** 163–174.

Horst WJ, Wagner A and Marschner H. 1982. Mucilage protects root meristems from aluminium injury. *Z. Pflanzenphysiol.* **105:** 435–444.

Howeler RH and Cadavid LF. 1976. Screening of rice cultivars for tolerance to Al toxicity in nutrient solutions as compared with field screening method. *Agron J.* **68:** 551–555.

Huang JW, Shaff JE, Grunes DL and Kochian LV. 1992. Aluminium (Al) effects on calcium fluxes at the root apex of Al tolerant and Al sensitive cultivars. *Plant Physiol.* **98:** 230–237.

Huett DO and Menary RC. 1980. Effect of Al on growth and nutrient uptake of cabbage, lettuce and kikuyu grass in nutrient solution. *Aust. J. Agric. Res.* **31**: 749–761.

Ishikawa S and Wahgatsuma T. 1998. Plasma membrane permeability of root tip cells following temporary exposure to Al ions is rapid measure of Al tolerance among plant species. *Plant Physiol.* **39**: 516–525.

Ishikawa S, Wagatmatsu T and Ikarashi T. 2003. Rapid changes in levels of mineral nutrients in root tip cells following short term exposure to Al. *Plant Soil.* **255**: 245–251.

Ishikawa S, Wagatmatsu T, Sasaki R and Manu PO. 2000. Comparison of the amount of citric and malic acids in Al media of seven plant species and two cultivars each in five plant species. *Soil Sci. Plant Nutr.* **46**: 751–758.

Jones DL, Gilroy S, Larsen PB, Howell SH and Kochian, LV. 1978. Effect of aluminium on cytoplasmic Ca^{2+} homeostasis in root hairs of *Arabidopsis thaliana* (L.). *Planta.* **206**: 378–387.

Kamprath EJ. 1970. Exchangeable aluminium as a criterion for liming leached mineral soils. *Soil Sci. Soc. Am. Proc.* **34**: 252–254.

Khatiwada SP, Sendhira D, Carpena AL, Zeigler SR and Fernandez PG. 1996. Variability and genetics of tolerance for Al toxicity in rice (*Oryza sativa* L.). *Theor. Appl. Genet.* **93**: 738–744.

Keser M, Neubauer BE and Hutchinson FE. 1975. Influence of Al ions on developmental morphology of sugarbeet roots. *Agron. J.* **67**: 84–88.

Kidd PS, Llugany M, Poschenrieder C, Gunse B and Barcelo J. 2001. The role of root exudates in aluminium resistance and silicon induced amelioration of aluminium toxicity in three varieties of maize (*Zea mays* L.). *J. Exp. Bot.* **52**: 1339–1352.

Kim BY, Baier AC, Somers DJ and Gustafson JP. 2001. Al tolerance in triticale, wheat and rye. *Euphytica.* **120**: 329–337.

Kinraide TB. 1993. Aluminium (Al) enhancement of plant growth in acid rooting media. A case of reciprocal alleviation of toxicity by two toxic cations. *Physiol. Plant.* **88**: 619–625.

Kinraide TB and Parker DR. 1987. Cation amelioration of aluminium toxicity in wheat. *Plant Physiol.* **83**: 546–551.

Klimashevskii EL. 1972. Physiological response to aluminium toxicity in root zone of pea varieties. *Agrochimica.* **16**: 487–496.

Kochian LV. 1995. Cellular mechanisms of aluminium toxicity and resistance in plants. *Ann. Rev. Pl. Physiol. Pl. Mol. Biol.* **46**: 237–260.

Kochian LV, Hoekenga OA and Pineros MA. 2004. How do crop plants tolerate acid soils? Mechanisms of aluminium tolerance and phosphorus efficiency. *Ann. Rev. Plant Biol.* **55**: 459–493.

Kochian LV, Miguel A, Owen P and Hoenka A. 2005. The physiology, genetics and molecular biology of plant aluminium resistance and toxicity. *Plant Soil.* **274**: 175–195.

Kumar K. 1995. Characterization of soil acidity and lime requirement of mid hill soils of Manipur with special reference to *Glycine max* and *Vigna radiata*. PhD Thesis, Manipur University, Chandipur, Imphal, India.

Lance JC. 1968. The effect of treatments with low concentrations of Al on root function in cotton. *Diss. Abstr.* **29B**: 446.

Larsen PB, Degenhardt J, Tai C-Y, Stenzler LM, Howell SH and Kochian LV. 1998. Aluminium resistance *Arabidopsis* mutant that exhibit altered pattern of Al accumulation and organic acid release from roots. *Plant Physiol.* **117:** 8–19.

Lazof DB, Goldsmidth JG, Rufty TW and Linton RW. 1994. Rapid uptake of aluminium into cells of intact soybean root tips. *Plant Physiol.* **106:** 1107–1114.

Lazof DB, Goldsmith JG, Rufty TW and Linton RW. 1996. The early entry of aluminium into cells of intact soybean roots. *Plant Physiol.* **112:** 1289–1300.

Le-Noble ME, Blevins DG, Sharp RE and Cumbie BG. 1996. Prevention of aluminium toxicity with supplemental boron. I. Maintenance of root elongation and cellular structure. *Plant Cell Environ.* **19:** 1132–1142.

Liang YC, Yang CG and Shi HH. 2001. Effects of silicon on growth and mineral composition of barley grown under toxic levels of Al. *J. Plant Nutr.* **24:** 2290û243.

Lidon FC, Azinheira HG and Barreiro MG. 2000. Aluminium toxicity in maize: modulation of biomass production and nutrient uptake and translocation. *J. Plant Nutr.* **23:** 151–160.

Lietuvos and Diroozomill. 1998. Agrocheminis savgbes ir ju kaita. *Red Mazvila J. Kaunas.* 14–50.

Lin Z and Myhre DL. 1991. Differential response of citrus rootstocks to aluminium levels in nutrient solutions. II. Plant mineral concentrations. *J. Plant Nutr.* **14:** 1239–1254.

Lindsay WL. 1979. Chemical equilibria in soils. John Wiley and Sons, New York.

Llugany M, Massot N, Wissemeir AH, Poschenrieder CH, Horst WJ and Barcelo J. 1994. Aluminium tolerance of maize cultivars assessed by callose production and root elongation. *Z. Pfanzenerahr Bodoenkd.* **157:** 477–451.

Llugany M, Poschenrieder C and Barcelo J. 1995. Monitoring of aluminium induced inhibition of root elongation in four maize cultivars differing in tolerance to aluminium and proton toxicity. *Physiol. Plant.* **93:** 265–271.

Lukaszewski KM and Blevins DG. 1996. Root growth inhibition in boron-deficient aluminium stressed squash may be a result of impaired ascorbate metabolism. *Plant Physiol.* **112:** 1135–1140.

Ma JF, Hiradate S, Nomoto K, Iwashita T and Matsumoto H. 1997. Internal detoxification mechanism of Al in *Hydrangea*. Identification of Al form in the leaves. *Plant Physiol.* **113:** 1033–1039.

Ma JF, Nagao S, Sato K, Ito H, Furukawa J and Takeda K. 2004. Molecular mapping of a gene responsible for Al-activated secretion of citrate in barley. *J. Exp. Bot.* **55:** 1335–1341.

Ma JF, Ryan P and Delhaize E. 2001. Aluminium resistance in plants and the complexing role of organic acids. *Trends Plant Sci.* **6:** 273–278.

Ma JF, Shen R, Zhao Z, Wissuwa M, Takeuchi Y, Ebitani T and Yano M. 2002. Response of rice to Al stress and identification of quantitative trait loci for aluminium tolerance. *Plant Cell Physiol.* **43:** 652–659.

MacLean AA and Chiasson TC. 1966. Differential performance of two barley varieties to varying Al concentrations. *Can. J. Soil Sci.* **46:** 147–153.

Magnavaca R, Gardner CO and Clark RB. 1987. Inheritance of aluminium tolerance in maize. In: Genetics aspects of plant mineral nutrition, p201–212. Gabelman HW and Loughman BC (Eds.), Dordrecht. The North Matinus Nijhoff.

Manivannan S and Singh D. 2008. Differential response of citrus rootstocks under aluminium stresses in hydroponics. In: Abstracts of the National Seminar on Sustainable Management of Acidic Soils for Higher Crop Productivity, p17. Singh D, Raju AS, Chaturvedi SK and Sharma S (Eds.) held during 22–24 September, 2008 at College of Horticulture and Forestry, Central Agricultural University, Pasighat, Arunachal Pradesh, India.

Marschner H. 1991. Mechanisms of adaptation of plants to acidic soils. *Plant Soil.* **134:** 1–20.

Marschner H. 1995. Mineral nutrition of higher plants. 2nd ed. Academic Press, London.

Mathan KK. 1980. Effect of various levels of aluminium on the dry matter yield, content and uptake of phosphorus, aluminium, manganese, magnesium and iron in maize. *Madras Agric. J.* **67:** 751–757.

Matsumoto H. 2000. Cell biology of aluminium toxicity and tolerance in higher plants. *Int. Rev. Cytol.* **200:** 1–46.

Matsumoto H, Hiraseva E, Morimura S and Takahashi E. 1976. Localization of aluminium in tea leaves. *Plant Cell Physiol.* **17:** 627–631.

Matsumoto H and Morimura S. 1980. Repressed template activity of chromatin of pea roots treated by Al. *Plant Cell Physiol.* **21:** 951–959.

Matsumoto H, Morimura S and Takahashi E. 1977. Less involvement of pectin in the precipitation of Al in pea root. *Plant Cell Physiol.* **18:** 325–335.

Meda AR and Furlani PR 2005. Tolerance to aluminium toxicity by tropical leguminous plants used as cover crops. *Braz. Archives Biol. Tech.* **48:** 309–317.

Meriga B, Reddy BK, Jageswar G, Reddy LA and Kishor PB. 2003. Alleviating effect of citrate on Al toxicity of rice seedlings. *Curr. Sci.* **85:** 383–385.

Michael M, Georia O and Lannoye R. 1995. Aluminium effects on photosynthesis and element uptake in an aluminium-tolerant and non-tolerant cultivars. *J. Plant Nutr.* **18:** 669–683.

Miftahudin G, Scoles J and Gustafson JP. 2002. AFLP markers tightly linked to aluminium tolerance gene Alt3 in rye (*Secale cereale* L.). *Theor. Appl.Genet.* **104:** 626–631.

Milla MAR and Gustafson JP. 2001. Genetic and physical characterization of chromosome 4DL in wheat. *Genome.* **44:** 883–892.

Minella E. 1989. Inheritance, chromosome location, genetic relationships of sources of diverse origins and breeding implications, p70, Dissertation (PhD)-Cornell University, Ithaca, New York.

Minella E. and Sorrells, ME. 1992. Aluminium tolerance in barley: Genetic relationships among genotypes of diverse origin. *Crop Sci.* **32:** 593–598.

Miyasaka SC, Buta JG, Howell RK and Foy CD. 1991. Mechanism of Al tolerance in snapbeans. Root exudation of citric acid. *Plant Physiol.* **96:** 737–743.

Moore DP. 1974. Physiological effects of pH on roots. In: The plants root and the environment, pp. 135–151. Carson EW (Ed), University Press of Virginia, Charlottesville.

Morimura S and Matsumoto H. 1978. Effect of Al on some properties and template activity of purified pea DNA. *Plant Cell Physiol.* **19**: 429–439.

Moustakas M and Ouzounido G. 1994. Increased non-photochemical quenching in leaves of aluminium-stressed wheat plants is due to Al^{3+} induced elemental loss. *Plant Physiol. Biochem.* **32**: 527–532.

Mugwira LM and Haque I. 1993. Screening forage and browse legumes germplasm to nutrient stresses II: Tolerance of *Lablab purpureus* to acidity and low phosphorus in two acid soils. *J. Plant Nutr.* **16**: 37–50.

Mullete KJ. 1975. Stimulation of growth in eucalyptus due to aluminium. *Plant Soil.* **42**: 495–499.

Nguyen BD, Brar DS, Bui BC, Nguyen TV, Pham LN and Nguyen HT. 2003. Identification and mapping of QTL for aluminium tolerance introgressed from the new source, *Oryza rufipgan* Griff, to indica rice (*Oryza sativa* L.). *Theor. Appl. Genet.* **106**: 583–593.

Nguyen V, Nguyen B, Sarkarung S, Matinez C, Paterson A and Nguyen H. 2002. Mapping of genes controlling aluminium tolerance in rice: Comparison of different genetic backgfrounds. *Mol. Genet. Genomics.* **267**: 722–780.

Ninamango-Cardenas FE, Guimaraes CT, Martinas PR, Parentoni SN, Carneiro NP, Lopes M A, Moro JR and Paiva E. 2003. Mapping QTLs for aluminium tolerance in maize. *Euphytica.* **130**: 223–232.

Nosko P, Brassard P, Kramer, JR and Kershaw KA. 1988. The effect of aluminium on seed germination and early seedling establishment, growth and respiration of white spruce (*Picea glauca*). *Can. J. Bot.* **66**: 2305–2310.

Ohki K. 1986. Photosynthesis, chlorophyll and transpiration responses in aluminium stressed wheat and sorghum. *Crop Sci.* **26**: 572–575.

Ota Y. 1968. Studies on the occurrence of the physiological disease of rice called bronzing. *Bull. Natl. Inst. Agric. Sci. Nishigahara*, Tokyo.

Pandey S, Magnavaca R, Bahia Filho AFC, Dugue-Varges J and Vinasco LE. 1994. Genetics of tolerance to soil acidity in tropical maize. *Crop Sci.* **34**: 1511–1514.

Parker DR, Kinraide TB and Zelazny LW. 1989. Aluminium speciation and phytotoxicity in dilute hydroxyl-aluminium solutions. *Soil Sci. Am. J.* **52**: 438–444.

Patel DU, Kumar SC, Ramchandran V and Athalye VV. 2002. Solution culture studies on the influence of aluminium on nutrients concentration in wheat seedlings. *Indian J. Plant Physiol.* **7**: 56–61.

Pavan MA and Bingham FT. 1982. Toxicity of aluminium to coffee seedlings grown in nutrient solution. *Soil Sci. Soc. AM. J.* **45**: 993–997.

Peaslee DE and Frink CR. 1969. Influence of silicic acid on uptake of Mn, Al, Zn and Cu by tomatoes (*Lycopersicon esculentum* L.) grown on acidic soils. *Soil Sci. AM Proc.* **33**: 569–571.

Pegtel DM. 1987. Effect of ionic Al in culture solutions on the growth of *Arnica montana* L. and *Deschampsia flexuosa* (L.). *Plant Soil.* **102**: 85–92.

Pellet DM, Papernik L and Kochian LV. 1996. Multiple Al resistance mechanisms in wheat. Role of root apical phosphate and malate exudation. *Plant Physiol.* **112:** 591–597.

Peters JL, Castillo FJ and Heat RL. 1989. Alteration of extracellular enzymes in *pinto* bean leaves upon exposure to air pollutant, ozone and sulfur oxide. *Plant Physiol.* **89:** 159–164.

Pineros M and Tester M. 1995. Characterization of a voltage-dependent Ca^{2+} selective channel from wheat roots. *Planta.* **195:** 478–488.

Pineros MA and Kochian LV. 2001. A patch-clamp study on the physiology of aluminium toxicity and aluminium tolerance in maize. Identification and characterization of aluminium induced anion channels. *Plant Physiol.* **125:** 292–305.

Pintro J, Barloy J and Fallavier P. 1996. Aluminium effects on the growth and mineral composition of corn plants cultivated in nutrient solution at low aluminium activity. *J. Plant Nutr.* **19:** 729–741.

Quellete GJ and Dessureaux. 1958. Chemical composition of alfalfa as related to degree of tolerance to manganese and aluminium. *Can. J. Plant Sci.* **38:** 206–214.

Ragland M and Soliman KM. 1997. Sali 5–4 a (Accession No U64866) and Sali 3–2 (Accession No U 89693): Two genes induced by aluminium in soybean roots (PGR 97–071). *Plant Physiol.* **11:** 395.

Raman HA, Karakousis JS, Moroni R, Raman B, Read BJ, Garvin DF, Kochian LV and Sorrells ME. 2003. Development and allele diversity of microsatellite markers linked with an aluminium tolerance gene *Alp* in barley. *Aust. J. Agric. Res.* **54:** 1315–1321.

Rengel Z. 1996. Uptake of aluminium by plant cells. *New Phytol.* **134:** 389–406.

Rengel Z and Elliott DC. 1992. Mechanism of aluminium inhibition of net 45 Ca^{2+} uptake by Amaranthus protoplasts. *Plant Physiol.* **98:** 632–638.

Rengel Z and Jurkic V. 1992. Genotypic differences in wheat Al tolerance. *Euphytica.* **62:** 111–117.

Rengel Z and Robinson DL. 1989. Comparative Al^{3+} inhibition of net Mg^{2+} uptake by intact *Lolium multiflorum* roots. I. Kinetics. *Plant Physiol.* **91:** 1407–1413.

Rhue RD and Grogan CO. 1977. Screening corn for aluminium tolerance. In Plant adaptation to mineral stress in problem soils, p420–422. Wright MJ and Ferrari, SA (Eds.), Cornell Univ. Agric. Exp. Stn., Ithaca, New York.

Rhue R, Grogan CO, Stockmeyer E and Evertte H. 1978. Genetic control of aluminium tolerance in corn. *Crop Sci.* **18:** 1063–1067.

Riede CR and Anderson JA. 1996. Linkage of RFLP markers to an aluminium tolerance gene in wheat. *Crop Sci.* **36:** 905–909.

Roy AK, Sharma A and Talukdar G. 1988. Some aspects of aluminium toxicity in plants. *Bot. Rev.* **54:** 145–177.

Ryan PR, Delhaize E and Randall PJ. 1995. Malate efflux from root apices and tolerance to aluminium are highly correlated in wheat. *Aust. J. Plant Physiol.* **22:** 531–536.

Ryan PR, Ditomaso J and Kochian L. 1993. Aluminium toxicity in roots: An investigation of spatial sensitivity and the role of the root cap. *J. Exp. Bot.* **44:** 437–446.

Ryan PR and Kochian LV. 1993. Interaction between aluminium toxicity and calcium uptake at the root apex in near isogenic lines of wheat (*Triticum aestivum* L.) differing in aluminium tolerance. *Plant Physiol*. **102**: 975–982.

Salinas JG. 1978. PhD Thesis, North Carolina Univ. Raleigh, NC, USA.

Sarkunan V and Bidappa CC. 1982. Effect of aluminium on the growth, yield and chemical composition of rice. *Oryza*. **19**: 188–190.

Sartain JB and Kamprath EJ. 1978. Aluminium tolerance of soybean cultivars based on root elongation in solution culture compared with growth in acid soil. *Agron. J*. **70**: 17–20.

Sharma PD and Sarkar AK. 2005. Managing acid soils for enhancing productivity. Publ. Director NBSS & LUP, Amravati Road, Nagpur 440010, India. p23.

Salisburry FB and Ross CW. 1992. Plant Physiology. Weds Worth Publ. Comp., Inc, Belmont.

Sledge MK, Bouton JH, Dall Agnoll M, Parrot WA and Kocher G. 2002. Identification and confirmation of aluminium tolerance QTL in diploid *Medicago sativa* subsp. Coerulea. *Crop Sci*. **42**: 1121–1128.

Severi A. 1997. Aluminium toxicity in *Lemma minor*: Effect of citrate and kinetin. *Environ. Exp. Bot*. **37**: 53–61.

Searcy KB and Mulcahy DL. 1990. Comparison of the response to Al toxicity in gametophyte and sporophyte of four tomato (*L. esculentus* Mill) cultivars. *Theor. Appl. Genet*. **80**: 289–295.

Sibov S, Gaspar M, Silva M, Ottoboni L, Aruda P and Souza A. 1999. Two genes control aluminium tolerance in maize: Genetic and molecular mapping analyses. *Genome*. **42**: 475–482.

Silva IR, Smith TJ, Maxley DF, Carter TE, Allen NS and Rufty TW. 2000. Aluminium accumulation at nuclei of cells in the root tip. Fluorescence detection using lumogallion and confocal laser scanning microscopy. *Plant Physiol*. **123**: 543–552.

Simen L, Smalley TJ, Jones Benton Jr and Lasseigne FT. 1994. Aluminium toxicity in tomato. Part I. Growth and mineral nutrition. *J. Plant Nutr*. **17**: 293–306.

Singh AL, Basu MS, Munda GC, Dutta M, Singh NP, Patel DP and Ray Chaudhary M. 2006. Groundnut cultivation technologies for North Eastern Hill of India. Technical Bulletin 24, National Research Centre for Groundnut Junagadh, Gujarat and ICAR Research Complex for NEH region, Umroi Road, Umiam, Meghalaya, India.

Singh D. 2007. Crop production in acidic soils. Technical Bulletin No. 5, College of Horticulture and Forestry, CAU, Pasighat, Arunachal Pradesh, India.

Singh D. 2008. Plant growth in aluminium stress environments, p.136. International Book Distribution Co. Lucknow, UP, India.

Singh D and Bhardwaj R. 2007. Screening of tomato and cabbage genotypes for their tolerance to aluminium toxicity. Final project report of College of Horticulture and Forestry, Central Agricultural University, Pasighat, Arunachal Pradesh, India.

Singh D and Chaturvedi SK. 2007. Rapid and effective screening technique for aluminium tolerance in chickpea at seedling stage. In: Abstract of the National Symposium on Legumes for ecologocal sustainability: Emerging challenges and opportunities, p107. Pramanik SC,

Singh, B, Singh IP, Naimuddin, Gupta S and Prakash B (Eds.) held during 3–5 November at Indian Institute of Pulses Research, Kanpur, India.

Singh D and Chaturvedi SK. 2008. Inheritance of aluminium tolerance in chickpea. In: Abstracts of the National Seminar on Sustainable Management of Acidic Soils for Higher Crop Productivity, p30. Singh D, Raju AS, Chaturvedi SK and Sharma S (Eds.) held during 22–24 September, 2008 at College of Horticulture and Forestry, Central Agricultural University, Pasighat, Arunachal Pradesh, India.

Singh D and Chauhan SK. 2008. Rapid screening technique for aluminium tolerance in baby corn. In: Abstracts of the National Seminar on Sustainable Management of Acidic Soils for Higher crop productivity, p29. Singh D, Raju AS, Chaturvedi SK and Sharma S (Eds.) held during 22–24 September, 2008 at College of Horticulture and Forestry, Central Agricultural University, Pasighat, Arunachal Pradesh, India.

Singh D, Rai AK and Panyang O. 2009. Hematoxylin staining as a potential screening technique for aluminium tolerance in pea (*Pisum sativum* L.). *Curr. Sci.* **96**: 1029–1030.

Singh D, Rai AK, Sureja AK and Bhardwaj R. 2007. Screening of tomato germplasm for tolerance to low pH and aluminium toxicity. In: Abstract and souvenir of 2nd *Indian Horticulture Congress*, p178. Chadha KL, Singh SK, Patel VB, Prasad KV and Asrey R (Eds.) held during 18–21 April 2007 at *ICAR Research Complex Barapani, Meghalaya, India*.

Singh D. 2012. Genetic control of aluminium tolerance in okra (*Abelmoschus esculentus* (L.) Moench). *Scientia Hort.* **138**: 134–137.

Singh D, Dikshit HK and Kumar A. 2015. Aluminium tolerance in lentil with monogenic inheritance pattern. *Plant Breed.* **134**: 105–110.

Singh D, Pal M, Singh R and Singh CK. 2015. Physiological and biochemical characteristics of *Vigna* species for Al stress tolerance. *Acta Physiol. Plant.* **37**: 87 (DOI 10.1007/s/11738-015-1834-7).

Singh D and Raje RS. 2011. Genetics of aluminium tolerance in chickpea. *Plant Breed.* **130**: 563–568.

Singh DP. 2001. Tolerance to soil acidity in field bean (*Phaseolus vulgaris*) under high rainfall conditions of Zambia. *Indian J. Agric. Sci.* **71**: 780–782.

Sirover MA and Loeb LA. 1976. Infidelity of DNA synthesis *in vitro*: Screening for potential metal mutagens or Carcinogenes. *Sci.* **194**: 1434–1436.

Sivaguru M, Baluska F, Volkamann D, Felle HH and Horst WJ. 1999. Impact of Al on the cytoskeleton of the maize root apex. Short-term effects on the distal part of the transition zone. *Plant Physiol.* **119**: 1073–1082.

Sivaguru M and Paliwal K. 1993. Differential aluminium tolerance in some tropical rice cultivars. I. Growth performance. *J. Plant Nutr.* **16**: 1705–1716.

Smalley TJ, Lasseigne FT, Mills HA and Hussey GG. 1993. Effect of aluminium on growth and chemical composition of marigolds. *J. Plant Nutr.* **16**: 1375–1384.

Song CL. 2006. Physiological responses and tolerance of plant shoot to aluminium toxicity. *J. Plant Physiol. Mol. Biol.* **32**: 143–155.

Subrahmanyam D. 1998. Effect of aluminium on growth, lipid peroxidation in sunflower tolerance into heavy metals. *Biol. Plant Prague.* **42**: 65–73.

Taiz L and Zeiger E. 2002. Plant Physiology, 3rd ed. Sinauer Associats, Inc. Publ. Sundelands, MA.

Tang Y, Garvin DF, Kochian LV, Sorrells ME and Carver BF. 2002. Physiological genetics of aluminium tolerance in the wheat cultivar Atlas 66. *Crop Sci.* **42:** 1541–1546.

Tang Y, Sorrells ME, Kochian LV and Garvin DF. 2000. Identification of RFLP markers linked to the barley Al tolerance gene. *Alp. Crop Sci.* **40:** 778–782.

Tasma IM, Warsun A and Asadi. 2008. Development and characterization of F_2 population for molecular mapping of aluminium toxicity tolerant QTL in soybean. *J. Agro. Biogen.* **4:** 1–8.

Taylor GJ. 1988. The physiology of aluminium phytotoxicity. In Metal ions in biological systems: Aluminium and its role in biology, p123–152. Sigel H and Sigel A (Eds.), Marcel Dekker, New York.

Taylor GJ. 1991. Current views of the aluminium stress response: The physiological basis of tolerance. *Curr. Top. Plant Biochem. Physiol.* **10:** 57–93.

Taylor GJ. 1995. Overcoming barriers to understanding the cellular basis of aluminium resistance. *Plant Soil.* **171:** 89–103.

Taylor GJ, Blamey FPC and Edwards DG. 1998. Antagonistics and synergistic interaction between aluminium and manganese on growth of cowpea (*Vigna unguiculata*) at low ionic strength. *Physiol. Plant.* **104:** 183–194.

Tesfaye M, Temple SJ, Allan DL, Vance CP and Samac DA. 2001. Overexpression of malate dehydrogenase in transgenic alfalfa enhances organic acid synthesis and confers tolerance to aluminium. *Plant Physiol.* **127:** 1836–1844

Thaworuwong N and Van Diest A. 1975. Influence of high acidity and aluminium on the growth of lowland rice. *Plant Soil.* **41:** 141–159.

Tice KR, Parker DR and Damason DA. 1992. Operationally defined apoplastic and symplastic aluminium fractions in root tips of aluminium intoxicated wheat. *Plant Physiol.* **100:** 309–318.

Tomioka R and Takenaka C. 2004. Difference in response to aluminium among Japanese coniferous species. *Soil Sci. Plant Nutr.* **50:** 755–761.

Varges A and Graham P. 1988. *Phaseolus vulgaris* cultivar and *Rhizobium* strains variations in acid pH tolerance and nodulation under acid conditions. *Field Crop Res.* **19:** 91–101.

Vazquez M, Poschenrieder C, Corrales I and Barcelo J. 1999. Change in apolastic aluminium during the initial growth response to aluminium by roots of a tolerant maize variety. *Plant Physiol.* **119:** 435–444.

Wagatsuma T, Ishikawa S, Obata H, Tawaraya K and Katohda S. 1995. Plasma membrane of younger and outer cells is the primary specific site for aluminium toxicity in roots. *Plant Soil.* **171:** 105–112.

Wagatsuma T, Kaneko M and Hayasok Y. 1987. Destruction process of plant root cells by Al. *Soil Sci. Plant Nutr.* **33:** 161–175.

Wang Y, Stars A and Horst WJ. 2004. Apoplastic binding of Al is involved in silicon-induced amelioration of Al toxicity in maize. *Plant Physiol.* **136:** 3762–3770.

Watnabe T and Osaki M. 2002. Mechanisms of adaptation to high aluminium conditions in native plant species growing in acid soils. *Soil Sci. Plant Anal.* **33:** 1247–1260.

Watnabe T, Osaki M, Yoshihara T and Tadano T. 1998. Distribution and chemical speciation of aluminium in the Al accumulator plant, *Melastoma malabatharicum* L. *Plant Soil.* **201:** 165–173.

Wehr JB, Menzies NW and Blamey FPC. 2004. Inhibition of cell wall autolysis and pectin degradation by cations. *Plant Physiol. Biochem.* **42:** 485–492.

Wheeler DM, Edmeades DC and Christic RA. 1992. Effect of Al on plant chemical concentrations in some temperate grasses grown in solution culture at low ionic strength. *J. Plant Nutr.* **15:** 387–402.

Wissemeier AH, Diening A, Hergenroder A, Horst WJ and Mixwagner G. 1992. Callose formation as parameter for assessment genotypical plant tolerance of aluminium and manganese. *Plant Soil.* **146:** 67–75.

Wissemeier AH, Klotz F and Horst WJ. 1987. Aluminium induced callose synthesis in roots of soybean (*Glycine max* L.). *Plant Physiol.* **129:** 487–497.

Wu P, Liao CY, Hu B, Yi KK, Jin WZ, Ni JJ and He C. 2000. QTLs and epistasis for aluminium tolerance in rice (*Oryza sativa* L.) at different seedling stages. *Theor. Appl. Genet.* **100:** 1295–1303.

Xiao XX, Chen LS, Cai YH, Huang Y and Xie YQ. 2005. The effect of Al stress on the absorption of nutrient elements in longan seedlings. *Acta Agri. Univ. Jiangxiensis.* **27:** 230–233.

Xue Y, Wan JM, Jiang L, Liu LL, Su N, Zhai HQ and Ma JF. 2006. QTL analysis of Al resistance in rice (*Oryza sativa* L.). *Plant Soil.* **287:** 375–383.

Yamamoto Y, Kobayshi Y and Matsumoto H. 2001. Lipid peroxidation is an early symptom triggered by Al but not the primary cause of elongation inhibition in pea roots. *Plant Physiol.* **125:** 199–208.

Zhang G, Hoddinolt J and Taylor GJ. 1994. Characterization of 1,3-β-D-glucan (callose) synthesis in roots of *T. aestivum* in response to Al toxicity. *J. Plant Physiol.* **144:** 229–234.

Zhang G and Taylor GJ. 1991. Effects of biological inhibitors on the kinetics of Al uptake by excised roots and purified cell wall material of Al tolerant and aluminium sensitive cultivars of *Triticum aestivum* L. *J. Plant Physiol.* **138:** 533–539.

Zheng SJ, Yang JL, He YF and Yu XH. 2005. Immobilization of aluminium with phosphorus in root is associated with high aluminium resistance in buckwheat. *Plant Physiol.* **138:** 297–303.

2 Aluminium Toxicity and Tolerance Mechanisms in Plants

Patiram

ABSTRACT

The physiology and biochemistry of Al-toxicity to plants are still not clear and occur when soil pH drops below 5.0, resulting in a poorly developed root system, which makes the plants susceptible to drought stress and nutrient deficiencies. The mechanisms of Al toxicity result from Al-ligand complex, which either inhibits the vital function of ligand that binds it (e.g. enzymes, calmodulin, tubulin, ATP, GTP, DNA), or the Al-ligand complex itself poisons other metabolic processes, and enhanced reactive oxygen species (ROS) inhibit the cell division and elongation. The external Al-tolerance (avoidance mechanisms) for toxic ions in plants includes an increase of pH around the roots, retention of ions within the root or within the cell wall of roots, compartmentation in the vacuole, Al-binding proteins, evolution of Al-resistant enzymes, elevated enzyme activity, Al-exclusion mechanisms and efflux of organic acids from root apices to chelate the toxic Al. The internal resistance mechanisms include chelating of Al in cystosol with organic acids or acidic polypeptides, compartmentation of Al in the vacuole, induction of protein synthesis, and synthesis of Al-resistant isoenzymes, Al-binding proteins within the root or within the cell wall of roots. Many native plant species and cultivars exhibit genetic-based variability for Al sensitivity that has allowed the plant breeders to develop Al-tolerant crops. Most of the farmers of acidic region soils are reluctant to use the lime as an amendment for acidic soils. Under such situations, the improvement of agricultural crops through molecular and/or physiological understanding of tolerance mechanisms to overcome this problem to a great extent by modifying the genotype of the plants (with superior root growth and vigor) adapted to the Al-toxic acid soil to achieve higher crop productivity without liming or with least amount of lime.

Key words: Aluminium toxicity tolerance, Al-ligand complexes, mechanisms.

INTRODUCTION

Food and Agriculture Organization (FAO) estimation, more than 99 per cent of the total worldwide human food supply is produced on land, whereas only 0.6 per cent comes from oceans and other aquatic ecosystems. The increasing human population and improvement of living standard will be required to develop management practices and utilize the acid soil regions resource in such a way to meet the needs of the population to maintain a balance with environment that is favourable both to humans and most other species (Hardwood 1990). Soil properties play the major role in determining the nutrient availability to plants and in many instances by specific mineral stress problems. Production constraints are more intense on acid soils, which cover 30 per cent of the world's land area (UexKull and Mutert 1995) and aluminium toxicity limits crop growth around 12 per cent of the world's cultivated lands. It is the important factor limiting the productivity of crops in humid northeastern region of India (Patiram 2007). The mineral stress in acid soils is primarily related to nutrient deficiencies and toxicities of aluminium (Al) and manganese (Mn). In acid soils, specific mineral stress phenomena are related to:

- Presence of the toxic concentration of Al and to a lesser extent Mn toxicity in many species,
- Deficiency of bases (Ca, Mg, K) and poor retention power of the bases,
- High P fixation power of soil on the surfaces of the highly active Al and Fe, rendering it unavailable to plants,
- Deficiency of Mo, especially for the growth of legumes,
- Reduction of soil biological activities, and
- Fe and Mn toxicities in submerged rice.

The once application of lime is not the permanent solution as compared to reclamation of alkaline soils. It is a recurring financial burden on resource poor farmers of humid tropical and subtropical regions of the world developing nations. Liming of acid soils is neither an economic option for poor farmers nor an effective strategy for ameliorating the subsoil acidity (Rao *et al.* 1993). The alternative strategy for improving crop productivity on Al-toxic acid soils is to select and develop crop species/genotypes with greater Al tolerance overcomes the Al-toxicity with least or without amendments to exploit the full yields potential. Lot of research works have been done in agronomy, physiology and molecular biology to understand the mechanism of Al toxicity and tolerance in plants in the last two decades of twentieth century. In this book an attempt has been made to review the aluminum tolerance mechanisms of plants to utilize this genetic potential to increase the productivity of aluminium-toxic acid soils of the tropics and subtropics for the food security without amendments and/or with least amount of amendments.

PHYTOTOXIC ALUMINIUM

Aluminium toxicity is associated with soluble aluminium. Attempts have been made recently to demonstrate the toxicity of individual Al species in solution. It is difficult to draw the conclusion, which Al monomer is the major phytotoxic species, and nearly all the monomer Al species (Al^{3+}, Al^{2+} and Al^+) have been considered toxic in one study or another (Kinraide 1991). Even with simple, low-ionic-strength nutrient solutions, various Al species can be predicted with more confidence, the conclusion can be confounded by the choice of equilibrium constants, the colinearity between the concentration of certain Al species, the formation of $Al(OH)_3$ and Al_{13}, the duration of experiments, and the difficulty of separating effects of pH from Al speciation. It has been well-documented that the addition of cations to growth solutions will ameliorate Al^{3+} toxicity, and this amelioration cannot be accounted for solely by ionic strength effects on Al^{3+} activity in solution. Calcium (Ca^{2+}) and magnesium (Mg^{2+}) are particularly more effective in ameliorating toxicity (Alva *et al.* 1986, Kinraide and Parker 1987). Kinraide *et al.* (1992) have developed a model based on modified Guoy-Chapman-Stern electrostatic interactions between Al^{3+}, other cations, and the negatively charged cell surface. This model was used on the assumptions that the negatively charged membrane surface would generate a strong attractive force for trivalent cations such as Al^{3+} and other cations had the ability to reduce the negative surface charge of plasma membrane, either through charge screening or charge neutralization. Based on this model, Al toxicity was best predicted with activity of Al^{3+} at the surface of plasma membrane than with the activity of Al^{3+} in the bulk solution. This model indicated the important role of negatively charged root-cell surface in toxicities not only to Al^{3+}, but also to other potentially toxic cations and anions. Kinraide *et al.* (1992) found that root growth was more closely related with the predicted activity of Al^{3+} at the surface of the plasma membrane with the activity in the bathing solution.

MECHANISMS OF ALUMINIUM TOXICITY

The most widely accepted measure of Al toxicity symptom in plants is the inhibition of root growth and associated with a swelling of root apex. Auxin is transported from auxin synthesizing shoot tissues via the phloem toward the root apical meristems, where it is considered to be unloaded to the elongation zone (Hasenstein and Evans 1988, Estelle 1998). Inhibition of basipetal auxin flow has been implicated in severe effects on root growth and morphology. These include swelling of root tips through uncontrolled periclinal divisions (Blancaflor and Hasenstein 1995, Ruegger *et al.* 1997) caused by auxin accumulation in the merismatic zone and distal transition zone (1–2 mm from the root tip) and reduction of the gravitropic response (Hasenstein and Evans 1988, Kollmeire *et al.* 2000).

The root apex (root cap, meristem, and elongation zone) accumulates more Al and attracts greater physiological damage than the mature root tissues (Delhaize and Ryan 1995). Bennet *et al.* (1987) and Bennet and Breen (1991) suggested that the root cap is a site of perception of Al injury, based on anatomical studies of maize root. They suggested that Al might inhibit root growth indirectly via a signal-response pathway involving the root cap, hormones, and secondary messengers. The mechanisms of Al toxicity result from either Al-ligand complex, which either inhibits the vital function of the ligand that binds it (e.g. enzymes, calmodulin, tubulin, ATP, GTP, DNA), or the Al-ligand complex itself poisons other metabolic processes (Delhaize and Ryan 1995). McQuattie and Schier (1990) examined the red spruce seedling to Al injury in nutrient solution and examination of root tips and 5–10 mm segments from the tips, revealed numerous cellular changes in Al-stress roots; premature vacuolation, accumulation of phenol-like material, loss of cells from peripheral cell layers, formation of intercellular spaces, increased disruption of cellular membranes and degeneration of the cytoplasm. Marschner (1991) described the possible inhibitory effects of Al on root growth; inhibition of cell division and elongation, replacement of Ca^{2+} and Mg^{2+} from the middle lamella, replacement of Ca^{2+} from the plasma membrane to cytosol through influx, and subsequently callose formation in root cap and rhizodermal cells. The possibility of Al transport through the Ca^{2+} channel might be convincing because Al^{3+} inhibited the specific Ca^{2+} channel, which responds to a specific channel blocker (Huang et al. 1992). Al^{3+} transport through the Mg^{2+} channel is also plausible because Mg^{2+} transport is strongly inhibited by Al^{3+} due to similar diameter of both (MacDiarmid and Gardner 1996). The antagonistic effect of Ca^{2+} on Al toxicity is well-known. The formation of callose (1, 3-beta-D-glucose) at plasma membrane is the rapid and sensitive marker of Al-induced injury (Zhang et al. 1994). In plant roots Al accumulates mainly in the cells located in the apical elongation zone and inhibits cell elongation rapidly. Blancaflor et al. (1998) opined that Al-induced microtubule orientation within the inner cortex cells might be a mechanism for root swelling. Yamamoto et al. (2002) reported that Al enhanced reactive oxygen species (ROS), which leads to respiration inhibition, ATP depletion and inhibition of the cell growth/elongation.

MECHANISMS OF ALUMINIUM TOLERANCE

Some species of plants have a much wider range of adaptation as compared to others. The plants that are adapted to acidic soils at high levels of aluminum do not usually show symptoms of Al toxicity. The plants were classified as Al-sensitive plant (*Hordeum vulgare*), Al-medium tolerants (*Leucaena leucocephala, Ischaemum barbatum, Stylosanthese guianensis,* and *Fagopyrum esculetum*), Al-tolerant plants which growth was not affected or stimulated by Al application (*Brachiaria ruziziensis*), and Al-stimulated plants (*Melastoma malabathricum, Melaleuca cājūputi, Acasia mangium, Hydrangea macrophylla, Vaccinium macrocarpon, Polygonum sachalinense* and *Oryza sativa*), respectively. Only a small fraction of plant species take up high levels of Al in their above ground tissues. The Al-tolerant plants were further classified on the basis of Al accumulation into Al-accumulators such as *Melastoma malabathricum, Hydrangea macrophylla, Vaccinium macrocarpon, Polygonum sachalinense* and *Fagopyrum esculetum*, Al-excluders such as *M. cajuputi, A. mangium, L. leucocephala, I. barbatum, S. guianensis* and *Oryza sativa*, and Al-root accumulators such as *V. macrocarpon, B. ruziziensis* and *P. sachalinense*.

Among the agricultural crops such as pineapple (*Ananas cosmosus*), coffee (*Coffea sp.*), tea (*Camellia sp.*), rubber (*Achra Zapata*), cassava (*Manihot sp.*), sweet potato (*Ipomea batata*), rice (*Oryza sativa*), finger millet (*Eleusine coracona*), buckwheat (*Fagopyrum esculentum*) as well pasture species such as guinea grass (*Panicum maximum*), jajagua (*Hypaahanea rufa*), molasses grass (*Melinis minutiflora*) and *Brachiaria decumbens* can grow in aluminium toxic soils where wheat, barley, maize and soybean can not grow well. Many plant species and cultivars of agricultural importance show an inheritable tolerance to Al stress, and these species and cultivars have become important resources for investigating Al toxicity and tolerance. There are several recent reviews that discuss mechanisms of Al tolerance and toxicity in plants (Kochian 1995, Matsumoto 2000, Ma *et al.* 2001, Ryan *et al.* 2001, Patiram *et al.* 2002, Kochian *et al.* 2004). The different physiological and molecular bases of plant tolerance mechanisms to Al toxicity are described below:

Plant Induced Increase in Rhizosphere pH

As we know that the phytotoxic form of Al^{3+} largely depends on pH, a mechanism based on increasing the pH around root apices should provide a degree of protection from Al^{3+}. The plant induced increases in rhizosphere pH is an attractive hypothesis for Al^{3+} exclusion barrier (Taylor 1991). All the previous studies in this support have measured changes in bulk solution pH, which is mainly influenced by mature root regions and not the root apex, which is the site of Al toxicity (Kochian 1995). At 4.5, an increase of rhizosphere pH of 0.1 to 0.2 units may lead to considerable decrease of toxic Al^{3+} activity (Kinraide, 1991), because the solubility of Al is strongly dependent on pH. Degenhardt *et al.* (1998) and Kollmeier *et al.* (2000) found a clear Al-induced increase in pH at the root surface by using a vibrating-sensitive microelectrode at the root tip surface. Kollmeier *et al.* (2000) explained the alkalization peak in distal transition zone (1–2 mm from the root tip) of maize Al-resistant cultivars. They hypothesized that the induced pH increase by two factors namely; either the physiological properties for maintenance of ionic currents, which are less affected by Al^{3+} in the Al-resistant as compared to the Al-sensitive cultivars or an Al-exclusion mechanism switched on in the Al-resistant cultivars promoting release of organic anions. The organic anions might bind free protons in the rhizosphere and hence lead to an increase in surface pH.

Role of Organic Acids to Detoxify the Aluminium Toxicity

Bruckert (1970) determined the presence of oxalic, citric, malic, manioc and others in water extract of strongly acidic forest soils. He divided the aliphatic acids into three groups according to their Al complexing capacities: (i) citric and oxalic as strong complexers; (ii) malic and manioc as moderate; (iii) lactic and succinic as weak. The first example of a chelating substance was the citrate from snap bean under Al stress (Miyasaka *et al.* 1991). Much of the current evidences pointed the major role of certain organic acids secreted from plant roots in response to Al treatment that can form complexes with Al^{3+} to protect plant roots (Ma 2000, Ryan *et al*. 2001) in the cystosol or at the root-soil interface.

Al-detoxifying capacities of these acids are highly related to the relative position on the main carbon chain of OH and COOH groups (Hue *et al*. 1986). The most effective detoxifying acids have either two pairs of OH/COOH attached to two adjacent carbons (citric and tartaric) or two COOHs directly connected (oxalic). The relative positions of OH/COOH for the effective Al-detoxifiers are the formation of stable 5- or 6-bond ring structures with Al. Organic acids, which can be synthesized in a large amount through photosynthesis (Larsen *et al*. 1998), are the powerful candidate to protect from Al toxicity by forming chelated complex with toxic Al^{3+} intra- or extracellular with the substances originating from plants before binding of Al^{3+} to cellular constituents. It has been found that resistant/tolerant varieties/cultivars exude much more organic acids (oxalic, citric or malic) from root apex as compared to Al-sensitive cultivars to reduce the activities of Al^{3+} in the rhizosphere. Citric acid and oxalic acid are produced in Krebs cycle and the tricarboxylic acid cycle (TCA cycle) in metabolic reaction. Malic acid is also a metabolite of the citric acid cycle. The binding capacity of these acids is dependent on the degree of their carboxyl groups and their ability to form bonds with Al^{3+}. Oxalic acid is relatively strong organic acid being about 10,000 times stronger than malic acid. Given its physicochemical properties, $citrate^{3-}$ (a tricarboxylic acid anion) chelates Al^{3+} more effectively than the dicarboxylic malate-2 anion, making it more effective at detoxifying Al.

At sufficient concentration, these organic acids can form complexes with Al ions, prevent the Al ions from binding to the fixed negative sites of the cell wall and plasma membrane, and confer tolerance to plants to maintain the normal functions of the cell wall and plasma membrane (Ishikawa *et al*. 2000). Aluminum tolerance mechanisms postulated to involve organic acids can be divided into external and internal detoxification with some plant species apparently using both types of mechanisms.

External Release of Organic Acids and Aluminium Tolerance

Although the amount of organic acids exuded from root apices may not be sufficient to detoxify all the Al^{3+} in the rhizosphere of the root system, yet it should be sufficient to detoxify the Al^{3+} that are in vicinity to root apices. However, efflux needs to continue to replace the organic acids that diffuse away from the root apices as well as replenish those which are broken down by microorganisms. Thus organic acids are protecting sheath around the root apex in Al tolerant plants as it moves through an acid soil. Ma *et al*. (2001) identified the two patterns of organic acid secretion from plant roots:

- In Pattern I, Al activates an anion channel on the plasma membrane permeable to organic acid anions. This stimulation could occur in one of the three ways: (1) Al^{3+} interacts directly with the channel protein to trigger its opening; (2) Al^{3+}

interacts with a specific receptor on the membrane surface or with the membrane itself to initiate secondary messenger cascade that then activates the channel; or (3) Al^{3+} enters the cytoplasm and activates the channel directly, or indirectly via secondary messenger.

- In Pattern II, Al interacts with the cell; encode proteins involved with metabolism of organic acids or their transport across the plasma membrane. Organic anions form a stable complexes with Al, thereby Al^{3+} detoxify in the rhizosphere.

The release of organic acids is quick in Pattern I and gets delayed for several hours in Pattern II after the addition of Al in nutrient solution. The Al-activated efflux from maize, trigger both a rapid efflux of citrate as well as a delayed release and induction of novel protein is not required for quick secretion (Ma 2000), whereas pattern II, protein induction is required (Ma *et al.* 2001).

At the prevailing neutral pH of the cytoplasm, organic acids in the cytoplasms are largely dissociated and exist as anions. Since the equilibrium potential for organic acid anions (as well as inorganic anions) is much more positive than that of the resting membrane potential in root cells, activation (i.e. opening) of plasma membrane anion channels will result in a large anion efflux down the outward electrochemical gradient. Ion channels are proteins that extend across membranes and allow the passive flow of ions down their electrochemical gradients. Ryan *et al.* (1997), Zhang *et al.* (2001) and Pineros and Kochian (2001) using the patch clamp theory provided the direct evidence for the presence of Al-activated anion channels in the root-cell plasma membrane of plants, which activate Al-induced organic anion exudation. The Al^{3+} activated anion channels are either the Al^{3+} bind activated channel protein, or the Al receptor and signal transduction pathway limited to the plasma membrane and are co-localized with the channel (Pineros and Kochian 2001). A complex cascade of events regulating this channel might be involved, such that in addition to the requirement of extracellular Al^{3+} for channel activation, other intracellular and extracellular factors may modulate the activity of this channel in the whole-cell mode (Pineros and Kochian 2001). The anion channel modulated by a wide range of signals such as changes in intracellular and/or extracellular Ca^{2+} and anion activities as well as protein phosphorylation or allosteric regulation by nucleotides.

Detoxification of Aluminium by Internal Organic Acids Secretion

Some plant species have the remarkable ability of accumulating Al in shoots and roots. Al binds mainly to the component of the cell wall and Lazof *et al.* (1994) indicated that Al could enter the symplasm of root cell quickly. Old leaves of tea can accumulate Al up to 30,000 ppm on dry weight basis (Matsumoto *et al.* 1976). Evidences show the role of organic acids in complexing internal Al in buckwheat, *Hydrangea macrophylla* and *Melastoma malabathricum*. The Al-tolerant indicator plant *Hydrangea*, which flower's colour changes from pink malabathricum to blue by increasing Al content in the leaves as much as 15.7 mmol kg^{-1} fresh weight, and 77 per cent of the total exist in cell sap (Ma *et al.* 1997). The blue colour results from a complex of Al, delphinidin 3-glucoside and 3-caffeoylquinic acid. The ligand in the *Hydrangea* leaves was determined to be citric acid approximately 1:1 Al-citrate complex according to measurement of ^{27}Al-NMR. The buckwheat with Al-tolerance, secretes organic acid that complexes Al differ in various tissues of the plant. The absorbed Al exists as Al:oxalate (1:3) complex that is completely detoxified in roots and leaves (Ma *et al.* 1997, 1998). In the xylem the predominant form is Al-citrate as 1:1 complex and once translocated to shoot cells, the 1:3 Al:oxalate is reformed. The organic that complexes Al differs in various tissues and the way they are translocated across the membrane is not known, but is likely to involve specific transporters. In *Melastoma malabathricum*, detoxify Al accumulate in leaves by forming Al-oxalate, Al- (oxalate)2 and Al- (oxalate)3 and accumulate in the apoplast and/or vacuole, in which the harmful effects of excess Al may be limited (Watanabe *et al.* 1998). The Al is transported from roots to shoots as Al-citrate complex, but is transformed into an Al-oxalate complex for its storage in the leaves (Watanabe *et al.* 2001). In tea leaves, most of aluminium was proposed to be bound to catechins, based on the observed signals of the ^{27}Al-NMR spectrum (Nagata *et al.* 1992).

The above findings suggest that Al^{3+} is transported across the plasma membrane into the symplasm in Al-accumulating plant species. Upon entering the symplasm, the prevailing pH (pH 6.5–7.5) and abundance of potential ligands will decrease the concentration of Al^{3+} at a very low concentration in the picomolar to nanomolar range (Martin 1988). Martin (1988) studies indicated that picomolar or nanomolar cytoplasmic Al^{3+} activities could be toxic as a result of Al interactions with sites regulated by Mg. Al binds almost 10^7 times more strongly to ATP than does Mg: therefore, very low concentration Al can compete with Mg for the P sites. The stability constants are 12.4 of 1:3 Al-oxalate (Nordstrom and May 1996) and 8.1 of 1:1 Al-citrate (Martin 1988) stability constant of later becomes 11.7 and 12.4 at pH 7.0 and pH 7.4, respectively. These constants are significantly higher than for the Al-ATP (10.9), could effectively reduce the activity of Al^{3+} in the cystosol at a pH above 7.0 and prevent the binding of the cellular components, thereby decrease Al^{3+} phytotoxic effects (Ma 2000).

The high rate of organic acid excretion involves several reactions, such as an increase in organic acid synthesis (Takita *at al.* 1999) and a superior ability for organic acid transport at the plasma membrane (Ryan *et al.* 1995). Mitochondrial CS (citrate synthase) and cystolic NADP-ICDH are two enzymes probably have a key role in controlling internal citrate concentration in plants. Number of genes relating to an increase in organic acid synthesis was isolated, thereafter introduced into several plants species (de la Fuente *et al.* 1997, Koyama *et al.* 2000, Tesfaye *et al.* 2001). These transgenic plants showed enhanced organic acid excretion from the roots and in turn could improve Al tolerance. Delhaize *et al.* (2003) reported that CS activity did not limit the accumulation of internal citrate and suggested that the transport of citrate across the plasma membrane was a more likely site for regulation of citrate efflux from tobacco roots.

SUPPRESSION OF LIPID PEROXIDATION

The involvement of oxidative stress in Al-toxicity has been suggested although Al itself is not a transition metal and cannot catalyse redox reactions. The stimulatory effect of Al on ferrous iron (Fe^{2+}) induced lipid peroxidation has been proposed as one of the possible mechanisms of Al-toxicity (Cakmark and Horst 1991, Yamamoto et al. 1997, 2002). The Al-enhanced Fe-mediated peroxidation of lipids leads to the loss of plasma membrane integrity and loss of viability in cultured tobacco cells (Ikegawa et al. 1998). Potential mechanisms of Al-toxicity measured as Al-induced inhibition growth in cultured tobacco cells (*Nicotiana tabacum*, nonchlorophillic cell line SL) and pea roots (*Pisum sativum* L.) by Yamamoto et al. (2002) suggested that the Al-triggered reactive oxygen species (O_2^-) leads to respiration inhibition, ATP depletion and the inhibition of cell growth/root elongation, respectively. In plant cells, O_2^- is mainly evolved in mitochondria (via respiration) and in chloroplast through photosynthesis.

Genetically biased studies in plants also suggest that Al enhances oxidative stress because Al induces the expression of several genes encoding antioxidant enzymes such as glutathiones S-transferase, peroxidase, and superoxide dismutase (Richards et al. 1998, Ezaki et al. 2000). Biological antioxidant molecules, which inhibit the peroxidation of lipids, may protect cells from Al-toxicity due to oxygen stress. It has been observed that over expression of some these induced proteins in *Arabiodopsis* resulted an increase of Al-tolerance to oxidative stress strengthened the link between Al-toxicity and oxidative stress (Ezaki et al. 2000). Hamilton et al. (2001) also reported the enhancement of activities of vacuolar H^+-ATPase and mitochondrial ATP synthase by Al specifically in an Al-resistant wheat (*Triticum aestivum* L.) cultivars, suggesting that the vacuolar H^+-ATPase responds specifically to Al stress with ATP supplied by mitochondrial ATP synthase.

MOLECULAR LEVELS

Differential uptake of Al into roots could account for differences in tolerance between genotypes. However, conflicting results have been reported. Apparent resistance of plants to adverse soil conditions is generally caused by avoidance mechanism rather than a tolerance. However, the information on the above at the molecular level is limited. Aniol (1984) suggested that plants could develop Al tolerance through the synthesis of proteins that bind or sequester Al and render it innocuous within the symplast. As Al tolerance is determined by potentially many genes, the task of identifying specific proteins that might confer Al tolerance is difficult. An understanding of genomic affinities helps to formulate effective breeding programmes designed to transfer desirable genes from wild relatives or primitive varieties of crop plants into otherwise superior cultivars. Rice shows the highest tolerance to Al toxicity among small-grain cereals crops, however, the mechanisms and genetics responsible for its high Al tolerance are not yet well understood. Carver and Ownby (1995) opined that some of the properties of a novel inducible 'Al tolerance' protein would include:

- Consistently high concentrations in tolerant lines and induced levels or absence in sensitive line;

- Co-segregation with tolerant phenotypes when tolerant and Al sensitive cultivars are crossed;

- Relatively specific to Al toxicity; and

- Physiological role that is consistent with proposed mechanisms for metal tolerance (e.g. a protein involved in production or secretion of chelating ligands or one that is part of an Al efflux pump or some other exclusion process).

The genetic analysis of Al-tolerance is the active area of research. Impressive interspecific diversification for Al-tolerance is well-known in many plant species (Foy 1988). The genetic architecture of tolerance is variable, being monogenic in some species and polygenic in others. To understand the genetic control of Al-tolerance and to determine the homology of Al-tolerance genes, molecular mapping has been initiated in different crops.

GENETICALLY CONTROL

Different genetic system may operate in seedlings vs. adult plant or at different levels of Al stress. Many plant species and cultivars show an inheritable tolerance to Al stress, and these species and cultivars have become important resources for investigating Al toxicity and tolerance. Utilizing this genetic variability in plant breeding and selection programmes, plants can be developed with resistance to many adverse acidic soil conditions. This is an important strategy for crop improvement in Al-toxic acidic soils is to select for cultivars with increased Al-tolerance. Among the small grains, barley is the most Al-sensitive species, while rye (*Secale cereale* L.) appears to possess highest degree of Al-tolerance (Foy 1983). Genotypic variation to Al-tolerance also exists within the species.

OTHER MECHANISMS

The meristem and cap region where Al-toxicity appeared dominantly are coated with mucilage that ranges in thickness from 50 μm to 1 mm (Matsumoto 2000). Mucilage consists of enormous molecules greater than 2×106 Da. Abundant sugars are glucose, galactose, arabinose, and uronic acids which are the characteristic sugars of mucilage. Mucilage has various protective functions against toxic metals in the soil. The diffusion of Al through mucilage droplets and its accompanying boundary layer would be rate-limiting step in the movement of Al to the root surface. Furthermore, organic acids released into a mucilage droplet by forming a region of high concentration of organic acids where Al could be chelated before it reached to the root surface (Henderson and Ownby 1991). The internal resistance mechanisms include chelating of Al in cystosol with organic acids or acidic polypeptides, compartmentation of Al in the vacuole, induction of protein synthesis, synthesis of Al-resistant isoenzymes and synthesis of specific Al-binding proteins (Taylor 1991).

The binding capacity of plasma membrane of Al^{3+} is attributed to the negativity of carboxyl groups and phosphate groups in the plasma membrane. The surface membrane potential may be one factor involved in the plant response Al^{3+}. Negatively charged cell surfaces of the root accumulate the toxic cations, and amelioration is affected by treatment that reduces the negativity of the cell surface potential by charge screening of cation binding. It has been found that the surface membrane potential of protoplast prepared from Al-tolerant species was less negative than that of Al-sensitive species (Wagastuma *et al.* 1995).

Induced exudation of organic acids has also been proposed as a potential mechanism of the Si-induced amelioration of Al toxicity in higher plants. Barcelo *et al.* (1993) observed that the roots of teosinte treated with Al and Si contained higher concentration of malate than roots treated with Al alone. Crocker *at al.* (1997) hypothesized that by Al/Si interactions at the cell wall, the exudation of malate or other organic compounds into the cell wall promotes the formation of aluminosilicate and hydroxyaluminosilicate, which detoxify the Al. The Al/Si co-deposition was detected in the outer tangenial walls of the root epidermis of wheat (Cocker *et al.* 1997) and inside the vacuoles of maize root cortical cells (Vazquez *et al.* 1999). Currently Kidd *et al.* (2001) concluded that Al and Si induced secretion of flavonoid-type phenolics, especially catechin, and quercetin by the root apex of maize could be a potential mechanism in the elimination of Al toxicity by silicon.

FUTURE STRATEGIES

Sufficient research works have already been done on liming of acid soil to increase the productivity of crops. However, most of the farmers of acidic uplands are reluctant to use the lime as an amendment for acidic soils. Under such situations, the improvement of agricultural crops will be a rewarding activity for plant breeders to overcome this problem to a great extent by modifying the genotype of the plants adapted to the Al-toxic acid soil mineral stress environment.

The genetic improvement of crops (cereals, pulses, and oilseeds) is justified where application of lime is out of question. Kochian *et al.* (2004) have forecasted the vision that researchers are on the verge of identifying some of the genes that confer Al-tolerant crop plants; these discoveries will open up new avenues of molecular/physiological understanding of tolerance mechanisms. Sasaki *et al.* (2004) isolated wheat's ALMT1 gene that encodes a membrane protein transporter that facilitates the release of malic acid in the root apices of the Al-tolerant line at greater level than the near isogenic but Al-sensitive line. This gene was introduced in barley in Australia and the developed cultivars performed well in controlled (hydroponic culture) as well as in field conditions (Delhaize *et al.* 2004). These findings provide additional evidence the ALMT1 is a major Al-tolerance gene and demonstrate its ability to confer effective tolerance to acid soils through a transgenic approach in an important crop species. However, ALMT1 did not confer enhanced Al-tolerance to rice plants despite conferring an Al-activated efflux of malate. This inability of

ALMT1 to confer Al-tolerance to rice was attributed to the already high endogenous Al-tolerance of this species (Sasaki *et al.* 2004). This breakthrough will provide new genetic resources for improving Al-tolerance via both molecular assisted breeding and biotechnology. This can be done in a systematic way to overcome the Al-toxicity on acidic soils through breeding of tolerant crops as follows:

- Efforts should be made to test or characterize tolerance limit of existing cultivars before breeding begins. The experience of other countries (Australia and American countries) can be utilized.

- What limit of tolerance are available with our own stock of crop varieties and this tolerance can be improved?

- Objectives must define research and development needs in screening and breeding in relation to needs of the farmers and researchers.

- Assay techniques to be adopted for screening should be precise with available methodologies and be capable of handling large numbers of germplasm.

- In field, where screening to be taken, the soil stress must be identified and characterized and sites must represent the characteristics of the region concerned with least spatial variation for better transfer of information from one site to other.

- We must also decide the part of the test area be limited to fertilizer or organic agriculture to suit the economic condition of the farmers.

- For the success of screening and breeding for Al-tolerance, a wide network of linked research and development programmes should be taken in different zones of acidic soils to identify the problems and to assess the best approaches to solve them. In this regards, the role of regional and international centers would be identified for tolerant strains or sources of germplasm to make germplasm stocks available.

- Generally plant breeders are accustomed to working individually, or in a multidisciplinary team, primarily with other biologists. Therefore, a well-integrated, multidisciplinary team of plant breeders, soil scientists and plant physiologists should be considered at planning stages so as to look at the problem in locality. The all team members should be considered in setting goals, defining objectives, making critical decisions and evaluating progress.

- Biotechnological approach to manipulate organic acid biosynthesis or catabolism, especially transgenic plants offer most optimistic in augmenting agricultural production in the present century.

REFERENCES

Alva AK, Asher CJ and Edwards DG. 1986. The role of calcium in alleviating aluminum toxicity. *Aust. J. Agric. Res.* **37:** 375–382.

Aniol A. 1984. Induction of aluminum tolerance in wheat seedlings by low doses of aluminum in the nutrient solution. *Plant Physiol.* **76:** 551–555.

Barcelo J, Guevara P and Poschenrieder Ch. 1993. Silicon amelioration of aluminium toxicity in teosinte (*Zea mays* L). *Plant Soil.* **154:** 249–255.

Bennet RJ, Breen CM and Fey MV. 1987. The effect of aluminium on root cap functions and root development in *Zea mays* L. *Eviron. Exp. Bot.* **27:** 91–104.

Bennet RJ and Breen CM. 1991. The aluminium signal: new dimensions to mechanisms of aluminium tolerance. *Plant Soil.* **134:** 153–166.

Blancaflor EB and Hasenstein KH. 1995. Time course and auxin sensitivity of cortical microtubule reorientaion in maize roots. *Protoplasma.* **185:** 72–82.

Blancaflor EB, Jones DL and Gilroy S. 1998. Alterations in the cytoskeleton accompany aluminum-induced growth inhibition and morphological changes in primary roots of maize. *Plant Physiol.* **118:** 159–172.

Bruckert S. 1970. Influence des composes organiguls sur la pedogenese en milieu acide. II. Expiriences dela labovatoir modalitis d' action des agents complexants. *Ann. Agron.,* Paris **21:** 725–757.

Cakmak I and Horst WJ. 1991. Effective aluminium on lipid peroxidation, superoxide dismutase, catalase and peroxidase activities in root tips of soybean (*Glycine max* L). *Physiol. Plant.* **83:** 463–468.

Carver RF and Ownby JD. 1995. Acid soil tolerance in wheat. *Adv. Agron.* **54:** 117–173.

Crocker KM, Hodson MJ, Evans DE and Sangster A. 1997. The interaction between silicon and aluminium in *Triticum aestivum* L (cv. Celtic). *Israel J. Plant Sci.* **45:** 285–292.

Degenhardt J, Larsen PB, Howell SH and Kochian LV. 1998. Aluminum resistance in the *Arabidopsis* mutant *alr*-104 is caused by an aluminum-induced increase in rhizosphere pH. *Plant Physiol.* **117:** 19–27.

de la Fuente JM, Ramirez-Rodriguez V, Cabreta-Ponce JL and Herreta-Estrella L. 1997. Aluminum tolerance in transgenic plants by alteration of citrate synthesis. *Sci.* **276:** 1566–1568.

Delhaize E and Ryan PR. 1995. Aluminum toxicity and tolerance in plants. *Plant Physiol.* **107:** 315–321.

Delhaize E, Ryan PR, Hebb DM, Yamamoto Y, Sasaki T and Matsumoto H. 2004. Engineering high-level aluminum tolerance in barley with the ALMT1. *Proc. Nat. Acad. Sci.*(USA) **101:** 152–15254.

Delhaize E, Ryan PR, Hocking PJ and Richardson AE. 2003. Effects of altered citrate synthase and isocitrate dehydrogenase expression on internal citrate concentrations of tobacco (*Nicotiana tabacum* L.) roots. *Plant Soil.* **248:** 137–144.

Estelle M. 1998. Polar auxin transport: New support for an old model. *Plant Cell.* **10:** 1775–1778.

Ezaki B, Gardner RC and Matsumoto H. 2000. Expression of aluminum-induced genes in transgenic *Arabidopsis* plants can ameliorate aluminum stress and/or oxidative stress. *Plant Physiol.* **122:** 657–666.

Foy CD. 1983. The physiology of plant adaptation in mineral stress. *Iowa State J. Res.* **57:** 355–391.

Foy CD. 1988. Plant adaptation to acid aluminium toxic soils. *Commun. Soil Sci. Plant Anal.* **19:** 959–987.

Hamilton CA, Good AG and Taylor GJ. 2001. Induction of vacuolar ATPase and mitochondrial ATP synthase by aluminum in an aluminum-resistant cultivar of wheat. *Plant Physiol.* **125:** 2068–2077.

Hardwood RR. 1990. A history of sustainable agriculture. In Sustainable agriculture system, p3–19. Edwards CA, Lal R, Madden P, Miller RH and House G (Eds), Soil Water Conservation Society of America, Ankeny, IA.

Hasenstein KH and Evans ML. 1988. Effects of cations on hormone transport in primary roots of *Zea mays*. *Plant Physiol.* **86:** 890–894.

Henderson M and Ownby JD. 1991. The role of root cap mucilage secretion in aluminum tolerance in wheat. *Curr. Top. Pl. Biochem. Physiol.* **10:** 134–141.

Huang JW, Shaff JE, Grunes DL and Kochian LV. 1992. Aluminum effects on calcium fluxes at the root apex of aluminum-tolerant and aluminum-sensitive wheat cultivars. *Plant Physiol.* **98:** 230–237.

Hue NV, Graddock GR and Adams F. 1986. Effect of organic acids on aluminum toxicity in subsoils. *Soil Sci. Soc. Am. J.* **50:** 28–34.

Ikegawa H, Yamamoto Y and Matsumoto H. 1998. Cell death caused by a combination of aluminum and iron in cultured tobacco cells. *Physiol. Plant.* **104:** 474–478.

Ishikawa S, Wagamatsu T, Sasaki R and Manu PO. 2000. Comparison of the amount of citric and malic acids in Al media of seven plant species and two cultivars each in five plant species. *Soil Sci. Plant Nutr.* **46:** 751–758.

Kidd PS, Llugani C, Poschenrieder B, Gunse B and Barcelo J. 2001. The role of root exudation in aluminium resistant and silico-induced amelioration of aluminium toxicity in three varieties of maize (*Zea mays* L.). *J. Exp. Bot.* **52:** 1339–1352.

Kinraide TB. 1991. Identification of the rhizotonic aluminium species. *Plant Soil.* **134:** 167–178.

Kinraide TB and Parker DR. 1987. Cation amelioration of aluminium toxicity in wheat. *Plant Physiol.* **83:** 546–551.

Kinraide TB, Ryan PR and Kochian L. 1992. Interactive effects of Al^{3+}, H^+, and other cations on root elongation considered in terms of cell-surface electrical potential. *Plant Physiol.* **99:** 1461–1468.

Kochian LV. 1995. Cellular mechanisms of aluminium toxicity and resistance in plants. *Annu. Rev. Pl. Physiol. Pl. Mol. Biol.* **46:** 237–260.

Kochian LV, Hoekenga OA and Pineros MA. 2004. How do crop plants tolerate acid soils? Mechanisms of aluminium tolerance and phosphorus efficiency. *Ann. Rev. Plant Biol.* **55:** 459–493.

Kollmeire M, Felle HH and Horst WJ. 2000. Genotypical difference in aluminium resistance of maize are expressed in the distal part of the transition zone. Is reduced basipetal auxin flow involved in inhibition of root elongation zone? *Plant Physiol.* **122**: 945–956.

Koyama H, Kawamura A, Kihara T, Takita E and Shibata D. 2000. Over expression of mitochondrial citrate synthase in *Arabidopsis thaliana* improved growth on phosphorus limited soil. *Plant Cell Physiol.* **41**: 1030–1037.

Larsen PB, Degenhardt J, Tai CY, Stenzler LM, Howell SH and Kochian LV. 1998. Aluminium–resistant *Arabidopsis* mutants that exhibit altered pattern of aluminium accumulation and organic acid released from roots. *Plant Physiol.* **117**: 743–75.

Lazof DB, Goldsmith JG, Ruty TW and Linton RW. 1994. Rapid uptake of aluminium into cells of intact soybean root tips. A microanalytical study using secondary ion mass spectrometry. *Plant Physiol.* **106**: 1107–1114.

Ma JF. 2000. Role of organic acids in detoxifying of aluminum in higher plants. *Plant Cell Physiol.* **41**: 383–390.

Ma JF, Ryan PR and Delhaize E. 2001. Aluminium tolerance in plants and the complexing role of organic acids. *Trends Plant Sci.* **6**: 273–278.

Ma JF, Zheng SJ, Hiradate S and Matsumoto H. 1997. Detoxifying aluminium with buckwheat. *Nature* **390**: 569–570.

Ma JF, Zheng SJ, Hiradate S and Matsumoto H. 1998. High aluminium resistance in buckwheat II. Oxalic acid detoxifies aluminium internally. *Plant Physiol.* **117**: 753–759.

Marschner H. 1991. Mechanisms of adaptation of plants to acid soil. *Plant Soil.* **134**: 1–20.

Martin RB. 1988. Bioinorganic chemistry of aluminium. In Metal ions in biological systems: Aluminium and its role in biology, p57. Sigel H and Sigel A (Eds), Marcel Dekker, New York.

Matsumoto H. 2000. Cell biology of aluminium toxicity and tolerance in higher plants. *Int. Rev. Cytol.* **200**: 1–46.

Matsumoto H, Hirasawa E, Morimura S and Takahashi E. 1976. Localization of aluminum in tea leaves. *Plant Cell Physiol.* **17**: 627–631.

MacDiarmid CW and Gardner RC. 1996. Al toxicity in yeast. A role of Mg? *Plant Physiol.* **112**: 1101–1109.

McQuattie C and Schier GA. 1990. Response of red spruce seedlings to aluminum toxicity in nutrient solution: alterations in root anatomy. *Can J. Forest Res.* **20**: 1479–1497.

Miyasaka SC, Bute JG, Howell RK and Foy C. 1991. Mechanism of aluminium tolerance in soybean: root exudation of citric acid. *Plant Physiol.* **96**: 737–743.

Nagata T, Hayatsu M and Kosuge N. 1992. Identification of aluminium form in tea leaves by ^{27}Al NMR. *Phytochem.* **31**: 1215–1218.

Nordstrom DK and May HM. 1996. Aqueous equilibrium data for mononuclear aluminium species. In: Environment chemistry of aluminium, p39–80. Sposito G (Ed), CRC Press, Boca Raton, Florida.

Patiram, Sarma BK and Dhiman KR. 2002. Plant genetic approaches for increasing crop productivity in aluminium toxic acid soil. *J. Hill Farming.* **15**: 1–10.

Patiram. 2007. Management and future research strategies for enhancing productivity of crops on the acid soils. *J. Indian Soc. Soil Sci.* **55:** 411–420.

Pineros MA and Kochian LV. 2001. A patch-clump study on the physiology of aluminium toxicity and aluminium tolerance in maize: identification and characterization of Al^{3+}-induced anion channels. *Plant Physiol.* **125:** 292–305.

Rao IM, Zeigler RS, Vera R and Sarakarung S. 1993. Selection and breeding for acid-soil tolerance in crops. *Biosci.* **43:** 454–465.

Richards KD, Schott EJ, Sharma AK, Davis KR and Gardner RC. 1998. Aluminium induces oxidative stress in *Arabidopsis thaliana. Plant Physiol.* **116:** 409–418.

Ruegger M, Dewey E, Hobbie L, Brown D, Bernasconi P, Turner J, Mudauy G and Estelle M. 1997. Reduced naphthylphthalmic acid binding in the tir3 mutant of *Arabidopsis* is associated with a regulation in polar auxin transport and diverse morphological defects. *Plant Cell.* **9:** 745–757.

Ryan PR, Delhaize E and Jones DL. 2001. Function and mechanism of organic anion exudation from plant roots. *Annu. Rev. Pl. Physiol. Pl. Mol. Biol.* **52:** 527–560.

Ryan PR, Delhaize E and Randal P. 1995. Characterization of Al-stimulated efflux from the root apices of Al-tolerant genotypes of wheat. *Planta.* **196:** 103–110.

Ryan PR, Skerrett M, Findlay GP, Delhaize E and Tyerman SD. 1997. Aluminium activates an anion channel in the apical cells of wheat roots. *Proc. Nat. Acad. Sci.* USA. **94:** 6547–6552.

Sasaki Y, Yamamoto Y, Ezaki B, Kastuhara M, Ahn SJ and Ryan PR. 2004. A wheat gene encoding an aluminium-activated malate transporter. *Plant J.* **37:** 645–653.

Takita E, Koyama H and Hara T. 1999. Organic acid metabolism in aluminium-phosphate utilizing cells of carrot (*Daucus carrota* L.). *Plant Cell Physiol.* **40:** 489–495.

Taylor GJ. 1991. Current views of the aluminium stress response; the physiological basis of tolerance. Curr. Top. *Plant Biochem. Physiol.* **10:** 57–93.

Tesfaye M, Temple SJ, Allan DL, Vance CP and Samac DA. 2001. Overexpression of malate dehyrogenase in transgenic alfalfa enhances organic acid synthesis and confers tolerance to aluminium. *Plant Physiol.* **127:** 1836–1844.

UexKull Von and Mutert E. 1995. Global extent, development and economic impact of acid soils. In Plant soil interactions at low pH: Principles and Management, p5–9. Dare RA (Ed), Kluwer Academic Publishers, Dorddrecht, Netherlands.

Vazquez MD, Poschenrieder C, Corrales I and Barcelo J. 1999. Changes in apoplastic Al during the initial growth response to Al by roots of a resistant maize variety. *Plant Physiol.* **119:** 435–444.

Wagatsuma T, Jujo K, Ishikawa S and Nakashima T. 1995. Aluminium-tolerant protoplasts from roots can be collected with positively charged silica microbeads: A method based on differences in surface negativity. *Plant Cell Physiol.* **36:** 1493–1502.

Watanabe T, Osaki M, Yoshihara T and Tadano T. 1998. Distribution and chemical speciation of aluminium in the Al accumulator plant, *Melastoma Malabathricum* L. *Plant Soil.* **201:** 165–173.

Watanabe T, Osaki M and Tadano T. 2001. Al uptake kinetics in roots of *Melastoma Malabathricum* L. – an Al accumulator plant. *Plant Soil.* **231:** 283–291.

Yamamoto Y, Hachiya A and Matsumoto H. 1997. Oxidative damage to membranes by a combination of aluminium and iron in suspension-cultured cells. *Plant Cell Physiol.* **38:** 1333–1339.

Yamamoto Y, Kobayashi Y, Devi S, Rikishi S and Matsumoto H. 2002. Aluminium toxicity is associated with mitochondrial dysfunction and the production of reactive oxygen species in plant cells. *Plant Physiol.* **110:** 1019–1025.

Zhang G, Hoddinott J and Taylor GJ. 1994. Characterization of 1, 3-beta – glucon (callose) synthesis in roots of *Triticum aestivum* L. in response to aluminium toxicity. *J. Plant Physiol.* **144:** 229–234.

Zhang W, Ryan P and Tyerman SD. 2001. Malate-permeable channels and cation channels activated by aluminium in the apical cells of wheat roots. *Plant Physiol.* **125:** 1459–1472.

3 Strategies for Screening for Evaluation of Aluminium Tolerance

Dharmendra Singh, RN Sehgal, Mahendra Singh, Rajendra Singh, NS Panwar and Muraleedhar Aski

ABSTRACT

Selection of crops for aluminium tolerance is a useful approach to increase production on acid soil. This requires a rapid and reliable system to discriminate between aluminium tolerant and aluminium sensitive genotypes. This chapter presents the various screening techniques to evaluate germplasm for aluminium tolerance.

Key words: Aluminium tolerance, evaluation, screening strategies.

INTRODUCTION

Reliable screening is an integral part of any successful program for biotic or abiotic stress breeding. A rapid screening technique is needed to select large populations for aluminium tolerance. Screening techniques vary with crop species and traits. For many traits, seedling stage is the most efficient for screening a large number of plants. To breed genotypes with improved Al-tolerance, reliable, efficient screening method must be available to the breeder. Several attempts have been made to establish a suitable test for assessing Al-tolerance in plants using different morphological, physiological and biochemical markers of aluminium toxicity. Al-toxicity in plant tops is often characterized by symptoms resembling those of phosphorus or calcium deficiencies, rendering these symptoms non-specific for use as a consistent measure of Al-toxicity. There have been various basic approaches to screen germplasm for tolerance to Al under solution culture (Furlani *et al.* 1982, Campbell and Lafever 1976, Howeler and Cadavid 1976), soil culture (Reid *et al.* 1969, Foy 1976), sand culture (Villagarcia *et al.* 2001, Singh 2009), *in vitro* (Conner and Meredith 1985), microplots and field evalaution. Solution culture has been divided into two types of screening, *viz.* long-term and short-term (pulse test). The long-term test studies assess the effect of aluminium ions on root elongation after several days or weeks of growth in a solution containing Al. The relative decrease of root growth under Al stress compared to control is a measure of tolerance. The main disadvantages are the time consumption and the necessity of adjusting the

pH of the medium twice daily. The short-term (pulse test) is based on the exposure of Al shocks to roots (24 to 48 h) after which the effect of such Al pulses on root elongation is recorded. In these tests the resistance of seedlings apical mersitems to Al-stress is the measure of Al-stress. Such tests allow one to rapidly screen a large numbers of plants in a short time.

Laboratory and greenhouse screening techniques for Al-tolerance are widely used because they are quick, highly accurate, non-destructive and can be applied at early developmental stages. Field based techniques are more laborious (Carver and Ownby 1995) than laboratory. The researchers have used various experimental conditions for screening of aluminium tolerance.

SHORT-TERM (PULSE TEST) SCREENING TECHNIQUES

Hematoxylin Staining Method

This method differentiates between aluminium resistant and aluminium sensitive genotypes on the basis of the staining pattern (Polle *et al.* 1978, Singh *et al.* 2007b, Singh *et al.* 2009). Visual evaluation of stained roots can be used to detect aluminium accumulation in root tissues. This is a simple method based on the staining pattern in which aluminium binds to form a purple complex in the root tips of sensitive genotypes and the absence of colour in root tips of the aluminium tolerant genotypes indicates that these genotypes either exclude aluminium or bind aluminium in complexes that are unavailable to hematoxylin. This reaction occurs by the oxidation of hematoxylin to hematyn, in the presence of sodium iodate ($NaIO_3$) which in the presence of aluminium produces nucleic acid coloration (Polle *et al.* 1978). The hematoxylin method is very common for the evaluation of aluminium tolerance in wheat (Delhaize *et al.* 1993), french bean (Singh and Sanwal 2008), pea (Singh *et al.* 2007), chickpea (Singh and Chaturvedi 2007), baby corn (Singh and Chauhan 2008), Okra (Singh and Sureja 2008), etc.

Hematoxylin staining is also employed as a means of measuring root re-growth. Singh *et al.* (2007) reported that hematoxylin with modified pulse method evaluates the tolerance based on the ability of aluminium tolerant seedlings to continue root growth after a short pulse treatment with high aluminium concentration. Aluminium sensitive seedlings do not show root re-growth because their apical meristem is damaged whereas tolerant genotypes showed continue root growth. This method can be applied to determine aluminium tolerance through measuring root re-growth (Aniol and Gustafson 1984).

Hematoxylin staining of the root tips in conjunction with hydroponic culture is a widely accepted technique for the evaluation of aluminium tolerance (Polle *et al.* 1978) who reported that the results of the hematoxylin test were in good agreement with those of the acid soil screening method in wheat. Singh *et al.* (2007) reported that scoring of aluminium tolerance of pea by the hematoxylin staining method strongly coincided with the scoring of aluminium tolerance in nutrient solution with aluminium. Cancado *et al.* (1999) used hematoxylin staining as a phenotypic index for selection of aluminium resistance in maize. Ownby (1993) reported that root-tips of an aluminium sensitive wheat variety did not intensely stain with hematoxylin when the roots were washed with citrate before the staining procedure.

Laboratory Protocol for the Hematoxylin Staining Method

- Sterilize the seeds by placing in 3 per cent sodium hypochlorite solution for 5 minutes and wash thoroughly with water.
- Soak the seeds in distilled water for 12 h and transfer to filter paper to germinate in the growth chamber until the cotyledonary leaves emerge.
- Transfer the germinated seedlings to planting trays and place them in plastic containers with nutrient solution (4 mM $CaCl_2$, 6.5 mM KNO_3, 2.5 mM $MgCl_2$, 0.1 mM $(NH_4)_2SO_4$ and 0.4 mM NH_4NO_3). Adjust the pH of the nutrient solution to 4.5 with 1M HCl solution. Keep seedlings in the nutrient solution for 24–31 h.
- Transfer seedlings to a fresh nutrient solution containing aluminium (pH 4.5) and keep in solution for 17–24 h.
- Place the seedlings in aerated distilled water for 30–60 min to remove the traces of Al from the root surface.
- Immerse the roots in hematoxylin staining solution (2 gl^{-1} hematoxylin powder and 0.2 gl^{-1} KIO_3 or $NaIO_3$) for 30 min.
- Place the roots of seedlings in distilled water for 30 minutes to remove excess stain.
- Rinse the roots 3 times in distilled water.
- Visually score the seedling root-tips based on the staining pattern, ranging from 0 to 3, 0: indicating no staining, 1: indicating partial staining, 2: moderate staining and 3: deep staining.
- Return seedlings to fresh nutrient solution for 48 h if measuring root re-growth.
- After 48 h, remove the seedlings from trays; measure root re-growth and rate the seedlings as tolerant (T), moderately tolerant (MT) and susceptible (S). The seedlings with all roots showing continuous growth are rated as tolerant, whereas seedlings showing no root re-growth are classified as sensitive to Al. Seedlings showing re-growth in a few roots are rated as moderately tolerant.

Eriochrome Cyanine R Stain

This method also discriminates between aluminium tolerant and aluminium sensitive genotypes based on the staining pattern. Root staining is also suitable for screening segregating populations (Hede *et al.* 2002). Eriochrome cyanine R staining is also used to assess root re-growth after aluminium stress. This technique is commonly used for evaluation of aluminium tolerance in wheat (Aniol 1995) and barley (Wang *et al.* 2006). Aluminium tolerant genotype is unstained because apical meristem is not damaged whereas in sensitive genotype root-tip is intensely stained because meristem is damaged. The root re-growth after aluminium shock is easily assessed from the existence of a stained ring along the root-tips.

Laboratory Protocol for the Eriochrome Cyanine R Stain Method

- Sterilize the seeds by placing in 3 per cent sodium hypochlorite solution for 5 min and wash thoroughly with water.
- Soak the seeds in distilled water for 12 h and transfer to filter paper to germinate in the growth chamber until the cotyledonary leaves emerge.
- Place seedlings in nutrient solution (0.65 mM KNO_3, 0.40 mM $CaCl_2$, 0.25 mM $MgCl_2$, 0.10 mM $(NH_4)_2SO_4$, 0.04 mM NH_4NO_3) for 4 days with daily pH adjustment.
- Transfer the germinated seedlings to planting trays placed in plastic containers with nutrient solution containing aluminium (pH 4.5) and keep seedlings in solution for 24 h.
- Wash the seedlings under a running tap water for 2–3 min to remove the traces of Al from the root surface.
- Stain the root-tip of seedlings with 0.1 per cent aqueous solution of eriochrome cyanine R for 10 min.
- After staining, remove the excess dye by repeated washing with tap water.
- Visually score the seedling root-tips based on the staining pattern and lateral root growth. Score the heavily stained roots with no lateral root growth as sensitive and roots with no staining and good lateral root growth as tolerant to aluminium.
- Return seedlings to aluminium free nutrient solution for 2 days with daily pH adjustments if measuring root re-growth.

Root Re-growth Method

Root re-growth method is also a good screening technique for aluminium tolerance (Tang *et al.* 2000, Singh *et al.* 2007). Tolerant plants showed continuous growth whereas sensitive genotype showed no root re-growth.

Laboratory Protocol for Root Re-growth Method

- Sterilize the seeds by placing in 3 per cent sodium hypochlorite solution for 5 min and wash thoroughly with water.
- Soak the seeds in distilled water for 12 h and transfer to filter paper to germinate in the growth chamber until the cotyledonary leaves emerge.
- Transfer the germinated seedlings to planting trays placed in plastic containers with Al-free nutrient solution for 48 h under continuous aeration. Adjust the pH of the nutrient solution to 4.5 with 1M HCl solution.
- Place the seedlings in a nutrient solution having aluminium and keep in solution for 48 h.
- Grow the seedlings for 72 h in the Al-free fresh nutrient solution at pH 4.5.

- Measure the root re-growth. The seedlings with all roots showing continuous growth are rated as tolerant, whereas seedlings showing no root re-growth are classified as sensitive to Al. Seedlings showing re-growth in a few roots are rated as moderately tolerant.

LONG-TERM SCREENING TECHNIQUES

Nutrient Solution

The solution culture is one of the most powerful and effective screening technique to discriminate tolerant and sensitive genotypes as compared to field screening. Diluted hydroponic, should be used because such solution more closely resembles the soil solution conditions than full strength nutrient solution (Simen *et al.* 1994). Some researchers have found a good correlation between nutrient solution and soil culture (Anas and Yoshida 2000, Bona *et al.* 1993) for aluminium tolerance in pea, tomato, cabbage (Singh, Unpublished data), wheat (Foy *et al.* 1969), barley (McLeod and Jackson 1967), cowpea (Horst *et al.* 1983) and sorghum (Furlani *et al.* 1991). However, some researchers have found a poor correlation between plant responses in soil culture and nutrient solution. The hydroponics assay is more repeatable, more easily accomplished and more cost effective than the sand and soil culture method.

Protocol for the Growth Response Method in Nutrient Solution

- Sterilize the seeds by placing in 3 per cent sodium hypochlorite solution for 5 min and wash thoroughly with water.
- Soak the seeds in distilled water for 12 h and transfer to filter paper to germinate in the growth chamber until the cotyledonary leaves emerge.
- Transfer the germinated seedlings (of similar root length) to planting trays placed in plastic containers with dilute nutrient solution: KNO_3 (0.5 mM), $Ca(NO_3)_2.4H_2O$ (0.5 mM), $MgSO_4.7H_2O$ (0.2 mM), KH_2PO_4 (0.1 mM), KCl (50 µM), H_3BO_3 (46 µM), Fe-EDTA (20 µM), $MnCl_2.4H_2O$ (2 µM), $ZnSO_4.7H_2O$ (1 µM), $CuSO_4.5H_2O$ (0.3 µM) and $NaMoO_4.2H_2O$ (0.5 µM) containing aluminium under continuous aeration (Simen *et al.* 1994). Seedlings are also kept in nutrient solution without Al for comparison.
- Maintain the pH of the nutrient solution at 4.5 with 1M HCl solution twice a day, in the morning and evening.
- Replace the nutrient solution every 4 days to maintain the concentration of aluminium and nutrients.
- After 14–70 days (according to the crop), remove the seedlings from the trays and measure the growth parameters (root, shoot length, etc.) of each seedling.

Soil Culture

Field heterogeneity in aluminium toxic soils hinders the reliability of the response of genotypes. Under such situations, it is necessary to create and maintain desired levels of aluminium in soils. It is a viable alternative approach to field screening (Scott and Fisher 1989). For aluminium screening, soils should be high in total aluminium at pH levels of 5.0 or below and it should be independent and free from nutritional deficiencies like, calcium, phosphorus, molybdenum and magnesium (Foy 1984).

The use of soil media has less attention than solution because of the complications of creating a soil environment with a specific type and amount of phytotoxicity (Foy 1976). Screening in soils representative of the targeted production area where soil acidity is a yield limiting factor provides a critical intermediate step in selection of tolerant genotypes after preliminary screening in nutrient solution but before more lengthy and costly screening under natural field conditions (Carver and Ownby 1995).

Protocol for the Growth Response Method in Soil Culture

- Sterilize the seeds by placing in 3 per cent sodium hypochlorite solution for 5 min and wash thoroughly with water.
- Collect homogenous soil and mix with aluminium chloride at various concentrations.
- Fill the treated soil in pots and sow the seeds.
- Irrigate the soils with deionized water if required.
- After 14–70 days (depending upon the duration of crop), seedlings are pulled from the pots by washing with tap water.
- Visual scoring of whole plant used as selection criterion based on the size of the root and shoot varies from 1 (very poor) to 5 (excellent).
- Measure growth parameters (root, shoot length, etc.).

Sand Culture

Sand culture is a viable alternative to hydroponics screening for aluminium tolerance. This method is useful with older plants than the hydroponics approach. It is more similar to field conditions, physically than hydroponics. In sand culture, aluminium and nutrients are supplied in solution form and because sand is almost inert, the level of aluminium applied to plants can be regulated and reproduced with consistency.

Previous results show that sand culture provides more accurate results. In contrast, results of sand culture are not well correlated with solution culture. Horst *et al.* (1990) found that sand culture required 10 folds higher concentration in order to inhibit sorghum root growth to the same degree as in solution culture. They found that this discrepancy may be due to slower movement of aluminium to the roots by diffusion in sand than by convection in aerated nutrient solution culture, increased formation of a gradient pH at the root surface leading to precipitation of aluminium, and enhanced release of root exudates which bind and inactivate aluminium (Horst and Klotz 1990). Villagarcia *et al.* (2001) also showed that about

100 times higher aluminium concentration is required to inhibit root elongation in sand culture in comparison with hydroponics. Horst and Klotz (1990) reported a poor correlation between aluminium resistance of 31 soybean genotypes in solution and sand cultures. However, the exact reason for the higher aluminium requirement in sand culture is still unclear.

Protocol for the Growth Response Method in Sand Culture

- Wash silica sand or quartz sand under running tap water and then treat with HCl and pass a continuous current of water stream under pressure until free from HCl acid.
- Seeds are either directly sown or seedlings raised on filter paper and then transferred to sand.
- Supply irrigation solution each day to the seedlings and flush sand with distilled water every seven days during the entire experimental period.
- After 14–70 days (depends upon the duration of crop), measure the root, shoot length, etc.

Field Screening

Naturally acidic soils are usually quite heterogenous in their aluminium toxicity levels for evaluating tolerance and this strategy has proved to be very expensive and time consuming besides the fact that results are highly unstable due to the natural variability of soils and climatic conditions. Spatial variability can greatly bias the interpretation of the field screening results. This strategy is more expensive and laborious, especially when a large number of genotypes are under evaluation (Garcia *et al.* 1979, Stolon and Anderson 1978, Ruiz-Torres *et al.* 1992).

In the field, artificially created gradient like lime and sulphur and/or sulphuric acid is normally used to achieve pH gradients (Howeler 1991). Cultivars are then grown to assess their relative growth over pH gradients.

Microplots

Sptial variability of acidic soils hinders the reliability of the response of genotypes. This attracted the development of mini-field environments with varying levels of controlled aluminium toxicity environments. It is possible to create and maintain desired levels of aluminium in these microplots simulating field conditions minus the soil heterogeneity. It is highly representative of the genotypic performance.

In Vitro Screening

In vitro screening for biotic and abiotic stresses holds a significant importance, as millions of cells can be screened in a single petridish, which reduces both time and space requirements. *In vitro* screening can be carried out throughout the year, without any seasonal constraints.

The use of cell and tissue culture may provide a way of screening for aluminium tolerance given that aluminium resistance can be expressed at the cellular level (Taylor 1995). It involves imposing a selection pressure on a population of cells, recovering variant cells which tolerate the stress and finally regenerating plants from the selected lines. The advantages of *in vitro* selection over the conventional methods include: (i) variation can be generated during culture, (ii) millions of cells can be screened in a single petridish and (iii) selection is done in controlled environments.

The exploitation of somatic variation by cell culture has become a new approach for stress tolerance breeding (Larken and Scowcroft 1981). Somaclonal variation can be used to improve aluminium tolerance (Moon *et al.* 1997, Van Sint Jan *et al.* 1997). The use of tissue culture screening to select aluminium tolerant genotypes at the cellular level has been reported in a number of crop species (Ojima and Ohira 1983, Smith *et al.* 1983, Duncan *et al.* 1995, Conner and Meredith 1985). Parrot and Bouton (1990) reported that alfalfa expressed aluminium tolerance at the callus stage and consequently the selection by tissue culture can be applied to identify aluminium tolerant plants. Ojima and Ohira (1983) developed aluminium tolerant cell lines of carrot by exposing the cells to Al-EDTA. Plants regenerated from selected calli were also tolerant to aluminium. It was noticed that selected lines secreted citric acid and malic acid. It was thought that citric acid chelates Al which prevents uptake.

Performance of aluminium tolerance in tissue culture may be more useful for breeding programme because selection can be earlier and faster than that in the field. Moreover, the selection by tissue culture can be applied to identify aluminium tolerant plants in segregating populations. There are only a few examples in the literature in which cell and tissue culture was applied (Conner and Meredith 1985, Parrot and Bouton 1990).

Protocol for *In Vitro* Method

- Select explant like seeds, etc.
- Surface sterilize using 0.1 per cent mercuric chloride for 2–8 min depending upon explant used followed by rinsing in sterile water 2–3 times to remove excess sterilant.
- Inoculate on MS+ 2, 4-D + kin medium using aseptic conditions.
- Raise cell suspensions in a flask kept on gravatory shaker for 80–120 rpm.
- Planting of cells on a medium containing aluminium for screening. Susceptible cells turn brown in colour and die while tolerant cells survive and continue to proliferate on selective medium.

CONCLUSION

Designing reliable and effective screening techniques is the most challenging task for developing and characterizing aluminium tolerant plants. Root staining technique is quite effective but the mechanisms behind the selectivity of hematoxylin and eriochrome R need to be understood for effective juvenile screening.

REFERENCES

Anas and Yoshida Y. 2000. Screening of Al tolerant sorghum by hematoxylin staining and growth response. *Crop Production Sci.* **3**: 246–253.

Aniol A and Gustafson JP. 1984. Chromosomal location of genes controlling aluminium tolerance in wheat, rye and triticale. *Can. J. Genet. Cytol.* **26**: 701–705.

Aniol AM. 1995. Physiological aspects of aluminium tolerance associated with the long arm of chromosome 2D of the wheat (*Triticum aestivum* L.) genome. *Theor. Appl. Genet.* **9**: 510–516.

Bona L, Baligar VC and Matuz J. 1993. Screening wheat and other small grains for acid soil tolerance. *Landscape and Urban Planning.* **27**: 175–178.

Campbell LG and Lafever HN. 1976. Correlation of field and nutrient culture techniques of screening wheat for aluminium tolerance. In Plant adaptation to mineral stress in problem soils, p277–286. Wright MJ and Ferrari SA (Eds), Cornell Univ. Agri. Expt. Sta. Ithaca, New York.

Cancado GMA, Loguercia LL, Martins PR, Parentoni SN, Paiva E, Borem A and Lopes MA. 1999. Hematoxylin staining as a phenotypic index for Al tolerance selection in tropical maize (*Z. mays* L.) *Theor. Appl. Genet.* **99**: 747–754.

Carver BF and Ownby JD. 1995. Acid soil tolerance in wheat. *Adv. Agron.* **54**: 117–173.

Conner AJ and Meredith CP. 1985. Large scale selection of aluminium resistant mutants from plant cell culture expression and inheritance in seedlings. *Theor. Appl. Genet.* **71**: 159–165.

Delhaize E, Craig S, Beaton CD, Bennet RJ, Jadish VC and Randall PJ. 1993. Aluminium tolerance in wheat (*T. aestivum* L.). Uptake and distribution of Al in root apices. *Plant Physiol.* **103**: 685–693.

Duncan PR, Wakson RM and Nabors MW. 1995. *In vitro* screening and field evalaution of tissue culture regenerated sorghum (*Sorghum bicolor* L. Moench) for soil stress tolerance. *Euphytica.* **85**: 373.

Foy CD, Flemming AL and Armiger WJ. 1969. Aluminium tolerance of soybean varieties in relation to calcium nutrition. *Agron. J.* **61**: 505–511.

Foy CD. 1976. General principle involve mineral stress in problem soils, p255–267. Wright MJ and Ferrari AS (Eds), Cornell Univ. Press, Ithaca.

Foy CD. 1984. Physiological effects of hydrogen, aluminium and manganese toxicities in acid soils. In Soil acidity and liming. Adams F (Ed), 2nd ed. *Soil Sci. Soc. Am. Soc. Agron. and Crop Sci of Am.*, Madison, WI.

Furlani PR, Quaggio IA and Gallo PB. 1991. Differential responses of high grain protein. *J. Plant Nutr.* **17**: 377–400.

Garcia J, Silva W and Massel M. 1979. An efficient method for screening maize inbred lines for Al tolerance. *Maydica.* **233**: 75–82.

Hede AR, Skovmand B, Ribout JM, Gonazales de lean D and Stolon D. 2002. Evaluation of aluminium tolerance in a spring rye collection by hydroponic screening. *Plant Breed.* **121:** 241–248.

Horst WJ and Klotz F. 1990. Screening soybean for aluminium tolerance and adaptation to acid soils. In Genetic aspects of plant mineral nutrition, p355–360. EI Bassam N. *et al.* (Eds), Kluwer Acad. Publ. Dordrecht, The Netherlands.

Horst WJ, Klotz F and Szulkiewicz P. 1990. Mechanical impedance increase aluminium tolerance of soybean (*Glycine max* L.) roots. *Plant Soil.* **124:** 227–231.

Horst WJ, Wagner A and Marschner H. 1983. Effect of aluminium on root growth, cell division and mineral element contents in roots of *Vigna unguiculata* genotypes. *Z. Pflanzenphysiol.* **109:** 95–103.

Howeler RH. 1991. Identifying plant adaptable to low pH conditions. In plant-soil Interactions at low pH, p885–904. Wright RJ, BaligarVC and Murrmann RP (Eds), Kluwer Academic Publishers Dordrecht, The Netherland.

Howeler RH and Cadavid LF. 1976. Screening of rice cultivars for tolerance to Al toxicity in nutrient solutions as compared with field screening method. *Agron J.* **68:** 551–555.

Larkin PJ and Scowcroft WR. 1981. Somaclonal variation a novel source of variability from cell cultures for plant improvement. *Theor. Appl. Genet.* **60:** 197–214.

MacLeod IB and Jackson LP. 1967. Effect of concentration of Al ion on root development and establishment of legume seedlings. *Can J. Soil Sci.* **6:** 259–279.

Moon DH, Ottoboni LMM, Souza AP, Sibov ST, Gaspar M and Arruda P. 1997. Somaclonal-variation-induced aluminum-sensitive mutant from an aluminum-inbred maize tolerant line. *Plant Cell Report.* **16:** 686–691.

Ojima K and Ohira K. 1983. Charcterization of aluminium and manganeses tolerant cell line selected from carrot cell culture. *Plant Cell Physiol.* **24:** 789–797.

Ownby JD. 1993. Mechanisms of reaction of hematoxylin with aluminium treated wheat roots. *Physiol. Plant.* **87:** 371–380.

Parrot WA and Bouton JH. 1990. Aluminium tolerance in alfalfa as expressed in tissue culture. *Crop Sci.* **30:** 387–389.

Polle E, Konzak CF and Kittrick JA. 1978. Visual detection of aluminium tolerance levels in wheat by hematoxylin staining of seedling roots. *Crop Sci.* **18:** 827–828.

Reid DA, Jones GD, Armiger WH, Foy CD, Hoch EJ and Sterling TM. 1969. Differential aluminium tolerance of winter barley varieties and selections in associated greenhouse and field experiment. *Agron. J.* **61:** 218–222.

Ruiz-Torres NA, Carver BF and Westerman RL. 1992. Agronomic performance in acid soils of wheat lines selected for hematoxylin staining pattern. *Crop Sci.* **32:** 104–107.

Scott BJ and Fisher JA. 1989. Selection of genotypes tolerant of Al and Mn. In Soil acidity and plant growth, p167–203. Robson AD (Ed), Academic Press, New York.

Simen L, Smalley TJ, Jones Benton Jr and Lasseigne FT. 1994. Aluminium toxicity in tomato part I. Growth and mineral nutrition. *J. Plant Nutr.* **17:** 293–306.

Singh D. 2009. Identification of aluminium and manganese resistant corn and pea genotypes adapted to acidic soils. Half yearly report of the project, College of Horticulture and Forestry, Central Agricultural University, Pasighat, Arunachal Pradesh, India.

Singh D and Chaturvedi SK. 2007. Rapid and effective screening technique for aluminium tolerance in chickpea at seedling stage. In abstracts of the National Symposium on Legumes for Ecologocal Sustainability: Emerging Challenges and Opportunities, pp 107. Pramanik SC, Singh, B, Singh IP, Naimuddin, Gupta S and Prakash B (Eds) held during 3–5 November at Indian Institute of Pulses Research, Kanpur, India.

Singh D and Chauhan SK. 2008. Rapid screening technique for aluminium tolerance in baby corn. In abstracts of the National Seminar on Sustainable Management of Acidic Soils for Higher Crop Productivity, p29. Singh D, Raju AS, Chaturvedi SK and Sharma S (Eds) held during 22–24 September, 2008 at College of Horticulture and Forestry, Central Agricultural University, Pasighat, Arunachal Pradesh, India.

Singh D, Rai AK and Panyang O. 2009. Hematoxylin staining as a potential screening technique for aluminium tolerance in pea (*Pisum sativum* L.). *Current Sci.* **96**: 1029–1030.

Singh D and Sanwal SK 2008. Hematoxylin staining as a phenotypic index for aluminium tolerance selection in French Bean. In abstracts of the National Seminar on Sustainable Management of Acidic Soils for Higher Crop Productivity, p28. Singh D, Raju AS, Chaturvedi SK and Sharma S (Eds) held during 22–24 September, 2008 at College of Horticulture and Forestry, Central Agricultural University, Pasighat, Arunachal Pradesh, India.

Singh D, Rai AK, Sureja AK and Bhardwaj R. 2007. Hematoxylin staining: A rapid method for assessment of aluminium tolerance in pea genotypes. In abstracts and souvenir of 2nd *Indian Horticulture Congress,* p178. Chadha KL, Singh SK, Patel VB, Prasad KV and Asrey R (Eds) held during 18–21 April 2007 at ICAR Research Complex for NEH region Barapani, Meghalaya, India.

Smith RH, Bhaskaron S and Schertz K. 1983. Sorghum plant regeneration from Al selection media. *Plant Cell Rep.* **2**: 129–132.

Stolon O. and Anderson S. 1978. Inheritance of tolerance to low soil pH in barley. *Hereditas* **88**: 101–105.

Tang Y, Sorrells ME, Kochian LV and Garvin DF. 2000. Identification of RFLP markers linked to the barley Al tolerance gene *Alp. Crop Sci.* **40**: 778–782.

Taylor GJ. 1995. Overcoming barriers to understanding the cellular basis of aluminium resistance. *Plant Soil.* **171**: 89–103.

Van Sint Jan V, Macedo de CC, Kinet JM and Bouharmont J. 1997. Selection of Al resistant plants from sensitive rice cultivars using somaclonal variation, *in vitro* selection and hydroponic culture. *Euphytica.* **97**: 303–310.

Villgarcia MR, Thomas E, Carter Jr, Rufty TW, Niewoehner AS, Jenette MW and Arrellano C. 2001. Genotypic ranking of Al tolerance of soybean roots. *Crop Sci.* **41**: 1499–1507.

Wang, J, Raman H, Read B, Meixue NZ, Mendhan S and Venkatanappa S. 2006. Comparison of root staining and root elongation in predicting aluminium tolerance using SSR markers in barley. *Aust. J. Agric. Res.* **57**: 89–100.

4 Biotechnological Approaches for Acid Soil Management

NP Singh, Indu Singh Yadav and Dharmendra Singh

ABSTRACT

Soil acidity is a major problem limiting performance of a large number of crops in many parts of the world. In India, 49 million hectares is affected by soil acidity of which 24 million hectares have pH below 5.5. The productivity potential of acidic soils is estimated to be far less than normal soil. The problems in acid soils are frequently due to aluminum (Al) and/or manganese (Mn) toxicities. Therefore, strategies have to be developed to make the plants adaptable to the acidic environments. The genetic variability among genotypes of crop species exists for soil acidity. The studies on the genetic basis of tolerance in plants for toxicity to Al and Mn revealed that variation in tolerance was genetically controlled and thus heritable in nature. The tolerance to aluminium toxicity has been reported to be controlled by both oligo-gene as well as polygene. There are also reports of development of transgenics expressing genes involved in chelation of aluminium tolerance in *Arabidopsis,* tobacco and alfalfa. Besides, loci controlling Al tolerance have been mapped using molecular markers, *viz.* RAPD, RFLP, AFLP, SCAR and SSR in wheat, maize, barley, rye, soybean, etc. In future, these developments will go a long way in developing Al-tolerant cultivars in crops to increase adoption of crops in acid affected soils of the country.

Key words: Acid Soil, Al-tolerance, molecular markers, transgenic, tissue culture.

INTRODUCTION

Acid soils are characterized by low pH and excess of aluminium and manganese hamper crop production in tropical and subtropical area. Acid soils pH below 5.0 are reported to occur throughout the world, with the largest area in tropical and subtropical regions. Several strategies have been pursued to manage acid soils. The primary method has been the application of large amount of lime to raise soil pH. However, liming does not remedy of subsoil acidity and it is not always economically feasible. The best way of solving this problem is to develop acid tolerant crop cultivars with increased aluminium and manganese tolerance. Development of acid tolerant crops will enhance food production in acidic regions. Breeding for acid tolerance has produced improved cultivars for acid stress environments, but progress has been slow due to the complex physiological/biochemical response to acid environments. The objective of this chapter is to provide an overview of biotechnological approaches that could be used to tag and dissect the genetic basis of acid tolerance traits in plants.

DISTRIBUTION OF ACID SOILS

Acid Soils will develop most rapidly in areas where rainfall is sufficiently abundant to leach away rapidly the bases liberated by ionic exchange and mineral decomposition. Acid soils occur in the tropics and subtropics as well as in moderate climates. Their formation depends on specific conditions of climate, topography, vegetation and parent material. Acrisols and Ferralsols are most common in old land surfaces in humid tropical climates. Acid sulphate soils occur in the tropics, in low-lying coastal land were formerly occupied by mangrove swamps. Podzols are typical soils of the northern coniferous forests but may occur in the tropics too. Acidic soils make up 26 per cent or 37.8 million square km of the global ice free surface land area. Acidic subsurface soils make up slightly less area than surface soils but consist of 20 per cent or 29.2 million square km of the global ice free land. The region with highest amounts of moderately to high surface soil acidity (pH < 5.5) is South America, with over half of the soils being classified in these categories. About 31 per cent of North American and about 43 per cent of European surface soils are moderately to highly acidic. Some soil orders are commonly associated with acidity (e.g. Oxisols, Ultisols, Alfisols, etc.) and these soils have the potential to impose fairly severe mineral deficiencies/toxicities on plants. In India, 49 million hectares is affected by soil acidity of which 24 million hectares have pH below 5.5 (Mandal 1997). In northeastern region of India, more than 90 percent area is affected by soil acidity (Sharma and Singh 2002).

STRATEGIES FOR IMPROVING ACID TOLERANCE

There are two basic approaches that are being employed to improve stress tolerance: (i) the use of genetic variations already present in existing crops either through direct selection in acidic environments or through linked genes and mapping quantitative trait loci (QTLs) and subsequent marker assisted selection, and (ii) the generation of transgenic plants to introduce novel genes or to change the tolerance levels of the existing genes. The progress made in this direction is described below:

Molecular Breeding

Conventional breeding methods have made little progress in improving aluminium tolerance. Identification of molecular markers tightly linked to Al-tolerant genes can serve as landmarks for the physical localization of such genes and facilitating marker assisted selection. Molecular markers like AFLP, RFLP, SSR, SCARs, etc.

would greatly facilitate more effective selection for desired genotypes possessing increased tolerance to aluminum toxicity (Raman *et al.* 2002, Tang *et al.* 2000, Riede and Anderson 1996, Miftahudin *et al.* 2002, Sibov *et al.* 1999, Nguyen *et al.* 2003, Wu *et al.* 2000). Molecular markers linked to genes or QTLs for aluminium tolerance have been identified in several crops including rice, wheat, maize, alfalfa, soybean, etc. which can be used for the selection of tolerant genotypes. These molecular markers are highly regarded as an efficient selection tool to indirectly select traits linked to Al-tolerance loci (Raman *et al.* 2002).

Molecular mapping of genes conferring Al-tolerance in rice suggested that Al tolerance was a complex multigenic trait. The major QTLs were detected by different molecular markers on chromosomes 1 and 12 (Wu *et al.* 2000), on chromosomes 1, 2 and 6 (Ma *et al.* 2002), or on chromosomes 1 and 8 (Nguyen *et al.* 2002). The common chromosome 1 did not seem to correspond to most of the genes that had been mapped for Al tolerance in other species (Nguyen *et al.* 2001) because homologous chromosome 4 of the *Triticeae* generally corresponds to chromosome 3 in rice. However, in later work, a major QTL explaining 24.9 per cent of the phenotype variation was found on chromosome 3 of rice, which is conserved across cereal species (Nguyen *et al.* 2003). In sorghum, a major Al-tolerance locus has been mapped on chromosome 3, which is not a syntenic region of group 4 chromosomes of wheat, barley and rye. Instead, it maps to a homologues region of *Triticeae* chromosome 3, rice chromosome 1 and maize chromosomes 3 and 8. QTLs associated with Al-tolerance in maize and rice has also been mapped on these chromosomes (Ninamango-Cárdenas *et al.* 2003). These studies indicate evolutional inheritance of Al-tolerance genes in different cereals.

Tang *et al.* (2000) reported three RFLP markers flanking the Al tolerance gene *Alp*, which were 2.1 cM proximal to the marker BCD1117 and 2.1 cM distal to the markers WG464 and CDO1395. RFLP-based marker-assisted selection (MAS) of the *Alp* is both time-consuming and labour intensive and generally involves radioactive isotopes labeling and hence is not suitable for high throughput analysis in breeding programme (Raman *et al.* 2003). Therefore, SSR markers (e.g. Bmag353, Bmac186 and Bmac310) were identified that showed tight linkage with the *Alp* locus (Raman *et al.* 2003). In an independent study, markers Bmac310, Bmag353, HVM68 and HVRCABG were found to be tightly linked to a major Al tolerance locus *Alt* in a F_2 population from Yambla (moderately tolerant of Al)/WB229 (tolerant of Al) (Raman *et al.* 2002). The *Alt* gene was 1.6 cM proximal to marker Bmag353 and HVM68 and 1.6 cM distal to HVM3. Two SSR markers (Bmac310 and HVRCABG) and six AFLP markers co-segregated with *Alt* (Raman *et al.* 2002). These SSR markers were used to distinguish other source for Al tolerance in different populations derived from Harrington (Al sensitive)/Brindabella (Raman *et al.* 2001), Ohichi/F6ant28B48-16 (Raman *et al.* 2005) and F6ant28B48-16/Honen (Wang *et al.* 2006). These markers have enabled fast tracking of Al tolerance alleles in different breeding programme in crops.

According to Kerridge and Kronstad (1968), a single dominant gene is responsible for Al tolerance in a cross between the two wheat varieties 'Druchamp' and 'Brevor'. Slootmaker (1974) was the first to locate genes for acid soil tolerance in wheat and found the D genome to be the most important genome followed by A and B genome in wheat. Riede and Anderson (1996) identified marker loci for the gene Alt$_{BH}$, which confers a high degree of Al tolerance in the Brazilian wheat cultivar 'BH1146'. Locus Xbcd1230, was the most approximately 1 centimorgan (cM) from Alt$_{BH}$, whereas the marker locus Xcdo1395 was approximately 10cM from Alt$_{BH}$. Luo and Dvorak (1996) used hematoxylin staining to map a gene conferring Al tolerance in the landrace Chinese spring. The gene was designated Alt2 was mapped by RFLP analysis to the long arm of the chromosome 4D. Mapping data ultimately reveals the presence of distinct Al tolerance loci among wheat cultivars, it may be possible to use the molecular markers to pyramid different Al tolerance genes in a single genotype and thereby obtain additive enhancement of Al tolerance.

In barley, Stolen and Andersen (1978) found that tolerance to soil acidity is controlled by a single dominant gene, designated *Pht* on chromosome 4. Al tolerance in barley cultivars 'Dayton' and 'Smooth Awn 86', were controlled by a single dominant gene, *Alp* (Reid 1971). Minella and Sorrells (1997) used trisomics analysis and found that the *Alp* gene is distally located from the centromere on chromosome 4. Because barley chromosome 4 is homologous to the wheat group 4 chromosomes, this suggested the possibility that Alp of barley and wheat Al tolerance genes Alt$_{BH}$ and *Alt*2 on the long arm of wheat chromosome 4D are orthologous. Until, no Al resistance gene had been cloned. However, Sasaki *et al.* (2004) cloned a gene with properties of an Al-induced channel and subsequently transformed barley and obtained high level of resistance (Delhaize *et al.* 2004). This may be the first Al tolerance gene to have been cloned.

Rye has one of the most efficient groups of genes for aluminum tolerance (Alt) among cultivated species of Triticeae. In rye (*Secale cereale*), aluminium tolerance is controlled by four dominant and independent genes (*Alt*1, *Alt*2 and *Alt*3 and *Alt*4) located on 6RS, 3RS and 4RL and 7RS, respectively (Aniol and Gustafson 1984, Gallego *et al.* 1998, Miftahudin *et al.* 2002, Matos *et al.* 2005). Aniol (2004) indicated that the major locus responsible for Al tolerance in rye is located on the short arm of chromosome 3R. Fontecha *et al.* (2007) suggested that the *Alt*4 locus encodes an aluminium activated organic acid transporter gene that could be utilized to increase Al tolerance in aluminium sensitive plant species. They cloned the rye ScALMT1 gene which is homologue to wheat TaALMT1 and mapped it on same position *i.e.* chromosome 7RS as the previously identified A*lt*4 locus. The ScALMT1 gene co-segregates with the aluminium tolerance phenotype in rye.

Tolerance to Al in maize is controlled by a smaller number of genomic regions. Sibov *et al.* (1999) identified two aluminium resistance genes *Alm*1 and *Alm*2 were associated on chromosome 10 and 6, respectively while Ninanmango Cardenas *et al.* (2003) mapped five QTLs on chromosome 2, 6 and 8 which explained 60 per cent of the phenotypic variation. The *Alm1* gene has a stronger impact on aluminium tolerance than the *Alm2* gene (Sibov et al. 1999). The most tightly linked markers to the Al tolerance genes *Alm1* and *Alm2* were cloned UMC 130 and CSU 70, respectively (Sibov *et al.* 1999). The *Alm1* gene was about 20.1 cM from UMC130, which is co-segregated with RZ141 (Wilson *et al.* 1999), a marker which maps on rice chromosome 11 (Causse *et al.* 1994). *Alm2* was located on maize chromosome 6, about 18.5 cM from CSU70, which is closely linked CDO580 (Wilson *et al.* 1999), a marker which on rice chromosome 5 (Causse *et al.* 1994).

Molecular markers such as Random Amplified Polymorphic DNA (RAPD) and Microsatellite Markers (Kassem *et al.* 2004) will facilitate to develop manganese resistant genotypes more effectively. Two hundred and forty microsatellite markers and 100 RILs were used to construct a map. The response of five plants per genotype to manganese was measured by leaf chlorosis (scored from 0–5) and root necrosis (scored from 0–5) from 7–28 days after treatment with 125 µM of manganese in hydroponics. Three genomic regions on different linkage groups were found to contain QTL for resistance to necrosis during manganese toxicity. The regions located on linkage groups C2 (BARCSatt291), I (BARCSatt239) and G (OPOEO2) were each significantly associated ($P<0.005$, $R^2 = 20\%$) with root necrosis at 7 days after treatment. All the regions derived the beneficial allele from Essex. One of the previously identified RAPD associated root necrosis QTL was also identified in this study. However, no QTL's for leaf chlorosis were detected ($P < 0.005$) and none of the RAPD could be identified for leaf chlorosis QTL. Therefore, it was concluded that root and leaf resistance to manganese toxicity are environmentally sensitive quantitative traits determined by separate loci of different number and magnitude of effect.

Kilo and Lightfoot (1996) found that twenty markers were associated with manganese in soybean cv. 'Essex' and it was controlled by 3–4 major QTLs for manganese tolerance. Wang *et al.* (2002) detected five QTLs for Mn tolerance, suggesting that tolerance is a quantitative trait.

Wang *et al.* (2002) did molecular marker analysis of manganese toxicity tolerance in rice under greenhouse conditions. Two hundred and seven markers covering 2419.5 cM of all 12 chromosomes of rice were used by single marker loci and interval mapping. These results indicated that the two parents differed in manganese tolerance index (MTI) and/or Mn content in shoots, and these parameters were associated with Mn toxicity tolerance. The RILs showed segregation for the above parameters. Molecular marker loci associated with variations in MTI values and Mn concentration/content in shoots were identified and eight QTLs associated with Mn toxicity tolerance were detected.

GENETIC ENGINEERING (GENE ISOLATION, CLONING AND TRANSGENIC DEVELOPMENT)

Genetic engineering uses the techniques of molecular cloning and transformation to alter the structure and characteristics of genes directly. Genetic engineering techniques have found some successes in numerous applications. Recent advances in gene transfer technology have provided a wide range of efficient systems for introducing foreign genes into crop plants. Genetic engineering provides an opportunity to enhance the Al-tolerance of sensitive species through the over-expression of endogenous genes or by the expression of foreign genes. These developments have facilitated studies on plant gene regulation and production of transgenic plants that are tolerant/resistant to aluminium. Many of the genes known to be involved in stress tolerance have been isolated initially from *Arabidopsis*. This has played a vital role in the elucidation of the basic processes underlying stress tolerance. Over 20 genes induced by Al stress have been isolated from a range of plant species, including wheat (*Triticum aestivum*) (Snowden and Gardner, 1993), tobacco (*Nicotiana tabacum*) (Ezaki *et al.* 1995) and *Arabidopsis* (Sugimoto and Sakamoto 1997). Ezaki *et al.* (2001) characterized the mechanism of action of four transgenes AtBCB (*Arabidopsis* blue copper-binding protein), par B (tobacco [*Nicotiana tabacum*] glutathione S-transferase), NtPox (tobacco peroxidase) and NtGDI1 (tobacco GDP dissociation inhibitor) which confer high degree of Al resistance on transgenic *Arabidopsis*. These four genes have different biochemical functions suggesting that there are several different Al-tolerance mechanisms in plants. Two of these genes AtBCB and parB and a peroxidase gene from *Arabidopsis* (AT Pox) also showed increased resistance to oxidative stress induced by diamide, while parB conferred resistance to copper (Cu) and sodium (Na). Aluminium (Al) content of Al treated root tips was reduced in the four Al-resistant lines which showed reduced staining of roots with 2', 7'-dichlorofluorescein diacetate, an indicator of oxidative stress. To determine the localization of these proteins, each gene was fused to the green fluorescent protein (GFP) gene. Transgenic lines over expressing the AtBCB gene showed constitutive lignin production in whole roots and microscopic observation of Al-treated roots indicated that the deposition of lipid peroxidase was clearly low in the area where lignin accumulated. The AtBCB expressing lines showed a lower deposition of malon dialdehyde after Al stress. It was also supposed that the NtGDI1 gene has also a similar function in plants. It was also speculated that the over expression of the NtGDI1 protein activates an Al efflux system that protects *Arabidopsis* against Al-toxicity. Most recently, an *ALMT1* gene, which encoded for an Al-activated malate transporter was isolated and characterized (Sasaki *et al.* 2004, Raman *et al.* 2005). This gene co-segregated with Al-tolerance in wheat and increased the tolerance of tobacco cells.

De la and Fuente *et al.* (1997) reported over expression of a citrate synthase gene (CSb) derived from *Pseudomonas aeruginosa* and targeted the bacterial CS to the cytoplasm rather than the mitochondria to avoid redistribution of carbon from citrate synthesis to the other components of the krebs cycle. This gene showed high citrate synthase citrate efflux and greater Al-tolerance than control. Transformed lines of tobacco expressing CSb had up to 10 folds greater internal citrate in their root tissues and one of the lines showed a fourfold release of citrate whereas in papaya citrate levels in the root was found to be 2–3 folds. Transgenic plants containing a bacterial citrate synthase gene produced elevated amounts of citric acid which was secreted from roots into the soils. Eventually citric acid binds Al and prevents its uptake by the roots.

Cruz-Ortega *et al.* (1997) suggested that synthesis of 1, 3-β-glucanase during Al stress in wheat could be as a protective response against pathogen attack. *TaMDR1* encoding multidrug resistance like protein was induced in both Al-sensitive and Al-tolerant wheat cultivars but the concentration of induced protein was lower in the Al-sensitive cultivar than in the Al-tolerant one (Sasaki *et al.* 2002). A clone *OsAR28* coding for an unknown protein could be a candidate gene for Al tolerance in rice (Mao *et al.* 2003).

Taylor *et al.* (1997) and Basu *et al.* (1999) demonstrated that a 51-kDa polypeptide and 23-kDa polypeptide, induced upon Al exposure in Al tolerant wheat cultivars appear to co-segregate with the Al-tolerance phenotype in segregating populations. This is an interesting finding but remains to be seen whether the gene encoding this polypeptide is also linked genetically with Al-tolerance segregation, which would strengthen the possibility that the polypeptide may be indeed be an Al-tolerance genes product. In addition to protein-based studies, several attempts have been made to clone Al-tolerance genes by molecular methods. This has included a number of studies that have approached the problem by searching for genes that exhibit increased expression upon Al exposure. Snowden *et al.* (1993) used differential complementary DNA (cDNA) screening of a root tip cDNA library from Al-stressed roots of the Al-sensitive cultivar 'Warigal', they isolated five cDNAs representing genes whose expression is induced by Al exposure. Constitutive expression of four of the five genes in the absence of Al was higher in the Al-tolerant cultivar 'Waalt' than in 'Warigal'. Interestingly, four of the five genes exhibited reduced levels of expression in 'Waalt' when exposed to non toxic levels of Al, whereas when toxic levels were used, the same four genes exhibited an increase in transcript abundance. Hamel *et al.* (1998) isolated several Al-induced cDNAs from the root tips of the Al-tolerant cultivar 'Atlas 66', including genes for peroxidase, cysteine proteinase, and oxalate oxidase. Tests of the ability of some of these genes to confer Al tolerance have been conducted by expressing these genes in plants and determining whether they confer an increased level of Al-tolerance. Ezaki *et al.* (2000) reported results of experiments in which they transformed *Arabidopsis* with a series of different Al-induced genes identified in several plant species, including one gene, a Bowman–Birk protease inhibitor, recovered from wheat. However, over expression of a few of the other genes from other plant species did increase Al-tolerance, although not dramatically and only across a narrow window of Al concentrations. Interestingly, two of these genes also conferred Al-tolerance in yeast (Ezaki *et al.* 1999). But it was suggested that this is due to an increase in basal stress tolerance and not to an increase in Al-tolerance *per se*. Thus, to date none of the genes recovered during the course of any of these molecular cloning efforts is likely to be a bonafide Al-tolerance gene.

Using genetic engineering, improvement in Mn tolerance was brought through detoxification mechanisms associated with CEC pectic polysaccharides and glycoprotein fractions in root cell walls (Wang *et al*. 1992), declaration or blocking of the enzymatic (IAA-oxidase), destruction of auxin (Morgan *et al*. 1966), or alteration of isoprenoid pathway biosynthetic reactions (Wilkinson 1991). Delhaize *et al*. (2003) reported genes encoding proteins of the Cation Diffusion Facilitator (CDF) family that confer Mn tolerance. The yeast *Saccharomyces cerevisiae* expressing a cDNA library was prepared from *Stylosanthes hamata* and was screened for enhanced Mn^{2+} tolerance. From this screen, they identified four related cDNAs that encode membrane-bound proteins of the Cation Diffusion Facilitator (CDF) family. One of these cDNAs (*ShMTP1*) was investigated in detail and found to confer Mn^{2+} tolerance to yeast by internal sequestration rather than by efflux of Mn^{2+}. Expression of *ShMTP1* in a range of yeast mutants suggested that it functions as a proton: Mn^{2+} antiporter on the membrane of an internal organelle. Similarly, when expressed in *Arabidopsis*, *ShMTP1* conferred Mn^{2+} tolerance through internal sequestration. The *ShMTP1* protein fused to green fluorescent protein was localized to the tonoplast of *Arabidopsis* cells but appeared to localize to the endoplasmic reticulum of yeast. They suggested that the *ShMTP1* proteins are members of the CDF family involved in conferring Mn^{2+} tolerance and that at least one of these proteins (*ShMTP1*) confers tolerance by sequestering Mn^{2+} into internal organelles.

SOMACLONAL VARIATION AND *IN VITRO* CELL SELECTION

Plant cell culture is one of the methods for studying how plants tolerate stress and for producing and selecting genetically superior plants. Use of cell culture technique in developing acid tolerant crop plants, and also studying tolerance at cellular level has aroused considerable excitement in recent years. This technique has advantage of performing selections in large cell mass that would take hundreds of acres if performed at the whole plant level. Hence, saving time and space moreover, in this approach, cells can be subjected to mutagenic agents in order to create genetic variability beyond existing gene pool. Disadvantages include the difficulty of selecting for characteristics at cell level that are manifested in subsequent growth stages such as yields. Thus the cells must be regenerated and grown to perform selection and evaluation. The exploitation of somatic variation by cell culture has become a new approach for stress tolerance breeding since very long (Larkin and Scowcroft 1981). Several tolerant crops have been obtained from somatic callus and microspore cultures. Somaclonal variation induced *in vitro* were used to enhance Al-tolerance toxicity in rice (Roy and Mandal 2005, Van Sint San *et al*. 1997), wheat (Dornelles *et al*. 1997) and tomato (Taghian and Enany 1996). The aluminium tolerance exhibited at cellular level is also maintained by adult plants as reported in tomato (Meredith 1978). Parrot and Bouton (1990) also reported that alfalfa expressed aluminium tolerance at the callus stage and consequently the selection through tissue culture cycles could be applied to identify aluminium tolerant plants. Roy and Mandal (2005) exploited somaclonal variability and generated toxicity tolerant plantlets by applying selection pressure both at callus and generated tolerant rice plantlets by using selection pressure both at callus and plantlets regenerated levels.

CONCLUSION

Soil acidity is major problems limiting performance of a large number of crops in many parts of the world, but neither an effective screening procedure nor highly tolerant cultivars in any crops are available to cope up with extreme soil acidity problems. As the plant problems in acid soils are frequently due to aluminum (Al) and/or manganese (Mn) excess, tolerance to acid soils is associated with tolerance to these elements. Plants vary greatly in their level of tolerance to Al and Mn toxicities so that the impact of acidity will depend upon the crop species involved. The genetics of tolerance to aluminium toxicity has been reported in limited number of crops such as barley, wheat, rice, maize, rye and alfalfa, sorghum, soybean, etc. The tolerance to Al-toxicity seems to be controlled by single dominant genes, and in some cases it appears to be under polygenic control. These information provide strong basis for breeding Al-tolerant cultivars in respective crops. DNA markers are of invaluable help in the process of mapping such major genes and provide the opportunity for tagging of Al-tolerance genes with linked markers which will eventually lead to expedite transfer such genes in agronomically useful background.

Generation of Al-tolerant plants through genetic engineering has been demonstrated to be valid approach. Some progress has been made in genetically modifying plants to enhance their Al-tolerance and future work is needed to ensure that sufficient levels of Al-tolerance are obtained in agronomically useful plant species. The production of transgenic plants with increased capacity to produce organic acids that chelate and detoxify aluminium in the rhizosphere is an appealing strategy to ensure sufficient level of tolerance for crop production.

REFERENCES

Aniol A. 2004. Chromosomal location of aluminium tolerance genes in rye. *Plant Breed.* **123**: 132–136.

Aniol A and Gustafson JP. 1984. Chromosome location of genes controlling aluminium tolerance in wheat, rye and triticate. *Can. J. Genet. Cytol.* **26**: 701–705.

Basu U, Good AG, Aung T, Slaski JJ, Basu A, Briggs KG and Taylor G J. 1999. A 23-kDa, root exudate polypeptide co-segregates with aluminium resistance in *Triticum aestivum* L. *Physiol. Plant.* **106**: 53–61.

Causse MA, Fulton TM, Cho YG, Ahn SN, Chunwongse J, Xu K, Xiang J, Yu Z, Ronald PC, Harrington SE, Second G, McCouch SR and Tanksley SD. 1994. Saturated molecular map of rice genome based on an interspecific backcross population. *Genetics.* **138**: 1251–1274.

Cruz-Ortega R, Cushman JC and Ownby JD. 1997. CDNA clones encoding 1,3-α-glucanase and a fimbrin-like cytoskeletal protein are induced by Al toxicity in wheat roots. *Plant Physiol.* **114**: 1453–1460

De la Fuente-J M, Ramirej-Rodriguez V, Cabrera-Ponce J and Herrera-Estrella L. 1997. Aluminium tolerance in transgenic plants by alteration of citrate synthesis. *Sci.* **276:** 1566–1568.

Delhaize E, Kataoka T, Hebb DM and White RG. 2003. Genes encoding proteins of the cation diffusion facilitator family that confer manganese tolerance. *Plant Cell.* **15:** 1131–1142.

Delhaize E, Ryan PR, Hebb DM, Yamamoto Y, Sasaki T and Matsumoto H. 2004. Engineering high level aluminium tolerance in barley with the *ALMTI* gene. *Proc. Natl. Acad. Sci.* USA. **101:** 15249–15254.

Dornelles ALC, Carvalho FIF de, Federizzi LC, Sereno MJC de M, Handel CL and Mittelmann A. 1997. Somaclonal variation for Al toxicity tolerance and gibberellic senstivity in wheat. *Pesquira Agropecuaria Brasileira.* **32:** 193–200.

Ezaki B, Gardner RC, Ezaki Y and Matsumoto H. 2000. Expression of aluminium-induced gene in transgenic *Arabidopsis* plants can ameliorate aluminium stress and/or oxidative stress. *Plant Physiol.* **122:** 657–665.

Ezaki B, Katsuhara M, Kawamura M and Matsumoto H. 2001. Different mechanisms of four Al resistant transgenes for Al toxicity in *Arabidopsis. Plant Physiol.* **127:** 918–927.

Ezaki B, Sivaguru M, Ezaki Y, Matsumoto H and Gardner RC. 1999. Acquisition of aluminium tolerance in *Saccharomyces cerevisiae* by expression of the *BCB* or *NtGDI1* gene derived from plants. *FEMS Microbiol Lett.* **171:** 81–87.

Ezaki B, Yamamoto Y and Matsumoto H. 1995. Cloning and sequencing of the CDNAs induced by Al treated and Pi starvation in cultured tobacco cells. *Physiol. Plant.* **93:** 11–18

Fontecha G, Silva-Navas J, Benito C, Mestres MA, Espino FJ. 2007. Candidate gene identification of an aluminium activated organic acid transporter gene at the Alt4 locus for aluminium tolerance in rye (*Secale cereale* L.). *Theor. Appl. Genet.* **114:** 249–260.

Gallego FJ, Lopez-Solanilla E, Figueiras AM and Benito C. 1998. Chromosomal location of PCR fragment as a source of DNA markers linked to aluminium tolerance genes in rye. *Theor. Appl. Genet.* **96(3–4):** 426–434.

Hamel F, Breton C and Houde M. 1998. Isolation and characterization of wheat aluminium-regulated genes: Possible involvement of aluminium as a pathogenesis response elicitor. *Planta.* **205:** 531–538.

Kerridge PC and Kronstad WE. 1968. Evidence of genetic resistance to aluminium toxicity in wheat (*Triticum aestivum* L. Vill., Host). *Agron.* **60:** 710–711.

Kassem MA, Meksem K, Kang CH, Njiti VN, Kilo V, Wood AJ and Lightfoot DA. 2004. Loci underlying resistance to manganese toxicity mapped in a soybean recombinant inbred line population of 'Essex' x 'Forrest'. *Plant Soil.* **260:** 197–204

Kilo V and Lightfoot DA. 1996. Genetic analysis of resistance to manganese toxicity in soybean molecular markers. *Soybean Genet. Newsltr.* **23:** 155–157.

Larkin PJ and Scowcroft WR. 1981. Somaclonal variation a novel source of variability from cell cultures for plant improvement. *Theor. Appl. Genet.* **60:** 197–214.

Luo MC and Dvorak J. 1996. Molecular mapping of an aluminium tolerance locus on chromosome 4D of Chinese spring wheat. *Euphytica.* **91:** 31–35.

Ma JF, Shen R, Zhao Z, Wissuwa M, Takeuchi Y, Ebitani T and Yano M. 2002. Response of rice to Al stress and identification of quantitative trait loci for aluminium tolerance. *Plant Cell Physiol*. **43**: 652–659.

Mandal SC. 1997. Introduction and historical overview. In: Acidic soils of India, p3–24. Mahapatra IC *et al*. (Eds), ICAR, New Delhi.

Matos M, Camacho MV, Perez-Flores V, Pernaute B, Pinto-Carnide O and Benito C. 2005. A new aluminium tolerance gene located on rye chromosome arm 7RS. *Theor. Appl. Genet*. **111**: 360–369.

Mao C, Yi K, Yang L, Zheng B, Wu Y, Liu F and Wu P. 2003. Identification of aluminium-regulated genes by cDNA-AFLP in rice (*Oryza sativa* L.): Al-regulated genes for the metabolism of cell wall components. *J. Exp. Bot*. **55**: 137–143.

Miftahudin G, Scoles J and Gustafson JP. 2002. AFLP markers tightly linked to the aluminium-tolerance gene *Alt₃* in rye (*Secale cereal* L.). *Theor. Appl. Genet*. **104**: 626–631.

Meredith CP. 1978. Selection and characterization of aluminium-resistant variants from tomato cell cultures. *Plant Sci. Lett*. **12**: 25–34.

Minella E and Sorrells ME. 1997. Inheritance and chromosome location of *Alp*, gene controlling aluminium tolerance in *Dayton* barley. *Plant Breed*. **116**: 465–469.

Morgan PW, Joham HE and Amin J. 1966. Effect of manganese toxicity on the indoleacetic acid oxidase system of cotton. *Plant Physiol*. **41**: 718–724.

Nguyen BD, Brar DS, Bui BC, Nguyen TV, Pham LN and Nguyen HT. 2003. Identification and mapping of QTL for aluminium tolerance introgressed from the new source, *Oryza rufipgan* Griff, to indica rice (*Oryza sativa* L.). *Theor. Appl. Genet*. **106**: 583–593.

Nguyen V, Nguyen B, Sarkarung S, Matinez C, Paterson A and Nguyen H. 2002. Mapping of genes controlling aluminium tolerance in rice: Comparison of different genetic backgrounds. *Mol. Genet. Genomics* **267**: 722–780.

Nguyen V, Burow M, Le H, Nguyen BT and Paterson A. 2001. Molecular mapping of genes conferring aluminium tolerance in rice (*Oryza sativa* L.) *Theor. Appl. Genet*. **102**: 1002–1010.

Ninamango-Cardenas FE, Guimaraes CT, Martinas PR, Parentoni SN, Carneiro NP, Lopes MA, Morò JR and Paiva E. 2003. Mapping QTLs for aluminium tolerance in maize. *Euphytica*. **130**: 223–232.

Parrot WA and Bouton JH. 1990. Aluminium tolerance in alfalfa as expressed in tissue culture. *Crop Sci*. **30**: 387–389.

Raman H, Karakousis A, Moroni JS, Raman R, Read B, Garvin DF, Kochian LV and Sorrells ME. 2003. Development and allele diversity of microsatellite markers linked with an aluminium tolerance gene *Alp* in barley. *Aust J. Agric Res*. **54**: 1315–1321.

Raman H, Moroni JH, Saito K, Read BJ and Scott B. 2002. Identification of AFLP and microsatellite markers linked with an aluminium tolerance gene in barley (*Hordeum vulgare* L.). *Theor. Appl. Genet*. **105**: 458–464.

Raman H, Moroni S, Raman R, Karakousis A, Read B, Sato K and Scott BJ. 2001. A genomic region associated with aluminium toxicity tolerance in barley. Proceedings of the 10th

Australian Barley Technical symposium. Http:// www.regional.org.au/au.abts/2001/t3 raman.htm.

Raman H, Wang JP and Read B. 2005. Molecular mapping of resistance to aluminium toxicity in barley. In Proc. plant and animal genome, p154, XIII Conference San Diego, USA.

Riede CR and Andreson JA. 1996. Linkage of RFLP markers to an aluminium tolerance gene in wheat. *Crop Sci.* **36:** 905–909.

Reid DA. 1971. Genetic control of reaction to aluminium in winter barley. In: International barley genetics symposium, 2. Pullman. Proc., p409–413, Pullman, Washington State University Press.

Roy B and Mandal BA. 2005. Towards development of Al-toxicity tolerant lines in indica rice by exploiting somaclonal variation. *Euphytica.* **145:** 221–227.

Sasaki T, Ezaki B and Matsumoto H. 2002. A gene encoding multidrug resistance (MDR)-like protein is induced by aluminium and inhibitors of calcium flux in wheat. *Plant cell Physiol.* **43:** 177–185.

Sasaki T, Yamamoto Y, Ezaki B, Katsuhara M, Ahn SJ, Ryan PR, Delahize E and Matsumoto HA. 2004. Wheat gene encoding an aluminium-activated malate transporter. *Plant J.* **37:** 645–653.

Sharma UC and Singh RP. 2002. Acid soils of India: Their distribution, management and future strategies for higher productivity. *Fert. News.* **47:** 45–52.

Sibov ST, Gaspar M, Silva MJ, Ottoboni LMM, Arruda P and Souza AP. 1999. Two genes control aluminium tolerance in maize: Genetic and molecular mapping analyses. *Genome.* **42:** 475–482.

Slootmaker ALJ. 1974. Tolerance to high soil acidity in wheat related species, rye and triticale. *Euphytica.* **23:** 505–513.

Snowden KC and Gardner RC. 1993. Five genes induced by aluminium in wheat (*Triticum aestivum* L.) roots. *Plant Physiol.* **103:** 855–861.

Stolen O and Anderson S. 1978. Inheritance of tolerance to low soil pH in barley. *Heriditas.* **88:** 101–105.

Sugimoto M and Sakamoto W. 1997. Putative phospholipids hydroperoxide glutathione peroxidase gene from *Arabidopsis thaliana* induced by oxidative stress. *Genes Genet. Syst.* **72:** 311–316.

Taghian AS and EI Enany AE. 1996. Genotypic differences and alteration of protein patterns of tomato explant under Al stress *in vitro*. *Aust. J. Agric. Sci.* **27:** 164–178.

Tang Y, Sorrells ME, Kochian LV and Garvin DF. 2000. Identification of RFLP markers linked to the barley Al tolerance gene *Alp*. *Crop Sci.* **40:** 778–782.

Taylor GJ, Basu A, Basu U, Slaski JJ, Zhang G and Good A. 1997. Al-induced, 51-kilodalton, membrane-bound proteins are associated with resistance to Al in a segregating population of wheat. *Plant Physiol.* **114:** 363–372.

Van Sint Jan V, deMacedo CC, Kinel JM and Bouharmont J. 1997. Selection of Al resistant plant from a sensitive rice cultivars using somaclonal variation *in vitro* and hydroponic cultures. *Euphytica.* **97:** 303–310.

Wang, J, Evangelou BP and Nielsen MT. 1992. Surface chemical properties of purified root cell walls from two tobacco genotypes exhibiting differential tolerance to manganese toxicity. *Plant Physiol*. **100**: 496–501.

Wang JP, Raman H, Read B, Zhou MX, Mendham NJ and Venkatanagappa. 2006. Validation of an *Alt* locus for aluminium tolerance scored with eriochrome cyanine R staining method in barley cultivar Honen (*Hordeum vulgare* L.). *Aust. J. Agric. Res.* **57**: 113–118.

Wang YX, Wu P, Wu YR and Yan XL. 2002. Molecular marker analysis of manganese toxicity tolerance in rice under greenhouse conditions. *Plant Soil*. **238**: 227–233.

Wilson AW, Harrington SE, WoodmanWL, Lee M, Sorrells M and McCouch SR. 1999. Inferences on the genome structure of progenitor maize through comparative analysis of rice, maize and the domesticated panicoids. *Genetics*. **153**: 453–473.

Wilkinson EE. 1991. Sorghum isoprenoid pathway responses to manganese concentration. *Canad. J. Plant Sci.* **71**: 973–981.

Wu P, Liao CY, Hu B, Yi KK, Jin WZ, Ni JJ and He C. 2000. QTLs and epistasis for aluminium tolerance in rice (*Oryza sativa* L.) at different seedling stages. *Theor. Appl. Genet.* **100**: 1295–1303.

5 Role of Organic Acids in the Evolution of Aluminium Tolerance in Crop Plants

Dharmendra Singh, Mahendra Singh, Rajendra Singh, NS Panwar and Muraleedhar Aski

ABSTRACT

Aluminium (Al) toxicity is a major worldwide constraint to crop production on acidic soils. A range of plant species exhibit aluminium tolerance by organic acids secretion that enable them to grow on acidic soils where toxic concentrations of Al can limit plant growth. Organic acids have been considered to play a central role in the detoxification of aluminium both externally and internally. Some plants detoxify aluminium by the secretion of organic acid from the roots. Other plants, including species that accumulate aluminium in their leaves, detoxify aluminium internally by forming complexes with organic acids. The advantages that plants get from the presence of organic acids in the rhizosphere are described and the genetic engineering approach to increase organic acid secretion is highlighted.

Key words: Aluminium toxicity, detoxification, organic acids.

INTRODUCTION

Aluminium (Al^{3+}) toxicity is one of the most deleterious factors for plant growth in acidic soils. This is particularly important in north eastern region of India, where more than 90 per cent of the soils are acidic, creating the potential for Al-toxicity etc. in surface and subsurface layers (Sharma and Singh 2002). The initial response to Al-toxicity is inhibition of root elongation, by destroying the root apex (Ryan *et al.* 1993) resulting in inefficient uptake of water and nutrients. Several studies provided the strong evidence that Al-tolerant genotypes have developed strategies to adapt to Al-toxicity and one of these strategies involves the efflux of organic acids (Ma *et al.* 2001, Ryan *et al.* 2001). The Al-dependent stimulation of organic acid efflux from roots has now been reported in many species, and this response has been associated with an increase in Al-tolerence. The biochemical, physiological and genetic bases of the mechanisms can produce and export organic acids to the root apoplast and rhizosphere. Such aspects are beginning to be understood and will be the main focus of this chapter.

STRATEGIES FOR THE DETOXIFICATION OF ALUMINIUM

There have been two strategies for the detoxification of aluminium by plants cells (Taylor 1991, Kochian 1995). One is the exclusion of aluminium from the root tips (Delhaize and Ryan 1995, Kochian 1995) and the other is tolerance to aluminium that absorbs the plant cells (Kochian *et al.* 2004). Thus organic acids play an important role in the external and internal neutralization of aluminium (Ma 2000, Ma *et al.* 1997).

A range of plant species are known to secrete organic acids from their roots in response to Al stress (Table 5.1). Two general patterns of Al stimulated efflux of organic acids have been observed from roots (Ma *et al.* 2001): First pattern, there is no discernible delay between the moment of aluminium addition and the onset of organic acid efflux. Activation of an anion channel located on the plasma membrane by aluminium is a possible mechanism responsible for quick secretion (Delhaize *et al.* 1993, Delhaize and Ryan 1995). This quick response suggests that all the necessary metabolic machineries are constitutively expressed in the root cells and that organic anion efflux is simple triggered by Al^{3+} and induction of novel protein is not required (Ma *et al.* 2002). Such pattern was observed in wheat (Delhaize *et al.* 1993), barley (Zhao *et al.* 2003), etc. In second pattern, organic acid efflux is delayed for several hours after exposure to aluminium. (Ma *et al.* 2001, Li *et al.* 2000, Yang *et al.* 2006) and protein induction is required (Ma *et al.* 2002). These induced proteins could be involved in organic acid metabolism or in the transport of organic acid anions. Such secretion pattern was observed in *Cassia tora* (Ma *et al.* 1997), rye (Li *et al.* 2000), triticale (Ma *et al.* 2000) and rice bean (Yang *et al.* 2006).

Table 5.1: *Organic acid exudation from different plant roots*

Crop	Organic acid released	Reference
Barley	Citrate	Zhao *et al.* 2003
Carrot	Citrate	Takashi *et al.* 2001
Citrus	Citrate	Deng *et al.* 2009
Eucalyptus	Citrate and malate	Silva *et al.* 2004
Maize	Citrate	Pellet *et al.* 1995
Pea	Citrate	Kobayashi *et al.* 2004
Oat	Malate and citrate	Zheng *et al.* 1998
Pineapple	Citrate, malate and succinate	Le-Van and Masuda 2004
Rapeseed	Malate and citrate	Zheng *et al.* 1998
Radish	Malate and citrate	Zheng *et al.* 1998
Rice	Citrate	Ma *et al.* 2002
Rice bean	Citrate	Yang *et al.* 2006

(Contd.)

Table 5.1: *Organic acid exudation from different plant roots (Contd.)*

Crop	Organic acid released	Reference
Rye	Malate and citrate	Li *et al.* 2000
Snapbean	Citrate	Miyasaka *et al.* 1991
Spinach	Oxalate	Yang *et al.* 2005
Tobacco	Citrate	Delhaize *et al.* 2001
Triticale	Citrate and malate	Ma *et al.* 2000

EXOGENOUS APPLICATIONS TO REDUCE ALUMINIUM TOXICITY

Organic acids play an important role in both internal and external aluminium detoxification. Meriga *et al.* (2003) observed that Al-tolerant reduced the root and shoot lengths of the control seedlings (without citrate) in rice tolerant cultivar by 26 per cent and 21 per cent respectively and that of sensitive by 51 per cent and 23 per cent respectively. However, corresponding seedlings grown in citrate-supplemented solution exhibited better root and shoot growth particularly at a citrate concentration of above 100 µM. At 200 µM citrate, the root and shoot length of tolerant and sensitive cultivar improved by 60 per cent over their respective control. Yang and Zhang (1998) observed that height of the mungbean seedlings treated with 5mM citric acid increased by 22.2 per cent or 102.8 per cent at 2 or 5 mM Al respectively.

ENHANCING THE ALUMINIUM TOLERANCE BY GENETIC ENGINEERING

The production of transgenic plants with an increased capacity to produce and/or excrete organic acids that chelate and detoxify Al in the rhizosphere is an appealing strategy to produce Al-tolerant plants. Genetically engineered plants that over express gene involved in the biosynthesis and transport of organic acid as well as aluminium toxicity events at the cell level have been produced. Plant breeders can take advantage of genetic engineering by which useful genes are made available in any species. This can be introgressed of new desirable traits into a crop species. Researchers have manipulated the biosynthesis capacity of cells which produce and accumulate higher amounts of organic acids. As a result, this will change root exudation profile and aluminium resistance of a genotype. The most well-known example of a successful achievement in this direction is the work of De la Fuente *et al.* (1997). They introduced a *Pseudomonas aurginosa* CSb gene into tobacco and papaya. As a result the transgenic plants showed enhanced citrate efflux and greater Al-tolerance than non-transformant lines. The transformed lines of tobacco expressing CSb had up to 10 folds greater internal citrate in their root tissues whereas in papaya citrate levels in the roots was only 2–3 folds. Increased production of citric acid was shown to result in aluminium tolerance in both the species. However, attempt to repeat the work using the same transgenic lines as De la Fuente *et al.* (1997) as well as tobacco transgenic expressing the *P. aeruginosa* CS gene to 10 folds greater levels, have shown neither increased citrate concentrations in roots nor increased citrate efflux. Thus no improvement of aluminium tolerance was achieved (Delhaize *et al*. 2001).

CONCLUSION

There is considerable evidence associating organic acids in the Al tolerance mechanisms of many species. The organic acids such as citrate, malate and oxalate play an important role for aluminium detoxification. However, the research on organic acid has also resulted in many questions that remain unanswered. For example, how do aluminium exposure activates or induces the secretion of specific organic acids out of root cells? How much organic acid secretion is sufficient to detoxify aluminium? Why do species release different organic acids as a response to Al stress?

Several researchers have attempted to manipulate citrate metabolism using genetic engineering to increase organic acid efflux. Citrate synthase gene has been identified, and the many yet to be discovered before targeted genetic modifications can be effectively designed.

REFERENCES

De la Fuente JM, Ramirej-Rodriguez V, Cabrera-Ponce J and Herrera-Estrella L. 1997. Aluminium tolerance in transgenic plants by alteration of citrate synthesis. *Sci.* **276:** 1566–1568.

Delhaize E, Hebb DM and Ryan PP. 2001. Expression of a *Psedomonas aeruginosa* citrate synthase gene in tobacco is not associated with either enhanced citrate accumulation or efflux. *Plant Physiol.* **125:** 2059–2067.

Delhaize E and Ryan PR. 1995. Aluminium toxicity and tolerance in plants. *Plant Physiol.* **107:** 315–321.

Delhaize E, Ryan PR and Randall PJ. 1993. Aluminium tolerance in wheat (*Triticum aestivum* L.): Part II. Aluminium–stimulated excretion of malic acid from root apices. *Plant Physiol.* **103:** 695–702.

Deng W, Luo K, Li Z, Yang Y, Hu N and Wu Y. 2009. Overexpression of *citrus junos* mitochondrial citrate synthase gene in *Nicotiana benthamiana* confer Al tolerance. *Planta* **230:** 355–365.

Kobayashi Y, Yamamoto Y and Matsumoto H. 2004. Studies on the mechanisms of aluminium tolerance in pea (*Pisum sativum* L.) using cultivar 'Alsaka' and Al-sensitive cultivar 'Hyogo'. *Soil Sci. Plant Nutr.* **50:** 197–204.

Kochian, LV 1995. Cellular mechanisms of aluminium toxicity and resistance in plants. *Ann. Rev. Pl. Physiol. Pl. Mol. Biol.* **46:** 237–260.

Kochian LV, Hoekenga OA and Pineros MA. 2004. How do crop plants tolerate acid soils? Mechanisms of aluminium tolerance and phosphorus efficiency. *Ann. Rev. Plant Biol.* **55:** 459–493.

Le-Van H and Masuda T. 2004. Physiological and biochemical studies on aluminium tolerance in pineapple. *Aust. J. Soil Res.* **42:** 699–707.

Li XF, Ma JF and Matsumoto H. 2000. Pattern of Al induced secretion of organic acids differs between rye and wheat. *Plant Physiol.* **123:** 1537–1543.

Ma JF. 2000. Role of organic acids in detoxification of aluminium in higher plants. *Plant Cell Physiol.* **41:** 383–390.

Ma JF, Hiradate S, Nomoto K, Iwashita T and Matsumoto H. 1997. Internal detoxification mechanism of Al in *Hydrangea*: Identification of Al form in the leaves. *Plant Physiol.* **113:** 1033–1039.

Ma JF, Ryan P and Delhaize E. 2001. Aluminium resistance in plants and the complexing role of organic acids. *Trends Plant Sci.* **6:** 273–278

Ma JF, Shen R, Zhao Z, Wissuwa M, Takeuchi Y, Ebitani T and Yano M. 2002. Response of rice to Al stress and identification of quantitative trait loci for aluminium tolerance. *Plant Cell Physiol.* **43:** 652–659.

Ma JF, Taketa S and Yang ZM. 2000. Aluminium tolerance genes on the short arm of chromosomes 3 R are linked to organic acid release in triticle. *Plant Physiol.* **122:** 687–694.

Ma JF, Zheng SJ and Matsumoto H. 1997. Specific secretion of citric acid induced by Al stress in *Cassia tora* L. *Plant Cell Physiol.* **38:** 1019–1025.

Meriga B, Reddy BK, Jageswar G, Reddy LA and Kishor PB. 2003. Alleviating effect of citrate on Al toxicity of rice seedlings. *Curr. Sci.* **85:** 383–385.

Miyasaka SC, Buta JG, Howell RK and Foy CD. 1991. Mechanism of Al tolerance in snapbeans. Root exudation of citric acid. *Plant Physiol.* **96:** 737–743.

Pellet DM, Grunes DL and Kochian LV. 1995. Organic acid exudation as an aluminium tolerance mechanisms in maize (*Z. mays* L.). *Planta* **196:** 788–795.

Ryan PR, Delhaize E and Jones DL. 2001. Function and mechanism of organic anion exudation from plant roots. *Annu. Rev. Pl. Physiol. Pl. Mol. Biol.* **52:** 527–560.

Ryan PR, Ditomaso JM and Kochian LV. 1993. Aluminium toxicity in roots: an investigation of spatial sensitivity and the role of the root cap. *J. Exp. Bot.* **44:** 437–446.

Sharma UC and Singh RP. 2002. Acid soils of India: Their distribution, management and future strategies for higher productivity. *Fert. News.* **47:** 45–52.

Silva IR, Novais QF, Jhem GN, Barros NF, Gebrim FO, Nunes FN, Neves JCL and Leite FP. 2004. Response of eucalyptus species to Al the possible involvement of low molecular weight organic acid in the aluminium tolerance mechanisms. *Tree Physiol.* **24:** 1267–1277.

Takashi K, Katsunori S, Hideki O, Kunihiko O and Masahiko S. 2001. Al tolerance of carrot (*Daucus carota* L.) S1 lines from selected cell cultures and locational variation of exuding citric acid from their roots. *Jpn. J. Soil Sci. Plant Nutr.* **72:** 49–55.

Taylor GJ. 1991. Current view of the aluminium stress response: The physiological basis of tolerance. *Curr. Top. Plant Biochem. Physiol.* **10:** 57–93.

Yang JL, Zhang L, Ya LY, You FJ, Wu P and Shao ZJ. 2006. Citrate transporters play a critical role in aluminium stimulated citrate efflux in rice bean (*Vigna umbellata*) roots. *Ann. Bot.* (Lond). **97:** 579–584.

Yang JL, Zheng SJ, He YF and Matsumoto H. 2005. Aluminium resistance requires resistance to acid stress: a case study with spinach that exudates oxalate rapidly when exposed to Al stress. *J. Experimental Bot.* **56:** 1197–1203.

Yang YH and Zhang HY 1998. Effect of citric acid on aluminium toxicity in the growth mungbean seedlings. *J Plant Nutr.* **21:** 1037–1044.

Zhao Z, Ma JF, Sato K and Takeda K. 2003. Differential aluminium resistance and citrate secretion in barley (*Hordeum vulgare* L.) *Planta.* **217:** 794–800.

Zheng S, Ma JF and Matsumoto H. 1988. Continuous seretion of organic acids is related to aluminium resistance during relatively long-term exposure to aluminium stress. *Physiol. Plant.* **103:** 209–219.

6 Manganese Toxicity in Crop Plants

Dharmendra Singh, RN Sehgal, Rajendra Singh, Ph Ranjit Sharma, SK Chauhan, Anil Kumar, NS Panwar and Muraleedhar Aski

ABSTRACT

Manganese toxicity is one of the important growth limiting factors in acidic soils. In general, the symptoms of manganese toxicity vary widely among plant species and varieties within species. Plant tops are affected to a greater extent than root growth in manganese stress environments. Toxic effects of manganese on plant growth have been attributed to several physiological and biochemical pathways. Such pathways have been suggested as important selection criteria to enhance the degree of Mn-tolerance. Variation for manganese tolerance exists in plant species which can be exploited through selection and breeding for improving manganese tolerance. The modem approaches being used to impart Mn-tolerance involves exploitation of natural variation and/or the generation of transgenic plants. These approaches would be rewarding in developing crop cultivars tolerant to manganese toxicity.

Key words: Acidic soil, manganese stress, plant growth.

INTRODUCTION

Manganese is an essential element required in plant nutrition. However, it becomes detrimental to plant growth when present in excess quantities as Mn^{2+} in soil. At low soil pH, MnO_2 is reduced to Mn^{2+} more so at pH <5.5. However, reports indicate that the toxicity can occur at pH values up to 6.0 particularly if the soils are poorly drained or compacted leading to low percolation and water logging thereby, setting in the reduced conditions. Such conditions are favourable for the formation of Mn^{2+} in soils and the plants absorb manganese in this form.

The amount of total Mn in most soils ranges from 200 to 30,000 mg kg $^{-1}$ (Mortvedt and Cunningham 1971). Its availability to plants depends upon pH, easily reducible Mn oxides, organic matter level, redox potential, population of Mn reducing micro-organisms and aeration (Foy 1984).

Manganese toxicity, in contrast to other toxic metals like aluminium cadmium, lead, mercury, etc. has received little attention from plant scientists. The present chapter deals with some important aspects such as growth, biochemical and physiological parameters, conventional and biotechnological approaches.

TOXIC EFFECTS OF MANGANESE ON PLANT GROWTH

Germination

Treatment with 0.05 per cent $MnSO_4$ hampered germination and seedling growth in tomato seeds (Foy 1984). Seeds soaked in 100, 1000, 10,000 mg kg^{-1} Mn as both $MnSO_4$ and $KMnO_4$ inhibited seed germination of *Pisum* (Joardar 1988, Joardar and Sharma 1989, Mukhopadhyay and Sharma 1991). However, Unni *et al.* (1995) found that Mn does not inhibit seed germination up to 200 ppm in rice cv. Jaya.

Root Growth

Mn does not injure roots directly but first affects shoots (Foy 1973) as Mn is readily taken up and transported to the shoots from the roots (Nable and Loneragan 1984). In severe cases of manganese toxicity, plant roots turned brown first followed by browning of lower leaves on the shoot. The root browning is attributed to accumulation of oxidized Mn on the root surface and oxidized phenolics in root cortical cells (Horst *et al.* 1999, Keil *et al.* 1986). The intensity of root browning increases with severity of toxicity. Usually, it will be darker near the root tips, gradually progressing upward and becoming localized on the older roots (Mortley 1993). Such roots are inefficient in absorbing nutrients and water.

There are contradictory reports about plant root browning first and shoots being severely injured later or vice versa (Morris and Pierre 1949, Foy *et al.* 1978). There is need to reassess.

Shoot Growth

Decrease in shoot growth is a well-documented effect due to Mn toxicity in crops. Necrotic brown spotting on leaves, petioles and stems is the typical symptom of Mn toxicity (Horst and Marschner 1978b, Wu 1994). Spotting starts on the lower leaves and progresses with time towards the upper leaves (Elamin and Wilcox 1986a, Elamin and Wilcox 1986b, Horiguchi 1987). Usually symptoms are more severe in the older leaves that have had the longest time to accumulate manganese. These symptoms have been used as an index of the degree of manganese toxicity tolerance in plants (Wang *et al.* 2002, Wissemeier and Horst 1982, Gonzalez and Lynch 1997, Horst *et al.* 1999).

The productivity decrease can also occur without exhibiting any visual symptoms (Miner and Sims 1983). The symptoms, however, differ for different plant species. Symptoms of manganese toxicity in various crops are given in Table 6.1.

Manganese Uptake, Translocation and Accumulation

Manganese tolerance is exhibited by two groups of crops. In the first group, the Mn tolerance is associated with more entrapment of Mn in the roots. The manganese gets oxidized and deposited in roots reducing its translocation to shoots thereby enhancing the tolerance of plant to excessive manganese concentration (Foy *et al.* 1978). It has been reported that tolerant clones of alfalfa contained lower concentration of manganese in their shoots and higher concentration in roots than was observed in more sensitive clones (Quellete and Dessureaux 1958). At adequate

Table 6.1: *Symptoms of manganese (Mn) toxicity in various plant species*

Species	Symptom	Reference
Alfalfa and lettuce	Marginal chlorosis and necrosis of leaves	Foy *et al. 1978*
Apple	Internal bark necrosis	Hoyt 1988, Miller and Schubert 1977, Scibisz and Sadowski 1979
Barley	Necrotic spots in the leaves	Vlamis and Williams 1964
Carrot	Marginal chlorosis, bronze necrotic speckling and scorching	Hewitt 1948
Cabbage and chickpea	Marginal chlorosis of old leaves often with brown necrotic spots	Foy *et al.* 1978
Common bean	Crinckle in young leaves and formation of brown speckles in mature leaves	Horst and Marschner 1978
Carnation	Leaf tip burning	Ishida and Masui 1976
Clover and sweet clover	Chlorosis of young leaves and speckling of older leaves	Morris and Pierre 1949
Cotton	Crinkle leaf	Foy 1973
Cowpea	Small dark brown spots on leaves followed by chlorosis, necrosis finally shedding of the leaves	Horst 1982
Pea	Brown and necrotic spots on leaves	Singh 2009, Rezai and Farboodnia 2008
Muskmelon	Fruit cracking at the blossom end	Mausi *et al.* 1976
Marigold and geranium	Small dark spots surrounded by irregular areas of chlorotic tissues in eaves	Albano *et al.* 1996
Potato	Dark brown streaks on the lower stems at the base of the petioles	Lee and McDonald 1978

(Contd.)

Table 6.1: *Symptoms of manganese (Mn) toxicity in various plant species (Contd.)*

Species	Symptoms	Reference
Rapeseed	Interveinal and leaf margin chlorosis, brown and necotic spots and the cupping or distortion of leaf shape	Colton *et al.* 1992, Fenton *et al.* 1996, Simon *et al.* 1974
Sweet potato and snapbean	Interveinal and leaf margin chlorosis, brown and necotic spots and the cupping or distortion of leaf shape	Colton *et al.* 1992, Fenton *et al.* 1996, Simon *et al.* 1974
Tobacco	Foliar chlorosis and necrotic spottings	Petolino and Collins 1985
Tomato	Dark brown/black spots in the leaves and cotyledons	Petolino and Collins 1985

and high levels of manganese supply, manganese concentrations are generally higher in roots than in leaves, higher in mature leaves than in younger leaves, and higher in leaves than in stems, flower and seeds (Nable 1983). Benac (1976) reported that transport of Mn from roots to leaves was responsible for superior tolerance to excess Mn.

In the second group, some plants may accumulate high amounts of Mn in their leaves. Leaves of tea plants with high but non toxic levels of Mn showed a much higher accumulation of Mn in the epidermis with relatively low levels in the parenchyma cells (Memon *et al.* 1980). Currently several Mn hyperaccumulators have been reported including 9 species listed by Reeves and Baker (2000) an unidentified *Eugenia* species (Proctor *et al.* 1989) and the newly found tree species *Austromyrtus* (Bidwell *et al.* 2002) and two herbaceous plants namely *Phytolacca acinosa* Roxb (Xue *et al.* 2003) and *Polygonum hydropiper* (Wang *et al.* 2007). Baker and Brooks (1989) defined Mn hyperaccumulators as species with concentration exceeding 10,000 mg kg^{-1} in the above ground tissue. Yang *et al.* (2008) also observed that leaves and stems contained 10,000 mg kg^{-1} in *Schima superba* a tree species.

Manganese Tolerance Behaviour and Critical Concentrations of Manganese Toxicity

Concentrations in the range of 0.2 to 12 mM can cause severe growth limitations in solution cultures among crops like cotton (Kennedy and Jones 1991), sweet potato (Mortley 1993), sorghum (Mgema and Clark 1995). Low concentration of 1 ppm can be toxic to tobacco, potato and bush clover when grown in solution culture (Berger and Gerloff 1947, Jacobson and Swanback 1932, Morris and Pierre 1949). Critical concentration of Mn in the leaves was associated with 10 per cent reduction in dry weight due to toxicity (Ohki 1981). Different plant species or even varieties within a species have different degrees of tolerance to Mn (Foy *et al.* 1988). Critical toxicity levels of Mn-toxicity in various crops are summarized in Table 6.2.

Factors Affecting Manganese Toxicity

Mn-toxicity to plants is dependent on several factors including soil pH, redox potential, soil moisture and microbial activity. The relative tolerance of plants to excess Mn is affected by climatic factors such as temperature and light intensity (Rufty *et al.* 1979). The threshold internal Mn concentration associated with Mn-

Table 6.2: *Critical toxicity levels of Mn in the leaves of various plant species*

Species	Critical toxicity (mg kg^{-1})	Reference
Bragg soybean	160	Foy *et al.* 1978
Carrot	7100–9600	Gupta *et al.* 1970
Cotton	750	Horst and Marschner 1990
Clover	650	Hannan and Ohki 1988
Cowpea, potato, peanut	500–1500	Cregan 1980
Cucumber	600–800	Sedberry *et al.* 1983
Lespedeza	200–300	Cregan 1980
Lettuce	200–400	Sedberry *et al.* 1983
Lowland rice	50000	Hannan and Ohki 1988
Maize	3500	Amberger and Yousry 1988
Muskmelon	900	Elamin and Wilcox 1986a
Peas	300	Horst and Marschner 1990
Sweet potato	1380	Horst and Marschner 1990
Soybean	600	Horst and Marschner 1990
Sunflower	5300	Horst and Marschner 1990
Tomato	1500–2000	Amberger and Yousry 1988
Urd bean	144	Kalyanaraman and Sivagurunathan 1993
Wheat, barley	400–500	Cregan 1980
Watermelon	1324	Elamin and Wilcox 1986a

toxicity is temperature dependent (Heenan and Carter 1977). Despite high Mn absorption, plant tolerance to Mn-toxicity increases with increasing temperature in tobacco and soybean because increasing temperature leads to faster growth rate (Ruftty *et al.* 1979, Foy 1984). In oats, at high temperature internal tolerance to Mn increases and toxicity is prevented (Cheng and Pesant 1977). However, high temperature increases Mn absorption and reduces the growth rate in potato (Marsh *et al.* 1989). Blatt and Diest (1981) noted more severe Mn-toxicity at higher temperature in lettuce varieties. Plants growing in low light displayed fewer symptoms of Mn toxicity than those growing in high light (Horiguchi 1988, Nable *et al*. 1988). High light intensity stimulates Mn absorption by plants and accentuates the severity of Mn toxicity (Horiguchi 1988).

Higher oxides of Mn are reduced in water-logged or flooded soil (Alam 1983, Ponnamperuma 1978). Under condition of poor soil aeration, Mn is reduced to the divalent form which is available to plants (Dionne and Pesant 1985, Patrick and Henderson 1981, Sparrow and Uren 1987).

Mechanisms of Manganese Tolerance

In general, the mechanisms of Mn tolerance can be classified into two categories, *viz*. exclusion and inclusion mechanisms. The Mn uptake and its translocation are prevented in the first one while the detoxification of Mn in vacuole occurs in the second. The plant tolerance to high concentrations of soil Mn operates by exclusion or restricting the Mn transport to plant shoots (Scott and Fisher 1989). Reduced transport of Mn from roots to leaves is responsible for superior tolerance to excess Mn (Benac 1976). The Mn-resistance of sunflower has been partially attributed to the secretion of Mn by the trichomes (Blamey *et al*. 1986). This indicates that an exclusion mechanism might be involved in this crop.

Plant species expressing resistance to high Mn have the capability to maintain normal growth under a high internal shoot Mn content in cowpea (Horst 1988), cotton (Foy *et al*. 1995), soybean (Brown and Jones 1977). These results indicated that physiological mechanism for resistance to high Mn is of tissue tolerance. The highest concentration of Mn occurs in the epidermis, collenchyma and bundle sheath cells in a Mn accumulator plant species (*Acanthopanax sciadophylloides)* (Memon *et al*. 1980). This localization may be due to internal tolerance mechanism which keeps Mn away from the key metabolic sites (Foy 1983, 1984). The tissue tolerance to excess Mn can be through the formation of metabolically inactive organic complexes, binding to cell walls and/or deposition in vacuoles or by tolerance of some vital enzyme systems to high concentration of ionic Mn (Scott and Fisher 1989). Ability of rice to oxidize Mn from divalent toxic state to tetravalent non-toxic state in its root zone imparts high internal tolerance to excess Mn (Engler and Patrick 1975). Mn-tolerance of several legumes is related with reduced Mn uptake and/or greater internal tolerance to excess Mn (Bromfield 1978, Hutton *et al*. 1978).

EFFECTS OF MANGANESE TOXICITY ON PHYSIOLOGICAL AND BIO-CHEMICAL PARAMETERS

Enzymes and Cell Metabolism

The effects of excess Mn can be through destruction of auxins (IAA, Indole-3-acetic acid) by increasing the activity of IAA oxidase; a possible amino acid imbalance; decreased activities of catalase, ascorbic acid oxidase, gluthione oxidase and cytochrome C oxidase and lowered ATP contents. (Foy 1983, 1984). Morgan *et al*.

(1966) reported that Mn-toxicity in cotton was associated with an increase in IAA oxidase activity and a decrease in IAA oxidase inhibitor activity.

Horiguchi and Fukomoto (1987) demonstrated that the increase in peroxidase activity was followed by the appearance of necrotic browning. They suggested that the increase in the peroxidase activity may, however, not be the only factor for the browning because the contact of peroxidase with the substrates, which are oxidized to form brown substances, is necessary. Rezai and Farboodnia (2008) observed close relationships between Mn concentration and antioxidant enzymes activity in pea.

Photosynthesis and Transpiration

Many studies have shown that Mn-toxicity inhibits the photosynthesis and decreases chlorophyll content in many plant species. Subrahmanyam and Rathore (2000) observed that net photosynthetic rate decreased with increasing concentration of Mn within 2 days of Mn supply in nutrient solution and transpiration rate and stomatal conductance were affected slowly in rice bean (*Vigna umbellata*). Critical Mn-toxicity levels for total chlorophyll and photosynthesis were 1030 and 1050 mg kg^{-1} respectively, in wheat (Ohki 1985). Gonzalez and Lynch (1997) found that Mn toxicity decreased total chlorophyll content only in immature leaves with consequent reduction of leaf CO_2 assimilation. They also observed that mature leaves showed brown speckles characteristic of Mn-toxicity, but did not suffer any detriment in their capacity to assimilate CO_2. Rezai and Farboodnia (2008) found that at 25 ppm Mn supplied in culture solution, decreased the chlorophyll content and at 50 ppm inhibited chlorophyll synthesis in the leaves.

Organic Acids

Researchers have found that organic acid levels can increase in both tolerant and sensitive cultivars depending on the species. Mn-tolerant cultivars of wheat did not enhance their production of malic, citric or aconitic acids when exposed to high solution Mn concentration while concentrations of the organic acids slightly increased in the sensitive cultivars (Burke *et al.* 1990). However, the exact role of organic acids for manganese tolerance is not yet clear. Hence, there is need to do work on this aspect.

Snejana *et al.* (2005) found that exogenous application of succinate above 1500 µM Mn in the nutrient solution decreased Mn uptake in the roots and was accompanied by a decrease in Mn translocation to the leaves and stems.

Callose

The formation of callose is a sensitive and reliable indicator for Mn-toxicity (Wissemeier and Horst 1982, Wissemeier *et al.* 1992, 1993). The occurrence of visible symptoms is preceded and accompanied by an early formation of callose. The concentration of extractable leaf callose, an indication of injury, correlates strongly with Mn-toxicity symptoms (Wissemeier *et al.* 1992). The Mn induced callose formation is more sensitive than the brown spots and it is increased slightly as early as 1 day and significantly after 2 days of Mn treatment (Wissemeier and Horst 1982). They found that callose deposition 20 times higher than of brown spots and early increase in total callose content indicate an early influence of Mn on the plasma membrane localized callose synthesis.

NUTRIENT INTERACTIONS

The interactions of manganese toxicity with other ions are very important for plant growth and development. Lidon (2000) found that excess Mn can interfere with the absorption, translocation and utilization of other mineral elements such as calcium (Ca), magnesium (Mg), iron (Fe), sodium (Na) and phosphorus (P).

Interaction with Nitrogen

Mn toxicity inhibits absorption of nitrate and promotes intensive accumulation of sulphate in grapevines (Khatiashvili *et al.* 1985). Effects of Mn toxicity were less in presence of N as NH_4^+ and NO_3 than the control in cabbage, spinach and tomato (Osava and Ikeda 1980). Increased Mn content was observed in vegetables as a consequence of nitrogen application (Taylor *et al.* 1983). The incidence of necrotic brown spots was reduced by an increase in the proportion of NH_4^+. NO_3^- enhanced Mn uptake and plant toxicity symptoms were observed (McGrath and Rorison 1982). In muskmelon, NH_4^+ decreased Mn concentration and alleviated Mn toxicity symptoms, but a concentration of NH_4^+ above 14 mg litre^{-1} decreased growth (Elamin and Wilcox 1986c).

Interaction with Calcium

There is evidence that 'crinkle leaf' is due to Mn induced Ca deficiency. 'Crinkle leaf' symptoms resemble symptoms of Ca deficiency (Foy *et al.* 1981, Horst and Marschner 1978a). Excessive supply of Mn, the translocation of Ca into the shoot apex is decreased (Horst and Marschner 1978a). This phenomenon might be related to the fact that high Mn level decreases the cation exchange capacity of the leaf tissue (Horst and Marschner 1978b) and decreases the IAA levels in the areas of new growth (Morgan *et al.* 1976). Auxin was reported to be responsible for the formation of new binding sites for the transport of Ca to the apical meristems (Horst and Marschner 1978a). Additional Ca reduced Mn concentration in muskmelon but failed to prevent decrease of yield by the excess Mn (Masui *et al.* 1976). Vose and Jones (1963) found that increasing the Ca level in the solution culture reduced the adverse effects of high Mn level on suppressing the number of nodules on white clover roots. However, Morris and Pierre (1947) found that Mn-toxicity was not alleviated by additional Ca and was even greater at high Ca concentrations.

Interaction with Magnesium

Toxic concentration of Mn in the medium can induce magnesium deficiency in roots (Heenan and Campbell 1981) possibly through competition for binding sites during uptake as well as for different metabolic reactions. Excess Mn may inhibit Mg uptake by up to 50 per cent (Kazda and Znacek 1989) due to competition for binding sites in the roots during absorption. Increase in Mn supply decreases the leaf concentration of Mg (Turner and Barkus 1983) in banana. "Golden Tip" necrosis in norway spruce is due to Mg deficiency, induced by Mn toxicity (Hecht-Buchholz *et al.* 1987). Large Mg application would prevent Mn toxicity, which could then lead to serious nutritional imbalance because Mg would interfere with Ca uptake.

Interaction with Potassium

The absorption of potassium is slightly reduced by an increasing in Mn concentration in comparison to other nutrients (Heenan and Campbell 1981). Mn toxicity symptoms were depressed by the reduced rate of Mn uptake at high potassium supply (Heenan and Campbell 1981) but there was no effect of potassium supply when Mn was absent. The uptake and distribution of K was independent of Mn concentration especially at below 5 ppm of Mn in tomato (Alvarez-Tinaut *et al.* 1979). High levels of K in the shoots of Mn-tolerant 'Lee' soybean alleviated the toxic effects of high internal Mn concentrations (Brown and Jones 1977).

Interaction with Phosphorus

Addition of phosphorus can detoxify excess Mn in plants through precipitation (Heintze 1968) or rendering it inactive within the plant (Foy 1984). Phosphorus concentration in rice plants increased significantly with increasing level of phosphorus in soil under flooding conditions, but was decreased by the highest Mn treatment under unflooded soil condition (Alam 1983). Application of soluble phosphates to soils or nutrient solutions containing high amounts of Mn increased crop yields and suppressed development of Mn-toxicity symptoms. This may be due to the additional available phosphorus and a decrease in soluble Mn in the medium by precipitation (Bortner 1935). Contrary to these findings, Morris and Pierre (1947) observed that the solubility of Mn in the nutrient solution was not affected by the additional phosphate. Such phosphorus does not have any effect in preventing Mn-toxicity, but may even accentuate it if added at a high concentration to the medium.

Interaction with Iron

Interaction between Mn and Fe is not always consistent and it varies among plant species. Increasing Fe supply decreased Mn uptake and could interfere with normal Fe metabolism without reducing Fe uptake (Masui *et al.* 1976). Excess Mn sometimes produces symptoms that resemble those of Fe deficiency. Either no interaction or positive interaction or negative interactions have been observed by several workers for Fe and Mn among different crops in different test conditions. A negative correlation was found between uptake of Mn and Fe in tomato, sorghum, rice and wheat (Jaurigui and Reisenauer 1982, Foy *et al.* 1978, Kuo and Mikkelson 1981, Sanchez-Ryan *et al.* 1974, Van Der Vorm and Van Diest 1979). Positive interaction

was observed between uptake of Mn and Fe in oats, wheat, and barley (Mashhady and EI-Damary 1981, Shuman and Anderson 1976, Singh and Pathak 1968) and negative interaction was found in pineapple, soybean, mustard, tobacco, rice, barley and flax (Beauchamp and Rossi 1972, Dekock and Inkson 1962, Heenan and Campbell 1983, Hiatt and Ragland 1963, Somers and Shive 1942, Vlamis and Williams 1964).

Mn induced Fe deficiency was related to the ratio of Fe/Mn (Leach and Taper 1954) as well as concentrations in the nutrients medium (Foy *et al.* 1995). Fe concentrations and Fe/Mn ratio were higher in the Mn-tolerant cultivar of cotton than in the Mn sensitive cultivar (Foy *et al.* 1995). Mn-toxicity internally induces interveinal chlorosis on young leaves due to Fe deficiency in beans, pepper spinach and tomato (Osawa and Ikeda 1976). Pronounced marginal chlorosis of old leaves often with brown necrotic spots due to accumulation of Mn is observed in lettuce, celery and cabbage and chickpea genotype 'T3' (Foy *et al.* 1978).

Interaction with Molybdenum

General similarities occur between Mo deficiency and Mn-toxicity (Anderson and Thompson 1946). Chlorosis with a necrosis of the margins of the lower leaves is Mn induced Mo deficiency symptom. Mn availability increases with acidity whereas Mo availability increases with soil alkalinity. Thus, the effect of soil reaction on Mo availability is the opposite of its effect on the availability of Mn (Touria and Douglas 1998). Milikan (1948) found that small applications of Mo to the medium prevented Mn-toxicity symptoms (lower leaf necrosis) of flax grown in strongly acid soil rich in $MnSO_4$.

Interaction with Sulphur

Browen (1981) has reported synergistic interaction between Mn and S in sugarcane, however, Ghosh *et al.* (1990) observed antagonism between Mn and S. In corn, sorghum and soybean, increasing rates of S applied to calcareous soils decreased the Mn uptake (Mahmoud *et al.* 1988). Wallace *et al.* (1974) reported that S significantly decreased the yields of soybeans suffering from Mn-toxicity.

Interaction with Silicon

Low level of silicon does not affect growth of bean plants but at 1.55 mg SiO_2 litre^{-1} severe growth depression induced by Mn toxicity is either prevented (in case of 5.0 µM) or reduced (10.0 µM Mn) by silicon application (Horst and Marschner 1978c). Supply of Si in nutrient solution reduced Mn toxicity symptoms (yellow spots) in sappo leaves of wheat (Lawton 1980). Si depresses the rate of Fe and Mn uptake in wetland rice (Horiguchi 1988a, Van der Vorm and Van Diest 1979). It has been observed that silicon increases the oxidizing power of the roots by increasing the rigidity and volume of aerenchyma and thereby enhancing O_2 transport from the shoots to the submerged root system exposed to toxic concentration of Mn (Marschner 1986).

Interaction with Copper

Application of Cu decreased the uptake of Mn (Hulagur and Danagrawda 1983) whereas Cu concentration reduced in presence of Mn (Harrison *et al*. 1983). Mn in combination with Cu, Zn, Cd and Ni exhibited protective, additive and synergistic effects in *Phaseolus vulgaris*, when single metal treatment produced little or no stress without any visual effects (Wallace 1982).

Interaction with Boron

The symptoms of boron deficiency were accentuated in the presence of normal levels of Mn (Alvarez-Tinaut *et al*. 1981) and symptoms of Mn-toxicity were accentuated in the presence of even moderately excess boron in tomato and spanish groundnut (Blamey and Chapman 1979). Significant inverse correlation between boron concentration in the solution and manganese content of leaves was obtained in sunflower (Gomez *et al*. 1981).

Interaction with Aluminium

Limited information is available on combined aluminium (Al) and manganese (Mn) interactions with other nutrients. Aluminium (Al) treatment decreased Mn concentration in barley plants except in stems (Alam 1981) and in many other plants (Thung *et al*. 1987, Walker 1979). It has been suggested that Mn competes effectively with aluminium for root absorption sites. Consequently, Mn concentration increased in roots but it decreased in plant tops with increasing amounts of Al (Alam 1983). Similarly, following aluminium treatment, Mn concentration was enhanced in roots but reduced in plant tops, grain and straw (Nambiar 1976, Sarkunan and Biddappa 1982).

Brassica crops are more susceptible to Mn-toxicity when Al is also present. The increase of available aluminium intensifies the toxic effects of Mn on the crop growth (Bromfield *et al*. 1983). The marked reduction in Mn uptake in the presence of Al suggests that within limits, aluminium might counter the toxic effects of Mn (Culvenor 1985). Protection by aluminium against manganese toxicity was also observed in *Atriplex hastat* (Rees and Sidrak 1961). However, Zhang *et al*. (1999) found no association between manganese and aluminium tolerance in *Triticale*. These apparently conflicting results illustrate limited understanding of the combined effects of aluminium and excess manganese.

BREEDING AND GENETIC CONTROL OF MANGANESE TOLERANCE

Breeding crop varieties for increased Mn-tolerance is realized as a more promising, energy efficient, economical and socially acceptable approach than soil amelioration technique. The basic requirements for breeding varieties for Mn-tolerance are: (i) availability of reliable and rapid screening techniques for identifying tolerance, (ii) availability of a reasonable range of variations and (iii) presence of a great magnitude of heritable variations.

Genetic variation is a prerequisite for the improvement in any trait through plant breeding. Differential Mn-tolerance among plant genotypes within the species have been reported for soybean (Ohki *et al.* 1981), wheat (Cregan 1980, Foy *et al.* 1973), bean (Kohno and Foy 1983), tobacco (Petolino and Collins 1985), cotton (Foy *et al.* 1981), cowpea (Horst 1982), pasture legume species (Andrew and Hegarty 1969), rice (Horiguch 1987), salt marsh plant (Singer and Havill 1985), Canadian spring wheat (Moroni *et al.* 1991), lucerne (Sale *et al.* 1992), common bean (Horst and Marschner 1978a), spinach, bean and various legumes (Horst 1988), pea and corn (Singh 2009) and tomato (Singh, unpublished results).

The level of Mn-tolerance is different in different plant species. This seems to be controlled by one or more genes. In lettuce, Mn-tolerance is controlled by one to four genes, depending upon the variation among lettuce species (Eenink and Garretsen 1977). Heenan *et al.* (1981) showed a single gene with possible involvement of minor genes controlling Mn-tolerance in soybean. In contrast, the control of tolerance to excess Mn appeared to be multigenic rather than single gene locus in soybean (Brown and Devine 1980, Devine 1982).

Khan and McNeilly (2000) found that dominance effects were greater for Mn-tolerance and maternal effects were either not involved or too small in the inheritance of Mn-tolerance and the degree of dominance was overdominance. However, reciprocal differences in progeny suggested that cytoplasmic inheritance influenced Mn-tolerance in soybean (Brown and Devine (1980).

Tolerance to Mn and Al was found to be opposite in screening of F_1 and F_2 generations of a cross between Mn-tolerant 'Siete Cerros' and Mn-sensitive 'BH 1146' cultivars of wheat (Camargo 1983, 1984). Similar findings with 'Atlas 66' (Mn-sensitive and Al-tolerant) and 'Monon' (Mn-tolerant and Al-sensitive) were found in wheat (Foy *et al.* 1973). This indicated that tolerance in acid soils (Al and Mn) is genetically independent and that selection in a breeding programme for one character will not co-select for the other.

Camargo (1983) found that broad sense heritability in response to both Mn and Al was high in wheat and concluded that selection for tolerance in early generations after crossing should be effective in increasing tolerance in this species.

CONCLUSION

Mn is an essential micronutrient for plants, but when in excess, it has toxic effects on plant growth on acidic soils of pH < 5.5. The morphological symptoms for both deficiency and toxicity are similar to a certain extent. Plants tolerate Mn either through external resistance mechanisms, by which Mn uptake and its translocation are prevented or internal tolerance mechanisms, conferring the ability of plants to tolerate Mn ion in the plant vacuole. Greater Mn-tolerance may be attributed to restricted absorption and translocation of excess Mn to the shoots, or greater tolerance to high Mn levels within plant tissue. Plants that tolerate high levels of Mn in their tissues may oxidize excess Mn to a metabolically inactive form. Studies of tolerance mechanisms may help to select or breed plants having greater tolerance to Mn-toxicity. In order to understand the exact mechanisms of Mn-toxicity, further work is needed on the phenomenon of Mn stress tolerance in plants, including the enzyme activities, chemical and physical compartmentation of the mineral elements in various plant fraction levels and the kind of organic acids and other exudates that may chelate Mn-toxicity.

Variation for tolerance to Mn-toxicity exists in crop species. A wide range of methods is potentially available to exploit such variation in the development of new varieties but to date conventional plant breeding methods are the only ones to have been used widely. Manganese tolerance is controlled by one or more genes. Manganese tolerance in most of the crops is under the control of polygenes or QTL. If these polygenes are closely linked to other genes with amplified effects, then the latter can be easily used as molecular markers to trace the inheritance of the linked polygene(s).

REFERENCES

Alam SM. 1981. Influence of aluminium on plant growth and mineral nutrition of barley. *Commu. Soil Sci. Plant Anal.* **12:** 121–138.

Alam SM. 1983. Effects of flooded and unflooded soil conditions, Fe and Mn application on growth and nutrient content by rice plants. *J. Sci. Techn.* **7:** 1–2.

Albano JP, Miller WB and Halbrooks MC. 1996. Iron toxicity stress cause bronze speckle, a specific physiological disorder of marigold (*Tagetes erecta* L.). *J. Am. Soc. Hort. Sci.* **121:** 430–437.

Alvarez-Tinaut MC, Leal A, Gomez M and Recalde L. 1979. Physiological effect of boron-manganese interaction in tomato plants III. Absorption and distribution of micro-elements, manganese, zinc and copper. *An. Edafol. Agrobiol.* **38:** 1013–1029.

Alvarez-Tinaut MC, Leal A and Recalde L. 1981. Physiological effects of the boron-magnesium interaction in tomato plants. *Agrochimica* **25:** 501–514.

Amberger A and Yousry M. 1988. Study on the effects of increasing manganese concentrations in nutrient solutions for tomato and corn under high iron levels. *Egyptian J. Agron.* **13:** 173–186.

Anderson AJ and Thomas MP. 1946. Plant responses to molybdenum as a fertilizer. I. Molybdenum and symbiotic nitrogen fixation. *Council of Sci. Industrial Res.* (Australia) *Bull.* 198.

Andrew CS and Hegarty MP. 1969. Comparative responses to manganese excess of eight tropical and four temperate pasture legume species. *Aust. J. Agri. Res.* **20:** 687–696.

Baker AJM and Brooks RR. 1989. Terrestrial higher plants which hyperaccumulate metallic elements—a review of their distribution, ecology and phytochemistry. *Biorecovery.* **1:** 81–126.

Beauchamp EG and Rossi N. 1972. Effects of Mn and Fe supply on the growth of barley in nutrient solution. *Canad. J. Plant Sci.* **52:** 575–581.

Benac R. 1976. Response of a sensitive (*Arachis hypogaea*) and a tolerant (*Zea mays*) species to different concentrations of manganese in the environment (Fr.) *Cah. ORSTOM. Ser. Biol.* **11**: 43–51.

Berger KC and Gerloff GC. 1947. Manganese toxicity of potatoes in relation to strong soil acidity. *Proc. Soil Sci. Soc. Am.* **2**: 310–314.

Bidwell SD, Woodrow IE, Batianoff GN and Sommer-Knudsen J. 2002. Hyperaccumulation of manganese in the rainforest tree *Austromyrdus bidwillii* (Myrtaceae) from Queesland. *Aust. Funct. Plant Biol.* **29**: 899–905.

Blamey FPC, Joyce DC, Edwards DG and Asher CJ. 1986. Role of trichomes in sunflower tolerance to manganese toxicity. *Plant Soil.* **91**: 171–180.

Blamey PPC and Chapman J. 1979. Boron toxicity in Spanish groundnuts. *Agrochemo physics Agron. J.* **71**: 57–59.

Blatt CR and Van Diest A. 1981. Evaluation of a screening technique for manganese toxicity in relation to leaf manganese distribution and interaction with silicon. *Netherlands J. Agric. Sci.* **29**: 297–304.

Bortner CE. 1935. Manganese toxicity in tobacco. *Soil Sci.* **39**: 15–33.

Bromfield SM. 1978. The oxidation of manganous ions under acid conditions by an acidophilous actinomycete from acid soil. *Aust. J. Soil Res.* **16**: 91–100.

Bromfield SM, Cumming RW, David DJ and Williams CH. 1983. The assessment of available manganese and aluminium status in acid soils under subterranean clover (*Trifolium subterraneum*) pasture of various stages. *Aust. J. Exp. Agric. Animal Husb.* **23**: 192–200.

Browen JE. 1981. Microelement nutrition of sugarcane II. Interactions in microelement accumulation. *Tropical Agric.* **58**: 215–220.

Brown JC and Devine TE. 1980. Inheritance of tolerance or resistance to manganese toxicity in soybeans. *Agron. J.* **72**: 898–904.

Brown JC and Jones WE. 1977. Fitting plant nutritionally to soils. I. Soybeans. *Agron. J.* **69**: 399–404.

Burke DJ, Watkins K and Scott BJ. 1990. Mn toxicity effects on visible symptoms, yield, manganese levels and organic acid levels in tolerant and sensitive wheat cultivars. *Crop Sci.* **30**: 275–280.

Camargo CE De O. 1983. Wheat breeding III. Evidence of genetic control over tolerance of toxic manganese and aluminium in wheat. *Bragantia.* **42**: 91–103.

Camargo CE De O. 1984. Wheat breeding X. Heritability estimates and correlation between both tolerance to aluminium toxicity and yield and other agronomic characters in wheat. *Bragantia.* **43**: 615–628.

Cheng BT and Pesant A. 1977. Manganese and copper nutrients in oats as affected by natural colour and texture of soil associated with temperature and aeration. *Agrochimica.* **21**: 170–179.

Colton RT and Sykes JD. 1992. Canola. Agfact P5.2.1 (4th ed) New South Wales Agriculture, Australia, p52.

Cregan PD. 1980. Soil acidity and associated problems. Guidelines for farmer recommendations. AG Bulletin 7, Oct 1980, Wagga Wagga, NSW.

Culvenor RA. 1985. Tolerance of *Phalaris aquatica* and some other agricultural species to excess manganese and the effect of aluminium and manganese tolerance in *Phalaris aquatica*. *Aust. J. Agric. Res.* **36**: 695–708.

Dekock PC and Inkson RHE. 1962. Manganese contents of mustard leaves in relation to iron and major nutrient supply. *Plant Soil.* **18**: 183–191.

Devine TE. 1982. Genetic fitting of crops to problem soils. In Breeding plants for less favourable environments, p143–173. MN Christiansen and CF (Eds), Lewis Willey, New York.

Dionne JL and Pesant AR. 1985. Effect of applications of manganese and aluminium: Soil pH and moisture regimes on alfalfa yield and the availability of manganese and aluminium. *Canad. J. Soil Sci.* **65**: 269–282.

Eenink AH and Garretsen GA. 1977. Inheritance of insensitivity of lettuce to a surplus of exchangeable manganese in steam sterilized soils. *Euphytica.* **26**: 47–53.

Elamin OM and Wilcox GE. 1986a. Effect of magnesium and manganese nutrition on muskmelon growth and manganese toxicity. *J. Am. Soc. Hort. Sci.* **111**: 582–587.

Elamin OM and Wilcox GE. 1986b. Effect of magnesium and manganese nutrition on watermelon growth and manganese toxicity. *J. Amer. Soc. Hort. Sci.* **111**: 588–593.

Elamin OM and Wilcox GE. 1986c. Manganese toxicity development in muskmelons as influenced by nitrogen form. *J. Am. Soc. Hort. Sci.* **111**: 323–327.

Engler RM and WH Patrick. 1975. Stability of sulfides of Mn, Zn, Cu and mercury in flooded and nonflooded soil. *Soil Sci.* **119**: 217–224.

Fenton G, Helyar K, Abbott T and Orchard P. 1996. Soil acidity and liming, *Agfact AC19* (2nd ed) New South Wales Agriculture, Australia, p24.

Foy CD. 1973. Manganese and plants. p51–76. National Academy of Science. National Research Council, Washington.

Foy CD. 1983. The physiology of plant adaptation to mineral stress. *Iowa State J. Res.* **57**: 355–391.

Foy CD. 1984. Physiological effects of hydrogen, aluminium and manganese toxicities in acid soils. In: Soil acidity and liming, Agronomy, p57–97. *Am. Soc. Agron.* Madison, WI.

Foy CD, Chaney RL and White MC. 1978. The physiology of metal toxicity in plants. *Ann. Rev. Plant Physiol.* **49**: 555–559.

Foy CD, Fleming AL and Schwartz JW. 1973. Opposite aluminium and manganese tolerances of two wheat varieties. *Agron. J.* **65**: 123–126.

Foy CD, Scott BJ and Fisher JA. 1988. Genetic differences in plant tolerance to manganese toxicity. In International symposium on manganese in soils and plants, p293–307. Graham RD, Hanan RJ and Uren NC (Eds), Kluwer Academic Publishers, Dordrecht, The Netherlands.

Foy CD, Webb HW and Jones JE. 1981. Adaptation of cotton genotypes to an acid, manganese toxic soil. *Agron. J.* **73**: 107–111.

Foy CD, Weil RR and Coradetti CA. 1995. Differential manganese tolerances of cotton genotypes in nutrient solution. *J. Plant Nutr.* **18**: 685–706.

Ghosh AK, Rai RK, Saxena RR and Srivastava AK. 1990. Effect of sulfur application on the nutritional status, yield and quality of sugarcane. *J. Indian Soc. Soil Sci.* **38**: 73–76.

Gomez RMV, Alvarez-Tinaut MC and Lune del Castillo J. 1981. Catalase, peroxidase and IAA oxidase activities and O diphenolic content in sunflower leaves grown with different boron levels. *J. Plant Nutr.* **4**: 375–383.

Gonzalez A and Lynch JP. 1997. Effects of Mn toxicity on leaf CO_2 assimilation of contrasting common bean genotypes. *Physiol. Plant.* **101**: 872–880.

Gupta U, Chipman EW and Mackay DC. 1970. Influence of iron and pH on the yield and iron, manganese, zinc and sulfur concentrations of carrots grown on sphagnum peat soil. *Plant Soil.* **44**: 559–566.

Hannan RJ and Ohki K. 1988. Detection of manganese deficiency and toxicity in plants. In managnese in soils and plants, p243–259. Graham RD *et al.* (Eds.), Kluwer Academy Publishers, Dordrecht, the Netherlands.

Harrison SJ, Lepp NW and Phipps DA. 1983. Copper uptake by excised roots: 3. Effect of Mn on copper uptake. *Z. Pflanzenphysiology.* **9**: 399–452.

Hecht-Buchholz CC, Jones A and Keil P. 1987. Effect of aluminium and manganese on norway spruce seedlings as related to magnesium nutrition. *J. Plant Nutr.* **10**: 1103–1110.

Heenan DP and Campbell LC. 1981. Influence of potassium and manganese on growth and uptake of magnesium by soybeans (*Glycine max* L. Merr cv. Bragg). *Plant Soil.* **61**: 447–456.

Heenan DP and Campbell LC. 1983. Manganese and iron interactions on their uptake and distribution in soybeans (*Glycine max* L. Merr). *Plant Soil.* **70**: 317–326.

Heenan DP, Campbell LC and Carter OG. 1981. Inheritance of tolerance to high manganese supply in soybeans. *Crop Sci.* **21**: 626–627.

Heenan DP and Carter OG. 1977. Influence of temperature on the expression of manganese toxicity by two soybean varieties. *Plant Soil.* **47**: 210–297.

Heintze JG. 1968. Manganese phosphate reactions in aqueous systems and the effects of application of monocalcium phosphate on the availability of manganese to oats in alkaline soils. *Plant Soil.* **24**: 407–423.

Hewitt EJ. 1948. Relation of manganese and other metal toxicities to the iron status of plants. *Nature.* **161**: 489–490.

Hiatt AJ and Ragland JL. 1963. Manganese toxicity of barley and tobacco. *Agron. J.* **55**: 47–49.

Horiguchi T. 1987. Mechanisms of manganese toxicity and tolerance of plants. II. Deposition of oxidized manganese in plant tissues. *J. Soil Sci. Plant Nutr.* **33**: 596–606.

Horiguch T. 1988a. Mechanisms of Mn toxicity and tolerance of plants. IV. Effects of silicon on alleviation of Mn toxicity of rice plants. *J. Soil Sci. Plant Nutr.* **34**: 65–73.

Horiguchi T. 1988b. Mechanisms of Mn toxicity and tolerance of plants. VII. Effect of light intensity on manganese induced chlorosis. *J. Plant Nutr.* **11**: 235–246.

Horiguchi T and Fukumoto T. 1987. Mechanism of manganese toxicity and tolerance of plants. III. Effect of excess manganese on respiration rate and peroxidase activity of various plant species. *J. Soil Sci. Plant Nutr.* **58:** 713–716.

Horst WJ. 1982. Quick screening of cowpea genotypes for manganese tolerance during vegetative and reproductive growth. *Z. Pflanzenernahrung Bodenkd.* **145:** 423–435.

Horst WJ. 1988. The physiology of manganese toxicity. In Manganese in soils and plants, p175–188. Graham RD, Hannan RJ and Uren NC (Eds), Kluwer Academic, Dordrecht, The Netherlands.

Horst WJ, Fecht M, Naumann A, Wissemeier AH and Maier P. 1999. Physiology of manganese toxicity and tolerance in *Vigna unguiculata* (L.) Walp. *J. Plant Nutr. Soil Sci.* **162:** 263–274.

Horst WJ and Marschner H. 1978a. Effect of excessive manganese supply on uptake and translocation of calcium in bean plants (*Phaseolus vulgaris* L.). *Z. Pflanzenphysiol.* **87:** 137–148.

Horst WJ and Marschner H. 1978b. Symptome von mangan Uberschu bei Bohnen *Phaseolus vulgaris* L. *Z. Pflanzenernahr. Dungung Bodenk.* **141:** 129–142.

Horst WJ and Marschner H. 1978c. Effect of silicon on manganese tolerance of bean plants (*Phaseolus vulgaris*). *Plant Soil.* **50:** 287–303.

Horst WJ and Marschner H. 1990. Mineral nutrition of higher plants. Academic Press, Boston, MA.

Hoyt PB. 1988. The relationship of internal bark necrosis in Delicious apples to tree characteristics and soil properties. *Commun. Soil Sci. Plant Anal.* **19:** 1041–1048.

Hulagur BF and Dangarwala RT. 1983. Effect of Zn, Cu and P fertilization on the uptake of iron, manganese and molybdenum by hybrid maize. *Madras Agric. J.* **70:** 88–91.

Hutton EM, Williams WT and Andrew CS. 1978. Differential tolerance to manganese in introduced and bred line *Macroptilium atropurpureum. Aust. J. Agric. Res.* **29:** 67–75.

Ishida A and Masui M. 1976. Studies on the manganese excess in carnation. II. Manganese excess in relation to certain soils, soil pH and two nitrogen forms. *Engei Gakkai Zasshi.* **45:** 283–288.

Jacobson HGM and Swanback TR. 1932. Manganese content of certain Connecticut soils and its relation to the growth of tobacco. *J. Am. Soc. Agron.* **24:** 237–245.

Jaurigui MA and Reisenauer HM. 1982. Calcium carbonate and manganese dioxide as regulators of available manganese and iron. *Soil Sci.* **134:** 105–110.

Joardar M. 1988. Cytotoxicity of certain environmental agents on plant systems. *J. Indian Bot. Soc.* **67:** 183–185.

Joardar M and Sharma A. 1989.Toxicological screening of a trace element, manganese *in vivo. Cytologia.* **55:** 135–139.

Kalyanaraman SB and Sivagurunathan P. 1993. Effect of cadmium, copper and zinc on the growth of blackgram. *J. Plant Nutr.* **16:** 2029–2047.

Kazda M and Znacek L. 1989. Aluminium and manganese and their relation to calcium in soil solution and needle in three norway spruce (*Picea abies* L. Karst.) stands of upper Australia. *Plant Soil.* **114:** 257–267.

Keil P, Hecht-Buchholz Ch and Ortmann V. 1986. Zum Elinfluâ von erhoehtem mangan-Angebot auf Fichtensaemlinge. *AFZ.* **34/35:** 855–858.

Khan AA and McNeilly T. 2000. Genetic analysis of aluminium and manganese tolerance in maize (*Zea mays* L.). *J. Genet. Breed.* **54:** 245–249.

Khatiashvili RM, Abulashvili JG, Burdzhanadze MB and Gogoladze NT. 1985. The effect of trace elements on the uptake of anions by the grapevines leaves *Soobshch Akad. Nauk Gruz. SSR.* **120:** 161–164.

Kennedy CW and Jones JE. 1991. Evaluating quantitative screening methods for Mn toxicity in cotton genotypes. *J. Plant Nutr.* **14:** 1331–1339.

Kohno Y and Foy CD. 1983. Manganese toxicity in bush bean as affected by concentration of manganese and iron in the nutrient solution. *J. Plant Nutr.* **6:** 363–386

Kuo S and Mikkelson DS. 1981. Effect of P and Mn on growth response and uptake of Fe, Mn and P by sorghum. *Plant Soil.* **62:** 15–22.

Lawton JR 1980. Silica in grasses. *Electron Microscopy Soc. South Africa Proc.* **10:** 67–68.

Leach W and Taper CD. 1954. Studies in plant mineral nutrition. II. The absorption of Fe and Mn by dwarf kidney beans, tomato, and onion from culture solutions. *Canad. J. Bot.* **32:** 561–570.

Lee CR and McDonald ML. 1978. Influence of soil amendment on potato growth, mineral nutrition and tuber yield and quality in very strongly acid soils. *Soil Sci. Soc. Am. J.* **41:** 573–577.

Lidon FC. 2000. Rice adaptation to excess manganese: Nutrient accumulation and implications of the quality of crops. *Plant Physiol.* **156:** 652–658.

Mahmoud K, Filsoof F and Rezai-Nejad Y. 1988. Effect of sulfur treatment on yield and uptake of Fe, Zn and Mn by corn, sorghum and soybean. *J. Plant Nutr.* **11:** 1353–1360.

Marschner H. 1986. Mineral nutrition of higher plants, Academic Press, New York, NY.

Marsh KB, Peterson LA and McCown BH. 1989. A microculture method for assessing nutrient uptake. II. The effect of temperature on manganese uptake and toxicity in potato shoots. *J. Plant Nutr.* **12:** 219–232.

Mashhady A and EI-Damaty AH. 1981. Biological availability of iron and manganese in some representative soils of Saudi Arabia. *Agrochimica.* **25:** 9–19.

Masui M, Nakaya A and Ishida A. 1976. Studies on the manganese excess muskmelon: V. The manganese, calcium and iron concentrations in nutrient solutions. *Engei Gakkai Zasshi.* **45:** 267–274.

McGrath SP and Rorison IH. 1982. The influence of nitrogen source on the tolerance of *Holeus lanatus* and *Bromus erectus* to manganese. *New Phytologist.* **9:** 443–452.

Memon AR, Chino M, Takeoka Y, Hora K and Yatazawa M. 1980. Distribution of manganese in leaf tissues of a manganese accumulator: *Acanthopanax sciadophylloides* as revealed by electron probe X-ray microanalyzer. *J. Plant Nutr.* **2:** 457–476.

Mgema WG and Clark RB. 1995. Sorghum genotypic differences in tolerance to excess manganese. *J. Plant Nutr.* **18:** 983–993.

Milikan CR. 1948. Effect of molybdenum on the severity of toxicity symptoms in flax induced by excess of manganese, zinc, copper, nickel or cobalt in the nutrient solution. *J. Aust. Institution of Agric. Sci.* **5**: 180–186.

Miller SS and Schubert OE. 1977. Plant manganese and soil pH associated with internal bark necrosis in apple. *Proc. West Virginia Academy of Sci.* **49**: 97–107.

Miner G and Sims J. 1983. Changing fertilization practices and utilization of added plant nutrient for efficient production of tobacco. *Recent Adv. Tobacco Sci.* **9**: 4–76.

Morgan PW, Joham HE and Amin J. 1966. Effect of manganese toxicity on the indoleacetic acid oxidase system of cotton. *Plant Physiol.* **41**: 718–724.

Morgan PW, Taylor DM and Joham HE. 1976. Manipulations of IAA oxidase activity and auxin deficiency symptoms in intact cotton plants with manganese nutrition. *Plant Physiol.* **37**: 149–156.

Moroni JS, Briggs KG and Taylor GJ. 1991. Pedigree analysis of the origin of manganese tolerance in Canadian spring wheat (*Triticum aestivum* L.) cultivars. *Euphytica.* **56**: 107–120.

Morris HD and Pierre WH. 1947. The effect of calcium, phosphorus and iron on the tolerance of lespediza to manganese toxicity in culture solutions. *Proc. Soil Sci. Soc. Am.* **12**: 382–386.

Morris HD and Pierre WH. 1949. Minimum concentrations of manganese necessary for injury to various legumes in culture solution. *Agron. J.* **41**: 107–113.

Mortley DG. 1993. Manganese toxicity and tolerance in sweet potato. *Hort Sci.* **28**: 812–813.

Mortvedt JJ and Cunningham HG. 1971. Production, marketing, and use of other secondary and micronutrient fertilizers. In Olson, R. A., (Ed.), Fertilizer Technology and Use, 2nd ed.: Madison, Wise., Soil Sci. Soc. America, Inc., p. 413–454.

Mukhopadhyay JM and Sharma A. 1991. Manganese in cell metabolism of higher plants. *Botanical Rev.* **57**: 117–149.

Nable RO. 1983. Translocation of manganese in subterranean clover and its relation to deficiency diagnosis. PhD Thesis, Murdoch University, West Australia.

Nable RO, Houtz RL and Cheniae GM. 1988. Early inhibition of photosynthesis during development of Mn-toxicity in tobacco. *Plant Physiol.* **86**: 1136–1142.

Nable RO and Loneragan JF. 1984. Translocation of manganese in subterranean clover (*Trifolium subterraneum* L cv. Seaton Park). I. redistribution during vegetative growth. *Aust. J. Plant Physiol.* **11**: 101–111.

Nambiar EKS. 1976. Genetic differences in the copper nutrition of cereals. I. Differential responses of genotypes to copper. *Aust. J. Agric. Res.* **27**: 453–463.

Ohki K. 1981. Manganese critical levels for soybean growth and physiological processes. *J. Plant Nutr.* **3**: 271–284.

Ohki K. 1985. Manganese deficiency and toxicity effects on photosynthesis, chlorophyll and transpiration in wheat. *Agron. J.* **25**: 187–191.

Osawa T and Ikeda H. 1976. Heavy metal toxicities in vegetable crops. I. The effect of iron concentrations in the nutrient solution on manganese toxicities in vegetable crops. *J. Japanese Soc. Hort. Sci.* **45**: 50–58.

Osawa T and Ikeda H. 1980. Heavy metal toxicities in vegetable crops. VIII. The effect of form of nitrogen supplied and pH level of the nutrient solution on manganese toxicities in vegetable crop. *Engei Gakkai Zasshi*. **49**: 197–202.

Patrick WH and Henderson RE. 1981. Reduction and reoxidation cycles of manganese and iron in flooded soil and in water solution. *Soil Sci. Soc. Am. J.* **45**: 855–859.

Petolino JF and Collins GB. 1985. Manganese toxicity in tobacco (*Nicotiana tabacum* L.) callus and seedlings. *Plant Physiol.* **118**: 139–144.

Ponnamperuma FN. 1978. Electrochemical changes in submerged soils and the growth of rice. In: *Soils and Rice,* p421–441. IRRI, Los Banos.

Proctor J, Philips C, Duff GK, Heaney A and Robertson FM. 1989. Ecological studies on Gunung Silam a small ultrabasic mountain in Sabah Malaysia. II. Some forest processes. *J. Ecology*. **77**: 317–331.

Quellette GJ and Dessureaux L. 1958. Chemical composition of alfalfa as related to degree of tolerance to manganese and aluminium. *Canad. J. Plant Sci.* **38**: 206–214.

Rees WJ and Sidrak GH. 1961. Interrelationship of aluminium and manganese toxicities towards plants. *Plant Soil* **14**: 101–117.

Reeves RD and Baker AJM. 2000. Metal-accumulating plants. In Phytoremediation of toxic metals: Using plants to clean up the environment, p193–229. John Wiley and Sons, New York.

Rezai K and Farboodnia T. 2008. Manganese toxicity effects on chlorophyll content and antioxidant enzymes in pea plant (*Pisum sativum* L., cv Qazvin). *Agric. J.* **3**: 454–458.

Rufty TW, Miner GS and Raner CD Jr. 1979. Temperature effects on growth and manganese tolerance in tobacco. *Agron. J.* **71**: 638–644.

Sale PWG, Couper DJ, Cachia PL and Larkin PJ. 1992. Tolerance to manganese toxicity among cultivars of lucerne (*Medicago sativa* L.). *Plant Soil*. **146**: 31–38.

Sanchez-Raya A, Leal A, Gomez-Ortega M and Recalde L. 1974. Effect of iron on the absorption and translocation of manganese. *Plant Soil*. **41**: 429–434.

Sarkunan V and Bidappa CC. 1982. Effect of aluminium on the growth, yield and chemical composition of rice. *Oryza* **19**: 188–190.

Scibisz K and Sadowski A. 1979. Internal bark necrosis in stark crimson delicious apple trees in relation to mineral nutrition. *Gartenbaughwissenschaft.* **44**: 177–181.

Scott BJ and Fisher JA. 1989. Selection of genotypes tolerant of aluminium and manganese. In Soil acidity and plant growth, p167–203. Robson AD (Ed.), Academic Press, Australia.

Sedberry JE, Bligh Jr BP, Muscagni HJ, Bruphacher RH, Marshall JG, Rabb JL, Phillips SA, Bertleson JL, Shelling PE and Morris D. 1983. Influence of soil reaction and manganese applications on yields and chemical composition of soybean plants. *Los Angeles Agricultural Experiment Station Bulletin.* **751**: 43.

Shuman LM and Anderson OE. 1976. Interactions of Mn with other ions in wheat and soybeans. *Commun. Soil Sci. Plant Anal.* **7**: 547–557.

Simen A, Cradock FW and Hudson AW. 1974. The development of manganese toxicity in pasture legumes under extreme climatic conditions. *Plant Soil*. **41**: 129–140.

Singer CE and Havill DC. 1985. Manganese as an ecological factor in salt marshes. *Vegetatio.* **62:** 287–292.

Singh D. 2009. Identification of aluminium and manganese resistant corn and pea genotypes adapted to acidic soils. Half yearly report of the project, College of Horticulture and Forestry, Central Agricultural University, Pasighat, Arunachal Pradesh, India.

Singh M and Pathak AN. 1968. Effects of manganese and iron application on their solubility, absorption and growth of oat plants. *Agrochimica.* **12:** 382–388.

Snejana D, Katya G, Vassileva V, Stoyanova Z, Popov N and Ignatov G. 2005. Effect of succinate on manganese toxicity in pea plants. *J. Plant Nutr.* **28:** 47–62.

Somers II and Shive JW. 1942. The iron-manganese relation in plant metabolism. *Plant Physiol.* **17:** 582–602.

Sparrow LA and Uren NC. 1987. The role of manganese toxicity in crop yellowing in seasonally waterlogged and strongly acidic soils in north-eastern Victoria. *Aust. J. Exp. Agric.* **27:** 303–307.

Subrahmanyam D and Rathore VS (2001). Influence of manganese toxicity on photosynthesis in ricebean (*Vigna umbellata*) seedlings. Photosynthetica. **38:** 449-453.

Taylor OA, Fetuga BL and Oyenuga VA. 1983. Accumulation of mineral elements in 5 tropical leafy vegetables as influenced by nitrogen fertilization and age. *Sci. Hort.*(Amstardam) **18:** 313–322.

Thung M, Ortega J and Erazo O. 1987. Breeding methodology for phosphorus efficiency and tolerance to aluminium and manganese toxicities for beans (*Phaseolus vulgaris* L.). In Proceedings workshop on evaluating sorghum for tolerance to Al-toxic tropical soils in Latin America, Colombia, p197–221. Gourley LM and Salinas JG (Eds.), Apartado, Aereo, Colombia.

Touria EI-J and Douglas AC. 1998. Manganese toxicity in plants. *J. Plant Nutr.* **21:** 353–386.

Turner DW and Barkus B. 1983. The uptake and distribution of mineral nutrients in banana in response to supply of K, Mg and Mn. *Fertilizer Res.* **4:** 89–99

Unni PN, Shanthakumar G and Naidu SR. 1995. Metal toxicity in acid soils of Kerala-effect of Mn on growth and physiology of rice (*Oryza sativa* L.) Cv. Jaya. *Int. J. Envi. Studies.* **47:** 151–158.

Van Der Vorm PDJ and Van Diest A. 1979. Aspect of the Fe and Mn nutrition of rice plants. I. Iron and manganese uptake by rice plants grown under aerobic and anaerobic conditions. *Plant Soil.* **51:** 233–246.

Vlamis J and Williams DE. 1964. Iron and manganese relation in rice and barley. *Plant Soil.* **20:** 221–231.

Vose PB and Jones DG. 1963. The interaction of Mn and Ca on nodulation and growth in varieties of *Trifolium repens*. *Plant Soil.* **18:** 372–385.

Walker GD. 1979. Occurrence of manganese with inclusions in the root cortex of white clover (*Trifolium*) *New Zealand J. Bot.* **17:** 1–4.

Wallace A, Mueller RT, Cha JW and Alexander GV. 1974. Soil pH, excess lime and chelation agent on micronutrient in soybeans and Bush beans. *Agron. J.* **66:** 698–700.

Wallace A. 1982. Additive, protective and synergistics effects on plants with excess trace elements. *Soil Sci.* **133**:319-323.

Wang H, Tang SM, Liao XJ, Cao G, Yang A and Wang TZ. 2007. A new manganese-hyperaccumulator. *Polygonum hydropiper* L. *Ecology Envi.* **16**: 830–834.

Wang YX, Wu P, Wu YR and Yan XL. 2002. Molecular marker analysis of manganese toxicity tolerance in rice under green house conditions. *Plant Soil.* **238**: 227–233.

Wissemeier AH, Diening A, Hergenroder A and Horst WJ. 1992. Callose formation as parameter for assessing genotypical plant tolerance of aluminium and manganese. *Plant Soil.* **146**: 67–75.

Wissemeier AH, Diening A, Hergenroder A, Mix-Wagner G and Horst WJ. 1993. Induction of callose formation by manganese in cell suspension culture and leaves of soybean (*Glycine max* L.). *Plant Physiol.* **142**: 67–73.

Wissemeier AH and Horst WJ. 1982. Effect of light intensity on manganese toxicity symptoms and callose formation in cowpea (*Vigna unguiculata* (L.) Walp. *Plant Soil.* **143**: 299–309.

Wu SH. 1994. Effect of manganese excess on the soybean plant cultivated under various growth conditions. *J. Plant Nutr.* **17**: 991–1003.

Xue SG, Chen YX, Lin Q, Xu SY and Wang YP. 2003. *Phytolacca acinosa* Roxb: A new manganese hyperaccumulator plant from south China. *Acta Entomologica sinica.* **5**: 935–937.

Yang SX, Deng H and Li MS. 2008. Manganese uptake and accumulation in a woody hyper-accumulator, *Schima superba*. *Plant Soil Envi.* **54**: 441–446.

Zhang X, Jessop RS and Ellisson F. 1999. Differential genotypic tolerance response to manganese stress in triticale. *Commun. Soil Sci. Plant Anal.* **30**: 2399–2408.

7 Acid Soil Tolerance in Legumes: Present Status and Future Strategies

Dharmendra Singh, NP Singh, SK Chaturvedi, RS Raje, NK Gautam and NS Panwar

ABSTRACT

Acid soils are one of the most important limitations to agricultural production in many areas of the world and limit legume productivity. One way to reduce the toxic effect of aluminium and manganese is to neutralize the acidity with application of lime. However, this practice is demanding and not very effective. The use of acid tolerant genotypes is the most effective strategy for crop production in acidic soils. This chapter presents the status and future strategies of acid soil tolerance in legumes.

Key words: Acid soils, legumes, aluminium, manganese toxicities.

INTRODUCTION

Acid soils (pH d "5.5") significantly limit crop production all over the world. Under acidic conditions, the adverse effects are due to mainly aluminium and manganese toxicities. Aluminium toxicity can cause P deficiency symptoms due to precipitation of alumino-phosphate complexes within the plant and in the soil. Legumes are considered very sensitive to aluminium toxicity. The ideal soil pH for growing pulses is between 6.5–7.5. In the pH range 5.0 to 6.0, where soluble aluminium is no longer problem, the root growth of some pulse species can still be slow. The reduction in shoot growth of grain legumes species at low pH is normally associated with more acute depression in root growth. Mahler and McDole (1987) reported that minimum acceptable pH (H_2O) for maximum grain yield of lentil and field peas were 5.65 and 5.52, respectively compared with 5.23 for barley and 5.19 for wheat. They also found that drop in soil pH by one unit below the threshold value (pH 5.5) caused a greater than 86 per cent reduction in seed yield of lentil and 93 per cent reduction in pea. This clearly showed that some legumes generally appear to be more sensitive than cereals (Mahler and McDole 1987, Yan *et al.* 1992).

TOXICITIES OF ALUMINIUM (AL) AND MANGANESE (MN)

Toxicities of Al^{3+} and Mn^{2+} are important growth limiting factors associated with acid soil infertility. These toxic factors may act independently and/or together to affect plant growth. Description of toxicities has been dealt herewith in details:

Aluminium Toxicity

Aluminium ions are regarded as a main toxic factor affecting plant growth in mineral soils at a pH below 5.5 (Foy *et al.* 1978). At low pH dissolution of Al-containing compounds is enhanced and the release of toxic Al ions into the soil solution can rapidly inhibit root growth and interfere with absorption of nutrients and water and consequently crop yield.

Aluminium taken up by plants is normally sequestered in roots and not easily translocated to shoots until at least the retaining capacity of roots is exceeded (Wagatsuma 1984). Roots are the first target for aluminium in most plant species particularly root elongation and lateral branching (Aniol 1984). Several reports indicated that inhibitory effects of Al on root growth was observed in cowpea (Horst *et al.* 1983), common bean (Buerkert *et al.* 1990), soybean (Foy *et al.* 1993), pigeonpea (Singh and Choudhary 2009), chickpea (Singh and Chaturvedi 2007), fababean (Gauer and Horst 1990), pea (Singh 2009), lentil (Singh *et al.* 2015) and *Vigna* species (Singh *et al.* 2015). Aluminium affected roots are short, stubby as a result of the inhibition of elongation and lateral branching (Foy 1984, Matsumoto 1991). Horst and Goppel (1986) observed that less than 1 mg Al g^{-1} dry weight is sufficient to inhibit root elongation in faba bean. In faba bean, root elongation is decreased by about 50 per cent in the presence of 9.3 mM m^{-3} $AlCl_3$ in the rooting medium (Gauer and Horst 1990), whereas in field pea, root elongation was completely inhibited by 100 mM m^{-3} $AlCl_3$ in the solution (Matsumoto 1991). Shallow root system was observed in the field (under acidic subsoil conditions) of faba bean (Hartman and Aldag 1989), chickpea and field pea (Seifu 1993), and therefore, inefficient in exploring nutrients and water from deeper soil layers. Singh and Choudhary (2009) observed that root length of 'IPA 7–10' and 'T7' showed only 31.8 per cent and 34.4 per cent decrease in their root length respectively compared to 'Bahar' (57.9 per cent) and 'Pusa' 9 (67.5 per cent) from 0–50 ppm Al concentrations in pigeonpea.

Manganese Toxicity

Mn-toxicity is probably the second most important growth limiting factor in acid soils. Managnese (Mn) is highly soluble at pH value lower than 5.5. Manganese absorbed by plant roots is easily transported to shoots. Thus, in most crop plants, including legumes, manganese toxicity first affect shoot growth (Foy 1984). However, roots may also be affected if the toxicity becomes severe (Suresh *et al.* 1987). The common symptoms of Mn-toxicity in grain legumes are interveinal chlorosis and crinckle in young leaves. Some of these symptoms appear due to induced deficiencies of Ca and Mg (Marschner 1995). Apart from the interferences with Ca and Mg nutrition, excess Mn disrupts phytohormone balance (e.g. activities of IAA), certain enzyme activities (e.g. RuBp carboxylase) and membrane functions in leaf tissues (Horst 1988).

Effects of Soil Acidity on Nodule Development and Symbiotic Nitrogen Fixation

Acid soils pose a major challenge to sustainable agriculture and particularly to the establishment of N_2 fixing symbiosis. Soil pH influences nodulation, nitrogen fixation and *rhizobium* survival. At low pH, rhizobial growth and survival in the soils as well as root nodule development are delayed or inhibited. Leguminous plants require neutral or slightly acidic soils for growth especially when they are dependent on symbiotic nitrogen fixation. Symbiotic nitrogen fixation can be seriously reduced in such soils due to the effects of H^+ concentration, toxic level of Al and Mn and induced deficiencies of Ca, P and Mo. The *rhizobium* species that infect field pea, faba bean, lentil and chickpea do not survive well in acidic soils. Furthermore, the strains that do survive well in acid soil may not fix nitrogen very efficiently even if they nodulate the plant.

Considerable genetic variation in response to acidity exists in rhizobia nodulating different cool season grain legumes, *viz.* lentil (Rai and Prasad 1983), chickpea (Rai 1991) and faba bean (Carter *et al.* 1995). Variations in acid tolerance within species of root nodulating bacteria imply a genetic basis to low pH tolerance and studies of acid sensitive mutants suggested that a large number of genes and regulatory systems could be involved (Glenn *et al.* 1998). Legume species vary markedly in their tolerance to Al^{3+} and Mn^{2+}, with some plants being significantly more strongly affected by these ions than are the rhizobia (Graham 1992). Therefore, for acid soils with high Al content, improvement can be achieved by manipulating the plant rather than the rhizobia (Taylor *et al.* 1991).

Nodulation and N_2 fixation are particularly more sensitive to aluminium than plant growth (Graham 1992). Aluminium has been shown to adversely affect rhizobium survival (Kim *et al.* 1985), nodulation initiation (Jarvis and Hatch 1985) and nitrogenase activity (Jarvis and Hatch 1985). Rhizobia appear to be varying in their symbiotic efficiency under acidic conditions. Acid-tolerant alfalfa-nodulating strains of rhizobia, isolated from acidic soils, were able to grow at pH 5.0 and formed nodules in alfalfa with a low rate of nitrogen fixation (Del *et al.* 1999). Evans *et al.* (1980) found that nodulation of *Pisum sativum* was 10 times more susceptible to acidity than was either rhizobial multiplication or plant growth.

Genetic Differences in Response to Aluminium Toxicity

Significant variation for Al-tolerance is well-known in many plant species and has led to a number of studies of inheritance for Al-tolerance (Foy 1988). Intraspecific variation in tolerance to soil acidity has been found in pea (Singh *et al.* 2009), chickpea (Singh and Chaturvedi, 2007), pigeonpea (Singh and Choudhary 2009), lentil (Singh *et al.* 2015) and *Vigna* species (Singh *et al.* 2015) Klimashevskii *et al.* (1970) found that in two fieldpea cultivars grown in nutrient solution having aluminium (supplied as $Al_2(SO_4)_3$, a relatively Al tolerant cultivars showed only 32 per cent reduction in growth (total dry matter) at 11 mg Al^{3+} l^{-1} whereas this level of Al^{3+} was completely detrimental to an Al-sensitive cultivars. Similarly, Rai (1991) found that at solution concentration of 5 ppm Al^{3+}, shoot dry weight of a sensitive cultivar reduced by 70 per cent, whereas that of a relatively tolerant cultivar reduced only by 27 per cent. These findings have been suggested that an impressive variation is present in chickpea and fieldpea.

GENETIC AND BIOTECHNOLOGICAL APPROACHES OF AL-TOLERANCE

Genetic studies have shown that tolerance to aluminium is a simply inherited trait governed by a single major dominant gene in pea (Singh and Choudhary 2010) and chickpea (Singh and Raje 2011) and by two major genes in pigeonpea (Singh *et al.* 2011). However, in alfalfa and soybean Al-tolerance was controlled by several genes.

No extensive work on molecular breeding has been done so far in legumes except soybean and alfalfa. Major loci and QTLs controlling Al-tolerance have been identified in alfalfa (Narsimhamoorthy *et al.* 2007) and soybean (Bianchi-Hall *et al.* 2000). The production of transgenic plants with an increased capacity to produce and or excrete organic acids that chelate and detoxify Al in the rizhosphere is an appealing strategy to produce Al tolerant plants. Such technique has been applied for improving aluminium tolerance in alfalfa. The over expression of phosphoenolpyruvate carboxylase (PEPC) and malate dehydrogense (MDH) enzymes resulted in enhanced aluminium tolerance in alfalfa due to organic acid synthesis and secretion (Tesfaye *et al.* 2001). A plant line containing the PEPC transgene with a 2-fold increase in PEPC activity had increased amounts of malate compared to the control. In acidic solution culture assays, plants expressing the MDH or PEPC transgene showed enhanced root elongation compared with the control untransformed line (Tesfaye *et al.* 2001). In such assay, transgenic lines of alfalfa increased 2–3 folds greater root growth in the presence of 20 µM aluminium level than the growth rate of the untransformed control. When subjected to culture with 100 µM $AlCl_3$, transgenic lines continued to grow, albeit at a reduced rate whereas the untransformed control plants did not show root growth (Tesfaye *et al.* 2001).

FUTURE STRATEGIES

The future research programmes for acid soil tolerance should consider the following strategies:

- There is urgent need for exploration of the plant genetic resources with attributes related to aluminium tolerance in different pulse crops and their characterization to facilitate transfer of desired traits through conventional plant breeding or biotechnological method.

- Attention should be concentrated on better understanding of physiological, biochemical and genetic basis of aluminium tolerance through expression level of enzymes, organic acids, proteins, etc.

- More comprehensive studies are needed in pulse crops to identify and validate useful selection criteria, including tissue culture, molecular and genetic engineering characteristics.

- Several symbiosis systems of legumes which are tolerant to extreme conditions of soil acidity need to be identified.

- Different genes responsible for organic acid secretion and synthesis conferring aluminium resistance should be considered for transfer in a crop plant at a time.

- To date genes encoding transporters for organic anions have not been cloned. Genes encoding these anion channels need to be cloned. Although considerable progress has been made in understanding Al-tolerance mechanisms based on organic acid efflux, much is still to be learned of the molecular mechanisms underlying the activation of anion channels by Al. For instance, better understanding of the processes is needed which are involved in how a cell initially senses Al that then leads to channel gating and organic acid efflux. There is need for a substantial increase in the efflux of organic acids for these approaches to have practical application in Agriculture.

- The transgenics with aluminium tolerance have been achieved in alfalfa. Extensive studies have to be carried out on other pulse crops.

- There should be more intense programme dealing with isolation of new genes, designing of vectors, transformation and identification of molecular markers in pulse crops.

- A significant number of QTLs/genes have been identified only in a few crops for aluminium tolerance. Such studies are needed on pulse crops. Mapping of new QTL/gene will provide key resources to improve aluminium tolerance to other genotypes.

- A multidisciplinary approach involving genetics, biochemistry, biotechnology, physiology, plant breeding and crop science will be appropriate to assess the complicated and integrated response of plants to aluminium and to evolve superior aluminium tolerant genotypes.

REFERENCES

Aniol A. 1984. Introduction of Aluminium tolerance into aluminium sensitive wheat cultivars. *Z. Pflanzen zuchtg.* **93**: 331–339.

Bianchi-Hall CM, Carter Te Jr, Bailey MA, Mian MAR, Rufty TW, Asley DA, Boerma HR, Arellano C, Hussey RS and Parrot WA. 2000. Aluminium tolerance associated with quantitative trait loci derived from soybean PI416937 in hydroponics. *Crop Sci.* **40**: 538–545.

Buerkert A, Cassmann K, Piedra RDL, Munns D, DE LPR and La PRD. 1990. Soil acidity and liming effects on sand, nodulation and yield of common bean. *Agron. J.* **82**: 749–754.

Carter J, Tieman J and Gibson A. 1995. Competitiveness and persistence of strains of rhizobia for faba bean in acid and alkaline soils. *Soil Biol. Biochem.* **27**: 617–623.

Del Papa MF, Balague LJ, Sowinski SC, Wegoner C, Segundo E, Aborca FM, Toro N, Nilehaus K, Puhler A, Aguillor OM, Martinez-Drets G and Lagares A. 1995. Isolation and characterization of alfalfa nodulation *rhizobia* present in acidic soils of Central Argentina and Uruguay. *Appl. Environ. Microbiol.* **65**: 1420–1427.

Evans LS, Lewin KF and Vella FA. 1980. Effects of nutrient medium pH on symbiotic nitrogen fixation by *Rhizobium leguminosarum* and *Pisum sativum*. *Plant Soil.* **56**: 71–80.

Foy CD. 1984. Physiological effects of hydrogen, aluminium and manganese toxicities in acid soils. In Soil acidity and liming. Adams F (Ed), 2nd ed. *Soil Sci. Soc. Am. Soc. Agron. and Crop Sci of Am.*, Madison, W.I.

Foy CD. 1988. Plant adaptation to acid Al toxic soils. *Commun. Soil Sci. Plant Anal.* **19**: 959–987.

Foy CD, Chaney RL and White MC. 1978. The physiology of metal toxicity in plants. *Ann. Rev. Plant Physiol.* **29**: 511–566.

Foy C.D, Shalunova L and Lee E. 1993. Acid soil tolerance of soybean (*Glycine max* L.) germplasm from the USSR. *J. Plant Nutr.* **16**: 1593–1617.

Gauer U and Horst W. 1990. Effect of pH and nitrogen source on aluminium tolerance of rye (*Secale cereale* L.) and yellow lupin (*Lupinus luteus* L.) *Plant Soil.* **127**: 13–21.

Glenn AR, Reeve WG, Tiwari RP and Dilworth MJ. 1998. Acid tolerance in root nodule bacteria. *Vavartis Found. Symp.* **221**: 112–126.

Graham PH. 1992. Stress tolerance in *Rhizobium* and *Bradyrhizobium* and nodulation under adverse soil conditions. *Can. J. Micro Biol.* **38**: 475–484.

Hartman C and Aldag R. 1989. N$_2$ fixation and yield structure of white lupin (*Lupins albus* L.) in comparison to *Vicia faba* L. and *Glycine max* (L.) on different sites. *J. Agron. Crop Sci.* **163**: 201–211.

Horst WJ. 1988. The physiology of manganese toxicity. In: Graham RD, Hannam RJ, Uren NJ (eds). Manganese in Soil and Plants. Kluwer Academic Publishers, Dordrecht, The Netherlands, pp. 175–188.

Horst W and Goppel H. 1986. Aluminium tolerance of horse bean, yellow lupin, barley and rye. 2. Mineral element concentrations in shoots and roots as affected by aluminium. *Z. Pflanzenernahrung Bodenkd.* **149**: 94–100.

Horst WJ, Wagner A and Marschner H. 1983. Effect of aluminium on root growth, cell division and mineral element contents in roots of *Vigna unguiculata* genotypes. *Z. Pflanzenernahrung Bodenkd.* **109**: 95–1–3

Jarvis SC and Hatch DJ. 1985. The effects of Al on the growth of white clover dependent upon fixation of atmospheric nitrogen. *J. Expt. Bot.* **36**: 1075–1086.

Kim MM, Asher CJ, Edward DG and Date RA. 1985. Aluminium toxicity, effect on growth and nodulation of subterranean clover. In Proc. 15th International grassland Congress, p501–53. Kuneh H, Kitahara T, Okuba T, Shiyonu M, Sugawata K, Tajima A and Yamaguchi (Eds.), Sci. Soc of Japan and Japanese Soc. of Grassland Sci. Tokyo, Japan.

Klimashevskii EL, Markova YA, Seregina ML, Grodzinskii DM and Kozarenko TD. 1970. Species of the physiological activity of pea in connection with unequal resistance of different varieties to mobile aluminium. *Soviet Plant Physiol.* **17**: 372–378.

Mahler RL and McDole RE. 1987. Effect of soil pH on crop yield in northern Idaho. *Agron. J.* **79**: 751–755.

Marschner H. 1995. Mineral nutrition of higher plants. 2nd ed. Academic Press, London.

Matsumoto H. 1991. Biochemical mechanisms of the toxicity of Aluminium and the sequestration of aluminium in plant cells. In Plant soil Interaction at low pH, p825–834. Wright *et al.* (Eds.), Kluwer Academic Publishers, Dordrecht, Netherlands.

Narasimhamoorthy B, Bouton JH, Olsen KM and Sledge MK. 2007. Quantitative trait loci and candidate gene mapping of Al-tolerance in diploid alfalfa. *Theor. Appl. Genet.* **114**: 901–913.

Rai R. 1991. Effect of soil acidity on interaction of chickpea (*Cicer arietinum* L.) genotypes and *Rhizobium* strains. Symbiotic N_2 fixation, grain quality and grain yield in acid soils. In Plant soil interaction at low pH, p619–631. Wright RJ, Baligar VC and Murr Mann RP (Eds), Kluwer Academic Publ., Netherlands.

Rai R and Prasad V. 1983. Effect of soil acidity factors on nodulation, active iron content of nodules and relative efficiency of symbiotic N_2 fixation by mutant strains of *Lens esculentus Rhizobium. J. Agric. Sci.* **100**: 607–611.

Seifu G. 1993. The effect of soil environment on plant performance and symbiosis by grain legumes in a Mediterranean environment. M.Sc. Thesis Univ, of Western Australia, Perth, Australia.

Singh D. 2009. Identification of aluminium and manganese resistant corn and pea genotypes adapted to acidic soils. Half yearly report of the project, College of Horticulture and Forestry, Central Agricultural University, Pasighat, Arunachal Pradesh, India.

Singh D and Chaturvedi SK. 2007. Rapid and effective screening technique for aluminium tolerance in chickpea at seedling stage. In abstracts of the National Symposium on "Legumes for Ecologocal Sustainability: Emerging Challenges and Opportunities, p107. Pramanik SC, Singh, B, Singh IP, Naimuddin, Gupta S and Prakash B (Eds) held during 3–5th November at Indian Institute of Pulses Research, Kanpur, India.

Singh D and Choudhary AK. 2009. Screening of pigeonpea genotypes for tolerance to aluminium toxicity. In abstracts of the international conference on Grain Legumes: Quality Improvement, Value Addition and Trade held during 14–16th February at Indian Institute of Pulses Research, Kanpur, Uttar Pradesh, India.

Singh D and Choudhary AK. 2010. Inheritance pattern of Al tolerance in pea. *Plant Breed.* **129**: 688–692.

Singh D, Dikshit HK and Kumar A. 2015. Aluminium tolerance in lentil with monogenic inheritance pattern. *Plant Breed*. **134**: 105–110.

Singh D, Pal M, Singh R and Singh CK. 2015. Physiological and biochemical characteristics of *Vigna* species for Al stress tolerance. *Acta Physiol. Plant.* **37**: 87 (DOI 10.1007/s/11738-015-1834-7).

Singh D, Rai AK, and Panyang O. 2009: Hematoxylin staining as a potential screening technique for aluminum tolerance in pea (*Pisum sativum* L.). *Current Sci.* **96:** 1029–1030.

Singh D and Raje RS 2011. Genetic of aluminium tolerance in chickpea. *Plant Breed.* **130:** 563–568.

Singh D, Raje RS and Choudhary AK. 2011. Inheritance of aluminium tolerance in pigeonpea. *Crop and Pasture Sci.* **62:** 761–764.

Suresh R, Foy C and Weidner J. 1987. Effects of excess soil manganese on stomatal function in two soybean cultivars. *J. Plant Nutr.* **10:** 749–760.

Taylor GJ. 1991. Current views of the aluminium stress response: The physiological basis of tolerance. *Curr. Top . Plant Biochem. Physiol.* **10:** 57–93.

Tesfaye M, Temple SJ, Allan DL, Vance CP and Samac DA. 2001. Overexpression of malate dehydrogenase in transgenic alfalfa enhances organic acid synthesis and confers tolerance to aluminium. *Plant Physiol.* **127:** 1836–1844.

Wagatsuma T. 1984. Characteristics of upward translocation of aluminium in plants. *Soil Sci. Plant Nutr.* **30:** 345–358.

Yan F, Schubert S and Mengel K. 1992. Effect of low root medium pH on net proton release, root respiration, and root growth of corn (*Zea mays* L.) and broad bean (*Vicia faba* L.). *Plant Physiol.* **99:** 415–421.

Response of Tree Seedlings Under Aluminium Toxicity Stress

RN Sehgal and Anil Kumar

ABSTRACT

Aluminium toxicity is the major factor in forest deterioration in acid soil. The present chapter is an attempt at collating information about researches mainly aimed at general effects and symptoms of Al-toxicity, Al uptake and localization in plants and cells, proposed mechanisms for adaptation/tolerance to aluminium toxicity, physiological and biochemical responses, comparative tolerance to Al-toxicity, important parameters for evaluation of Al-tolerance and variation for aluminium tolerance in tree seedling.

Key words: Aluminium toxicity, forest deterioration, tree seedlings.

INTRODUCTION

Aluminium (Al) toxicity is considered an important factor in forest decline caused by acidification of the soil solution (Ulrich *et al.* 1980). Soil acidification leads to increasing concentrations of Al and decreasing concentrations of the base cations (BC), K, Ca, Mg in the soil solution (Puhe *et al.* 2000). When the soil pH drops below 5.0, aluminium is solubilized as the phytotoxic Al^{3+} species from non toxic aluminium silicates and oxides (Lindsay 1979). This may negatively influence forest tree species in acidic soils. Several forest decline, studies have focused on minimum Al solution concentration limiting conifer growth and various values have been reported depending on experimental conditions (Hentschel *et al.* 1993). In general, aluminium is toxic to many plants (Kochian 1995) and restricts root growth within minutes or hours of exposure to about 10 to 50 µM Al in most crop species. On the other hand, it has been reported that Al inhibits root growth in tree species at levels higher than 0.3 mM (Thornton *et al.* 1986a). Therefore, tree species are considered to be more tolerant than crop species to aluminium and to harbor some mechanisms of aluminium resistance.

Al is not essential for plant growth, although low concentrations (2 and 5 mg l^{-1}) sometimes increase plant growth or produce some other beneficial effects (Foy and Flemming 1978). Thornton *et al.* (1986b) also reported enhancement of growth in sugar maple seedlings at low Al levels in solution culture. Such stimulation of growth has been reported in hardwoods like eucalyptus (Huang and Bachelard 1993), silver birch (Kidd and Proctor 2000), red oak and American beech (Thronton *et al.* 1989) and softwoods like radiata pine (Huang and Bachelard 1993), eastern white pine (Hutchinson *et al.* 1986), Douglas fir (Keltjens 1990) red spruce (McCanny *et al.* 1995) and white spruce (Nosko *et al.* 1988). The beneficial effects of Al on plant growth are however, less important than the detrimental effects.

GENERAL EFFECTS AND SYMPTOMS OF ALUMINIUM TOXICITY

The negative effect of aluminium on germination and growth of seedlings is in contrast to the report by Henriksen *et al.* (1992) who found no effects of aluminium on germination but on seedlings establishment in Norway spruce, which was in line with reports for white spruce (*Picea glauca* (Moench) Voss) (Nosko *et al.* 1988) and red spruce (*Picea rubens* Sarg.) (Scherbatskoy *et al.* 1987).

The primary effect of aluminium is inhibition of root elongation (Wagatsuma *et al.* 1987, Kochian 1995). Lateral root initiation typically occurs near the apex of the main axis. Al-injury inhibits branching and the roots are characteristically stubby and brittle, brown in colour and occasionally necrotic (Foy 1984). Root-tips may additionally turn brown in the most severe circumstances in forest tree species, the above ground organs may wilt and die due to inhibition of water uptake (Foy 1984). The root systems lack fine branching are reduced in size and coralloid in appearance (Foy 1984). Coralloid roots due to Al-injury are not reported for tree species and specific symptoms can not be found. Tepper *et al.* (1989) found that the effect of Al on root elongation was limited to the distal 4 mm of honeylocust and loblolly pine seedling roots due to decreased mitotic activity. In honeylocust, secondary root formation was reduced by 50 per cent when seedlings were grown in solution containing 50 µM Al. A reduction of similar magnitude was measured in loblolly pine grown in single salt solutions at 370 µM Al (Paganelli *et al.* 1987).

Secondary effects that can arise as the result of the abnormal root system include inhibition of nutrient and water uptake (Kochian 1995). In leaves of many plants, the symptoms may resemble phosphorus deficiency, including small leaf size, purple coloration and chlorosis and necrosis of leaf tips. Leaves may exhibit a chlorotic appearance and it was demonstrated that yellowing of some European conifers was due to magnesium deficiency (Landmann *et al.* 1987), the latter being related either to base cation depletion or to Al or Mn toxicity (Schlegel *et al.* 1992). In Norway spruce, symptoms of decline are premature loss of the older needles and discoloration of the remaining needles. In older needles the discoloration ranges from a yellowing of the tips to complete yellowing of the whole needles. Discoloration can often be associated with nutritional imbalance in particular with lack of Mg and Ca in the needles. Severe Al-induced shoot damage has been reported for peach (Edwards *et al.* 1976), coffee (Pavan and Bingham 1982) and honeylocust (Thornton *et al.* 1986a). In coffee shoots, Al-toxicity symptoms include marginal chlorosis and necrosis of younger leaves and spotty chlorosis of older leaves. In the presence of 150 µM Al, young honeylocust leaves emerged normally but after unfolding the leaflets turned brown and abscissed, leaving only a naked rachis which too finally abscissed. At higher concentrations of Al (600 ppm) the terminal meristem was killed after 2 to 3 weeks of exposure. In peach leaf symptoms of Al-toxicity were similar to those in coffee but developed first on the 4th and 5th (Edwards *et al.* 1976) leaves. For species such as sugar maple (Thornton *et al.* 1986b) and loblolly pine (Ryanal *et al.* 1990), aluminum may affect dry weight and size of shoots more than roots.

ALUMINIUM UPTAKE AND LOCALIZATION IN PLANTS

Chenery (1948) assayed the Al content in the leaves of thousands of plant species and classified them into Al accumulators with leaf aluminium content (> 1000 mg/kg DW) and non-accumulator with leaf content (< 1000 mg/kg DW). Sixty-five tree species in 25 families and 12 unidentified trees are referred to as aluminium (Al) accumulators. Aluminium (Al) content is higher in the leaves than that in the bark for most of the aluminium accumulators, but the reverse is the case in some species of Euphorbiaceae, Melastomaceae and Ulmaceae (Masunaga *et al.* 1998). Although the aluminium content of most plants is not more than 200 mg kg^{-1} DW, aluminium content of the leaves or barks in some aluminium accumulators such as *Acisanthera uniflora, Henriettea sucosa, Miconia acinodendron, A. maingayi, A. nigricans, Eugenia bisulea, Eurya acuminata, Maschalorymbus corymbus* (Masunaga *et al.* 1998), *Chamaecrista repens* (Geoghegan and Sprent 1996), tea (*Camellia sinensis*) and *Faramea marginata* (Watnabe and Osaki 2002) is more than 15000 mg kg^{-1} DW, suggesting that these species must possess some mechanisms to tolerate toxic levels of aluminium in their tissues.

Aluminium tolerance is associated with aluminium accumulation in plant shoot as seen in pine trees and tea (Foy *et al.* 1978), *Arnica montana, Deschampsia flexuosa* L. (Pegtel 1987), Melastoma m*alabathricum* (Watnabe *et al.* 1998) and *Hydrangea* (Matsumoto *et al.* 1976). Such aluminium accumulating species detoxify the internal Al^{3+} by forming aluminium organic complexes. In tea leaves, most aluminium was chelated to the catechin group of polyphenols, and to a lesser extent to phenolic and organic acids and as Al-F complexes (Nagata *et al.* 1992). Hydrangea (*Hydrangea macrophylla*), a woody plant has more than 3,000 mg kg^{-1} DW aluminium in both leaves and sepals during a several month growth period (Ma *et al.* 1997). Flowers of hydrangea turn from pink to blue by the application of aluminium. The bluing was thought to be due to the formation of delphinidin 3-glucoside-Al-3-caffeoylquinic acid. *Hydrangea* leaves from plants with blue sepals contain 15.7 mmol kg^{-1} FW Al, whereas those from plants with pink sepals contain only 0.23 mmol/kg FW. Over 2/3 of the Al in *Hydrangea* leaves from plants with blue sepals is localized in the cell sap, where Al concentration can be as high as 13.7 mmol^{-1}. In *Hydrangea macrophylla* leaves, Al was found as a complex with citrate (Ma *et al.* 1997) and in the hyperaccumulator *Melastoma malabathricum,* it was bound to oxalate (Watnabe *et al.* 1998). It is known that aluminium mainly is retained in the roots of Norway spruce and only very little is translocated to the shoot (Hentschel *et al.* 1993). Hodson and Wilkinson (1991) showed that accumulation of aluminium in Norway spruce roots is confined to the cell walls. Nevertheless, if small amount of Al ions below the detection limit of EDX enter the symplast, they will be chelated by the organic acid present. The major site of aluminium accumulation in root apices of slash pine and loblolly pine seedlings was the cell wall. Of the total Al in root-tips only 12 per cent was in the symplasmic fraction, whereas 88 per cent of Al was associated with the apoplasm (Nowak and Friend 2005). Large amount of monomeric Al exists in *Melastoma malabathricum* leaves, suggesting that Al is distributed in some parts, which are acidic, such as the vacuoles (Watnabe *et al.* 1998).

PROPOSED MECHANISMS FOR ADAPTATION/TOLERANCE TO ALUMINIUM TOXICITY

Plant species growing naturally on acid soils have developed strategies to cope with high concentrations of available Al in soil solution. The following hypotheses have been proposed to explain mechanisms. In exclusion mechanisms, immobilization of aluminium at the cell wall, selective permeability of the cell membrane, formation of a plant induced pH barrier in the rhizosphere and the exudation of chelating ligands are main. In acid soils, the pH near the root surface may be higher than the soil average (Schaller and Fischer 1985). Because high pH leads to aluminium precipitation, it has been suggested that Al-resistant plants are able to maintain a higher pH near the root surface than Al-sensitive plants (Mugwira and Patel 1977). Kochian (1995) also proposed several hypotheses, *viz.* alteration of rhizosphere pH, low cell wall CEC, Al efflux across the plasma membrane and Al-induced release of organic acids from the root apex. The best mechanism of aluminium tolerance is exclusion based on the release of organic acids from roots into the rhizosphere that complex Al (De la Fuente-Martinez and Herrera-Estrella 1999). Organic acids such as citric and malic acids are good chelators and can be synthesized in large amounts (Larsen *et al.* 1998). The predominant Al-resistance mechanism in plants is aluminium exclusion from root-tips (Taylor 1987). This mechanism mediated through organic acid exudation in response to aluminium stress, has been demonstrated in several crops and tropical woody species (Nguyen *et al.* 2003) as well as in red spruce (*Picea rubens* Sarg) cell suspension cultures (Minocha and Long 2004). The exuded organic acids chelate Al externally and prevent it from entering roots of Al resistant genotypes.

Internal tolerance mechanisms include Al-complexation chelation in the cytosol, compartmentation in the vacuole, Al-binding proteins and Al-tolerant enzymes. Chelation of aluminium by organic ligands in the cytoplasm could efficiently reduce the activity of aluminium and thus its phytotoxic effects (Scott and Fisher 1989). In certain woody Al-accumulator species, Al in the cytosol is complexed by organic molecules without disrupting cell metabolism. Once the Al is complexed, it might remain in the cytoplasm or be deposited elsewhere, e.g. in old xylem vessels or on cell walls (Helyar 1978). In the tea plant (*Camellia sinensis*), most of the aluminium is bound to catechins, but some portions are bound to phenolic and organic acids (Nagata *et al.* 1992). Tea can tolerate very high Al concentration (30, 000 mg Al kg^{-1}) in the tops by using this mechanism.

PHYSIOLOGICAL AND BIOCHEMICAL RESPONSES

Organic Acids

The organic acids secreted by plant roots play an important role in the external and internal neutralization of aluminium. A well-characterized mechanism of resistance to Al is the specific release of organic acid anions such as malate, citrate and oxalate from the roots of aluminium resistant plants (Pellet *et al.* 1995). Citrate concentration in *Melastoma malabathricum* xylem sap increases with increasing aluminium concentration whereas malate, succinate and ketoglutarate concentrations decrease (Watnabe and Osaki 2002). Oxalate a ligand of aluminium in *Melastoma mala-bathricum* leaves, is not detected in the xylem sap treated with or without aluminium (Watnabe and Osaki 2002). Responses of organic acids metabolisms to aluminium are probably related to the fact that *Melastoma malabathricum* has higher aluminium accumulation capacity in shoots. It has been reported that aluminium treatment increases citrate, oxalate and malate contents in the leaves of *Melastoma malabthricum* (Watnabe and Osaki 2002). Minocha and Long (2004) in their study on cell suspension cultures of red spruce (*Picea rubra*) have found that Al does not significantly affect the cellular concentrations of malate, ascorbate and citrate which were not present in detectable quantities in the medium. Exogenous succinate alone or with Al had no effects on cellular free polyamine concentrations or cell mass. However, a significant increase in cellular putrescine concentrations was observed with Al. Addition of malate had a positive effect on growth and completely reversed the effects of Al on cell physiology. Addition of oxalate and citrate only partly reversed the effects of Al.

Callose

Root callose content can be used as an indicator of sensitivity of aluminium stress (Wissemeier *et al. 1992)* and is useful for evaluating Al sensitivity in many crops. Callose in root tips of forest trees is one prospective physiological parameter of Al toxicity (Hirano *et al.* 2006). Callose synthesis is dependent on both depolarization of the plasma membrane and an increase in intracellular Ca^{2+} concentrations in root cells. In the chestnut seedlings, the concentrations of callose increased significantly in root tips after one day exposure of 168 mM Al (Hirano *et al.* 2006). Callose has also been shown to form in root tips of Norway spruce (*Picea abies*) seedlings exposed to Al after 6 h (Hirano *et al.* 2004). Under forest field conditions, callose concentrations in short roots of Norway spruce was positively correlated with Al concentration but not with Ca/Al molar ratios in the soil solution (Wissemeier *et al.* 1998) who reported that there was a significantly positive relationship between the callose content in the short roots of Norway spruce and free Al concentrations in the soil solution. Negative correlation was observed between root growth and callose accumulation (Horst *et al.* 1997). However, Tomioka and Takenaka (2004) observed a positive correlation between the relative root callose content and relative root growth in conifers. Using an *Arabidopsis* mutant, Larsen *et al.* (1996) indicated that Al induced callose accumulation was not always correlated with Al-induced root growth inhibition.

Phenolics

McQuattie and Schier (1990) found accumulation of phenolics by microscopical observation of aluminium treated red spruce (*Picea rubens* Sarg.) root cells. Karolewski and Giertych (1994) studied total phenolic levels in scots pine (*Pinus sylvestris* L.) after Pb and Cd treatment, but were not significantly affected by aluminium. The catechol (o-dihydroxyphenyl) unit of many phenolic substances is a potent chelator of aluminium (Tang *et al.* 1992). Phenolics constituents in tree bark have been shown to effectively bind heavy metals (Gaballah and Kilbertus 1998).

Mineral Nutrition

The presence of aluminum in the root environment and its uptake by roots tends to reduce the concentration of other mineral nutrients in the plant especially Ca, Mg and P (Foy *et al.* 1978). Nutrient deficiencies are induced by Al in some plants, e.g. Mg deficiency in Norway spruce (Jorns 1988) and possibly red spruce (Thornton *et al.* 1987), Ca deficiency in loblolly pine (Raynal *et al.* 1990), and P deficiency in American beech and European beech (Thornton *et al.* 1989). In many species a reduction in tissue nutrient composition generally occurs at lower concentrations of Al than a reduction in growth (Pavan and Bingham 1982, Thornton *et al.* 1987). Tissue nutrient composition effects may result from co-precipitation of Al with an ion, e.g. the precipitation of phosphate in roots as Al phosphate (Foy *et al.* 1978). This may result in a high P content in root tissues (McCormick and Borden 1972) and a phosphate deficiency in shoot tissues. Precipitation of Al in roots and possibly other tissues depends largely on external phosphate and Al concentrations, pH and ionic strength. The observed pattern of $AlPO_4$ interactions therefore varies from system to system (Roy *et al.* 1988). Not all elemental nutrient concentrations are reduced with increasing concentrations of Al. In many studies, K increased with increasing Al concentration (Truman *et al.* 1986). Aluminium may also interfere directly with uptake and translocation of ions (Haug 1983, Roy *et al.* 1988). However, a reduction in content is insufficient evidence to prove direct inhibition of transport because Al may change root morphology thereby reducing the absorbing surface and thus the rate of nutrient uptake. In seedlings exposed to Al, the content of Mg and Ca in the needles was significantly reduced (Godbold *et al.* 1988).

Relationships Between Ca/Al Ratio in Fine Roots and Aboveground Tree Response

In forest ecosystems, usually solution Al or Ca/Al is regarded as the parameter determining Al effects on tree health (Cronan and Grigal 1995). Cronan and Grigal (1995) reviewed relationships between soil and soil solution chemistry with root parameters such as biomass, growth, and nutrients. They found that molar Ca/Al ratios in foliar and root tissues are positively correlated with the solution Ca/Al molar ratios under controlled conditions. In general, foliar Al concentrations are far lower than root Al concentrations. This suggests that there is a root barrier to Al translocation at lower external Al concentrations (Cronan and Grigal 1995). Increased Al concentration in roots is manifested both as decreased Ca/Al ratio in roots and as decreased translocation of different nutrient elements to shoots. So far, little information is available on the relationships between the root Ca/Al ratios and the parameters of aboveground parts. Fine root Ca/Al below 0.2 and foliar Ca/Al below 12.5 (when soil solution Ca/Al is below 1) were suggested by Cronan and Grigal (1995) to be associated with risk of Al toxicity. Jentschke *et al.* (2001) reported a decrease in root biomass in the mineral soil (20–40 cm soil depth) with decreasing Ca/Al ratios. Decreased fine root Ca/Al (50.5) ratio in *Pinus sylvestris* was associated with signifcantly increased root necromass (Varguelova *et al.* 2005). These results clearly encourage the use of root Ca/Al molar ratio as an indicator of Al toxicity. Fine roots of European chestnut (*Castania sativa*) seedlings decreased significantly their Ca/Al molar ratios after an exposure of 168 mM Al for 28 days but did not after 7 days exposure (Hirano *et al.* 2006), indicating an accumulative effect.

Ratio of Base Cation to Aluminium (Al) in the Soil Solution

A ratio of base cations (BC) to Al in the soil solution lower than 1 is widely used as an indicator for potentially adverse effects on tree health. Adverse effects on tree health are expected below a threshold value of 1 for BC:Al (Sverdrup *et al.* 1992b). Scier and Mc Quattie (2002) reported enhanced growth of sugar maple (*Acer saccharum*) seedlings with 2.5 and 5.0 mh L^{-1} of Al at pH 3.8. But at higher levels of Al, reduced foliar concentration of Ca and Mg and some injury to roots and leaves was observed. Hirano *et al.* (2007) while reviewing the effects of soil acidification and aluminium toxicity on the roots of some Japanese forest trees have recommended that the specific root response to the Ca/Al molar ratio of the roots should be considered as a parameter for long-term monitoring of forest sites because nutritional status and physiological changes are better indicators of Al stress than the biomass and morphological responses.

Important Parameters for Evaluation of Aluminium Tolerance

Root morphology was a better indicator of toxic response than root length or weight. Ranking of aluminium resistance among tree species have been compiled based on growth response from many studies. However, Macedo *et al.* (1997) reported that multiple growth parameters would be necessary to determine the relative Al toxicity between genotypes of the same species. Stem measurements could be variable due to restricted or promoted root development. Using a necrosis criterion may be the only reliable method to gauge Al-toxicity in long-term experiments at high concentrations of Al. At low concentrations and short intervals of exposure, plants would be categorized best by weight parameters, not length parameters. However, physiological differences among genotypes within a tree species have received less attention.

COMPARATIVE ALUMINIUM TOXICITY

The trees have been grouped into three categories according to their growth response to Al (c.f. McLean and Gilbert 1927) as presented below:

Sensitive species: The growth is affected by solution Al concentrations of 150 µM or less, as found in acid soils.

Intermediate species: The growth is affected by solution Al concentrations of 150 to 800 µM, as have been reported in only a few soils.

Resistant species: The growth is affected by solution Al concentration of 800 µM.

The wide variety of different physical, chemical and biological conditions used in these studies further reduces the comparability of the information presented in Table 8.1.

Table 8.1: *Summary of the response of tree seedlings to aluminium in sensitive species*

Species	System	Toxic Al concentration (µM)		Reference
		Growth effect	Nutrient composition effect	
Sensitive species				
Honey locust	Solution	50^3	50^3	Thornton *et al.* 1986a
Populus	Solution	111	ND^4	Steiner *et al.* 1984
Coffee	Solution	35	35	Pavan and Bingham 1982
Norway spruce	Solution	150	170^3	Rost-Siebert 1983
White spruce	Solution	50^3	ND	Nosko *et al.* 1988
Peach	Solution	111^3	111^3	Edwards *et al.* 1976
Intermediate species				
Sugar maple	Solution	800–1000	300	Thornton *et al.* 1986b
Red spruce	Solution	185^3	250^3	Thornton *et al.* 1987, Hutchinson *et al.* 1986
Black spruce	Sand	370	185^3	Hutchinson *et al.* 1986
European beech	Solution	500^3	500^3	Thornton *et al.* 1989

(Contd.)

Table 8.1: *Summary of the response of tree seedlings to aluminium in sensitive species (Contd.)*

Species	System	Toxic Al concentration (µM)		Reference
		Growth effect	Nutrient composition effect	
Loblolly pine	Solution	600[3]	500	Tepper *et al.* 1989
Resistant species				
Jack pine	Sand culture	1480	740	Hutchinson *et al.* 1986
White pine	Sand culture	1960	ND	Hutchinson *et al.* 1986
Slash pine	Solution	2222	555[3]	Williams 1982
Longleaf pine	Solution	1111	1111[3]	Williams 1982
Sand pine	Solution	1111	555[3]	Williams 1982
Scot pine	Solution	300–5000	ND	Eldhuset *et al.* 1987
White birch	Solution	3000	1000	Goransson and Eldhuset 1987
Douglas fir	Solution	3100	NS[5]	Ryan *et al.* 1986
Western hemlock	Solution	2170	NS	Ryan *et al.* 1986
Western red cedar	Solution	3700	NS	Ryan *et al.* 1986
Sitka spruce	Solution	3700	NS	Ryan *et al.* 1986
American beech	Solution	2000	500	Thornton *et al.* 1989
Red oak	Solution	2500	500	Thornton *et al.* 1989
Balsam fir	Soil	1850	1050	Entry 1987
Resistant species (classification based on limited data)				
Yellow birch	Solution	4400	ND	McCormick and Steiner 1978
Paper birch	Solution	4400	4400	Steiner *et al.* 1980
Gray birch	Solution	4400	ND	McCormick and Steiner 1978
Pin oak	Solution	7400	ND	McCormick and Steiner 1978
Virginia pine	Solution	4400	ND	McCormick and Steiner 1978
Pitch pine	Solution	4400	ND	McCormick and Steiner 1978
White ash	Sand	2375	ND	Stanturf 1984
Black cherry	Sand	4800	ND	Stanturf 1984

(Adapted from Schaedle *et al.* 1989)

[1] A decrease in root or shoot tissue Ca, Mg, P or K.

[2] Could be sensitive.

[3] The lowest Al concentration tested.

[4] ND = not determined.

[5] NS = no significant effect.

VARIATION FOR ALUMINIUM TOLERANCE

In all cases, resistance is under genetic control, but the expression of resistance depends on complex interactions between the organism and its environment. Aluminium stress resistance is a common phenomenon in trees and elucidation of the detailed molecular processes controlling resistance would facilitate development of Al-tolerant strains of valuable Al-sensitive species. Selection for Al-tolerant varieties of wheat, barley and soybeans has been highly successful in expanding production of these crops on acid soils containing high concentrations of Al (Rhue 1979). No similar programme has been initiated with woody plants although genes for Al-resistance exist in woody plants. Heritability of aluminium tolerance has been demonstrated for Populus families (Steiner *et al.* 1984) and varietal differences have been reported for Norway spruce (Makkonen-Spiecker 1985), paper birch (McCormick and Steiner 1979) and citrus root stock (Worku *et al.* 1982).

CONCLUSION

Trees are more tolerant to aluminium toxicity because of their general hardiness and long life span. However, most of sensitivity is exhibited either at the seedling stage or by fine roots in a grown up plant. It is very important to study Al-tolerance in species and provenances if afforestation is to be extended successfully to marginal areas. At the physiological level it will be very interesting if we find tolerance mechanisms to be different from crops. So investigation in this direction must continue. There is need to develop special screening techniques for tree seedlings as their growth and morphology is different from crop seedlings.

REFERENCES

Chenery EM. 1948. Al in the plant . Part I. General survey in dicotyledons. *Kew Bull.* **2**: 173–183.

Cronan CS and Grigal DF. 1995. Use of calcium/aluminium ratios as indicators of stress in forest ecosystems. *J. Environ. Qual.* **24**: 209–226.

De la Fuente-Martinez, JM and Herrera-Estrella L. 1999. Advances in the understanding the aluminium toxicity and the development of aluminium tolerant transgenic plants. *Adv. Agron.* **66**: 103–120.

Edwards JH, Horton BD and Kirpatrick HC. 1976. Aluminium toxicity symptoms in peach seedlings. *J. Am. Soc. Hort. Sci.* **101**: 139–142.

Eldhuset T, Goranson A and Ingestad T. 1987. Aluminium toxicity in forest tree seedlings. In Effects of atmospheric pollutants on forests, wetlands and agricultural ecosystems, p401–409. Hutchinson TC and Meema KM (Eds), Springer-Verlag, Berlin.

Entry JA. 1987. The effect of pH and aluminium concentration on ectomycorrhizal formation of *Abies balsamea* (L.) Mill. *Can. J. For. Res.* **17**: 865–871.

Foy CD. 1984. Physiological effects of hydrogen, aluminium and manganese toxicities in acid soils. In Soil acidity and liming. Adams F (Ed), 2nd ed. Soil Sci. Soc. Am. Soc. Agron. and Crop Sci. of Am., Madison, WI.

Foy CD, Chaney RL and White MC. 1978. The physiology of metal toxicity in plants. *Ann. Rev. Plant Physiol.* **29:** 511–566.

Foy CD and Fleming AL. 1978. The physiology of plant tolerance to excess available aluminium and manganese in acidic soils. In crop tolerance to suboptimal land conditions, p301–328. Jung GA (Ed), ASA Spec. Publ. 32. ASA, CSSA and SSSA, Madison, WI.

Gaballah I and Kilbertus G. 1998. Recovery of heavy metal ions through decontamination of synthetic solutions and industrial effluents modified barks. *J. Geochem. Explor.* **62:** 241–286.

Geoghegen IE and Sprent JI. 1996. Aluminium and nutrient concentrations in species native to central Brazil. *Commun. Soil Sci. Plant Anal.* **27:** 2925–2934.

Godbold DL, Friz E and Huttermann A. 1988. Aluminium toxicity and forest decline. *Proc. Natl. Acad. Sci., USA.* **85:** 3888–3892.

Goranson A and Ekihuset TD. 1987. Effects of aluminum on Betulupehdu seedlings. *Physiol. Plant.* **69:** 193–199.

Haug A. 1983. Molecular aspects of aluminium toxicity. Critical Rev. *Plant Sci.* **1:** 345–373.

Helyar KR. 1978. Effect of aluminium and manganese toxicities on legume growth. In mineral nutrition of legumes in tropical and subtropical soils, p208–231. Andrew CS and Kamprath FJ (Eds), CSIRO, Melbourne, Australia.

Henricksen TM, Eldhuset TD, Stuanes AO and Langerud BR. 1992. Effects of Al and Ca on *Piecea abies* seedlings. *Scand. J. Res.* **7:** 63–70.

Hentschel E, Godbold DL, Marshchner P, Schlegel H and Jentschke G. 1993. The effect of *Paxillus involutus* Fr. on Al sensitivity of norway spruce seedlings. *Tree Physiol.* **12:** 379–390.

Hirano Y, Mizoguchi T and Brunner I. 2007. Root response of cyperus seedlings to various levels of Ca/Al molar ratios. *Environ. Sci.* **7:** 71–82.

Hirano Y, Pannatier EG, Stefan Z and Brunner I. 2004. Induction of callose in roots of norway spruce seedlings after short-term exposure to aluminium. *Tree Physiol.* **24:** 1279–1283.

Hirano Y, Walthert L and Brunner I. 2006. Callose in root apices of European chestnut seedlings: A physiological indicator of Al stress. *Tree Physiol.* **26:** 431–440.

Hodson MJ and Wilkins DA. 1991. Localization of Al in the roots of norway spruce (*Picea abies* (L) Karst) inoculated with *Paxillus involutus* Fr. *New Phytol.* **118:** 273–278.

Horst WJ, Puschel AK and Schmohl N. 1997. Induction of callose formation is a sensitive marker for genotypic aluminium sensitivity in maize. *Plant Soil.* **192:** 23–30.

Huang J and Bachelard EP. 1993. Effects of Al on growth and cation uptake in seedlings of *Eucalyptus manifera* and *Pinus radiata*. *Plant Soil.* **149:** 121–127.

Hutchinson TC, Bozic L and Munoz-Vega G. 1986. Response of five species of conifer seedlings to aluminum stress. *Water Air Soil Poll.* **31:** 283–294.

Jentschke G, Drexhage M, Fritz HW, Fritz E, Schella B, Lee DH, Gruber F, Heinmann J, Kuhr M, Schmidt J, Schmidt S, Zimmermann R and Godbold DL. 2001. Does soil acidity reduce subsoil rooting in Norway spruce (*Picea abies*). *Plant Soil.* **237:** 91–108.

Jorns AC. 1988. Aluminium toxizitat bei Samlingen der Fichte (*Picea abies* (L.) Karst) in Nohrlosung. PhD Thesis. Technical Univ of Berlin, FRG.

Karolewski P and Giertych MJ. 1994. Influence of toxic metal ions on phenolics in needles and roots and on root respiration of scots pine seedlings. *Acta Soc. Bot. Polo*. **63**: 29–35.

Keltjens WG. 1990. Effect of Al on growth and nutrient status of Douglas fir seedlings grown in culture solution. *Tree Physiol*. **6**: 165–175.

Kidd P and Proctor J. 2000. Effects of Aluminium on the growth and mineral composition of *Betula pendula* Roth. *J. Expt. Bot*. **51**: 1057–1066.

Kochian LV. 1995. Cellular mechanisms of aluminium toxicity and resistance in plants. *Ann. Rev. Pl. Physiol. Pl. Mol. Biol*. **46**: 237–260.

Landmann G, Bonneau N and Adrian M. 1987. le deprissement du sapir pectine et de lepicea commun dans le massifvosgien estil en relation avec l ' *et al*. nutritional des peuplements? *Rev. For Fr*. **39**: 5–11.

Larsen PB, Degenhardt J, Tai C, Stenzler LM, Howell SH and Kochian LV. 1998. Aluminium resistant Arabidopsis mutant that exhibit altered pattern of aluminium accumulation and organic acid release from roots. *Plant Physiol*. **117**: 8–19.

Larsen PB, Degenhardt J, Tai C, Stenzler LM, Howell SH and Kochian LV. 1998. Aluminium resistant Arabidopsis mutant that exhibit altered pattern of aluminium accumulation and organic acid release from roots. *Plant Physiol*. **117**: 8–19.

Larsen PB, Tai CY, Kochain LV and Howell SH. 1996. *Arabidopsis* mutants with increased sensitivity to aluminium. *Plant Physiol*. **110**: 743–751.

Lindsay WL. 1979. Chemical equilibria in soils. John Wiley & Sons, New York.

Macedo CEC, Kinet JM and Van Sint Jan V. 1997. Effects of duration and intensity of Al stress on growth parameter in four rice cultivars differing in Al sensitivity. *J. Plant Nutr*. **20**: 181–193.

Ma JF, Hiradate S, Nomoto K, Iwashita T and Matsumoto H. 1997. Internal detoxification mechanism of Al in *Hydrangea*: Identification of Al form in the leaves. *Plant Physiol*. **113**: 1033–1039.

Makkonen-Spiecker K. 1985. Auswirkungen der Aluminums auf junge Fichten (*Picea abies* Karst) verschiedener Provenienzen. *Forstw. Chl*. **104**: 341–353.

Masunaga T, Kubota D, Hotta M and Wagatsuki T. 1998. Mineral composition of leaves and bark in aluminium accumulators in a tropical rain forest in Indonesia. *Soil Sci. Plant Nutr*. **44**: 347–358.

Matsumoto H, Hiraseva E, Morimura S and Takahashi E. 1976. Localization of aluminium in tea leaves. *Plant Cell Physiol*. **17**: 627–631.

McCanny SJ, Hendershot WH, Lechomicz MJ and Shipley B. 1995. The effects of Al on *Picea rubens*: factorial experiments using sand culture. *Can J. For. Res*. **25**: 8–17.

McCormick LH and Borden FY. 1972. Phosphate fixation by aluminium in plant roots. *Soil Sci. Soc. Amer. Proc*. **36**: 799–802.

McCormick LH and Steiner KC. 1978. Variation in aluminium tolerance among six tree species. *For. Sci*. **24**: 565–568.

McCormick LM and Steiner KC. 1979. Differential response of paper birch provenances to aluminum in solution culture. *Can. J. For. Res*. **10**: 25-29.

McLean FT and Gilbert BE. 1927. The relative aluminium tolerance of crop plants. *Soil Sci.* **24**: 163–175.

Mc Quattie CJ and Schier GA. 1990. Response of red spruce seedlings to aluminium toxicity in nutrient solution: alterations in root anatomy. *Can J. For. Res.* **20**: 1001–1011.

Minocha R and Long S. 2004. Effects of Al on organic acid metabolism and secretion by red spruce cell suspension cultures and the reversal of Al effects on growth and polyamine metabolism by exogenous acids. *Tree Physiol.* **24**: 15–64.

Mugwira LM and Patel SU. 1977. Root zone pH changes and ion uptake imbalances by triticale,wheat and rye. *Agron. J.* **69**: 719–722.

Nagata T, Hayatum M and Kosuga N. 1992. Identification of Al form in tea leaves by ^{27}Al NMR. *Phytochem.* **31**:1275-1298.

Nguyen NT, Nakabayashi K, Thompson J and Fujita K. 2003. Role of exudation of organic acid and phosphate in Al tolerance of four tropical woody species. *Tree Physiol.* **23**: 1041–1050.

Nosko P, Brassard P, Kramer JR and Kershaw KA. 1988. The effect of aluminium on seed germination and early seedlings establishments, growth and respiration of white spruce *Picea glauca. Can. J. Bot.* **66**: 2305–2310.

Nowok J and Friend A. 2005. Aluminium fractions in root tips of slashpine and loblolly pine families differing in Al resistance. *Tree Physiol.* **25**: 245–250.

Paganelli DJ, Seiler JR and Feret PP. 1987. Root regeneration as an indicator of aluminum toxicity in globally pine. *Plant Soil.* **102**: 115–118.

Pavan MA and Bingham FT. 1982. Toxicity of aluminium to coffee seedlings grown in nutrient solution. *Soil Sci. Soc. Am. J.* **45**: 993–997.

Pegtel DM. 1987. Effect of ionic Al in culture solutions on the growth of *Arnica montana* L. and *Deschampsia flexuosa* (L.) Trin. *Plant Soil.* **102**: 85–92.

Pellet D, Grunes D and Kochian LV. 1995. Organic acid exudation as an aluminium tolerance mechanisms in maize (*Z. mays* L.). *Planta.* **196**: 788–795.

Puhe J, Ulrich B and Dohrenbusch A. 2000. Global climate and human impacts on forest ecosystems: Postglacial development, present situation and future trends in central Europe. Berlin, Springer.

Raynal DJ, Joslin JD, Thornton FC, Schaedle M and Henderson GS. 1990. Sensitivity of tree seedlings to aluminum: III. Red spruce and loblolly pine. *J. Environ. Qual.* **19**: 180–187.

Rhue RD. 1979. Differential aluminum tolerance in crop plants. In stress physiology of crop plants, p62–80. Mussel H and Staples RC (Eds), Wiley Interscience Publication, New York.

Rost-Sibert K. 1983. Aluminium-toxizitatund-toleranz an Keimpflanzen Von fichte (*Picea abies* Kasst.) und Buche (*Fagus sylvatica* L.). *AFZ.* **38**: 686–689.

Roy AK, Sharma A and Talukdar G. 1988. Some aspects of aluminium toxicity in plants. *Bot. Rev.* **54**: 145–177.

Ryan PJ, Gessell SP and Zasoski RJ. 1986. Acid tolerance of Pacific North West conifers in solution culture II. Effect of varying aluminium concentrations at constant pH. *Plant Soil.* **96**: 259–277.

Schaller G and Fischer WR. 1985. pH-Andenmgen in der Rhizosphere von Mais-und Erdnusswurzeln. *Z. Pflanzener. Bodenk.* **148**: 306–320.

Scherbatskoy T, Klein RM and Badger GJ. 1987. Germination responses of forest tree seed to acidity and metal ions. *Env. Exp. Bot.* **27**: 157–164.

Schier GS and Mc Quattie CJ. 2002. Stimulating effects of aluminium on growth of sugarmaple seedlings. *J. Plant Nutr.* **25**: 2583–2589.

Schlegel H, Amuodson RG and Hultermann A. 1992. Element distribution in red spruce (*Picea rubens*) fine roots, evidence for Al toxicity at white face mountain. *Can J. Res.* **22**: 1132–1138.

Scott BJ and Fisher JA. 1989. Selection of genotypes tolerant of aluminium and manganese. In Soil acidity and plant growth, p167–203. Robson AD (Ed), Academic Press, Australia.

Stanturf JA. 1984. The effect of Al on the growth of blackberry and white ash in sand culture. *Agron. Abst.* **76**: 226.

Steiner KC, Barbour JR and McCormick LH. 1984. Response of Populus hybrids to aluminium toxicity. *For. Sci.* **30**: 400–410.

Steiner KC, McCormick LH and Canavera DS. 1980. Differential response of paper birch provenances to aluminium in solution culture. *Can. J. For. Res.* **10**: 25–29.

Sverdrup H, Warfvinge P, Fronger T, Haoya AO, Johansson M and Andersen B. 1992. Critical loads for forest soils in Nordic countries. *Ambio* **21**: 348–355.

Tang H, Hancock RA and Covington AD. 1992. Complexation between polyphenols and aluminium salts. In Plant polyphenols: Synthesis, properties, significance, p437–445. Hemingway R and Lakhs PE (Eds.), Plenuspress, New York.

Taylor GJ. 1987. Aluminium tolerance, rhizosphere pH and nitrogen nutrition in *Triticum aestivum* L; correlation without casuality? In Proc. Int. conf. on heavy metals in the environment, p473–475. Lindberg SE and Hutchinson TC (Eds.), New Orleans CEP Consultants LTP, Edinburg.

Tepper HB, Yang CS and Schaedle M. 1989. Effect of Al on growth of root tips on honeylocust and loblolly pine. *J. Env. Expt. Bot.* **29**: 165–173.

Thornton FC, Schaedle M, Raynal DJ and Zipperer C. 1986a. Effects of Al on honeylocust (*Gleditsia triacanthos* L.) seedlings in solution culture. *J. Expt. Bot.* **37**: 755–785.

Thornton FC, Schaedle M and Raynal DJ. 1986b. Effect of Al on the growth of sugarmaple in solution culture. *Can. J. For. Res.* **16**: 892–896.

Thornton FC, Schaedle M and Raynal DJ. 1987. Effects of aluminium on red spruce seedlings in solution culture. *Env. Expt. Bot.* **27**: 489–498.

Thornton FC, Schaedle M and Raynal DJ. 1989. An evaluation of the Al tolerance of red oak, american beech and european beech using solution culture. *J. Env. Qual.* **18**: 541–545.

Tomioka R and Takenga C. 2004. Difference in response to aluminium among japanese coniferous species. *Soil Sci. Plant Nutr.* **50**: 755–761.

Truman RA, Humphreys FR and Ryan PJ. 1986. Effect of varying solution ratios of Al and Ca on the uptake of phosphorus by *Pinus radiata*. *Plant Soil* **96**: 109–123.

Ulrich B, Mayer R and Khanna PK. 1980. Chemical changes due to acid precipitation in a less derived soil in central Europe. *Soil Sci.* **130:** 193–199.

Varguelova EI, Nortcliff S, Moffat AJ and Kennedy F. 2005. Morphology, biomass and nutrient status of fine roots of scots pine (*Pinus sylvestris*) as influenced by season fluctuations in soil moisture and soil solution chemistry. *Plant Soil.* **270:** 233–247.

Wagatsuma T, Kaneko M and Hayasak Y. 1987. Destruction process of plant root cells by aluminium. *Soil Sci. Plant Nutr.* **33:** 161–175.

Wissemeier AH, Diening A, Hergenroder A, Horst WJ and Mixwagner G. 1992. Callose formation as parameter for assessment of genotypical plant tolerance of Al and Mn. *Plant Soil.* **146:** 67–75.

Wissemeier AH, Hahn G and Marschner H. 1998. Callose in roots of norway spruce (*Picea abies* L.) is a sensitive parameter for Al supply at a forest site. *Plant Soil.* **199:** 53–57.

Watnabe T and Osak M. 2002. Mechanisms of adaptation to high aluminium conditions in native plant species growing in acid soils. *Commun. Soil Sci. Plant Anal.* **33:** 1247–1260.

Watnabe T, Osaki M, Yoshihara T and Tadano T. 1998. Distribution and chemical speciation of aluminium in the Al accumulator Plant, *Melastoma malabatharicum* L. *Plant Soil* **201:** 165–173.

Williams KA. 1982. Tolerance of four species of southern pine to aluminum in solution culture. MS Thesis. p129, Univ. Florida.

Worku Z, Warner RM and Fox RL 1982. Comparative tolerance of three citrus root stocks to soil aluminium and manganese. Coll. of Trop. Agric. Morman Resou. Research Series 017. Univ. Hawaii.

9 Iron Toxicity in Crop Plants

KN Das, BN Hazarika and Dharmendra Singh

ABSTRACT

Iron toxicity is a syndrome of disorder associated with large concentrations of reduced iron (Fe^{2+}) in the soil solution. Effective measures to overcome Fe-toxicity include periodic surface drainage, liming, good fertilizer management and use of tolerant genotypes. If toxicity is not severe, the use of tolerant varieties alone may serve as an alternative to these measures. Based on the available literature, this chapter reviews the manifestation of iron toxicity, its plant symptoms, current knowledge of crop adaptation mechanisms, nutritional interaction and breeding for Fe stress tolerance in crop plants.

Key words: Adaptive mechanism, iron toxicity, nutrient interaction.

INTRODUCTION

Iron is the fourth abundant mineral in the earth's crust after oxygen, silicon and Al. Plants derive 2.5 per cent concentration of iron from all the elements they derive from the soil. Iron is classified as a trace element or micro nutrient because it is only needed in small amount. Excess amount of iron can be toxic to plants. Iron toxicity is a widespread nutrient disorder affecting the growth of wetland rice in Asia, Africa, and South America (Sahrawat 2005, Sahu 1968, Barbosa Filho *et al*. 1983, Fageria 1984, Fageria and Rabelo 1987, Fageria *et al*. 2003b, Sahrawat 2004). In India 11.7 m ha land is affected by Fe-toxicity (Prasad and Biswas 2000). Iron is present in aerobic soils as Fe^{3+} but a large part of this element could be reduced to Fe^{2+} in waterlogged soils characterized by anaerobic conditions and low pH. Iron toxicity may then appear in plants due to excessive Fe^{2+} absorption by roots (Ponnamperuma 1972).

Iron toxicity occurs mostly in ultisols, oxisols, and acid sulfate soils which have high in active iron and potential acidity, irrespective of organic matter and texture. But texture, cation exchange capacity, and organic matter content influence the concentration of ferrous iron in soil solution, in which iron toxicity occurs (Breemen and Moormann 1978). Iron (Fe) toxicity may be attributed to low soil pH, low soil fertility as well as by accumulation of harmful organic acids and/or hydrogen sulphides (Sahu 1968, Tanaka *et al.* 1966). Fe is also abundantly found in heavy soil (Tanaka and Yamaguchi 1973). A concentration of 300–500 ppm dissolved iron in the root zone generally causes bronzing. However, with low nutrients levels, especially K and P or with respiratory inhibitors such as hydrogen sulphides, and Fe concentration as low as 30 ppm may be toxic to rice (Breeman and Moormann 1978). Concentrations of 500–1000 ppm of ferrous iron are very common under reduced conditions (Ponnamperumma 1976). A concentration above 500 ppm of ferrous iron is considered toxic. The critical toxicity contents are above 500 mg Fe kg^{-1} leaf dry weight and consequently yield reduce (Marschner 1995, Mengel and Kirby 1987). The Asian rice species *Oryza sativa* L. is rather sensitive to high Fe^{2+} levels: Typical symptoms called "bronzing" appear on old leaves of stressed plants which also exhibit a stunted growth, limited tillering (Dorlodot *et al.* 2005, Thongbai and Goodman 2000), nutritional disorders (Ottow *et al.* 1983, Genon *et al.* 1994) and ethylene overproduction (Yamauchi and Peng 1995). Fe-toxicity can reduce rice yield by 12–100 per cent depending on the intensity of the stress and tolerance of cultivars (Becker and Asch 2005, Sahrawat 2004).

Another study conducted by Dobermann and Fairhurst (2000) showed that Fe content in affected plants is usually (but not always) high (300–2,000 mg Fe kg^{-1}), but the critical Fe content depends on plant age and general nutritional status. The critical threshold is lower in poor soils where nutrition is not properly balanced. Fe-toxic plants have low K content in leaves (often < 1% K). A K:Fe ratio of < 17–18:1 in straw and < 1.5:1 in roots may indicate Fe-toxicity. The critical concentration for the occurrence of Fe-toxicity is > 300 mg Fe L^{-1} soil. Critical Fe solution concentrations for the occurrence of Fe toxicity vary widely. Reported values range from 10 to 1,000 mg Fe L^{-1}, which implies that Fe toxicity is not related to the Fe concentration in soil solution alone. The difference between critical solution Fe concentrations is caused by differences in the potential of rice roots to resist the effects of Fe-toxicity, depending on crop growth stage, physiological status of the plant, and variety grown (root oxidation power). No critical levels for soil test results have been established, but soils with pH < 5.0 (in H_2O) are prone to Fe-toxicity. Similarly, soils containing small amounts of available K, P, Ca, and Mg contents are prone to Fe-toxicity.

LAND SITUATIONS FOR MANIFESTATION OF ACUTE IRON TOXICITY

Iron is the most important element in the earth's crust. It is especially concentrated in the lowland soils of toposequence, however, many of the upland slopes also have high concentrations of iron. But, just because iron is present in the soil does not necessarily mean that there will be a toxicity problem. In the uplands and on the slopes, iron is typically in ferric form [Fe^{3+}]. This form is non-soluble, and therefore not available to the plants. In other words, ferric iron is harmless to rice, and iron toxicity is not a problem on the upper slopes. Meanwhile, if the fields are not adequately flushed with fresh water, iron in the lowlands is subjected to an environment depleted of oxygen, and tends to become converted into ferrous [Fe^{2+}]

iron. Ferrous iron is soluble in water, and so is available for uptake by the rice plants. In a typical iron-toxic valley, ferric iron is washed down into the valley lowland, either by seepage through the soil (known as interflow), or else by run-off and erosion of the upper slopes into the valley bottom (Fig. 9.1). Either route (for interflow) or else upon arrival in the valley bottom (for run-off), the ferric iron encounters waterlogged conditions, and becomes ferrous iron. Thus the already high concentrations of ferrous iron in the valley bottom are increased by the iron coming down the slope. A vast area in Andaman, including Island swamps and valleys, is also constrained with Fe-toxicity (Mandal and Roy 2000).

Srivastava *et al.* (2009) studied the response of lowland rice to iron toxicity at different slope position in West Africa. Their results showed that in 2006, effect of plot position was significant on grain yield. The plot situated on the upper slope registered 2.5 Mg ha^{-1} of grain yield, which was 21 per cent than yields from downward plots. The probable reason behind such an observation could be the significant higher nitrogen concentration on upper slope compared to that on lower slope and negative impact of iron toxicity on the growth of crop on the lower slope.

The same patterns of results were also observed in 2007 and 2008 (Fig. 9.2a and b). In these years, plots on upper slope registered significantly higher grain yield (34 and 45 per cent respectively) than that obtained from the down slope plots (Fig. 9.3).

This was because plots on the lower parts of the slope have iron concentration above the toxicity threshold level (500 ppm) in the rice leaves leading to reduced biomass development and yields. In the leaf, such quantities of iron cause increased production of radicals that can irreversibly damage cell structural components and cause an accumulation of polyphenylene oxides (Yamauchi and Peng 1993).

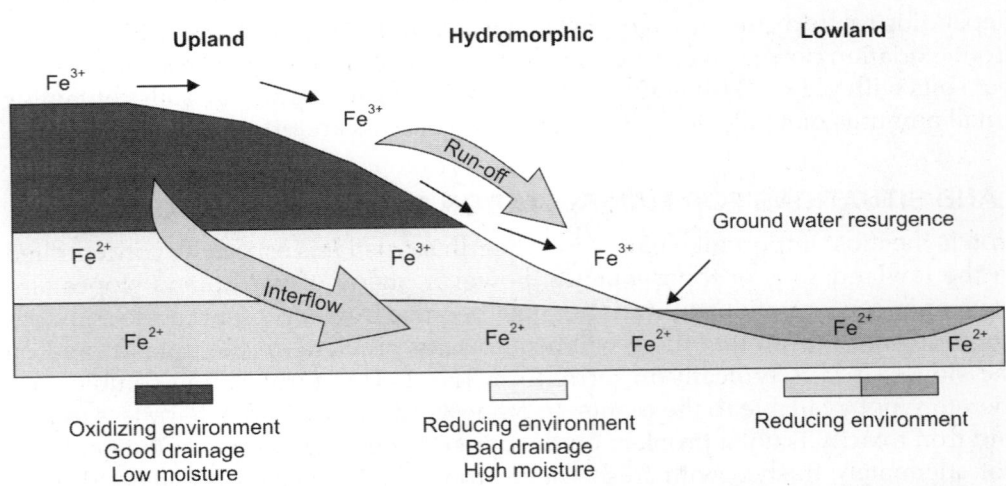

Fig. 9.1: Cross-section of toposequence showing movement of iron and reduction process

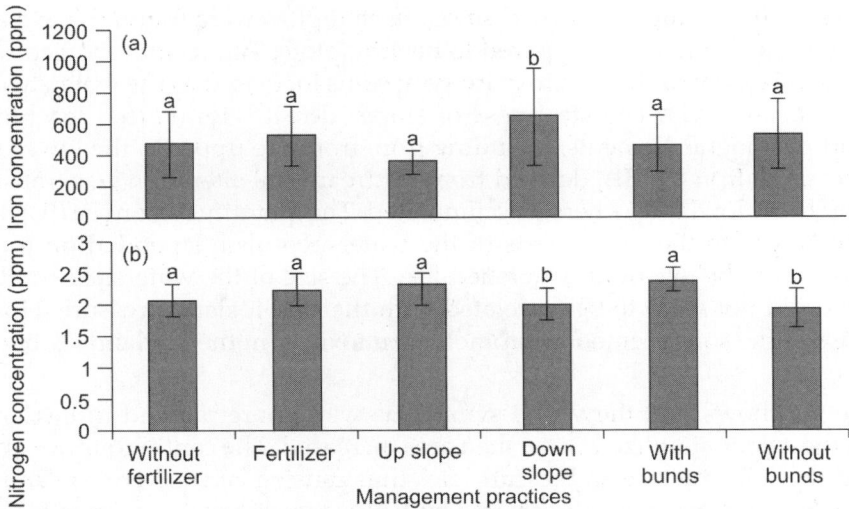

Fig. 9.2 (a) and (b): Fe and N concentrations in leaves of rice plant under different management practices (mean over two years, 2007 and 2008). Values with same letter within the group are not significantly different (p = 0.05).

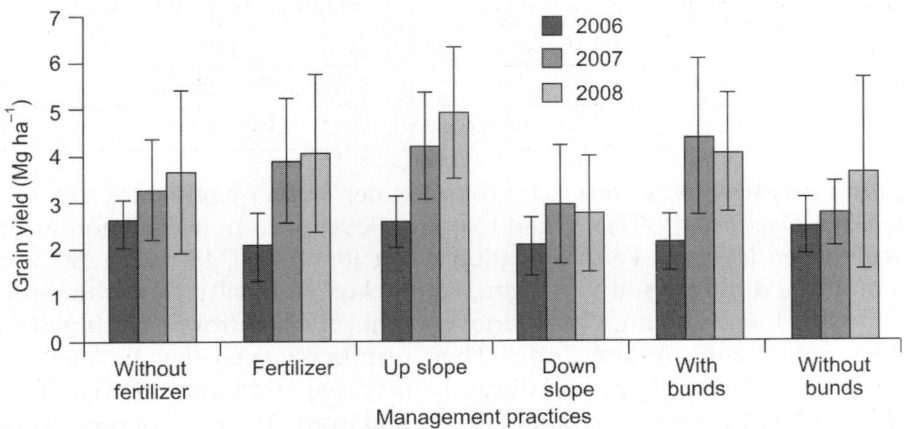

Fig. 9.3: Rice grain yield under different management practices over three growing seasons

A survey was conducted to quantify the effects of iron toxicity on rice in three countries (Guinea, Ivory Coast and Ghana) in the West African subregion (Chérif *et al.* 2009). It was confirmed that iron toxicity is a major edaphic constraint in cultivated lowlands as it affects more than 50 per cent of lowlands and about 60 per cent of cultivated rice plots on average. About 10 per cent of lowland crop fields were even abandoned due to high iron toxicity stress. Studies have also shown that more than 55 per cent of rice-growing areas are affected by excess iron. There is also a significant impact on yield since affected plots were found to have a mean 54 per cent lower yield as compared to healthy plots. The results showed that the visibility and extent of the iron toxicity symptoms increased as the watershed slope increased (Table 9.1). The steepness of slopes directly influenced leaching and transport of mineral elements, including iron, from the upper to the lower part of the watershed. Iron [Fe (II)] derived from upstream soil alteration was transported by runoff to the lowlands where it accumulated. The quantity of iron [Fe (II)] drained from the upper to the lower parts of the watershed also depended on the slope conditions and the extent of watershed use. The size of the watershed or the total area used did not seem to be correlated with the iron toxicity pressure. However, major use of the soils seemed to promote iron toxicity in the lowlands (Cherif *et al.* 2006).

Table 9.1 shows that the visual symptoms were more marked in lowland rice plots as the extent of utilized watershed area increased. The continuous use of slopes changed the soil structure and texture, etc., thus causing accrued erosion and Fe (II) leaching. Hence, steep slopes associated with high watershed use seemed to increase the iron toxicity risk in lowlands.

Table 9.1: *Iron toxicity intensity in lowlands as a function of the watershed slope and use*

Infection	High slopes (> 5%) (%)	Extent of watershed use (%)
Low	60	64
Medium	66	77
High	72	82

Long-term irrigation with iron rich ground water further aggravates iron toxicity in rice crop. Das *et al.* (1997) studied tolerance level of iron in irrigation water for rice with seven levels of Fe in irrigation water (0, 50, 100, 150, 200, 250 and 300 ppm) on three different soil types, *viz.* sandy clay loam, silty clay loam and clay each having a low and a high initial iron content collected from experimental field of RARS, Shillongani, Assam, India. Their results revealed that Fe levels in the irrigation water above 50 ppm significantly increased Fe concentration in the plant from 140.1 to 942.6 ppm at maximum tillering and from 216.9 to 905.4 ppm at harvest with 0 and 300 ppm Fe in irrigation water, respectively. Rice plants exhibited their tolerance to Fe in irrigation water only up to 50 ppm in all the soils except in light textured soils containing high initial iron content. In general iron toxicity symptoms in rice plant increased progressively with the increasing levels of iron in irrigation water. The severity of toxicity was very pronounced with higher Fe level in irrigation water and thus produced about 84.4 per cent sterile grain resulting in 82 per cent decrease in grain yield under 300 ppm Fe level (Table 9.2). Ahmed (1997) and Borah *et al.* (2000) also recorded similar effects in rice with increasing Fe levels in irrigation water in soil of Assam.

Table 9.2: *Effect of soil type (S), initial iron content (I) and Fe level in irrigation water on grain yield of rice (g pot^{-1}) var. Mahsuri)*

Fe level in irrigation water	Sandy clay loam		Silty clay loam		Clay		Mean
	I_1	I_2	I_1	I_2	I_1	I_2	
0	15.02	14.67	17.08	15.05	17.02	15.95	15.78
50	15.01	13.42	16.17	14.82	16.75	14.65	15.11
100	10.13	9.54	11.53	10.05	11.58	10.68	10.59
200	7.06	4.01	8.09	4.26	8.28	4.55	6.06
300	2.61	2.66	2.73	2.67	3.33	3.11	2.84
Mean	8.86	7.91	9.82	8.36	10.24	8.77	8.99
CD (P = 0.05)							
S	0.63			I		0.66	
Fe	0.68			S × I		NS	
Fe × S	NS			Fe × I		0.97	
Fe × S × I	1.43						

Source: Das *et al.* (1997).

SYMPTOMS OF IRON TOXICITY

Visual toxicity symptoms on plants, soil and plant tissue test are major diagnostic techniques for identifying iron toxicity (Fageria *et al.* 2008). Iron toxicity symptoms are manifested as tiny brown spots starting from the upper tips and spreading over the whole leaves causing the lower leaves to turn dark gray and die. The whole leaf becomes orange to brown or purple brown when the toxicity is severe (Fairhurst and Witt 2002). These symptoms commonly develop at the maximum tillering and heading growth stage, but may be observed at any growth stage of the rice crop. Symptoms of iron toxicity in tomato plants include yellowing stunted and delayed flowering (Albano *et al.*1996). These symptoms usually appear in more mature leaves. Equally important, the roots of rice plants affected by iron toxicity become stunted (ragged root system), coarse and reddish-brown or dark brown (a coating of iron oxide reduce root surface and decrease capacity to absorb soil nutrients) in color; with the alleviation of the stress, the roots may slowly recover to the usual white color. Figures 9.4–9.6 show iron toxicity symptoms in rice plant.

IRON TOXICITY TOLERANCE MECHANISMS

The possible tolerance mechanisms towards Fe-toxicity have been presented below. To make iron more available, plants have evolved various adaptation mechanisms

Fig. 9.4: Rice plant with iron toxicity symptoms in bronzed flag leaves and small panicles

Fig. 9.5: Iron toxicity symptoms in rice: (a) Tiny brown spots develop on the leaf tip and spread towards the lower base, (b) Leaves turn orange-brown and die, (c) Symptoms first appear on older leaves, (d) Under sever Fe-toxicity, the whole leaf surface is affected and (e) Panicle with bronzed leaf (left) compared to healthy panicle (right).

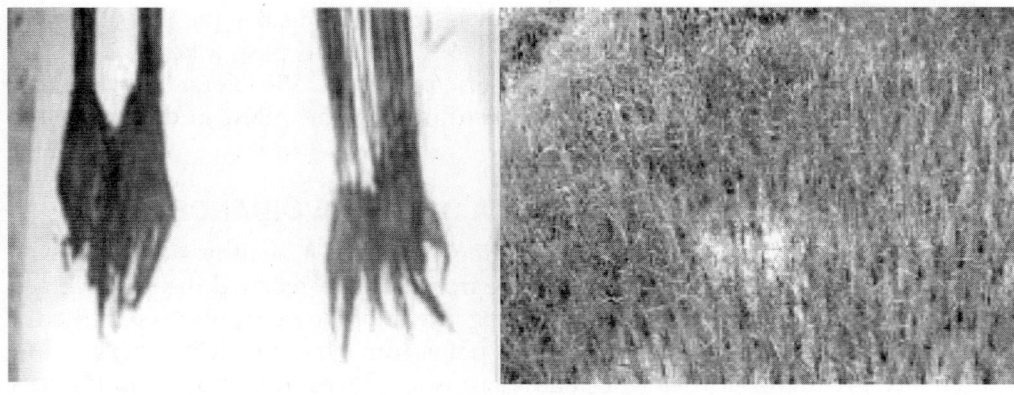

Fig. 9.6: Bushy brown roots and plants affected by iron toxicity

that mobilize iron at the root-soil interface (rhizosphere). The physiological status of a rice plant growing under submerged soil conditions greatly modifies its ability to tolerate high concentrations of Fe. Tadano (1975) suggested that three functions of rice roots were involved in counteracting Fe toxicity:

- Oxidation of Fe in the rhizosphere, which helps to keep Fe concentration low in the growth media.
- Iron-excluding power of the roots, which excludes Fe at the root surface and thus prevents Fe from entering the root.
- Iron retaining power of the roots, which retains Fe in the root tissue and thus decreases the translocation of Fe from the root to the shoot.

OXIDATION IN THE RHIZOSPHERE

Rice roots diffuse molecular oxygen into the root medium through air chambers and aerenchyma in the leaves, stems, nodes, and roots, which makes the rhizosphere more oxidative than the bulk growing media. Ferrous iron in soil solution is also oxidized to Fe (III), which can be seen as deposits on the surface of the rice roots. The oxidizing power of the rice roots is greater at the growing points and at the elongating parts of the roots than at the basal parts (Yoshida 1981). Under controlled conditions in pots, it was observed that the redox potential of soil solution was higher in pots with plants than without. The increase in redox potential was more prominent when plants were supplied with K than when K was not added. Thus it is concluded that rice roots maintain supplying rice plants with nutrients such as K (Tadano 1975) can further increase high redox potentials. Fe toxicity tolerant cultivars show superior performance under Fe toxic environment partly to avoidance (less iron accumulation in leaves) and tolerance (superior photosynthetic potential in the presence of absorbed iron in the leaves). The precipitation of Fe^{3+} hydroxide in the rhizosphere by healthy roots (indicated by reddish brown coatings on the roots).

Consequently, such roots prevent excessive Fe^{2+} uptake. In soils, the physiological status of the plant and particularly of the roots seems to play a key role in the control of types and intensities of rhizospheric processes. Vice versa the chemical properties of the soil determine the physiology of the plant and the proper functioning of the root system.

IRON EXCLUDING POWER OR PHYSIOLOGICAL AVOIDANCE

Tadano (1976) reported that the Fe-excluding power of a healthy rice plant was 87 per cent, implying that 87 per cent of the iron that had reached the root surface by mass flow was excluded. The Fe-excluding power of the rice roots was markedly decreased by respiratory inhibitors such as potassium cyanide (KCN) and sodium azide (NaN_3). The iron-tolerant rice cultivar absorbed less iron or transported less from roots to leaves, indicating the presence of a physiological avoidance (Audebert and Sahrawat 2000). Further they reported that physiological avoidance mechanisms can be enhanced through application of nutrients (P, K and Zn).

IRON RETAINING POWER OF THE ROOTS

Similarly, the ability of rice roots to retain Fe by reduced translocation of absorbed Fe from root to shoot can affect plant tolerance to Fe. The Fe-retaining power of the rice roots is inversely related to the translocation percentage, i.e. the amount of Fe translocated to the shoot relative to the total amount of Fe absorbed by the plant. Salts such as sodium chloride and respiratory inhibitors decrease the Fe-retaining power of the root (Tadano 1981). The nutritional status of the plant, especially with regard to Ca, Mg, K, Mn, and P, greatly modifies the rice roots' Fe-excluding and Fe-retaining power. The role of K in Fe toxicity has been suggested to be very important because K is not only involved in exclusion of Fe, but also in its translocation from roots to shoots (Yamauchi 1989, Tadano 1981).

ABILITY TO TOLERATE HIGH IRON CONCENTRATION

Another mechanism is involved in which the rice plant is able to tolerate a high concentration of Fe in the tissue. For example, Jayawardena *et al.* (1977) tested 17 tropical rice varieties for their tolerance to Fe toxicity, Fe content in plant tissue and Fe-oxidizing power of roots. They found that the majority of the tolerant varieties contained a high concentration of Fe in the plant tissues and this led them to suggest that the varietal tolerance for Fe toxicity is a degree of tolerance for excess Fe rather than a mechanism of resisting the entry of Fe into roots.

ENZYMATIC OXIDATION

Enzymatic oxidation of Fe was found to be the principal mechanisms for higher oxidation activity of rice roots (Armstrong 1969). Root oxidation power includes the excretion of O_2 (transported from the shoot to the root through aerenchyma) from roots and oxidation mediated by enzymes such as peroxidase or catalase.

Glycolic acid pathway present in the rice root system was reported to be chiefly for the root oxidation power in addition to catalase and peroxidase enzymes (Mitsui *et al.* 1962). Rice cv. TRC229-F41 (*Oryza Oryza rupipogon* and *Oryza sativa*) with higher glycolic acid oxidase and leaf nitrate reductase activities were found to be more tolerant to the adverse effects of higher concentration of Fe (Nath and Borah 1999). Hu *et al.* (1997) observed that Fe stress significantly increased the activities of ascorbate peroxidase, dehydroascorbate reductase, glutathione dehydrogenase (ascorbate) and glutathione reductase. Activities of ascorbate peroxidase, dehydroascorbate reductase, glutathione dehydrogenase (ascorbate) and glutathione reductase in the tolerant lines were higher than those in sensitive lines and significantly negatively correlated with a relative decrease in shoot dry weight. Thus, they concluded that the ascorbate-specific H_2O_2 scavenging system may play an important role in the detoxification of Fe toxicity in rice.

NUTRITIONAL INTERACTION

Iron toxicity is a complex nutrient disorder and the deficiencies of other nutrients, especially phosphorus (P), potassium (K), calcium (Ca), magnesium (Mg), and zinc (Zn), are considered to affect its incidence (Ottow *et al.* 1983, Tanaka *et al.* 1966, Yamauchi 1989). Other nutrients may play an important role not only in reducing the effect of iron toxicity but also in the expression of iron tolerance by various rice cultivars (Sahrawat *et al.* 1996, Sahrawat 2004). Deficiencies of P, K, Ca, Mg, and manganese (Mn) decrease the iron-excluding power of rice roots and can thus affect the rice plant's tolerance of iron toxicity (Yoshida 1981, Sahrawat 2004). Sahrawat *et al.* (2001) showed that applications of N, P, K and Zn in various combinations reduced iron toxicity and increased yields of iron tolerant and susceptible rice cultivars. The increase in grain yields of iron-susceptible cultivars was more than that of iron tolerant cultivars. Silica also alleviates Fe-toxicity by promoting Fe^{2+} oxidation by the roots, resulting in the deposition of iron oxides on the root surface. Silica treated rice plants had lower Fe contents in the shoots and higher Fe contents in the roots than untreated plants (Okuda and Takahashi 1965).

A high concentration of iron in soil solution can cause nutrient imbalance through antagonistic effects on the uptake of nutrients, including K and Zn. The deficiency or lack of availability of other nutrients can also affect the rice plant's ability to decrease uptake of iron in the tops through physiological functions carried out by roots such as iron oxidation, iron exclusion, and iron retention (Yoshida 1981, Audebert and Sahrawat 2000, Sahrawat 2004). Thus, it is not entirely surprising that the application of other nutrients reduces iron toxicity and improves yield of rice on iron-toxic soils. Several reports show that applications of nutrients such as P, K and Zn reduce iron toxicity, improve growth and increase rice yield (Sahrawat *et al.* 2001, Nayak *et al.* 2004, Sahrawat 2004). Sahrawat *et al.* (2001) showed that applications of N, P, K and Zn in various combinations reduced iron toxicity and increased yields of iron tolerant and susceptible rice cultivars. The increase in grain yields of iron-susceptible cultivars was more than that of iron tolerant cultivars (Table 9.3).

Table 9.3: *Effects of field applications of nutrients on grain yield of iron-tolerant (CK 4) and susceptible (Bouake 189 and TOX 3069-66-2-1-6) rice cultivars on an iron-toxic soil at Korhogo, Côte d'Ivoire (1995–98).*[a]

Treatment	Grain yield (t ha^{-1})		
	CK 4	**Bouake 189**	**TOX 3069-66-2-1-6**
No fertilizer	4.3 (3)[b]	3.4 (5)	2.9 (7)
N	4.4 (3)	4.1 (5)	3.3 (7)
N + P	5.3 (2)	4.3 (4)	4.2 (5)
N + K	4.8 (2)	4.4 (4)	3.8 (5)
N + Zn	4.8 (2)	4.6 (4)	4.6 (5)
N + P + Zn	5.0 (2)	4.4 (4)	4.2 (4)
N + K + Zn	5.2 (2)	4.6 (3)	4.6 (4)
N + P + K	5.4 (2)	4.5 (3)	4.5 (3)
N + P + K + Zn	5.7 (2)	4.7 (3)	4.7 (3)
LSD (0.05)	1.01	1.02	1.15

[a] The data are an average of four years (1995–98). All cultivars received a uniform application of N (100 kg ha^{-1}), P (50 kg ha^{-1}), K (80 kg ha^{-1}) and Zn (10 kg ha^{-1}).

[b] Iron toxicity scores are given in parentheses on a scale of 1 to 9, where 1 = normal growth and 9 = most plants are dead or drying.

Source: Sahrawat *et al.* (2001).

Benckiser *et al.* (1984) studied the effect of N, P, K, Ca and Mg fertilization on the performance of rice grown in pots using an Fe-toxic soil and a non Fe-toxic soil. They found that dehydrogenase activity, the number of nitrogen fixing, Fe-reducing bacteria, and Fe (II) production and the uptake of Fe by rice decreased with increased supply of K, Ca and Mg. This effect was clearer with the rice variety 'IR 22', which is susceptible to Fe toxicity compared to the relatively tolerant variety 'IR 42'. Data on the effects of plant nutrients on Fe uptake at maximum tillering stage by 'IR 22' and 'IR 42' rice plant tops (Table 9.4) showed that the application of K, Ca and Mg together greatly reduced Fe uptake and accumulation compared to the control. A low supply of other plant nutrients and high Fe supply in a growth chamber experiment increased exudation (a measure of metabolic root leakage) and Fe uptake by rice variety 'IR 36'. It was concluded that nutritional conditions, exudation by rice roots, and the Fe reducing activity of the rhizosphere were clearly related to Fe uptake by wetland rice. It was further concluded that Fe toxicity in wetland rice is a physiological disorder caused by multiple nutritional soil stress rather than by a low pH and high Fe supply *per se*.

Table 9.4: *Effects of nutrients on iron uptake in 'IR 22' and 'IR 42' rice plants grown in pots with an iron-toxic soil. Relative iron uptake (%) over control at 6 weeks after transplanting (Benckiser et al.1984)*

Treatment[a]	IR 22	IR 42
N	124	115
P	179	125
K	97	115
Ca + Mg	93	77
K + Ca + Mg	91	88

[a] Soil was fertilized with 100 mg N kg^{-1} as urea, 500 mg P kg^{-1} as ammonium phosphate, 100 mg K kg^{-1} as KCl, 50 mg Ca kg^{-1} as $CaCO_3$, and 20 mg kg^{-1} of soil as $MgCl_2$

BREEDING FOR IRON STRESS TOLERANCE

Selection and breeding to improve the tolerance for Fe^{2+} has two prerequisites: (i) a selection parameter that is straight forward to measure and a reliable indicator of specific mechanisms for the tolerance and (ii) understanding of the genetic basis for this tolerance mechanisms. The degree of leaf bronzing has been suggested as a good measure of the degree of toxicity ('IRRI 1965', 'Ota 1968') but little is known about the genetic basis for tolerance mechanisms associated with degree of bronzing. Molecular marker technology makes it possible to investigate the genetic basis of both single gene and polygenic traits and to locate and manipulate individual genetic factors and epistasis interactions underlying the traits of interest (Tanksley 1983). Inheritance of Fe toxicity tolerance in rice was found to be simple. Two different genes (dominant and recessive) were reported to govern Fe toxicity tolerance in rice genotypes (Abifarin 1989). Camargo (1985) reported partial dominance of Fe toxicity tolerance in wheat, with high broad sense heritability. Gorsline *et al.* (1964) found that the additive gene action was more important in maize. Nipah *et al.* (1997) found that the most genes responsible for tolerance of Fe toxicity were dominant, but epistemic effects were also observed.

Genetic differences in adaptation to and tolerance for iron toxic soil conditions have indeed been exploited for developing rice cultivars with tolerance for iron toxicity (Gunawardena *et al.* 1982, De Datta *et al.* 1994). Breeding and screening efforts at the International Rice Research Institute in the Philippines and at WARDA (West Africa Rice Development Association) in Côte d'Ivoire have identified a number of rice cultivars for growing in iron-toxic soils (De Datta *et al.* 1994, Sahrawat 2004).

Sahrawat *et al.* (1996) evaluated 20 lowland rice cultivars for tolerance of iron toxicity at an iron-toxic site in Korhogo, Côte d'Ivoire, under irrigated conditions. The cultivars differed in tolerance of iron toxicity. Grain yields varied from 0.10 to 5.04 t ha^{-1} and iron toxicity scores, based on the extent of bronzing symptoms on foliage, ranged from 1 to 9 (1: indicates normal growth and 9: indicates that most plants are dead or dying). Further, evaluation of rice cultivars during 1992–97 showed that, among three promising iron-tolerant cultivars, 'CK 4' was the top yielder (mean grain yield 5.33 t ha⁻¹), followed by 'WITA 1' (4.96 t ha⁻¹) and 'WITA 3' (4.46 t ha⁻¹), and tolerant check 'Suakoko 8' (3.80 t ha⁻¹) (Table 9.5). These and other results suggest that high rice yields and iron toxicity tolerance are physiologically compatible (Sahrawat *et al.* 2000, Audebert and Sahrawat 2000).

Table 9.5: *Grain yields (t ha⁻¹) of WITA 1 and WITA 3 rice cultivars during 1992–97 relative to the performance of iron-tolerant ('Suakoko 8' and 'CK 4') and iron-susceptible (Bouake 189) check cultivars under irrigated conditions in the wet season at an iron-toxic site in Korhogo, Côte d'Ivoire.*[a]

Year	CK 4	WITA 1	WITA 3	Bouake 189	Suakoko 8	LSD (0.05)
1992	–	4.33	5.04	2.87	4.85	1.080
1993	5.87	5.53	5.17	4.08	5.07	0.630
1994	6.05	6.66	4.30	4.69	3.73	1.100
1996	3.76	3.24	3.21	2.81	2.57	0.760
1997	5.63	5.02	4.59	4.99	2.79	1.345
Mean	5.33	4.96	4.46	3.88	3.80	

[a] Each season, all cultivars received a uniform application of 100 kg N ha⁻¹, 50 kg P ha⁻¹, and 10 kg Zn ha⁻¹.
Source: Sahrawat *et al.* (2000).

Work done at WARDA in West Africa showed that some *Oryza glaberrima* cultivars, adapted to lowland rice-growing conditions, possess a higher tolerance for iron toxicity than their *O. sativa* counterparts. Sahrawat and Sika (2002) conducted experiments at an iron-toxic site (Korhogo, Côte d'Ivoire) during the 2000 wet and dry seasons to evaluate the performance of promising *O. sativa* (CK 4, tolerant check; 'Bouake 189', susceptible check) and *O. glaberrima* (CG 14) cultivars. While 'CK 4' and 'Bouake 189' showed typical iron toxicity symptoms in varying degrees, 'CG 14' plants did not show any iron toxicity symptoms at all as measured by iron toxicity scores. Although 'CG 14' did not give high grain yields because of its lower harvest index, lodging of the crop, especially under the application of nutrients, and shattering of seeds at maturity, it showed remarkable tolerance for iron toxicity. Research shows that 'CG 14' has a high tolerance for iron toxicity and remains an obvious choice as a donor for iron tolerance in breeding programs (Sahrawat and Sika 2002, Sahrawat 2004).

Tissue tolerance for Fe toxicity in rice was considered to be an important parameter for genetic studies. Wu *et al.* (1998) mapped the QTLs by using a double haploid population, which revealed that Fe toxicity tolerance as measured by the leaf bronzing index (LBI) was associated with two loci of chromosome 1. Results revealed that Fe-toxicity tolerance is located on two loci of chromosome 1 based on single marker loci and interval mapping analysis. The first gene locus was flanked by RG 345 and RG 381 which showed 31 per cent of the total variation in leaf bronzing index across populations and second gene locus flanked by RG 810 and RG 331 which explained 16 per cent variation. The first gene locus was found to be associated with Fe-induced enzyme glutathione-S-reductase involve in ascorbate-specific H_2O_2 scavenging system. The second gene locus was also detected for the variation in total iron content in plants. Wan *et al.* (2005) were detected 20 QTLs for LBI, PH and MRL under the Fe^{2+} stress over 10 of the 12 rice chromosomes, reflecting multigenic control of these traits.

In rice, 96 populations of backcross inbred lines (BILs) derived from a Nippobare (japonica) × Kasalath (indica) for molecular mapping (Wan *et al.* 2003). Fe toxicity tolerance was measured by leaf bronzing index, stem dry weight, tiller number and root dry weight under Fe stress conditions. They identified four QTLs on chromosome 1 and 3. The QTLs were located at the region of C955-C885 on chromosome 1 and their contributions to whole variations were 20.5 per cent, 36.9 per cent, 43.9 per cent and 38.8 per cent for LBI, SDW, TN and RDW respectively. The QTL located at the region of C955-C885 on chromosome 1 may be important to ferrous iron-toxicity tolerance in rice. Another QTL for SDW and RDW was located at the region of C25-C515 on chromosome 3 with respective contributions of 47.9 per cent and 35 per cent to whole variations. Further Two QTLs on chromosome 1 were located for RDW at the region of R2329-R210 and for TN at the region of R1928-C178.

A QTL analysis for iron-toxicity tolerance was conducted by Shimizu (2009) in rice. Bronzing scores, which are regarded as an index of sensitivity to iron toxicity, were converted to digital data *via* a scanner and quantified to parametric data using chromaticity coordinates. On the basis of quantified score, QTL analysis for bronzing tolerance was conducted using F_3 lines from a cross between a japonica cultivar 'Gimbozu' (tolerant) and an indica cultivar 'Kasalath' (susceptible). A single QTL near RM221 marker on chromosome 2 was detected by composite interval mapping and additional five QTL were detected by multiple interval mapping. These QTL explained 99 per cent of the total phenotypic variance and they will be used to develop tolerant varieties.

Molecular marker loci associated with variations in index values and in relative decrease in shoot dry weight (RDSDW), and gene loci for tolerance were detected using 175 markers mapped on all 12 chromosomes by single marker loci and interval mapping (Wu *et al.* 1997). Two gene loci were identified as flanked by RG345 and RG381 and linked to RG810 respectively, on chromosome 1 for index value and RDSDW. These explained 32 and 13 per cent of the total variation in the index values and 15 and 21 per cent in the RDSDW in the population respectively. The variation in RDSDW was also explained by a locus linked to RG978 on chromosome 8 by about 10 per cent.

Cell and tissue culture techniques have been successfully used to develop NaCl tolerant lines in tobacco, wheat and oats. A similar approach may also help in obtaining genotypes with higher level of tolerance to Fe-toxicity.

CONCLUSION

The intensified use of iron-toxic wetlands in the future is inevitable for meeting the food needs of the ever-growing population in tropical regions, where iron-toxic soils are an important natural resource for food production. Iron toxicity can be reduced by using iron-tolerant cultivars and by applying other nutrients whose availability is negatively affected by a high concentration of iron in soil solution. An integrated use of tolerant genotypes and improved soil and nutrient management is more practical for sustainable increases in productivity.

REFERENCES

Abifarin AO. 1989. Progress in breeding for tolerance to iron toxicity. Annual Report, 1989, p34–39. West Africa Rice Development Association Bouake, Cote d'Ivoire.

Ahmed S. 1997. Effect of levels of iron in irrigation water and organic matter treatment on the yield and uptake of nutrients by rice plants. MSc. (Agric.) Thesis, Assam Agricultural University, Jorhat, Assam.

Albano JP, Miller WB and Halbrooks MC. 1996. Iron toxicity stress causes bronze speckle, a specific physiological disorder of Marigold (*Tagates erecta* L.). *J. Am. Soc. Hort. Sci.* **121:** 430–437.

Armstrong W. 1969. Rizhosphere in rice: An analysis of intervarietal difference in oxygen flux from the root. *Physiol. Plant.* **59:** 285–291.

Audebert A and Sahrawat KL. 2000. Mechanisms for iron toxicity tolerance in lowland rice. *J. Plant Nutr.* **23:** 1877–1885.

Barbosa Filho MP, Fageria NK and Stone LF. 1983. Water management and liming in relation to grain yield and iron toxicity. *Pes. Agro. Brasi.* **18:** 903–910.

Becker M and Asch F. 2005. Iron toxicity in rice-condition and management concepts. *J. Plant Nutr. Soil Sci.* **168:** 558–573.

Benckiser G, Santiago S, Neue HU, Watanabe I and Ottow JCG. 1984. Effect of fertilization on exudation, dehydrogenase activity, iron-reducing populations and Fe (1I) formation in the rizosphere of rice (*Oryza sativa* L.) in relation to iron toxicity. *Plant Soil.* **79:** 305–316.

Borah N, Das KN, Bordoiloi PK and Goswami J. 2000. Effect of added iron in irrigation water on iron content of rice plant in relation to soil iron and clay content. *Ann. Agri Bio. Res.* **5:** 15–18.

Breemen NV and Moormann FR. 1978. Iron-toxic soils. In *Soils and Rice*, p781–800. (Ed). International Rice Research Institute,. Los B⁻anos, Philippines.

Camargo CEDO. 1985. Genetic studies of tolerance to iron toxicity in wheat. *Bragantia.* **44:** 87–96.

Chérif M, Audebert A, Fofana M and Zouzou M. 2009. Evaluation of iron toxicity on lowland irrigated rice in West Africa, *Tropicultura.* **27:** 88–92.

Cherif M, Fofana M, Audebert A and Zouzou M. 2006. Significant aspects of iron toxicity in West Africa, p141–148. Audebert A, Narteh LT, Kiepe P, Millar D and Beks B (Eds), In Iron Toxicity in Rice-basedSystems in West Africa, Africa Rice Center (WARDA), Cotonou, Benin.

Das KN, Bordoiloi PK and Bora N. 1997. Tolerance level of iron in irrigation water for rice crop. *Int. J. Trop. Agric.* **15**: 159–166.

De Datta SK, Neue HU, Senadhira D and Quijano C. 1994. Success in rice improvement for poor soils. In Proceedings of the workshop on adaptation of plants to soil stresses, p248–268, University of Nebraska, Lincoln, Nebraska. INTSORMIL Publication No. 94–2. Lincoln, Nebraska (USA): University of Nebraska.

Dobermann A and Fairhurst T. 2000. Rice: Nutrient disorders and nutrient management, p191. Handbook series. Potash and Phosphate Institute (PPI), Potash & Phosphate Institute of Canada (PPIC) and International Rice Research Institute, phillipines, Manils.

Dorlodot S, Lutts S and Bertin P. 2005. Effects of ferrous iron toxicity on the growth and mineral composition of and interspecific rice. *J. Plant Nutr.* **28**: 1–20.

Fageria NK 1984. Fertilization and mineral nutrition of rice. Goîania/Rio de Janeiro, Brazil: EMBRAPA-CNPAF/Editora Campus.

Fageria NK and Rabelo NA. 1987. Tolerance of rice cultivars to iron toxicity. *J. Plant Nutr.* **10**: 653–661.

Fageria NK, Santos AB, Barbosa Filho MP and Guimar̄aes CM. 2008. Iron toxicity in lowland rice. *J. Plant Nutr.* **31**: 1676–1697.

Fageria NK, Stone LF and Santos AB. 2003b. Fertility management of irrigated rice. Santo Antônio de Goiás, Goiás, Brazil: Embrapa Arroz e Feij̄aodoi: 10.1023/A:1023915710103.

Fairhurst TH and C Witt. 2002. Rice: A practical guide to nutrient management. International Rice Research Institute, Philippine, Manila.

Genon JG, de Hepcee N, Duffey JE, Delvaux B and Hennebert PA. 1994. Iron toxicity and other chemical soil constraints to rice in highland swamps of Burundi. *Plant Soil.* **166**: 109–115.

Gorsline GW, Thomas WI and Baker DE. 1964. Inheritance of P, K, Mg, Cu, B, Zn, Mn, Al and Fe concentrations by corn (*Zea mays* L.) leaves and grains. *Crop Sci.* **4**: 207–210.

Gunawardena I, Virmani SS and Sumo FJ. 1982. Breeding rice for tolerance to iron toxicity. *Oryza.* **19**: 5–12.

Hu B, Zhu J, Wu Y, Luo A and Wu P. 1997. Effect of POD on tolerance to ferrous iron toxicity in rice (English abstract). *J. Zhejiang Agric. Univ.* **23**: 557–560.

International Rice Research Institute 1965. Annual Report, 1964, p335. Los Banos, Philippines.

Jayawardena SDG, Watabe T and Tanaka K. 1977. Relation between root oxidizing power and resistance to iron toxicity. *Rep. Crop Sci. Soc. Breed.* Kinki, Japan, **22**: 38–47.

Mandal AB and Roy B. 2000. Development of Fe tolerant rice somaclones through *in vitro* screening, p356. In 4th Intl. Rice Genet Symp (IRRI, Philippines).

Marshner H. 1995. Mineral nutrition of higher plants, 2nd edition; Academic Press: London.

Mengel K and Kirkby E. 1987. Principles of plant nutrition, p685. International Potash Institute.

Mitsui S, Kumazawa K, Varaki J, Hirala H and Ishizuka K. 1962. Dynamic aspects of NPK uptake and oxygen secretion in relation to the metabolic path ways within the plant roots, *Soil Sci. Plant Nutr.* **8:** 25–30.

Nath T and Borah RC. 1999. Effect of application of iron on glycolic acid oxidase and nitrate reductase in rice. *Oryza.* **36:** 167–168.

Nayak SC, Sahu SK, Mishra GC and Sandha B. 2004. Comparison of different amendments for alleviating iron toxicity in rice. *Int. Rice Res. Notes.* **29:** 51–53.

Nipah JO, Jones MP, Singh BN, Kantaka OS and Sahrawat KL. 1997. Screening for tolerance for iron toxicity. *Int. Rice Res. Notes.* **22:** 26–27.

Okuda A and Takahashi E. 1965. The role of silicon. The mineral nutrition of the rice plant, p123–146. In International Rice Research Institute, phillipines, Johns Hopkins Press, Baltimore, Maryland.

Ota Y. 1968. Studies on the occurrence of the physiological disease called 'bronzing'.Bull. *Natl Inst Agric Sci* (Japan). **18:** 31–104.

Ottow JCG, Benckiser G, Watanabe I and Santiago S. 1983. Multiple nutrient stress as the prerequisite for iron toxicity of wetland rice (*Oryza sativa* L.). *Trop. Agric.* (Trinidad). **60:** 102–106.

Ponnamperuma FN. 1972. The chemistry of submerged soils. *Adv. Agron.* **24:** 29–96.

Ponnamperuma FN. 1976. Specific soil chemical characteristics for rice production in Asia. International Rice Research Institute, Manila, Philippines. IRRI Res. Paper Ser. 2.

Prasad RN and Biswas PP. 2000. Land resources in sustainable agricultural development. *Indian Farming.* **49:** 9–13.

Sahrawat KL. 2004. Iron toxicity in wetland rice and the role of other nutrients. *J. Plant Nutr.* **27:** 1471–1504.

Sahrawat KL. 2005. Managing iron toxicity in lowland rice: The role of tolerant genotypes and plant nutrients. Rice is life: Scientific perspectives for the 21st century. In Proceedings of the world rice research conference, p452–454. Toriyama K, Heong KLand Hardy B (Eds.), Tsukuba, Japan.

Sahrawat KL, Diatta S and Singh BN. 2000. Reducing iron toxicity in lowland rice through an integrated use of tolerant genotypesand plant nutrient management. *Oryza.* **37:** 44–47.

Sahrawat KL, Diatta S and Singh BN. 2001. Nutrient application reduces iron toxicity in lowland rice in West Africa, p51–52. *IRRN* 26.2 Soil, nutrient, and water management.

Sahrawat KL, Mulbah CK, Diatta S, DeLaune RD, Patrick WH Jr, Singh BN and Jones MP. 1996. The role of tolerant genotypes and plant nutrients in the management of iron toxicity in lowland rice. *J. Agric. Sci.* **126:** 143–146.

Sahrawat KL and Sika M. 2002. Comparative tolerance of *Oryza sativa* and *O. glaberrima* rice cultivars for iron toxicity in West Africa. *Int. Rice Res. Notes.* **27:** 30–31.

Sahu BN. 1968. Bronzing disease of rice in Orissa as influenced by soil types and manuring and its control. *J. Indian Soc. Soil Sci.* **16:** 41–54.

Shimizu A. 2009. QTL analysis of genetic tolerance to iron toxicity in rice (*Oryza Sativa* L.) by quantification of bronzing score. *J. New Seeds.* **10:** 171–179.

Srivastava AK, Kanninko C and Gaiser T. 2009. Response of lowland rice to iron toxicity at different slope positions: A case study in Upper Oueme Basin, Benin Republic. *Agric. J.* **4:** 226–230.

Tadano T. 1975. Devices of rice roots to tolerate high iron concentrations in growth media. *JARQ.* **9:** 34–39.

Tanado T. 1976. Studies on the methods to prevent iron toxicity in lowland rice. Mem. Fac. Agric. Hokkaido Univ. **10:** 22–68.

Tanaka A, Loe R and Navasero SA. 1966. Some mechanisms involved in the development of iron toxicity symptoms in the rice plant. *Soil Sci. Plant Nutr.* **12:** 32–38.

Tanaka A and Yamaguchi K. 1973. A note on the nutritional status of the rice plant in Italy, Portugal, and Spain. *Soil Sci. Plant Nutr.* **19:** 161–171.

Tanksley SD. 1993. Mapping polygenes. *Annu. Rev. Genet.* **27:** 205–233.

Thongbai P and Goodman BA. 2000. Free radical generation and post-anoxic injury in rice grown in an iron-toxic soil. *J. Plant Nutr.* **23:** 1887–1900.

Wan J, Zhai H, Wan J and Ikehashi H. 2003. Detection and analysis of QTLs for ferrous iron toxicity tolerance in rice, *Oryza sativa* L. *Euphytica.* **131:** 201–206

Wan SC, Basten J and Zeng ZB. 2005. Windows QTL Cartographer 2.5. Raleigh: Department of Statistics, North Carolina State University. http://statgen.ncsu.edu/qtlcart/WQTLCart.htm.

Wu P, Hu B, Liao CY, Zhu JM, Wu YR, Senadhira D and Paterson AH. 1998. Characterization of tissue tolerance to iron by molecular markers in different lines of rice. *Plant Soil.* **203:** 217–226.

Wu P, Ni J, Luo A, Jin G and Tao Q. 1997. Investigation of QTLs underlying rice tolerance for potassium deficiency *via* molecular markers. *Plant Nutr Fert. Sci.* **3:** 209–217.

Yamauchi M. 1989. Rice bronzing in Nigeria caused by nutrient imbalances and its control by potassium sulfate application. *Plant Soil.* **117:** 275–286.

Yamauchi M and Peng XX. 1993. Ethylene production in rice bronzing leaves induced by ferrous iron. *Plant Soil.* **149:** 227–234.

Yamauchi M and Peng XX. 1995. Iron toxicity and stress-induced ethylene production in rice leaves. *Plant Soil.* **173:** 21–28.

Yoshida S. 1981. Fundamentals of rice crop science. Manila (Philippines): International Rice Research Institute. p269.

10

Soil Amendments to Increase the Productivity of Acid Soils

Patiram

ABSTRACT

Generally, lime is used for the amendment of acid soils to increase the productivity of crops to overcome the acidity stress. The application of agricultural liming materials increases the soil pH and decreases soil acidity and frequently alleviates the problems of soil infertility stresses of harmful elements. Agricultural liming materials contain compounds of carbonates, hydroxides, or oxides of calcium and magnesium. The lime requirement (LR) of acidic soils is generally determined by buffer solutions to raise the desired pH by liming materials. The field experiments conducted on acidic soils revealed that the optimum yield of crops can be obtained on acidic soils lime rates based on either 25 per cent of LR determined by buffer methods or 1–2.5 equivalent of exchangeable Al. The above optimum rate of lime application is found to be sufficient for two years in high rainfall areas and thereafter half rate of lime is needed to sustain the productivity. The furrow application lime of 1/10th to 1/20th of LR to each crop is equally effective to increase the productivity of crops at par with 25 per cent lime of LR. It has also been found that the continuous application of organic manure to every crop can eliminate Al-toxicity on Al-toxic soils and yield can be further increased by the application of lime. Therefore, most of the farmers of northeast India take the good crop of maize around their settlements because they recycle the organic matter in these areas from their animals and house refuse. Northeast India has a vast reserve of limestone totaling about 6,686 million metric tonnes, which can be utilized to amend the acidic soils for increasing the crops productivity.

Key words: Acid soils, productivity, soil amendments.

INTRODUCTION

In general amendment usually includes those substances that enhance any or all of the physical, biological, and nutritional properties of soil. There are two categories of amendments, organic and inorganic. The organic amendments are made from natural products. The common organic amendments are animal manures, sphagnum peat, crop residues, sawdust, compost, sewage sludge and industrial wastes such as press mud from sugarcane and paper sludge. The inorganic amendments are man made and they include chemicals that are used for making the soil fertile, e.g. lime, gypsum, etc. Soil amendments keep the soil tillable, fertile, and chemically and biologically healthy. Amendments generally do not degrade the soil and their values are often long-term. Technically fertilizers are soil amendments but conventionally they are not referred as amendment.

As the soil pH drops below 5.0, toxic forms of Al become soluble into the soil solution, interfering with a wide range of physical and cellular processes resulting in the inhibition of root growth and function and thus reducing crop yields. Soils are becoming more acidic by certain farming practices, e.g. the application of ammonium-based fertilizers, and accumulation of organic matter. The adverse effects of soil acidity can be solved either by addition of lime to counteracts the anomalies of such soils or to manipulate the agricultural practices to obtain optimum crops production. The high level of Al in acid soil leads to soil infertility was demonstrated during the early part of twentieth century and effects of liming were very often due to elimination of Al-toxicity (Hartwell and Pember 1918, Conner 1921). Crops such as maize, beans, soybean, wheat, barley, oilseeds, cotton, etc. do not grow well in the acid soils because of their high sensitivity to acidity and productivity of these crops suffer too much. The application of lime has been advocated to farmers around the world to combat the problems. The later approach includes breeding and selecting cultivars of crops and pasturing grasses that can grow well with the existing soil conditions. However, it offers a temporary solution, because growing tolerant crops continuously may aggravate the acid conditions severely. It is the tendency of farmers to plant the best-adopted crops and follow the cropping pattern to vary somewhat with acidity of the soil. The liming of acid soils periodically, replenishes the calcium and magnesium and neutralizes the soil acidity and other toxic nutrients to plants.

LIMING AND NEUTRALIZATION OF SOIL ACIDITY

The application of agricultural liming materials (commonly referred to as lime) to acidic soils, increases soil pH and decreases soil acidity and frequently alleviates the problems of soil infertility stresses without addition of harmful elements. Agricultural liming materials contain compounds of carbonates, hydroxides, or oxides of calcium and magnesium. Liming materials include limestone, burned lime, marl, dolomitic lime, oyster shells, basic slag, cement plant flue dust, mining tailings, sugarcane press mud, wood ashes, and paper mill lime sludge. It can be categorized into carbonates, oxides, hydroxides, and by-product materials. If a soil is low in magnesium, dolomitic lime should be used; otherwise calcic lime can be used.

The anions of these compounds neutralize the hydrogen ions in solution and on the exchange sites of soil colloids and remove toxic materials from solution by precipitation. The reaction of calcite ($CaCO_3$) in acid soil occurs by the following reaction:

$$CaCO_3 + H_2O \longrightarrow Ca^{2+} + 2OH^- + HCO_3^-$$

The Ca^{2+} (Ca^{2+} and Mg^{2+} in dolomite) helps to displace the H^+ and Al^{3+} from the exchange sites, and OH ions react to neutralize the acidic components by the following reactions:

$$Al^{3+} + 3OH^- \longrightarrow Al(OH)_3$$
$$OH^- + H^+ \longrightarrow H_2O$$

Neutralization is the function of the reaction of the limestone or with the carbonate or hydroxides formed by the dissolution of the limestone. As such calcium or magnesium of limestone does not bring the neutralization, but these ions replace the hydrogen and aluminium ions from soil colloids to soil solution where they react with limestone, bicarbonate, or hydroxide and be neutralized.

$$[\text{Colloid}] \, H^+, Al^{3+} + Ca^{2+} + 2HCO_3^- \longrightarrow [\text{Colloid}] \, 2Ca^{2+} + Al(OH)_3 + H_2O + CO_2$$

The quick lime (CaO) is also called burnt lime or garden lime. The heat from the burning material decomposes the carbonates of limestone to oxides with loss of CO_2 to the air. The calcium and magnesium oxides formation depends on the proportion to the amount of their carbonate present.

$$CaCO_3 + Heat \longrightarrow CaO + CO_2$$

Reacting quicklime with water forms hydrated lime.

$$CaO + H_2O \longrightarrow Ca(OH)_2$$

For rapid neutralization of soil acidity or to raise the soil pH higher than 6.5, there use of quicklime or hydrated lime can be considered. Generally, they are not in common use, because in most of tropical acid soils there is no need to raise the pH around neutrality.

Marl and oyster shells are also carbonate materials. Marl is naturally occurring mixture of clays, carbonates of Ca and Mg and shells remnants. Oyster shells are pure calcium carbonate but are important only in coastal regions. These liming materials are not in common use.

LIME REQUIREMENT OF SOILS

The optimum soil pH for optimum yield depends on the type of crop grown, soil, but even with cultivars. It is also affected by economic feasibility and profitability. Not all acid soils need lime, and also it is not necessary to limed all the soils to the same pH. Such differences in response of crops to lime at different pH to get the maximum yield vary according to degree of weathering of soil and associated differences in certain physical and chemical properties (McLean 1971). The highly weathered tropical and subtropical oxisols and ultisols which are dominated in hydrous oxides of Al and Fe, the soil pH around 5.5 with the exchangeable of aluminium saturation of less than 20 per cent of effective CEC would produce satisfactory plant growth (Adams 1984), while liming to pH 6.5 to 6.8 is desirable for those soils which are rich in heavy clay minerals.

Lime requirement (LR) refers to the amount of lime required to neutralize the acidic components present in the soils of low pH. Some chemical methods depend on measuring the buffering capacity of the acidic components found in soil, others on determining the amount of exchangeable hydrogen ions held by the soil particles using a titration procedure, and exchangeable aluminium based for highly leached tropical soils. The criteria behind the use of any one of these methods is based upon the type of soil to be limed.

The methods used for LR should be based on soil properties, accuracy of the method, and the time and labour required for the test. Generally, test methods have been divided into following categories:

- The soil-lime incubated method consists of mixing incremental amounts of lime ($CaCO_3$) with appropriate amounts of soil and determining soil pH after incubation. The LR is determined based on the selected pH. This method is considered normally reliable but takes months to complete the reaction of added lime with soil acidity constituents.

- Soil based-titration involves directly titrating an acid soil with a base, or mixing incremental amounts of base such as $Ca(OH)_2$ with predetermined aliquots of soil and LR is determined based on the pH measurement after equilibration.

- Lime requirement (LR) methods consisting of buffer solutions merely determine a proportion of the exchange acidity of soil. The amount of lime ($CaCO_3$) required to achieve a soil pH is then obtained by calibrating the pH of the soil-buffer against the LR established by titrating soils with $Ca(OH)_2$, or incubating them with various amounts of $CaCO_3$.

BUFFER METHOD OF LR

As buffer tests are a rapid and convenient means of estimating the LR compared with titrating or incubating soils, several methods have been proposed over the years (Quigley 1998), but no single method is suitable for all soils under all conditions. Among the different buffer methods, Woodruff (1948), Adams and Evans (1962) and Shoemaker et al. (1961) have become popular (SMP) as quick-test methods. However, SMP method is commonly recommended for routine soil testing because of its speed and simplicity.

LIME REQUIREMENT TO ACHIEVE THE SOIL pH 5.5

It has been observed from the field trials that the optimum yield of crops can be achieved by applying the limestone 1 to 2.5 equivalents of exchangeable Al^{3+} and soil pH around 5.5 depending on soil characteristics (Patiram et al. 1989, 1990a, b, c and d). It is difficult to assess the LR based on exchangeable Al^{3+}, because the applied limestone does not only neutralize the acidity produced by the hydrolysis of Al compounds but also reacts to other sources of soil acidity. Therefore, it is more practical to use buffer-pH methods to evaluate the LR to achieve the soil pH 5.5. The author determined LR of acidic Sikkim soils to achieve the soil pH 5.5 and found that the SMP initial buffer pH of 5.5 gave the best results for measuring the lime rates to achieve the soil pH 5.5 (Patiram and Prasad 1991). The ready reckoner of the lime dose to get the soil pH 5.5 for acid soils has been prepared (Patiram 1991), taking into account pH, organic matter and clay content of the soil, because exchangeable Al^{3+} did not improve the predictability. This reckoner (Table 10.1) can be utilized by the State Soil Testing Laboratories to advice the farmers how much lime would be needed to raise the soil pH 5.5 for getting the optimum production.

Table 10.1: *Lime requirement of soils to achieve the pH 5.5 as affected by pH, organic matter and clay content of soils (t ha⁻¹)**

(Patiram, 1991)

Soil pH	Organic matter, 2%				Organic matter, 4%				Organic matter, 6%				Organic matter, 8%			
	Clay (%)				Clay (%)				Clay (%)				Clay (%)			
	10	15	20	25	10	15	20	25	10	15	20	25	10	15	20	25
4.5	3.56	3.83	4.11	4.39	3.72	4.00	4.28	4.56	3.89	4.17	4.44	4.72	4.05	4.33	4.61	4.89
4.6	3.15	3.42	3.70	3.98	3.32	3.59	3.87	4.14	3.49	3.77	4.04	4.32	3.66	3.93	4.21	4.49
4.7	2.74	3.01	3.29	3.60	2.91	3.18	3.34	3.62	3.08	3.36	3.63	3.91	3.24	3.52	3.80	4.08
4.8	2.25	2.53	2.81	3.09	2.42	2.70	2.98	3.26	2.59	2.87	3.14	3.42	2.76	3.03	3.31	3.59
4.9	1.93	2.22	2.49	2.75	2.10	2.38	2.66	2.93	2.27	2.54	2.82	3.10	2.43	2.71	3.00	3.27
5.0	1.52	1.80	2.08	2.35	1.69	1.97	2.24	2.52	1.86	2.13	2.41	2.69	2.02	2.30	2.58	2.86
5.1	1.11	1.40	1.68	1.94	1.29	1.56	1.84	2.12	1.46	1.73	2.01	3.29	1.62	1.90	2.18	2.46
5.2	0.71	1.00	1.27	1.56	0.90	1.16	1.43	1.71	0.06	1.33	1.61	1.90	1.22	1.50	1.78	2.06
5.3	0.31	0.59	0.86	1.13	0.48	0.76	1.03	1.31	0.64	0.92	1.20	1.48	0.81	1.09	1.37	1.64
5.4	0.12	0.18	0.44	0.72	0.07	0.34	0.62	0.90	0.23	0.51	0.82	1.10	0.40	0.68	0.96	1.23

*Agricultural dolomitic limestone passed through 100-mesh sieve and average neutralizing power 90% equivalent to pure limestone.

QUALITY OF LIMING MATERIALS

The quality of liming materials depends on its chemical composition, purity, and particle size of grind liming source. The purity of liming material (its acid neutralizing capacity or neutralizing value) is determined by its CCE (calcium carbonate equivalence). The neutralizing value of liming materials related to its molecular composition and purity. Pure $CaCO_3$ is the standard against which other liming materials are measured and its CCE value is taken 100 per cent. Consider the following reactions:

$$CaCO_3 + 2H^+ \longleftrightarrow Ca^{2+} + H_2O + CO_2$$
$$MgCO_3 + 2H^+ \longleftrightarrow Mg^{2+} + H_2O + CaCO_3$$

In each reaction, one mole of CO_3^{2-} will neutralize two moles of H^+. On the basis of molecular weight 84 g $MgCO_3$ will neutralize 100 g of $CaCO_3$. Therefore, the CCE of equal weights of the two materials is calculated by

$$84/100 = 100/X$$
$$X = 119$$

Therefore, $MgCO_3$ will neutralize 1.19 times more as compared to similar weight of $CaCO_3$. The liming material used as the amendments for acidic soils and their CCE values are given in Table 10.2.

The CCE may also be expressed by its Ca or Mg oxide equivalent. The pure $CaCO_3$ contains 40 per cent calcium. CaO has a molecular weight of 56, which means that 16 g of O is combined with 40 g of Ca. Therefore, if the Ca in $CaCO_3$ are expressed as the oxide, it will contain $(56/100) \times 100$, or 56 per cent CaO equivalent. For example, assume that a dolomitic limestone contains 60 per cent $CaCO_3$ and 35 per cent $MgCO_3$, its total content would be 95 per cent. The conversion factors, by which the value of CCE can be estimated in any way are given in Table 10.3.

The fineness of agricultural liming materials determines its rate of reaction with soil particles to a great extent, because the reaction rate depends on the surface area in contact with the soil. As particle size decreases, lime dissolves most rapidly and changes in pH occur in short time. Lime fineness is measured by using sieves with mesh sizes. Although, there are no provisions in the law as to what percentages passing the sieves. The best results can be obtained with the liming materials should pass the 90 per cent through 10-mesh sieve and 50 per cent through 60-mesh sieve. At least 20 per cent should pass a 100-mesh sieve.

SOIL FACTORS AFFECTING LIME REQUIREMENT (LR)

The lime requirement of soils has to be determined for correct rate of lime to raise the desired soil pH. In addition to soil pH, the amount of lime to applied is affected by a number of factors including the following:

Table 10.2: *Liming materials for agricultural soils and their CEC*

Materials	Formula	$CaCO_3$ equivalency
Calcite	$CaCO_3$	90–100
Dolomite	$CaCO_3 \, MgCO_3$	90–108
Quicklime	CaO	150–180
Hydrated lime	$Ca(OH)_2$	120–135
Wood ashes	Oxides and carbonates of Ca, Mg, and K	30–50
Basic slag	$CaCO_3.X$	50–70
Sludges	$CaCO_3.X$	30–50

Table 10.3: *Limestone conversion factors for determining CCE*

%		%	Multiply by factor
Ca	To	CaO	1.40
Ca	To	Ca(OH)$_2$	1.85
Ca	To	CaCO$_3$	2.50
Mg	To	MgO	1.67
Mg	To	Mg(OH)$_2$	2.42
Mg	To	MgCO$_3$	2.42
Mg	To	Ca	1.67
Mg	To	CaCO$_3$	4.17
MgO	To	CaCO$_3$	2.50
MgCO$_3$	To	CaCO$_3$	1.19

- Surface and subsurface texture and structure,
- Clay content,
- Cation exchange capacity,
- Base saturation,
- Amount of organic matter,
- Crops to be grown,
- Kind and fineness of liming materials, and
- Economic return from the lime application.

The texture and organic matter content of soils are the important factors because they are important indices of adsorption capacity and buffering capacity of soil. The low buffering capacity of sandy soils with low content organic matter will require LR less than that of fine textured or high organic matter soil. Naturally, for higher buffering capacity of soils (fine textured and high organic matter), the higher amount of lime is required to attain the similar pH than that of coarse textured and poor in organic matter soils.

At a given base saturation, the calcium ion is held strongly by montmorillonite as compared to kaolinite. Therefore, the base saturation of montmorillonite must be raised to 70 per cent to release of the calcium from the exchange complex to meet plant requirement. The kaolinite clay on the other hand liberates much more calcium easily for the satisfactory growth of crops at a much lower percentage base saturation. Therefore, the lime requirement of soils differs in two different types of clay minerals composition.

METHOD AND TIME OF LIME APPLICATION

The application of lime can be made in any season to a crop/cropping provided there is sufficient moisture in the soil to permit the reaction of lime to soil. Lime must be uniformly applied and mixed into the deep furrow (10–15 cm) of soil. Lime is not mobile in soils and will only change the pH where it contacts the soils. The reaction of lime and soils takes months together, therefore, often the benefit will not be so pronounced until the second crop after liming. Applying lime to the surface of soil will not significantly change subsurface soil pH.

RESPONSE OF CROPS TO LIMING

Low productivity of acid soils has been attributed to low availability of P, Ca, Mg, and Mo and to toxicity of Al, Fe, and Mn. Acid soils are base unsaturated and consequently do not sustained the crop productivity even the application of inorganic fertilizers. Therefore, satisfactory crop yields are not obtained unless these soils are properly amended with lime (Mandal and Sinha 1975). The permanent manorial experiment started on an acid red loam Alfisol at Ranchi to study the effect of continuous use of farmyard manure and fertilizer either alone on in combinations in presence or absence of lime, on crop yield and soil properties. It was observed that fertilizers alone increased the yields of maize and wheat up to 15th year but sharp reduction was found in subsequent two years in N, NP and NPK treatments (Lal and Mathur 1988). Maize grain was not produced at the end of 27 years while wheat still continued to give 0.8 t ha^{-1} yield from NPK treatment. It has happened because there was decrease of soil pH from 5.7 to below 4.5 after the continuous fertilizer applications, which was responsible for this effect. Application of NPK with lime maintained higher yield of crops and soil fertility. Organic manure alone or in combination with fertilizer also maintained yield and soil fertility.

LIMING ON LIME REQUIREMENT BASIS

The entire earlier field experiments were conducted on the basis the 1 LR lime application, it led to confusion about the rate of liming. The field experiments conducted at higher altitude of Meghalaya (1800 m) indicated that liming of acid soils at the rate of 25 per cent of the lime requirement (LR) determined by calcium acetate buffer method of Woodruff gave optimum yield of maize and was at par with 50 and 100 per cent application of dolomitic limestone (Prasad *et al.* 1983). The same rate of lime also gave the residual effects for the next two years. The 25 per cent dolomitic limestone of LR was enough to neutralize the exchangeable Al and augmented the uptake of phosphorus and calcium. The field experiments also conducted on an acid clay loam soil (*Alfisols*) of Bhubaneswar revealed that high productivity of crops can be obtained by the lime either as paper mill sludge or as limestone in the crop rotation of pigeonpea plus black gram wheat, little millet-niger-French bean and finger millet-rape seed-green gram (Sahu and Pal 1987).

Lime dose at 0.25 LR proved to be optimum dose and over liming at 1.5 LR had detrimental effect on the crop yield. Residual effect of liming was also beneficial to the succeeding crops in the rotation.

EXCHANGEABLE ALUMINIUM BASED LIMING

The use of exchangeable Al^{3+} as the criteria of lime dose has been proposed for acid soils with low permanent charge and relatively high in pH-dependent charge (Kamprath 1971). Field experiments were conducted to lime the acid soils based on exchangeable Al^{3+} to wheat, maize and soybean test crops (Patiram *et al.* 1989, 1990a, b and c). The crops well-responded to the dolomitic limestone rates and depending on soils, highest yield of crops were obtained when lime rates were 1.0 to 2.5 equivalent of exchangeable Al^{3+} (Table 10.4) and soil pH around 5.5. The buffer method of LR over estimated the lime rates. The rate of dolomitic limestone based on exchangeable Al^{3+} was considerably lower than the buffer method of LR. The lime rate equivalent to 2 exchangeable Al^{3+} completely neutralized the Al^{3+} on exchange complex. The analysis of plant tissues also indicated that Al was the main factors of poor crop growth on acid infertile soils.

Table 10.4: *Effect of dolomitic limestone on crops yield on three soils*

Dolomite (t ha^{-1})	Crops yield (kg ha^{-1})											
	Maize				Soybean				Wheat			
	1	2	3	Mean	1	2	3	Mean	1	2	3	Mean
	Soils				Soils				Soils			
0	4403	2943	2866	3340	874	1833	1134	1313	554	3847	2253	2218
0.5 L	4823	3780	3550	4051	1445	2142	1634	1794	975	4367	2693	2445
1.0 L	6586	4826	4470	5294	1781	2367	1933	2060	1404	4567	3033	3001
1.5 L	6137	4950	4541	5212	1936	2467	2067	2228	1627	4800	3333	3282
2.0 L	6212	5298	4324	5278	1924	2433	1967	2178	1955	4600	3200	3252
2.5 L	6081	4874	3964	4973	1943	2450	2075	2228	2092	4667	3047	3269
3.0 L	6069	4806	3837	4931	1820	2492	2018	2173	2098	4500	3033	3222
0.25 LR					1900	2356	2148	2209				
0.5 LR	6378	4051	3837	4723	1856	2550	2050	2134	2009	4600	3100	3203
1.0 LR	6180	3868	3923	4658	1825	2222	1846	2141	2147	4600	2867	3205
CD (P = 0.05)	1716	969	640		283	346	246		468	439	393	

(Contd.)

Table 10.4: *Effect of dolomitic limestone on crops yield on three soils (Contd.)*

Dolomite (t ha^{-1})					Crops yield (kg ha^{-1})							
	Maize				Soybean				Wheat			
	1	2	3	Mean	1	2	3	Mean	1	2	3	Mean
	Soils				Soils				Soils			
Soil properties												
pH	5.1	4.7	4.9		4.8	5.2	5.1		4.9	5.1	5.0	
Exch. Ca + Mg	3.6	2.1	1.7		2.2	2.7	2.7		2.1	3.0	2.9	
Exch. Al^{3+}	1.4	1.9	1.5		1.4	0.8	1.1		1.4	1.2	0.8	
Al sat. of CEC (%)	27	43	43		37	22	27		37	29	19	
Lime requirement (LR, t/ha)												
1 L	1.4	1.9	1.5		1.4	0.8	1.1		1.4	1.2	0.8	
1 LR	8.2	10.8	8.4		7.6	4.3	5.4		8.4	7.9	6.7	

L and LR were the lime rates based on exchangeable aluminium and buffer method of lime requirement respectively.

Exchangeable Ca + Mg and Al were expressed in me/100 g soil.

FURROW APPLICATION OF LIME

It has been found that applying only 250–500 kg limestone ha^{-1} in furrows every year as compared to high rates of broadcasted limestone (Table 10.5) can optimize the yield of crops (Patiram 1994, 1996a). However, in our country as such no regulation exists to control the quality of lime, different grades of liming materials are available in the market. It is very difficult for farmers to apply the lime in furrows in large areas uniformly. There is a need to develop the implements for applying the lime in furrows with mixing facility in soil in addition to separate arrangement for seed dropping and fertilizer application. If such type of implements can be made available to farmers, no doubt this technology can be adopted by the farmers in large areas. In hilly terrain inputs are carried to distant agricultural field by head load. Therefore, furrow application at lower rates suits their requirement and can be carried to their distant fields.

FREQUENCY OF LIME APPLICATION

It is very much essential to know the frequency of lime applied once for sustaining the soil productivity. It has been found that under the high rainfall condition of the north east India, the optimum rates of lime applied once are sufficient for two years only (Table 10.6) receiving annual rainfall around 3,000 mm/annum, because the

Table 10.5: *Efficacy of furrow application of limestone on crops productivity (pooled mean of three years)*

Limestone (t ha^{-1})	Crops yield (t ha^{-1})		
		Soybean-wheat sequence	
	Maize	Soybean	Wheat
Broadcast once before the sowing of 1st crop			
0	2.86	1.38	1.20
1		2.34	2.38
2	5.69	2.31	2.79
3		2.45	2.18
4	5.74		
6	5.70		
In furrows every year			
0.25	4.98	2.00	1.70
0.50	5.18	2.28	2.29
0.75	5.21	2.20	2.39
1.00	5.23	2.20	2.52
CD (P = 0.05)	1.08	0.297	0.324
Soil properties			
pH	4.6	5.0	
Exch. Al (me/100 g soil)	1.30	0.70	
% Al saturation of CEC	30	18	

Table 10.6: *Crops performance as a function of dolomitic limestone applied before the first crop*

Limestone (t ha^{-1})	Crops yield (kg ha^{-1})				
	1985–86		1986–87		1987–88
	Wheat	Maize	Wheat	Maize	Wheat
0	593	2432	313	1657	107
0.4	656	2695	340	1721	110
0.8	847	3295	363	1909	143
1.2	1044	3458	573	2081	187
1.6	1263	3626	953	2137	240

(Contd.)

Table 10.6: *Crops performance as a function of dolomitic limestone applied before the first crop (Contd.)*

Limestone (t ha^{-1})	Crops yield (kg ha^{-1})				
	1985–86		1986–87		1987–88
	Wheat	Maize	Wheat	Maize	Wheat
2.0	1565	4031	1006	2471	243
4.0	2102	4989	1654	3454	943
8.0	1771	3895	1835	3658	1567
CD (P = 0.05)	344	441	222	651	230

precipitated exchangeable Al started to reappear as the cropping number increased, and after two years half rate of limestone needed for sustained productivity (Patiram *et al.* 1990e). The areas which are getting rainfall of less than 2,000 mm / annum, the frequency of lime application can be 3 to 4 years depending on the crops grown.

ORGANIC MANURE AS AMENDMENT

The application of organic manures to acid soils temporarily forms the organo-Al-complexes that reduce the toxicity of soil solution Al^{3+} to plant roots. The farmers of the hilly region are using organic manures to upland crops by their tradition. It has been observed that the benefit of fertilizer could be increased by continuous application of farmyard manure (FYM) to each crop in Al-toxic acid soils (Table 10.7). The periodic analysis of soil samples indicated that application of FYM initially decreased the soluble Al without affecting soil pH and favoured growth of plant roots. However, the difference was eliminated with time as a result of release of Al from unstable organo-Al-complexes and subsequent adsorption on soil colloid. So, the application of FYM to each crop is needed to eliminate the Al toxicity of acidic soils. This is the common practice for the production of organic food. So, most of the farmers of the acid soils of north eastern region take maize as a homestead crop.

Table 10.7: *Effect of single application of limestone and FYM on yield of crops grown in Sequence (Patiram 1996b)*

Limestone (L) and FYM (t ha^{-1})	Grain yield (t ha^{-1})		
	Maize (1st crop)	Soybean (2nd crop)	Maize (3rd crop)
L_0	24.25	3.70	12.00
L_1	31.70	7.10	12.00
L_2	37.95	10.90	17.20

(Contd.)

Table 10.7: *Effect of single application of limestone and FYM on yield of crops grown in Sequence (Patiram 1996b) (Contd.)*

Limestone (L) and FYM (t ha^{-1})	Grain yield (t ha^{-1})		
	Maize (1st crop)	Soybean (2nd crop)	Maize (3rd crop)
L$_3$	43.60	12.00	18.50
FYM$_{10}$	34.44	5.74	12.40
FYM$_{20}$	38.55	9.64	14.75
FYM$_{10}$ + L$_1$	46.20	13.24	21.75
FYM$_{20}$ + L$_1$	48.60	16.74	23.00
CD (P = 0.05)	5.34	2.56	4.71
CV (%)	9.51	17.61	19.85

UTILIZATION OF PRESSMUD AS AN AMENDMENT

Pressmud was utilized as an amendment in acid soils of Nagaland. Pressmud produced through carbonation process in sugar mill contained 41.7 per cent CaO, 13.11 per cent organic matter, 0.66 per cent N, 0.37 per cent P and 0.36 per cent K indicating the superiority of this material to lime. The application of 2 tonnes pressmud ha^{-1} in an acidic soil along with fertilizers gave higher yield of maize-wheat crop sequence (Datta *et al.* 1983).

LIME REQUIREMENT (LR) INDICES

The critical limits of soil acidity indices for liming were calculated statistically for the preceding crops indicated that these crops would response to added lime when soil pH drops below 5.2 (Table 10.8). If acid soils contain exchangeable aluminium more than 0.70, 0.55 and 0.41 me/100 g of soil, and if the aluminium saturation of ECEC is more than 17 per cent, 13 per cent and 11 per cent, the productivity of maize, soybean and wheat, respectively, will be affected by excessive soil aluminium. It can be seen from the Table 8, that maize was comparatively more tolerant to soil acidity as compared to soybean and wheat.

Table 10.8: *Critical limits of lime requirement indices*

Indices	Crops		
	Maize	Soybean	Wheat
Soil pH	5.2	5.2	5.2
Exch. Al^{3+}, me/100 g	0.70	0.55	0.41
% Al saturation of ECEC	17.2	13.0	10.6

BENEFITS OF LIMING

The proper liming of acid soils provides the number of benefits:

- Nutrient solubility and availability are improved by raising soil pH. The optimum pH range for tropical acid soils is around 5.5. The pH higher than 6.0, the micronutrients required by plants become less soluble excepting Mo and deficiencies may occur.

- Plants develop healthier roots because they are exposed to reduced toxicity of Al and Mn. The better development of roots improves the nutrient uptake and enhances drought tolerance.

- Lime is also an economical source of essential calcium as well as beneficial magnesium if dolomitic limestone has been applied as liming material.

- The native as well as applied phosphorus is used more efficiently caused by its lesser fixation by active Al and Fe oxides surfaces through liming increased soil pH.

- It causes an increase in soil cation exchange capacity (CEC), which reduces the leaching of base cations, particularly potassium.

- Nodulation of legumes is enhanced, which improves N-fixation by bacteria *Rhizobium* in nodules of legume roots. N-fixation provides an economical source of nitrogen and may supply the succeeding crop with substantial residual nitrogen.

- Molybdenum an essential element to *Rhizobia* in N-fixing process increases with increasing soil pH after liming.

- Triazine herbicide, such as atrazine and simazine, work better in a higher pH environment.

- Some nemacides may work better.

- Optimum pH allows the breakdown of some herbicides, preventing damage to rotational crops.

- Increase soil pH favours the microbial activities and increases the decomposition of organic matter and nutrient transformation for root growth.

- The activities of deep burrowing and soil eating worm species perform their duties well in soils free from acid stress soil fertility constraints.

ECONOMIC RETURN OF LIMING ON FARM TRIALS

Large number of field trials conducted at the farmers' field on acidic soils of Meghalaya to find out the benefit of lime, fertilizer and manure on the basis of prevailing market price of crops. The rate of N, P_2O_5 and K_2O were taken at the rate of Rs 10.50, 18.70 and 7.42/unit nutrients from the applied sources of urea, diammonium phosphate (DAP) and murate of potash, respectively. The rate of limestone was taken @ Rs 1 kg^{-1} dolomite. The cost of labourers for application of fertilizer and lime was taken @ Rs 100/each, respectively.

The first set of farmer's field trials were taken on maize and mustard consisting the treatments of:

T_1 = Farmer's practice only (FP)
T_2 = Farmers practice + lime (1/10th LR) (FP + L)
T_3 = Recommended dose of fertilizers only (RF)
T_4 = Recommended dose of fertilizers + lime (1/10th LR) (RF + L)

The doses of fertilizers were 100:60:60 N, P_2O_5 and K_2O/ha and 40:40:20 kg N, P_2O_5 and K_2O/ha for maize and mustard respectively.

The calculated benefit cost (BC) ratio for maize and mustard are given in Tables 10.9 and 10.10.

Table 10.9: *Benefit cost ratio (B:C) for maize (pool mean of 40 sites and LR 18.3 t ha^{-1})*

Treatments	Grain yield (q ha^{-1})	Extra yield over FP (q ha^{-1})	Price of grain (Rs)	Cost of inputs (Rs)	B:C ratio
FP	10.65	–	–	–	–
FP + L	14.15	3.5	2450	1930	1:1.27
RF	22.31	11.66	8162	2280	1:3.58
RF + L	31.41	20.76	14532	4210	1:3.45

Rate of maize Rs 7 kg^{-1}.

Table 10.10: *Cost benefit ratio for mustard (pool mean of 23 sites and LR 18.9 t ha^{-1})*

Treatments	Grain yield (q ha^{-1})	Extra yield over FP (q ha^{-1})	Price of grain (Rs)	Cost of inputs (Rs)	B:C ratio
FP	0.59	–	–	–	–
FP + L	1.22	0.63	1260	1990	1:0.63
RF	1.44	0.85	1700	1290	1:1.32
RF + L	4.42	3.83	7600	3259	1:2.35

Rate of mustard Rs 20 kg^{-1}.

Second set of farm trials were taken on groundnut, soybean and maize. The treatments consisted of:

T_1 = Farmer's practice only (FP).
T_2 = Recommended dose of fertilizers only (RF).
T_3 = 50 per cent recommended dose of fertilizers only (RF) + Lime (1/10th in furrows).
T_4 = 50 per cent recommended dose of fertilizers + lime (1/10th LR) and 5 t FYM/ha (RF + L + FYM).

The recommended doses of fertilizers are 100:60:60 kg N, P_2O_5 and K_2O/ha for maize and 40:60:40 kg N, P_2O_5 and K_2O/ha for soybean and groundnut.

The calculated benefit cost ratio for these crops is given in Tables 10.11, 10.12 and 10.13.

The applications of fertilizers to each above crops gave the benefit:cost ratio between 1:1.32 and 1:4.67. The application of lime along with 100 per cent

Table 10.11: *Benefit cost ratio for soybean (LR = 17.4 t ha^{-1})*

Treatments	Grain yield (q ha^{-1})	Extra yield over FP (q ha^{-1})	Price of grain (Rs)	Cost of inputs (Rs)	B:C ratio
FP	7.32	–	–	–	–
100% RF	11.34	4.02	6030	1693	1:3.56
50% RF + L	17.50	10.18	15270	2810	1:5.43
50% RF + L + FYM	19.26	11.94	29910	5110	1:5.85

Cost of soybean grain Rs 15 kg^{-1}.

Table 10.12: *Benefit cost ratio for groundnut (pooled 15 site, LR 16.83 t ha^{-1})*

Treatments	Grain yield (q ha^{-1})	Extra yield over FP (q ha^{-1})	Price of grain (Rs)	Cost of inputs (Rs)	B:C ratio
FP	8.65	–	–	–	–
100% RF	14.15	5.50	5500	1693	1:3.25
50% RF + L	20.90	12.25	12250	2625	1:4.67
50% RF + L + FYM	24.99	16.34	16340	5225	1:3.13

Rate of groundnut pod @ Rs 10 kg^{-1} and FYM @ Rs 500 tonne^{-1}.

Table 10.13: *Benefit cost ratio for maize (pool mean of 24 sites and LR 15.4 t ha^{-1})*

Treatments	Grain yield (q ha^{-1})	Extra yield over FP (q ha^{-1})	Price of grain (Rs)	Cost of inputs (Rs)	B:C ratio
FP	14.44	–	–	–	–
100% RF	23.36	8.92	6244	2280	1:2.83
50% RF +L	28.06	13.62	9534	2780	1:3.43
50% RF + L + FYM	33.67	19.23	13463	5280	1:2.55

Rate of maize grain @ Rs 7 kg^{-1} and FYM @ Rs 500 t^{-1}.

recommended dose of fertilizers gave the better output for mustard as compared to maize, which although gave maximum grain yield yet benefit: cost ration lower than the 100 per cent application of fertilizers alone. This indicated that the benefit could be increased by lowering dose of lime from 1/10th to between 1/15th and 1/20th. The lime determined was very high, so the cost of its application increased @ 1/10th LR, which reduced the benefit:cost ratio.

In case of second on-farm trials the reduction of 50 per cent recommended fertilizer and application of lime (1/10th LR in furrows) resulted the maximum benefit: cost ratio for the tested crops of maize, soybean and groundnut. This ratio decreased with the application of 5 tonnes FYM/ha (excepting soybean) might be the higher cost of FYM.

LIMESTONE RESERVES IN NORTHEAST REGION

Northeast India has a vast reserve of limestone totaling about 6,686 million metric tonnes (Table 10.14). The limestone found in the region is mostly organic, originated from nummilite shells in those areas, which were under intermediated sea condition during Mesozoic period. These sources can be utilized to amendment the acidic soils in addition to meet the requirement of cement factories.

Table 10.14: *Limestone reserves of northeastern region in India*

State	Reserves (million tonnes)
Arunachal Pradesh	1503.00
Assam	135.02
Nagaland	450.0
Meghalaya	4665.00
Manipur	4.60
Sikkim	2.1
Total reserves of the region	6,686

In Assam, limestone occurs in a number of places in the Karbi plateau. In the border region between Meghalaya, North Cachar Hills and Hamren subdivision there are limestone deposits in the Kopili and Kharkhor river valleys. The Garampani-Umrangshu area of North Cachar Hills and has a reserve of about 154 million tonnes of good quality limestone. The Diphu and Bokajan subdivisions of Karbi Anglong also have rich reserves of limestone. The Kailajan and Dilai area of Bokajan subdivision have high quality limestone, which is used in the Bokajan cement factory. In the Diphu subdivision limestone is found in the Sibheta area (26°00′ N.93°18′) which contains about 52 million tonnes of limestone.

A very large extensive limestone deposit is found in Meghalaya along the Southern part of the state almost all through its length from the Southern Garo

Hills to the border of Meghalaya and Assam and beyond. It extends from the Western parts, namely the West Garo, Hills to the eastern Jaintia Hills, and continues into Karbi Anglong (Mikir Hills) of Assam. This belt is said to be 400 km long. The limestone occurring in this belt is not only of good quality, but it is found in thick workable layer of 7 m to 230 m. In Garo Hills limestone is found exposed along the Simsang river george near Siju (25°3 N 90°43 E). In fact, the Siju area has coal, clay, sandstone and limestone in close proximity. In Khasi Hills, there is a 64 km long belt of limestone from the north of Lamgaon through Therriaghat and Mawlong-Isamati areas (25°11 N 91°45 E) to Shella river. In Jaintia Hills, there is a large bed of limestone (Lakadong and Lumshnong areas) about 22 km long.

In Arunachal Pradesh, limestone has been discovered at Tela-Tidding area of Lohit district, where an estimated reserve of 9.1 million tonnes of the mineral occurs. The Tezu area of this district is also said to contain a reserve of high-silica and high magnesia marble containing about 74 million tonnes. Dali, Mega and Kabbu in Siang districts also have rich deposit of limestone. Limestone is available in Manipur in Chandel and Ukhrul districts. The total reserve in these two districts, up to workable depth, is estimated at 4.5 million tonnes. Out of this, 2.2 metric tonnes occur in Ukhrul while the remainder is found in isolated pockets at Hungdung, Mova and Khangoi of Chandel district. The deposits of Manipur generally carry 34 per cent to 53 per cent of lime.

In Nagaland, high grade limestone deposits have been discovered in various places of Phek and Tuensaang district. Out of them, the deposits of Wazeho in Phek district and Nimi (375 million tonnes) in Tuensang district are really large. There is calcareous tufa type of limestone is Chakhabam of Kohima and Dibuia of Mokokchung. The total reserve of limestone so far discovered in this state is estimated at 450 million tonnes. Mizoram also has limestone deposits in several places. Of these ones found at Muthi, Tuirial, Vakku and Kawrthan areas are more important. In Tripura siliceous limestone deposits have been located at Shankan Range, but no production has so far been achieved.

REFERENCES

Adams F. 1984. Crop response to lime in the southern United States. *In* Soil Acidity and Liming. Adams F (ed.), ASA-CSSA-SSSA, Madison, WI, pp. 211–265.

Adams F and Evans CE. 1962. A rapid method for measuring the lime requirement of Red-Yellow Podzolic soils. *Soil Sci. Soc. Am. Proc.* **26:** 355–257.

Conner SD. 1921. Liming in its relation to injurious inorganic compounds in the soil. *J. Amer. Soc. Agron.* **13:** 113–124.

Datta M and Gupta RK. 1983. Utilization of pressmud as amendment of acid soil in Nagaland. *J. Indian Soc. Soil Sci.* **31:** 511–516.

Hartwell BL and Pember F. 1918. Aluminium as a factor influencing the effect of acid soils on different crops. *J. Am. Soil Sci. Proc.* **10:** 25–47.

Kamprath EJ. 1971. Exchangeable Aluminium as a criterion for liming leached mineral soils. *Soil Sci. Soc. Am. J.* **34**: 252–254.

Lal S and Mathur BS. 1988. Effect of long term manuring, fertilization and liming on crop yield and some physicochemical properties of acid soil. *J. Indian Soc. Soil Sci.* **36**: 113–119.

Mandal SC and Sinha MK. 1975. Acid Soils of India and Liming. ICAR Technical Bulletin **51**, New Delhi.

McLean EO. 1971. Potentially beneficial effects from liming: chemical and physical. *Soil Crop Sci Soc. Florida. Proc.* **31**: 189–199.

Patiram. 1991. Liming of acid soils and crop production in Sikkim. *J. Hill Res.* **4**: 6–12.

Patiram. 1994. Efficacy of furrow-applied limestone on maize production on an acid inceptisol of Sikkim. *J. Indian Soc. Soil Sci.* **42**: 309–313.

Patiram. 1996a. Efficacy of furrow application of limestone on soybean and wheat grown in sequence on an acid soil. *Indian J. Agric. Sci.* **66**: 81–85.

Patiram. 1996b. Effect of limestone and farmyard manure on crop yields and soil acidity on an acid inceptisol of Sikkim, India. *J. Trop. Agric* (Trinidad). **73**: 238–241.

Patiram and Prasad RN. 1991. Evaluation of lime requirement to achieve the soil pH 6.0 and 5.5 for the acidic soils of Sikkim, India. *J. Trop. Agric* (Trinidad). **68**: 284–288.

Patiram, Singh KP and Rai RN. 1989. Liming for maize production on acid soils of Sikkim. *J. Indian Soc. Soil Sci.* **37**: 121–125.

Patiram, Singh KP, Rai RN and Prasad RN. 1990a. Liming for production of wheat (*Triticum aestivum* L.) in acidic soils of Sikkim. *Indian J. Agric. Sci.* **60**: 40–44.

Patiram, Rai RN and Prasad RN. 1990b. Effect of liming on aluminium and yield of wheat in acidic soil. *J. Indian Soc. Soil Sci.* **38**: 719–722.

Patiram, Rai RN and Prasad RN. 1990c. Response of soybean to liming in acid soils of Sikkim. *J. Indian Soc. Soil Sci.* **38**: 499–503.

Patiram, Rai RN and Prasad RN. 1990d. Effect of liming on aluminium and yield of wheat in acid soil. *J. Indian Soc. Soil Sci.* **38**: 719–722.

Patiram, Rai RN and Prasad RN. 1990e. Frequency of lime application to wheat-maize crop sequence on an acid soil of Sikkim. *J. Indian Soc. Soil Sci.* **38**: 723–727.

Prasad RN, Patiram, Barooah RC and Ram M. 1983. Direct and residual effect of liming on yield of maize and uptake of nutrients in acid soils of Meghalaya. *J. Indian Soc. Soil Sci.* **31**: 233–235.

Quigley MN. 1998. Testing soils for lime requirement. In *Hand book of soil conditioners: Substances that enhance the physical properties of soils*, p293–308. Wallace A and Terry AE (Eds.), Marcel Dekker Inc., New York.

Sahu SK and Pal SS. 1987. Direct and residual effect of paper mill sludge and limestone on crop yield under three different crop rotations on an acid red soil. *J. Indian Soc. Soil Sci.* **35**: 46–51.

Shoemaker HE, McLean EO and Pratt PF. 1961. Buffer methods for determining the lime requirement of soils with appreciable amounts of extractable aluminium. *Soil Sci. Soc. Am. Proc.* **25**: 274–277.

Woodruff CM. 1948. Testing soils for lime requirement by means of a buffered solution and the glass electrode. *Soil Sci.* **66**: 53-63.

11

Soil Acidity, Acidification and its Implications on Soil Fertility

Patiram

ABSTRACT

Acid soils cover 30 per cent of the world's ice-free land area and aluminium toxicity limits crop growth around 12 per cent of the world's cultivated lands. About 68 per cent of these acidic soils occur in the humid tropics. Acidic soils below pH 5.5 occupy around 25 million ha of arable land in India and are mainly concentrated in North-eastern (NE) region (54 per cent). The soil acidity may be divided into active, exchangeable and non-exchangeable (titrable or pH dependent). Active acidity (pH) is due to H$^+$ ions in the soil solution and exchangeable or potential acidity consists of H and Al ions adsorbed on the soil exchange complex and it becomes active when H$^+$ and Al^{3+} ions are exchanged to soil solution. The titratable acidity arises from dissociation of weak acid functional groups of soil organic matter, deprotonation of hydroxyl-Al-polymers associated with the internal and external surfaces of phyllosilicate minerals, from short range ordered aluminosilicates (allophonic materials) and from ruptured surfaces of oxides and silicates. Acid soils are the characteristics of high rainfall humid areas caused by loss of exchangeable bases from the exchange complex and occupied by Al^{3+} and H$^+$ ions. This process of acidification is accelerated by the use of nitrogenous fertilizers, removal of bases from the harvested biomass, mining tailing, acid rainfall, etc. The hydrated Al ion (Al hexahydronium ion, $[Al(H_2O)_6]^{3+}$) is an acid in general sense because it contains protons (H ions) removable from six water molecules ($-OH_2$) surrounding the Al in an octahedral coordination. As solution pH increases, $[Al(H_2O)_6]^{3+}$ hydrolyzes to Al^{3+} below pH 5, whereas the Al(OH)$^{2+}$ and Al(OH)$_2{}^+$ species form as soil pH increases. At near-neutral pH, solid phase gibbsite [Al(OH)$_3$] may occur, whereas aluminates [Al(OH)$_4{}^-$] dominates in alkaline conditions. It is well-proved that Al^{3+} is the main cause of toxicity among Al-monomers. Acid soil infertility is a syndrome of problems that affect plant growth in soils at low pH namely, toxicities of Al^{3+} and Mn, deficiency and low status of bases, low P availability, Mo deficiency, and lower microbiological activities, etc. The relative importance of these constraints may vary with soil type, parent material, soil pH, soil structure and texture, and plant species. The toxicity of Al^{3+} results into poorly developed root system, which causes susceptibility to drought stress and nutrient deficiencies. The Al toxicity produces a range of symptoms in the top plant, including small dark green leaves, stunted growth and delayed maturity, purpling of leaves, wilting, and induced deficiencies of Ca. The foliar symptoms in some plants resemble those of phosphorus deficiency manifested by overall stunting, small dark green leaves, late maturity, purpling of stems, leaves and leaf veins and yellowing and death of leaf tips. In majority of the acidic soils, the P deficiency may limit the crop productivity after soil acidity.

Key words: Acid soil, forms of soil acidity, soil fertility.

INTRODUCTION

Soil acidity and associated infertility and mineral toxicities are major constraints to agricultural production in various parts of the world, which cover 30 per cent of the world's land area (Von UexKull and Mutert 1995) and aluminum toxicity limits crop growth around 12 percent of the world's cultivated lands. Eswaran *et al.* (1997) estimated the global area of 26 per cent, which are limiting the productivity of crops by acidity stress. Although, a large portion of about 68 per cent of these acidic soils occur in the humid tropics yet a considerable portion is also distributed in Australia, North America, and Europe.

The acid soils of the world consists large areas of potentially arable land, which are concentrated in Brazil (called Cerrados), Columbia, Venezuela, Central Africa and Southeast Asia (Borlaug 1997). In India, most of the acid regions soils are sedentary and are found in hilly terrains. Generally, these are common in/on hill tops, hill slopes, terraced and unterraced uplands, medium lands or valley floors (Mandal 1996). The acid soils (pH < 6.5) in India occupy approximately 90 million ha of the geographical area (Sharma and Sarkar 2005). Acidic soils below pH 5.5 occupy around 25 million ha of arable land. Such type of problematic soils in India are mainly concentrated in northeastern (NE) region and Western Ghats, Jharkhand, Chhattisgarh, Uttaranchal with sporadic distribution in Himachal Pradesh, Odisha, West Bengal, etc. In northeastern region, the acid soils below pH 5.5 occupy 54 per cent of the total area of the country (Table 11.1).

The toxicity of soil Al has been recognized one of the important factors limiting the productivity of crops on acid soils having pH below 5.5. In the Himalayan region, the acidity of soil increases from West to East with increasing rainfall and almost neutral alkaline soil reaction occurs in Jammu and Kashmir. The improvement of such type of soils for agriculture is one of the issues to get the optimum productivity of crops in this region.

Table 11.1: *Extent of the acid soil in northeastern region (m ha)*

State	pH <5.5	pH 5.5–6.5	Total acid soil	Geographical area	Per cent geographical area of acid soil
Arunachal Pradesh	6.52	0.27	6.79	7.786	81.08
Assam	2.33	2.33	4.66	7.844	59.41
Manipur	1.87	0.32	2.19	2.233	98.07
Meghalaya	1.19	1.05	2.24	2.243	99.87
Mizoram	1.27	0.78	2.05	2.208	97.20
Nagaland	1.60	0.05	1.64	1.658	99.50
Sikkim	0.60	–	0.60	0.710	84.51
Tripura	0.81	0.24	1.05	1.049	100.00
Total NE	16.19	5.04	21.23	26.219	80.97
India	30.00	58.94	89.95	328.726	27.36
% NE of India	53.97	8.41	23.60	7.97	6.45

Source: NBSS & LUP.

NATURE OF SOIL ACIDITY

In the beginning of 20th century, soil acidity was thought to be caused by exchangeable hydrogen because this could be leached out of acid soils by neutral salts. Johnson (1888) declared that all permanently productive soils were calcareous, but his results revealed that 1N NaCl did not replace all the acidity as measured by $Ca(OH)_2$ equilibrations and estimated the lime requirement of mineral soils. Most importantly he discovered that the acidity replaced by NaCl was primarily $AlCl_3$, not HCl. He got only full credit for his remarkable observations only after 60 years. Cameron and Bell (1905) speculated that acid soils are artifacts caused by the selective adsorption of cations, leaving the acid anions in solution. Truog (1916) opined that acid soils are natural consequence of the removal of exchangeable cations by dilute H_2CO_3 during weathering, and quantities of acid removed by salts depended on the anions not the cations.

Several workers (quoted by Thomas 1977) extracted the soils with neutral salts and related the quantity of Al extracted to the growth of plants. Kelley and Brown (1925) and Page (1926) explained that the Al was dissolved by exchangeable H^+ during the salt-extraction. However, their own data showed that addition of $AlCl_3$ to a neutral soil ultimately resulted in almost complete Al saturation of the soil. Paver and Marshall (1934) showed that electrodialysed bentonite and Putnam clay did not adsorb much Al^{3+} from solution but adsorbed $Co(NH_2)_6^{3+}$ from solution and Fe^{3+} from highly acidified solution. On this basis they concluded that electrodialysed clay was aluminium saturated. However, Marshall seems to have had doubts, as evidence by the fact that he devoted only two paragraphs to these results in his book written 15 years later (Marshall 1949).

Dr JN Mukherjee and his associates from India between 1940 and 1950 also suggested that acid clays were weak acid and H^+ adsorbed on clays, when exchanged by neutral salts immediately dissolved hydrated alumina in the soil released Al^{3+} in the extracts. However, their works could not be recognized in the western countries due to lack of information (Jenny 1961). Schofield (1949) also believed that "acid mineral soils and clays are aluminium not hydrogen soils". He found that Rothamsted soil leached with 0.2N NH_4Cl at pH 3.0 did not buffer and the CEC was invariant between pH 2.5 and 5 thus refuted the concept of clays as weak acids. The soil leached with 0.01N HCl resulted larger buffer effect which he attributed to Al^{3+} released by the acid treatment and then reabsorbed.

The publication of the book written by Chernove (1947) of Russia, who promulgated the Al theory and claimed H-clay must get converted Al-clays due to its stronger adsorption on clay than H^+ ions. The concept of exchangeable aluminium as the major source of the acidity in mineral soils was developed by NT Coleman and his colleagues (1952–54) of the North Carollina State University, USA, after the discovery of Chernove book. Coleman and Harward (1953) discovered that by measuring heats of neutralization and titration curves of H-and Al-resins, 0.1N HCl clays or clays leached rapidly with 1N HCl entirely indifferent properties than clays prepared by electrodialysis and dilute acid leaching. They concluded that clay prepared by concentrated HCl or H-resin treatment is a strong acid which get changed on storage to an Al-clay. In most of the acid mineral soils, the pH dependent charge is largely caused by polymerized hydroxyl-Al, which is non-exchangeable by KCl, but which can be titrated with a base (Coleman and Thomas, 1967). So, the nature of soil acidity has been resolved: acid soils are aluminium-saturated materials with apparent weak acid characteristics due to the hydrolysis of adsorbed Al^{3+}. H-saturated clays are in fact strong acid but get reverted on standing to Al-clays (Jenny 1961, Coulter 1969). The exchangeable H^+ dominates in very acid soils (< pH 4.8 in KCl) and at higher pH Al^{3+} dominates (Yuan 1963), both ions become negligible about pH 5.8. So, only significant amount of exchangeable H^+ occurs naturally in very acid soil and generally acid soils contain exchangeable Al^{3+} only. The relationship between soil pH and exchangeable Al^{3+} in the acidic soils of Meghalaya are given in Fig. 11.1. It can be seen from the Fig. 11.1, a sharp decline of exchangeable Al^{3+} as the soil pH increased from 4 0 to 5.6 and thereafter almost disappear from the exchange complex.

TYPES OF SOIL ACIDITY

The soil acidity may be divided into active, exchangeable and non-exchangeable (titrable or pH dependent). Active acidity (pH) is due to H^+ ions in the soil solution. The exchangeable or potential acidity [measured in cmol (p+)kg^{-1}] consists of H and Al ions adsorbed on the soil exchange complex (clay and organic matter) and it becomes active when H^+ and Al^{3+} ions are exchanged to soil solution. Active and potential acidity are related, but it may vary across soils. It is influenced by type and amount of clay and organic matter and free lime in the soil. The ratios of potential and active acidity are related to the buffering capacity of soil.

The titratable acidity arises from dissociation of weak acid functional groups of soil organic matter, deprotonation of hydroxyl-Al-polymers associated with the internal and external surfaces of phyllosilicate minerals, from short range ordered aluminosilicates (allophonic materials) and from ruptured surfaces of oxides and silicates. According to Jackson (1963) the various groups in soil are considered responsible for the production of titratable acidity are:

(i) Strong acids, soil pH below 4.2:
   - Mineral colloidal electrolytes
   - Free H_2SO_4 and FeS_2 or S

(ii) Weak acids, soil pH below 5.2:
   - Aluminohydronium ions
   - Possibly some humus carboxyl

(iii) Very weak acid, soil pH 5.2–6 or 7
   - Humus carboxyl
   - Polyalumino edge $OH_2^{0.5+}$
   - H_2CO_3, basic aluminium sulphate

(iv) Very, very weak acids, soil pH 6.5 or 7 to 9.5:
   - Humus phenol
   - Polyaluminohydronium edge pair $—OH_2^{0.5+}$
     $—OH_2^{0.5-}$

   - $Ca(HCO_3)_2.NaHCO_3$

(v) Extremely weak acids, soil pH > 9.5:
   - Humus alcoholic hydroxyl
   - Silicic $—OH$
   - Gibbsite $—OH$

Fundamentally, all the acidic groups depend on proton association, but differ only in acid strength of the functional groups. Group (i) derives from the presence of exchangeable H^+ ions, while groups (ii) and (iii) are of most concern in practice as sources of acidity which have important effects on crops productivity from the agronomic point of view.

The hydrated Al ion (Al hexahydronium ion) is an acid in the general sense that it contains protons (hydrogen ions) removable from the six water molecules ($—OH_2$) surrounding the Al in an octahedral coordination. Exchangeable Al^{3+} is in equilibrium with soluble Al^{3+} (present as Al hexahydronium ion, $Al(H_2O)_6^{3+}$) in the soil solution that can react with water to produce H^+ and thus acidify the soil, as shown below:

$$Al^{3+} + H_2O \longleftrightarrow Al(OH)^{2+} + H^+$$
$$Al(OH)^{2+} + H_2O \longleftrightarrow Al(OH)_2^+ + H^+$$
$$Al(OH)^+ + H_2O \longleftrightarrow Al(OH)_3^0 + H^+$$

Most of the soil acidity in soils occurs between pH 4.0 and 7.5 due to hydrolysis of Al^{3+}. In extremely acidic soils (pH < 4.0), strong acids such as H_2SO_4 are a major component of soil acidity. At pH 5.5 to 7.0 hydroxy-Al polymers predominate, exchangeable acidity is absent and only non-exchangeable and titrable acidity are present in measurable quantities. Significant quantities of such acidity as R-COOH and R-OH groups of soil organic matter can be present even in soils of pH more than 7.0 (Panda 1987).

ACIDIFICATION OF SOIL

Soil acidification is a natural process in soils from both acidic and basic parent materials. Soil acidification is defined as a decrease of base saturation of effective cation exchange capacity of soil. Low base saturation of acid soils indicates the low concentration of base cations (Ca, Mg, and K) in soil solution, which can lead to deficiency of cations in plants. Low base saturation of soil is also indicative of high concentration of Al in soil solution, which is harmful to growth of plant roots. High concentration Al in the run-off water can also cause the toxic effects on the biota of surface water bodies.

Once soil pH is lowered much below 5.5, aluminosilicate clays and aluminium hydroxide minerals begin to dissolve, releasing aluminium-hydroxyl cations and then exchange with other cations from soil exchange complex. The fraction of exchange sites occupied by Al monomer and polymer species and its hydrolysis products can become large once the soil pH falls below 5.0. The larger the percentage of exchange sites occupied by aluminium, the greater the percentage of hydrogen formed, thus the lower pH and increase the acidity of soil.

$$Al^{3+} \ Ca^{2+} \ Mg^{2+} \ K^+ \ H^+ + water \longrightarrow Ca^{2+} + Mg^{2+} + K^+ + Al^{3+} + Al\,(OH)x + H^+$$

$\uparrow$

clays and organic

Exchangeable acidity   Soil solution active acidity

(Al^{3+}, H^+) (H^+)

De Vries and Breeussma (1987) divided the soil acidification into actual and potential acidification. Actual soil acidification is the decrease of acid-neutralizing capacity (ANC) of soil, which is the total amount of cations is soil. Potential soil acidification is defined as an increase in the base-neutralizing capacity (BNC) of the soil. BNC is the total amount of the acidic components in soil, including sulphur and nitrogen in organic matter, adsorbed sulphur and carbon in organic matter.

The amount of base cations in soil (BC) is important for the long-term susceptibility of a soil to acidification, because the release of base cations from minerals during weathering processes buffer the system.

Weathering and dissolution of parent materials by hydrolysis of CO_2 followed by leaching of basic cations (Na, Ca, and Mg) with bicarbonate (HCO_3^-), is the dominant soil acidification process in nature. Soils usually become more acidic with time due to weathering. Highly weathered soils are often more acidic. The initial factors responsible for the development of soil acidity are parent material, rainfall and type of vegetation. Many soils of tropical regions are acidic primarily because they are millions of years old and have been exposed to continuous weathering under high rainfall conditions, which allow the leaching of cations Ca, Mg and K from the surface layer of soil. The cation exchange sites vacated by leached cations, leaving Al^{3+} as the dominant exchange cation. Inorganic soil components such as aluminosilicate clay minerals and sesquioxides (R_2O_3) produce titratable acidity through deprotonation from hydroxyl groups at clay surfaces and edges. In the leaching environment the dissolution of clay occurs as follows:

$$[Xa - Alb - Sic]clay + dH^+ \longleftrightarrow bAl^{3+} + cH_4SiO_4 + aX^{n+}$$

where [ ] represents a generalized clay and X represents non-Al cations.

In igneous rocks, Al is largely bonded with oxygen ions in tetrahedral coordination. As the rocks weather, Al progressively acquires more octahedral bonding. Many aluminosilicate minerals contain base cations, and weathering of these minerals in relatively young acidic soils, released cations as they weather.

$$CaAl_2Si_2O_8 + 8H^+ = Ca^{2+} + 2Al^{3+} + 2H_4SiO_4$$

(anorthite)

The weathering of this mineral releases 1 mole of Ca^{2+} for every 2 moles of Al^{3+}. If the reaction is not rate limiting and no secondary reactions occur, and conditions are favourable for reduction of exchangeable bases or mobilization of Al^{3+} in solution, the soil would become eventually acidic.

Montmorillonite, kaolinite and gibbsite represent successive stages of increasing weathering. High rainfall is one of the characteristics of the more intense weathering situations where gibbsite forms.

$$Al_2(Si_2O_5)_2(OH)_2 + 4H_2O + 6H^+ = 2Al^{3+} + 4H_4SiO_4$$

(montmorillonite)

$$Al_2Si_2O_5(OH)_4 + 6H^+ = 2Al^{3+} + 2H_4SiO_4 + H_2O$$

(kaolinite)

The weathering releases the aluminum from 2:1 layer silicates in soils is enhanced by inputs of acids from the natural decomposition of organic matter and acid deposition. Once soil pH drops below 5.5 aluminosilicate clays and aluminium hydroxide minerals begin to dissolve and exchange with other cations from the soil colloid exchange complex. The rate of soil acidification is influenced by the following natural and human induced processes.

PARENT MATERIALS

Soil acidification is a natural process in soil from both acidic and basic parent materials. Soil usually become more acidic with time caused by weathering and frequently more weathered soils are more acidic. If other factors of soil formation (climate, time, vegetation, etc.) remain constant (Schroeder 1984) pH decreases in the order of:

On igneous rocks　:　basalt > diorite > granite

On sediments　　　:　limestone > boulder clay > aeolian sand

The calcareous geologic materials (e.g. limestone) resist acidification more than those of granite and gneiss predominant parent materials.

LEACHING OF BASES

In the high rainfall and humid zones, the leaching losses of exchangeable bases (Ca^{2+}, Mg^{2+}, K^+ and Na^+) out of the effective root zone is also a contributing factor to increased soil acidity. This is a major problem in sandy soils of high rainfall areas with low cation exchange capacity. Excessive rainfall influences the rate of soil acidification depending on the rate of percolation of water through the soil profile. These basic cations are replaced by acidic cations such as aluminium and hydrogen ions. So, the soils formed under high rainfall conditions are more acid than those formed under arid conditions.

NITROGENOUS FERTILIZERS

The natural process of soil acidification is often intensified by agricultural practices, particularly nitrogen fertilization. The pioneering work of Pierre (1928a, 1928b) demonstrated that use of ammonium-based nitrogenous fertilizers in excess of crop removal induced acidification in agricultural soils. The magnitude of soil acidification resulting from the residual acidity of fertilizers is a function of N source, rate and placement (Mahler and Harder 1984).

Soil acidity does not develop in a year or two, but the rate of acidification varies among the soils. A long-term field experiment started in 1956 at Kanke, Ranchi, India on a Paleustalfs (acid red loam) of pH 5.8 with different combinations of N, NP, NPK, farmyard manure (FYM), and lime (Lal and Mathur 1989). Lime is applied at the rate of 2.5 t ha^{-1}, once in four years, and FYM is equivalent to N dose. The N, P_2O_5, and K_2O were applied at the levels of 44 kg each ha^{-1} up to 1969–70, thereafter increased to 100, 60, and 40 kg ha^{-1} respectively. The continuous application N alone or in combination with P and K decreased the soil pH from 5.8 to 4–3.8 in 28 years. Even the application of FYM only maintained the initial soil pH.

ACID PRECIPITATION

The combustion of oil, coal, fuel in vehicles, smelting of S-containing ores, forest fire, burning of crop residues, etc. which contain N and S are combusted, oxidation results in the formation of nitric oxide (NO), nitrogen dioxide (NO_2) and sulphur dioxide (SO_2) which in the presence of light and moisture converted to HNO_3 and H_2SO_4 and when they fall to earth constitute acid rain. In the industrialized areas, acid precipitation contributes around 1 kmol H^+ ha^{-1} $year^{-1}$, but in some of very highly areas the precipitation can be as high as 6 kmol H^+ ha^{-1} $year^{-1}$.

$$SO_2 + H_2O \longrightarrow H_2SO_4 \longrightarrow H^+ + HSO_3^-$$

$$SO_2 \xrightarrow[O_2]{\text{Sunlight}} SO_3 \xrightarrow{H_2O} H_2SO_4 \longleftrightarrow 2H^+ + SO_4^{2-}$$

$$2N_2O + O_2 \longrightarrow 4NO \longrightarrow 4O_2 \longrightarrow 4NO_3$$

The soils of low buffering capacity, such as acid sands with low cation exchange capacity are most sensitive to acid rain. In general, tropical soils are high in sesquioxides (Fe- and Al-oxides) and already highly acidic, so the small contribution from precipitation will have minimal effect.

REMOVAL OF BASE CATIONS BY CROPS

The uptake of cations by plants can either reduce or increase the soil acidity produced by nitrification of NH_4^+ from fertilizers, crop and animal wastes or in organic matter. Generally, excess base (EB)/N ratio is used as a tool to estimate the contribution of crop production to soil acidity (Westerman 1981). This ratio is obtained by dividing the total cations minus total anions with total N expressed as cmol (p+)kg^{-1} of plant material.

$$(Ca^{2+} + Mg^{2+} + K^+ + Na^+) - (Cl^- + S + P + NO_3—N)/Total\ N$$

Plants with an EB/N ratio less than one would decrease the acidity produced by nitrification of NH_4^+ to NO_3 and if this ratio is greater than one would enhance the acidity.

In the case of forage and grain considerable N is removed, leaving behind in the soil the basic residues of Ca, Mg, K and Na that neutralize the acidity produced by nitrification of fertilizer N. Removal of straw, however, depletes the bases in soil faster than removal of nitrogen, which further enhances the acidification of fertilizer N. Leguminous plants are particularly more acidifying because the anion/cation uptake from the soil is more imbalance towards cations as compared to non-leguminous plants.

Nitrogen plays a major role in the cation-anion balance, because it is the nutrient that is taken up at the highest rate by more plant species. The plants supplied with NO_3^- will counterbalance the corresponding excess of negative charges by releasing equivalent amounts of OH^- or HCO_3^- into rhizosphere, thereby increase the rhizosphere pH. The plants receiving NH_4^+ will counterbalance the corresponding excess of positive charges by releasing equivalent amount of H^+ in the rhizosphere, thereby decrease rhizosphere pH

Root + NO_3^- Root (NO_3^-) + OH^-

Root + NH_4^+ Root (NH_4^+) + H^+

In a similar manner, plants relying on atmospheric N_2 such as legumes, take up more cations than anions, therefore, the release of excess of positive charges (H^+ ions) acidify the rhizoshere.

DECOMPOSITION OF ORGANIC MATTER

The decomposition of organic residues in soil also contributes to increased soil acidity. Carbon dioxide (CO_2) is released from organic residues during the decomposition process, respiration of soil organisms and plant roots. The CO_2 combines with water to form carbonic acid (H_2CO_3). Carbonic acid dissociates into hydrogen (H^+) and bicarbonate (HCO_3^-), resulting in another source of H^+ for increasing soil acidity in a cropping system.

$$CO_2 + H_2O \longrightarrow H_2CO_3 \longleftrightarrow HCO_3^- + H^+ \longrightarrow pKa = 6.35$$

Some plant residues contain significant quantities of organic acids, and after decomposition naturally affect the soil acidity. Other plants are acidifying simply because of the low concentrations of their bases. If plant does not contain enough bases to satisfy microbial needs the decomposition of plant residues will not only give off CO_2, but will also remove base nutrients such as calcium and magnesium from the soil in the decomposition process.

MINE TAILINGS

Mining often exposes sulfide-bearing minerals (pyrite, pyrrhotite, chalcopyrite, arsenopyrite and cobaltite) to the atmosphere. Mining tailings from the working of sulphide ores are extremely acid and pollute surface waters with acid, aluminium, iron, and heavy metals. Coal mine spoil is also pyritic and pH values of 3.0 commonly occur. Metal processing also does not remove all pyretic minerals and tailings, therefore, they often have significant sulphide concentrations. Oxidation of pyrite and production of acid can be illustrated using FeS_2 as an example in the general equations:

$$2FeS_2 + 2H_2O + 7O_2 = 2FeSO_4 + 2H_2SO_4$$
$$2FeSO_4 + H_2SO_4 + 1/2O_2 = Fe_2(SO_4)_3 + H_2O$$
$$Fe_2(SO_4)_3 + 6H_2O = 2Fe(OH)_3 + 4H_2SO_4$$

$$\rule{6cm}{0.4pt}$$

$$2FeS_2 + 15/2\ O_2 + 7H_2O = 2Fe(OH)_3 + 4H_2SO_4$$

Formation of sulphuric acid decreases the pH of the tailing environment and results in increased solubility of metals and minerals that are present.

Acid Mine Drainage (AMD) is the main source of soil pollution in the mining areas. The United States' Environmental Agencies have classified the AMD into following categories (Table 11.2) and the same is used in Indian condition for all practical purposes.

Table 11.2: *Classification of acid mine drainage*

Attributes	Class 1 (Acid drainage)	Class 2 (Partially oxidized and/or neutralized)	Class 3 (Oxidized and neutralized and/or alkaline)	Class 4 (Neutralized and not oxidized)
pH	2.0–4.0	3.5–6.6	6.5–8.5	6.5–8.5
Acidity, mg L^{-1}	1,000–15,000	0–1,000	0	0
F^{2+}, mg L^{-1}	500–1,000	0–500	0	50–1,000
F^{3+}, mg L^{-1}	0	0–1,000	0	0
Al^{3+}, mg L^{-1}	0–2,000	0–20	0	0
SO_4^{2-}, mg L^{-1}	1,000–20,000	500–10,000	500–10,000	500–10,000

LAND USE

The production of agricultural crops increases the acidification through the addition of acidifying fertilizers, increases nitrate leaching and removal of total biomass above ground portions for consumption. Forested watersheds tend to contribute more acidity than those dominated by meadows, pastures and agricultural crops. Trees and other vegetation in forests, 'scavenge' (retain on leaves and stems) acidic compounds in fogs, mists and atmospheric particulate matter. These compounds are later delivered to forest soils, and they get leached by rainfall water from the surface of the vegetation.

ALUMINIUM IN SOIL SOLUTION AND ITS TOXICITY

The role of soil solution of Al in acid soil infertility is now well-recognized for its agronomic significance. Although, Al solubility is pH-dependent, soil pH is a poor measure of Al toxicity or soil solution Al concentration. So, attention has shifted to concentrations and chemical activities of Al and its species in soil solution as predictors of Al toxicity. Al in aqueous systems exists in a variety of mononuclear and polynuclear forms, some of which are toxic to plants. The soil solution Al exists in inorganic and organic monomeric and polymeric forms.

The Al^{3+} ion, which is released from Al-bearing minerals to soil solutions, and natural water octahedrally coordinated with six molecules of water as an $[Al(H_2O)_6]^{3+}$ ion, which can exist as unhydrolyzed $[Al(H_2O)_6]^{3+}$ below pH 3.0. The hydrated Al ion (Al hexahydronium ion, $[Al(H_2O)_6]^{3+}$) is an acid in the general sense because it contains protons (H ions) removable from the six water molecules (—OH$_2$) surrounding the Al in an octahedral coordination. As the solution pH increases, $[Al(H_2O)_6]^{3+}$ can be hydrolyzed extensively:

$$[Al(H_2O)_6]^{3+} + nH_2O \longleftrightarrow [Al(OH)_n (H_2O)_{2-n}]^{(3-n)+}$$

where n is defined as the molar ratio of hydrolysis, which is equivalent to the OH:Al ratio in the solution. The stable mononuclear species in solution correspond to the series, n = 0–4, although n = 2 and 3 species are significant only in very dilute solutions.

For simplicity these hydrolysis species are generally written without the hydrated water even though the water is present. In solution, aluminium ions are hydrated and readily lose protons forming hydroxo complexes and can exist in many different ionic forms. Al hydrolyzes to Al^{3+}, dominates below pH 5.0, whereas the $Al(OH)^{2+}$ and $Al(OH)_2^{+}$ species form as the soil pH increases. At near-neutral pH the solid phase gibbsite $[Al(OH)_3]$ may occur, whereas aluminate $[Al(OH)_4^{-}]$ dominates in alkaline conditions without the water molecules normally as written.

It is difficult to draw the conclusion, which Al monomer is the major phytotoxic species, and nearly all the monomer Al species listed above have been considered toxic in one study or another (Kinraide 1991). Kinraide *et al.* (1992) have developed a model based on modified Guoy-Chapman-Stern analysis electrostatic interactions between Al^{3+}, other cations and the negatively charged cell surface on the assumptions that the negatively charged membrane surface would generate a strong attractive force for trivalent cations such as Al^{3+} and other cations to reduce the negative surface charge of plasma membrane, either through charge screening or charge neutralization. Based on this model, Al toxicity was best predicted with activity of Al^{3+} at the surface of plasma membrane than with the activity of Al^{3+} in the bulk solution. This model indicated the important role of negatively charged root-cell surface in toxicities not only to Al^{3+} but also to other potentially toxic cations and anions. There are some evidences to suggest that solution containing more than one Al atom polynuclear forms of Al can form, the most important of which is triskaideaaluminium $[AlO_4Al_{12}(OH)_{24}(H_2O)^{7+}]$, also referred as Al_{13}, which appears to be considerably more toxic than Al^{3+} in the plant species. However, still there is no direct evidence of it.

Monomeric Al also form low molecular weight complexes with a number of ligands, such as organic acids, proteins, lipids, PO_4^{3-}, SO_4^{2-}, and F^- and are much less toxic than soluble Al^{3+} or Al-hydroxyl cations.

SOIL ACIDITY ASSOCIATED FERTILITY STRESS

The soil acidity plays major role in determining the nutrient availability to plants and in many instances by specific mineral stress problems. Acid soil infertility is a syndrome of problems that affect plant growth in soils with low pH. This complex of problems arises from toxicities and deficiencies in acid soils are related to:

- Presence of the toxic concentration of Al and to a lesser extent Mn toxicity in many species,
- Deficiency of bases (Ca, Mg, K) and their poor retention power,
- High P fixation capacity of soil caused by highly active Al and Fe surfaces, rendering it unavailable to plants,
- Deficiency of Mo, especially for the growth of legumes,
- Reduction of soil biological activities,
- Impairment of N_2-fixation by legumes caused by poor survival of microsymbiont and inhibition of nodulation,
- Fe and Mn toxicities in submerged rice,
- Bacterial growth is inhibited by nutrient toxicities and low nutrient availability in acidic soils, and
- Soil acidification changes the decline balance between groups of living organisms in the soil, due to the preference of soil fauna for specific pH environment. Generally, soil fauna has the capacity to tolerate the soil acidity to cope with large changes in soil pH, however, most macrofauna including deep burrowing species such as worms and termites tend to decrease in abundance in acidic soil conditions.

The relative importance of these constraints may vary with soil type, parent material, soil pH, soil structure and texture, and plant species. The toxicity of Al^{3+} results into poorly developed root system, which causes susceptibility to drought stress and nutrient deficiencies. The primary response of Al stress in plants occurs in roots, as reduced elongation at the tip, followed by swelling and deterioration of differentiated cells, as well as root disclouration (Foy *et al.* 1978). The Al toxicity produces a range of symptoms in the top of plant, including small dark green leaves, stunted growth, delayed maturity, purpling of leaves, wilting and induced deficiencies of Ca. The foliar symptoms in some plants resemble those of phosphorus deficiency manifested by overall stunting, small dark green leaves, late maturity, purpling of stems, leaves and leaf veins and yellowing and death of leaf tips (Foy 1992). The Al induced Ca deficiency causes curling or rolling of leaves, inhibited growth of lateral branches, or collapse of growing points or petiole.

The deficiencies and toxicities may act independently or together to reduce plant growth. Al toxicity is particularly severe at soil pH values of 5.0 and below, but it can also occur at high pH 5.5 in smectitic (clay mineral) soils. In most cultivated crops, the symptoms of Al injury are first expressed by reduced root growth later the affected roots thicken and don't branch normally. The root tips disintegrate and turn brown, and adventitious roots proliferate as long as crown is alive.

In acidic soils, it is frequently the growth reduction is attributed to Al toxicity in terms of its important for growth reduction as compared to Mn toxicity. Unlike Al, Mn is easily transported to shoot from the absorbed roots. It produces more characteristics symptoms in plant tops and often foliage injury is proportional to

accumulated Mn. The toxicity symptoms of Mn have been reported from the acidic soils include marginal chlorosis and necrosis of leaves and necrotic spots on leaves. However, in the acidic soils of northeast India, the toxicity of Mn toxicity so far not reported. In acid soils, apart from low pH and toxicities of Al and Mn, the deficiencies of Ca, Mg, P and Mo may also limit the productivity of crops. Deficiencies of these elements at low pH occur either due to reduced availability in the soil or interactions with high concentrations of H^+, Al^{n+} and Mn^{2+}. The high concentration of Al^{n+} and Mn^{2+} can compete with Ca^{2+} and Mg^{2+} for binding at cation exchange sites in the apoplasm, reduce the uptake of Ca^{2+} and Mg^{2+}.

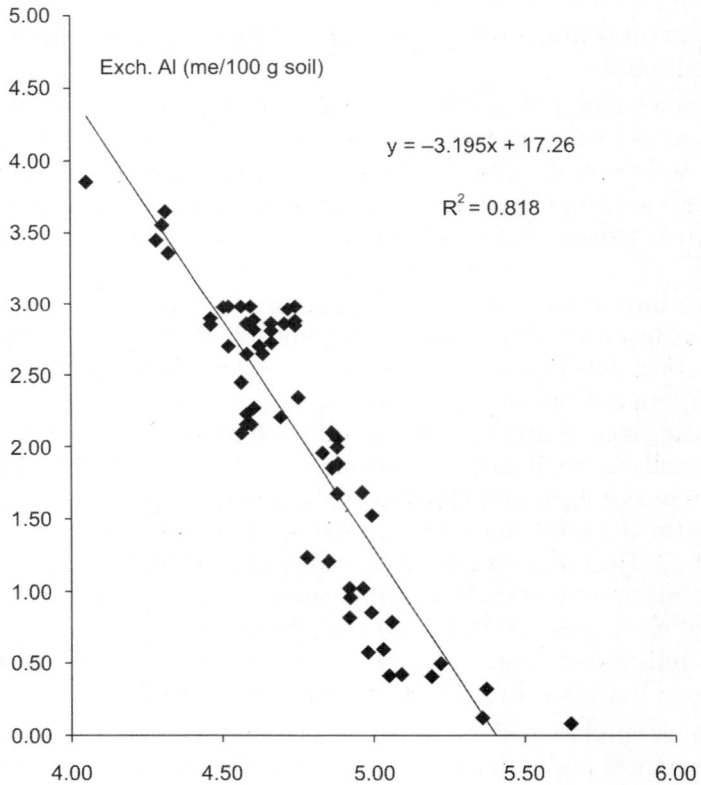

Fig. 11.1: Relationship between exchangeable Al and soil pH

In majority of the acidic soils, the P deficiency may limit the crop productivity after soil acidity. In the acidic soils, the availability of phosphorus is reduced due to high P fixation capacity and/or precipitation of P to less soluble Fe- and Al-phosphates. Moreover, Al can immobilize P on root surfaces, cell walls and in the free spaces of plant roots as insoluble Al-P, preventing the translocation of P from roots to shoots and limit the uptake of relatively immobile P in the soil to plants.

REFERENCES

Borlaug NE. 1997. Feeding a world of 10 billion people: the miracle ahead. *Plant Tissue Cul. Biotech.* **3:** 19–127.

Cameron FK and Bell JM. 1905. The mineral constituents of the soil solution. *U S Agric. Bur. Soils Bull.* **30.**

Chernov VA. 1947. The Nature of soil acidity. (English Translation Sciences, USSR, Moscow. *Soil Sci. Soc. Amer.*

Coleman NT and Howard ME. 1953. The heats of neutralization of acid clays and cation exchange resins. *J. Am. Soc. Chem.* **75:** 6045–6046.

Coleman NT and Thomas GW. 1967. The basic chemistry of soil acidity. In Soil acidity and liming, p1–41. Pearson RW and Adams F (Eds.), *ASA* Madison, Wisconsin.

Coulter BS. 1969. The chemistry of hydrogen and aluminium ions in soil, clay minerals and resins. *Soil Fertil.* **32:** 214–223.

De Vries W and Breeussma A. 1987. The relation between soil acidification and element cycling. *Water Air Soil Poll.* **35:** 293–310.

Eswaran H, Reich P and Beinroth F. 1997. Global distribution of soils with acidity. In Plant-soil interactions at low pH, p159–164. Moniz AC, Furlani AMC, Schaffert RE, Frageria NK, Rosolem CA and Cantarella H (Eds.), Brazillion Soil Science Society, Campinas.

Foy C. 1992. Soil chemical factors limiting plant root growth. *Adv. Soil Sci.* **19:** 97–149.

Foy CD, Chaney RL and White MC. 1978. The physiology of metal toxicity in plants. *Ann. Rev. Plant Physiol.* **29:** 511–566.

Jackson ML. 1963. Aluminium bonding in soils: a unifying principle of soil science. *Proc. Soil Sci. Soc. Am.* **27:** 1–10.

Jenny H. 1961. Reflections on the soil acidity merry-go-round. *Soil Sci. Soc. Am. Proc.* **25:** 428–432.

Johnson SW. 1888. How crops feed. Orange Jud and Comp., New York.

Kelley WP and Brown SM. 1925. Ion exchange in relation to soil acidity. *Soil Sci.* **21:** 289–302.

Kinraide TB. 1991. Identification of the rhizotonic aluminium species. *Plant Soil.* **134:** 167–178.

Kinraide TB, Ryan PR and Kochian L. 1992. Interactive effects of Al^{3+}, H^+, and other cations on root elongation considered in terms of cell-surface electrical potential. *Plant Physiol.* **99:** 1461–1468.

Lal S and Mathur BS. 1988. Effect of long term manuring, fertilization and liming on crop yield and some physicochemical properties of acid soil. *J. Indian Soc. Soil Sci.* **36:** 113–119.

Mahler RL and Harder RW. 1984. The influence of tillage methods, cropping sequence and N rates on the acidification of northern Idaho soil. *Soil Sci.* **137:** 52–60.

Mandal SC. 1996. Introduction and historical review. In Acid soils of India, p3–24. Mahapatra IC, Mandal SC, Mishra C, Mitra GN and Panda N (Eds.), Indian Council of Agricultural Research, New Delhi.

Marshall CE. 1949. The colloid chemistry of silicate minerals. Academic Press, New York.

Page MJ. 1926. The nature of soil acidity. *Intern. Soc. Soil Sci.* (Groningen, Holland) IIA: 232–244.

Panda N. 1987. Acid soils of Eastern India-their chemistry and management. *J. Indian Soc. Soil Sci.* **35:** 568–581.

Paver H and Marshall CE. 1934. The role of aluminium in the reactions of the clays. *Chem. Indust.* **12:** 750–760.

Pierre WH. 1928a. Nitrogenous fertilizers and soil acidity: 1. Effects of various nitrogenous fertilizers on soil reaction. *Agron. J.* **20:** 254–269.

Pierre WH. 1928b. Nitrogenous fertilizers and soil acidity: 2. The use of fertilizer combinations, lime and basic slag in correcting the acidity formed by various nitrogenous fertilizers. *Agron. J.* **20:** 270–279.

Schofield RK. 1949. Effect of pH on electric charges carried by clay particles. *J. Soil. Sci.* **23:** 252–254.

Schroeder D. 1984. Soil- Facts and Concepts. p140. International Potash Institute, Bern/Switzerland.

Sharma PD and Sarkar AK. 2005. Managing Acid Soils for Enhancing Productivity, p23. Indian Council of Agricultural Research, NRM Division, Krishi Bhavan-II, New Delhi.

Thomas GW. 1977. Historical developments of soil chemistry: Ion exchange. *Soil Sci. Soc. Am. J.* **41:** 230–238.

Truog E. 1916 . Soil acidity. *J. Physic. Chem.* **20:** 457–484.

Yuan TL. 1963. Some relationships among hydrogen, aluminum and pH in solution and soil systems. *Soil Sci.* **95:** 155–163.

Westerman RL. 1981. Factors affecting soil acidity. *Solution.* **25:** 64–81.

Von Uexkull HR and Mutert E. 1995. Global extent, development and economic impact of acid soils. *Plant Soil.* **171:** 1–15.

12 Strategies for Production of Horticultural Crops on Acidic Soils

DS Rathore

ABSTRACT

Poor crop productivity of acid soil is due to mineral toxicities (Al and Mn) and deficiencies (P, Ca, Mg and Mo). Combining the use of acid tolerant genotypes with management practices is often the most effective strategy for improving horticultural crop productivity on acid soils.

Key words: Acidic soils, horticultural crops, production.

INTRODUCTION

Acidic soils are the main constraints of crop productivity in the country. The acidic soil of India are mainly found in North Eastern Region and Western Ghats with sporadic distribution in Jharkhand, Himachal Pradesh, Odisha, West Bengal and Chhattisgarh, etc. According to an estimate, about one-third of the Indian soils (49 m ha) are acidic out of which 25 m ha have pH below 5.5. Acid soils are widely prevalent in the hill region of the country due to leaching of bases from the exchange ion complex under prevailing high rainfall and sloping topography. The percentages of acidic soils in different states of northeastern hill region are 84, 77, 76, 60, 57 and 47 in Arunachal Pradesh, Manipur, Meghalaya, Mizoram, Sikkim and Tripura respectively (Panda 1998).

Parent materials, presence of elements creating acidity, high rainfall, vegetation and continuous application of acid producing fertilizers, are the various factors, which cause the formation of acid soils. Soil acidity can be corrected by applying agricultural lime; however, liming is both costly and cumbersome in application, a combination of reduced quantity of lime application and cultivation of acid tolerant genotypes will be an ideal approach for future research to combat the problem of soil acidity in the world.

TYPES OF SOIL ACIDITY

There are two types of acidities in soil, *viz.* pH dependent/active acidity and reserve/potential acidity. The H^+ ion concentration in soil solution is called pH dependent acidity. The H^+ and Al^{3+} ions present on the exchange complex of the colloid cause reserve/potential acidity. Reserve acidity is the main acidity in the soil, which is several times higher than the active acidity. Active acidity indicates the need of lime whereas potential acidity determines the amount of limestone to neutralize soil acidity. As potential acidity increases, a larger amount of lime is required to raise pH of a given soil. When cation exchange capacity (CEC) increases due to higher clay and organic matter, the quantity of liming material needed to change soil pH also increases. Soils with low CEC may require only 1 tonne of agricultural limestone to change a pH from 4.5 to 6.5 whereas a soil with a higher CEC may require 2 tonnes of lime to make the same change.

Formation of Acidic Soils

The following five factors have been found responsible for creating acidity in soils:

Parent Material

Parent materials such as granite produce acidity in soils on weathering.

Presence of Elements Creating Acidity

Aluminium, manganese, and iron release protons on hydrolysis resulting into soil acidity.

High Rainfall

High rainfall accelerates leaching of bases like Ca, Mg, Na and K, which results into poor base saturation, and thus increasing acidity in soils.

Vegetation

Coniferous vegetation generally found in hills is rich in silica and produces silicic acid on decomposition that is one of the main causes of soil acidity.

Continuous Application of Acid Producing Fertilizers

Nitrogenous fertilizers such as ammonium sulphate, ammonium chloride and urea produce acidity in the soils. During mineralization process, when ammonium converts into nitrate by the action of nitrosomonas in the presence of water, there is release of hydrogen ions causing acidity in the soil.

CHARACTERISTICS OF ACIDIC SOILS

The common features of acid soils are given below:

Low pH

Descriptive ranges of pH in acid soils are under:

Ultra acid below	:	3.5
Extremely acid	:	3.5–4.5

Very strongly acid : 4.5–5.5
Moderately acid   : 5.6–6.0
Slightly acid   : 6.1–6.5

The pH ranges of a soil help in identifying suitable crops for cultivation.

Toxicity of Elements

Acid soils often contain soluble forms of aluminium, manganese and iron. As soil acidity increases (pH decreases), soluble aluminium, manganese and iron increase to toxic levels. Aluminium toxicity is more pronounced which restricts root growth and phosphorus uptake and inactivates phosphorus within the plant roots. Manganese toxicity causes black necrotic spots or streaks on leaves of cereals and chlorosis on leaf margins and cupping of leaves of canola and legumes. Aluminium and manganese toxicity generally reduces the yield of crops grown on acid soils.

Deficiency of Nutrient Elements

Phosphorus, calcium, molybdenum, magnesium and boron are found generally deficient in acid soils. Aluminium toxicity renders phosphorus immobile and unavailable to plants. Consequently, plants show phosphorus deficiency symptoms like purplish colouring on dark green leaves due to accumulation of sugars which favours anthocyanin synthesis. Calcium deficient cabbage plants are stunted and margins of young leaves become necrotic.

Microbial Activity

Soil acidity has a direct effect on the survival and growth of rhizobium bacteria which fix nitrogen in association with legumes. The rhizobium bacteria associated with alfalfa and sweet clover are especially sensitive to acidity. However, the activity of fungi, actinomycetes is much more as compared to the activity of bacteria than the neutral soils.

Soil Structure

Since soil structure is the arrangement of soil particles, i.e. sand, silt and clay, the Al, Fe and Mn ions act as binding agent in the soil and thus affect soil structure.

STRATEGIES FOR PRODUCTION ON ACID SOILS

Soil acidity affects many aspects of soil and plant health causing significant decline in the crop productivity. Crops vary greatly in their tolerance to some of the components of the problematic acid soils. Differences in the reaction of both crop species and varieties within a species to varying levels of aluminium and manganese have been measured under field and laboratory conditions. The expression of some acid soil problems therefore is not merely one of the soil chemical characteristics but rather the result of a complex interaction between the plant and the soil. Horticultural crops have been found more remunerative than agricultural crops in the hill region. Therefore, suitable strategies are required to be adopted to produce horticultural crops more profitably in the acidic soils.

CULTIVATION OF HORTICULTURAL CROPS TOLERANT TO SOIL ACIDITY

The aim of management of acid soils is to realize their crop production potential to a large extent. Thus, the problem of soil acidity is addressed either by addition of the amendments to counteract the abnormalities of such soils or to manipulate the agricultural practices to obtain optimum crop yields under the acidic conditions. In the latter case, the most important approach is to cultivate acid tolerant crops. A large number of horticultural crops can be cultivated successfully on acid soils (Table 12.1). However, some of these crops require acidic soil reaction for their good growth and production whereas others are merely tolerant to the acidic conditions of the soil. Azolea, blueberry, cherries and tea need acid soils for high productivity.

GROWING GENOTYPES TOLERANT TO ACID SOILS

Growing of aluminium tolerant crop varieties or genotypes is the potential approach to enhance the crop productivity. These can be obtained through traditional breeding or by genetic engineering. Some genotypes release organic acids into the soil, which

Table 12.1: *Suitable horticultural crops for growing in acid soils*

1. **Fruits:**	3. **Plantation crops:**
Apple	Cardamom
Blueberry	Coffee
Cherries	Tea
Cranberry	Rubber
Pummelo	
Pineapple	
Strawberry	
2. **Vegetables:**	4. **Ornamentals:**
Brinjal	Azalea
Bittergourd	Croton
Carrot	Bougainvillea
Capsicum	Orchids
Cucurbits	Rose
Bean	Hydrangea
Turnip	
Potato	
Radish	

bind aluminium within complexes that cannot enter the root. In this way the metal does not remain toxic. On the basis of this observation, it is possible to produce transgenic crop genotypes with increased organic acid release. The transgenic approach has been used in several crops (papaya, tobacco, rice, alfalfa) to produce genotypes that overexpress organic acids. Furthermore, it is possible to increase aluminium tolerance by crossing a traditional variety that is naturally aluminium tolerant with a line engineered to tolerate aluminium. A list of tolerant genotypes of horticultural crops to acid soils is given in Table 12.2.

Transgenics have also been used to tackle the problem of manganese toxicity in acid soils. The strategy involves introducing a gene into a crop plant that causes manganese to remain sequestered in a cell compartment (the vacuole) where it can do no harm to the plant. Similar research work is being postulated to make much more phosphate available to the plants.

APPLICATION OF LIME

Liming has long been regarded as an essential component of good management of acid soils. Lime purely is calcium oxide but in practical terms it is material containing

Table 12.2: *Tolerant genotypes of different horticultural crops to acidic soils*

Crop	Genotype	Tolerance	Reference
Tomato	Pant Bahar	Al tolerant	Singh and Bhardwaj R 2007a
Cabbage	Pusa Drum Head	Al tolerant	Singh and Bhardwaj 2007
Citrus	Volkamer lemon	Al resistant	Toon *et al.* 2003
	Cleopetra Mandarin Rough lemon	Al resistant	Lin and Myre 1991
Pea	PC-55-11-1-2	Al tolerant	Singh *et al.* 2007b
Okra	Prabhani Kranti	Al tolerant	Singh and Sureja 2008
Vegetable cowpea	Bhaya Lakshmi	Acid tolerant	Sharma and Sarkar 2005
French bean	HUR-15	Acid tolerant	Sharma and Sarkar 2005
	F-15 and Supere	Al tolerant	Massot *et al.* 1999
	VRA 81054, Uyole 84, 2AV 8313, ACV 55, ACV 8312, (Climbing type), ICA PIJAO, MCM 1015, (Black seeded), Lusale white A197, BAC 76 (Dwarf type)	Al tolerant	Singh *et al.* 1996
	Contender, RCFB-31 A, RCFB-43	Al tolerant	Singh and Sanval 2008

carbonates, hydroxides of Ca and Mg which is capable of neutralizing the acidity of soil. Farmers can improve the quality of acid soils by liming to adjust pH to the levels needed by the crop to be grown. The effectiveness of liming material is based on two factors, i.e. calcium carbonate equivalent and fairness of the material. Benefits of liming are given below:

- Reduces the possibility of Al and Mn toxicities
- Improves microbial activity
- Improves physical condition of the soil
- Improves symbiotic nitrogen fixation by legumes
- Provides an inexpensive source for Ca and Mg
- Improves nutrients availability of P and Mo.

An annual application of 2–5 tonnes of lime ha^{-1} $year^{-1}$ is sufficient to maintain the level the calcium and magnesium in the soil under continuous cropping (Somani 1996). However, the amount required for reclamation of any particular field must be accurately determined through soil testing. Amount of lime required will vary depending on current soil pH, soil types, lime quality and crops to be grown. Adequate soil moisture is required for lime to react with soil. Effects of lime application will be slower in a dry soil. Lime must be thoroughly mixed with the soil. Since neutralization involves a reaction between soil particles and lime particles, the better lime is mixed with soil the more efficiently, the acidity is neutralized. It takes about 6 to 12 months to have an effect on the soil pH because lime is less soluble in water. It is important to apply lime immediately after crop harvest to allow lime to react and correct the soil pH before the next growing season. Lime can be highly effective in alleviating aluminium toxicity in acid soils but is an additional input that can induce serious problems if not done correctly. Incorporating lime into the surface 15 cm of soil before planting is a recommended strategy for horticultural crops.

APPLICATION OF ORGANIC MATERIAL

Maintenance of high soil organic matter levels through the return of crop residues, cover cropping or mulching will help as components in the organic matter being capable of binding free Al into non-toxic complexes. Organic matter also helps to slow the rate of acidification of the soil which may result from sequential cropping. The continuous application of farmyard manure (FYM) in aluminium toxic soils decreases soil aluminium and also favours the growth of plant roots (Patiram, 1996). The combination of limestone and FYM enhances yields by increasing the base status of soil and surface charge. FYM increases Ca, Mg, P and K content of plants through beneficial influence on physicochemical properties of the soil and nutrient release.

Regular application of organic residues will induce a long-term increase in the soil organic matter content. Complexation of Al by the newly formed organic matter will tend to reduce the concentration of exchangeable and soluble Al present. As organic residues decompose, P is released and this can become adsorbed to oxide surfaces. This will in turn, reduce the extent of adsorption of subsequently added P thus increasing P availability. The practical implication of the processes discussed is that organic residues could be used as a strategic tool to reduce the rates of lime and fertilizer P required for optimum crop production on acidic, P-fixing soils. Further research is, however, warranted to investigate the use of organic residues in the management of acid soils (Haynes and Mokolobate, 2001).

APPLICATION OF FERTILIZERS

The low pH soils exhibit severe phosphorus deficiency emanating from high P-fixation and low P mobility and availability. Phosphate in the soil has long been known to be less available to crops in some extremely acid soils because it reacts with aluminium and/or manganese, which are available in acid soils. When phosphate reacts with these metals, the compound formed is a very insoluble solid (such as aluminium phosphate). As a result, not only is the phosphote unavailable, but the aluminium and manganese are also unavailable. For these reasons, when phosphate fertilizers are blended with the seed at planting time, the harmful effects of toxic Al and Mn are greatly reduced, and near normal yield may be obtained. Phosphate forms insoluble complexes with Al.

Deficiency of other nutrients such as nitrogen (N), potassium (K), Calcium (Ca), magnesium (Mg) and sulphur (S) has also been reported in acid soils. Depending on the soil analysis, the application of deficient nutrients is required to be applied to obtain proper crop yields.

Although liming is very effective in elimination of aluminium toxicity, yet the quantity of lime required to neutralize the soil acidity is high for optimum productivity. Majority of farmers can neither obtain nor afford it. Further, it is difficult to place lime deep in the soil. Hence, use of limited amount of lime and fertilizers along with nutrient efficient and elemental toxicity tolerant crops is the right strategy for improving crop productivity on acid soils. Recent research findings have shown the existence of inter and intraspecific differences in acidic tolerance and nutrient use efficiency of many crops' varieties and genotypes. Genotypes that have high nutrient use efficiency under soil acidity stress may be useful in breeding varieties with high yield potentials for acid soils. Best Management Practices (BMP) such as crop rotations, improvement of organic matter content in soil and control of soil erosion, insect pests, diseases and weeds can improve crop yields and optimize nutrient use efficiency on degraded infertile acid soils. The development of new varieties with high nutrient use efficiency and tolerance to acidity with BMP's will contribute to economically viable and environmentally sustainable crop production systems for the vast acid soil ecosystems of the world.

CONCLUSION

Soil acidity occurs throughout the world and it can be made more productive if soil acidity are minimized. Since genetic variation present in crop plants, perhaps the best measure for soil acidity would be a combination of acid tolerant genotype with liming. However, more information is needed on the plant component of this approach especially a better understanding of acid tolerance mechanisms and how these can be incorporated into productive cultivars. It is essential that there should be a team plant breeder, plant nutritionists, soil scientist, agronomist for bringing fruitful results in solving this soil toxic problem.

REFERENCES

Haynes RJ and Mokolobate MS. 2001. Amelioration of Al toxicity and P deficiency in acid soils by additions of organic residues: a critical review of the phenomenon and mechanism involved. *Nutr. Cyc. agroeco.* **591:** 47–63.

Lin Z and Myhre DL. 1991. Differential response of citrus rootstocks to Al levels in nutrient solutions: I. Plant Growth. *J. Plant Nutr.* **14:** 1223–1238.

Massot N, Llugany M, Paschenrieder C and barcelo J. 1999. Callose production as an indicator of Al toxicity in bean cultivars. *J. Plant Nutr.* **22:** 1–10.

Panda N. 1998. Soils of north eastern region and their management for sustainable production. Paper presented in Symp., ICAR Res. Complex for NEH Region, Umiam, Meghalaya.

Patiram 1996. Effect of limestone and farmyard manure on crop yields and soil acidity or on acid Inceptosols in Sikkim, India. *Trop. Agric.* (Trinidad) **73:** 238–241.

Sharma PD and Sarkar AK. 2005. Managing acid soils for enhancing productivity. Published by, Director NBSS and LUP, Amravati Road, Nagpur 440 010, Maharashtra.

Singh D and Bhardwaj R. 2007a. Screening of tomato and cabbage genotypes for their tolerance to aluminium toxicity. Final project report of College of Horticulture and Forestry, Central Agricultural University, Pasighat, Arunachal Pradesh, India.

Singh D, Rai AK, Sureja AK and Bhardwaj R. 2007b. Hematoxylin staining: A rapid method for assessment of aluminium tolerance in pea genotypes. In Abstract and Souvenir of 2nd Indian Horticulture Congress, p178. Chadha KL, Singh SK, Patel VB, Prasad KV and Asrey R (Eds) held during 18–21 April 2007 at ICAR Research Complex for NEH region, Barapani, Meghalaya, India.

Singh D, Rai AK, Sureja AK and Bhardwaj R. 2007b. Screening of tomato germplasm for tolerance to low pH and aluminium toxicity. Paper Presented in 2nd Indian Horticulture Congress held in ICAR Research Complex for NEH region, Barapani, Meghalaya from 18–21 April, 2007.

Singh D and Sureja AK. 2008. Identification of *okra* genotypes tolerant to aluminium toxicity. In abstract of the National Seminar on Sustainable Management of Acidic Soils for Higher Crop productivity, pp. 28. Singh D, Raju AS, Chaturvedi SK and Sharma S (Eds) held during 22–24 September, 2008 at College of Horticulture and Forestry, Central Agricultural University, Pasighat, Arunachal Pradesh, India.

Singh DP, Mapiki A, Musanya JC, Mulila J and Javaheri F. 1996. Screening of bean varieties for tolerance to Al toxicity. 2nd Crop Sci. Cong. Abstract, 262.

Singh D and Sanval SK 2008. Hematoxylin staining as a phenotypic index for aluminium tolerance selection in French Bean. In Abstract of the National Seminar on Sustainable Management of Acidic soils for Higher Crop Productivity, p28. Singh D, Raju AS, Chaturvedi SK and Sharma S (Eds) held during 22-24 September, 2008 at College of Horticulture and Forestry, Central Agricultural University, Pasighat, Arunachal Pradesh, India.

Somani LL. 1996. Crop Production in acid soils, p223. Agrotech Publishing Academy, Udaipur, Rajasthan, India.

Toon NB Debergh P and Ve NB. 2003. Al tolerance of citrus seedlings in the Mekonga Delta, Vietnam. *South African J. Bot.* **69**: 526–537.

13

Acid Soils of Himachal Pradesh— Management Options for Higher Productivity

SP Sharma and SK Bhardwaj

ABSTRACT

The state of Himachal Pradesh, in India, is a mountainous terrain receiving high precipitation (rainfall/snow) in its most parts. Soil acidity is one of the major constraints in crop production in agriculturally important districts of the state. The cultivated area under acid soils having pH below 5.5 is about one lakh hectare, which is about 16 per cent of the total cultivated area in the state. These areas need special attention for increased crop productivity *vis-à-vis* soil quality. These soils have taxonomically been classified in Alfisol, Mollisol, Spodosol and Inceptisol soil orders and occur primarily in areas receiving high rainfall. The texture of the soils varies from loamy sand to clay loam. The soils had organic carbon content low to very high, cation exchange capacity (CEC) 8.3 to 14.9 cmol (p+) kg^{-1}, base saturation 43.4 to 56.1 per cent and exchangeable Al 0.01 to 1.03 cmol (p+) kg^{-1}. The soils are prone to soil erosion due to their occurrence, generally, on hilly terrains. Maize and wheat are the main crops in the state contributing about 42 per cent towards total food grain production. The average productivity of some of the important crops grown is still very low compared to the achievable yields. The crop production suffers due to poor availability of nutrients, toxicities of aluminium and iron, poor biological activity of soils and frequent moisture stress.

Liming to ameliorate soil acidity or planting acid tolerant crops could be the viable technological options for improving productivity of acidic soils. Among various lime requirement methods, Shoemaker *et al.* (1961) buffer method, commonly known as SMP method, holds good for determining lime requirement of acid soils of Himachal Pradesh. The marketable lime used normally for whitewashing of houses and other domestic purposes, is the only lime source available in the state of Himachal Pradesh which could be used for the amelioration of acid soils for increasing productivity. The average lime requirement of acid soils of the region determined by SMP buffer method varied from 3.0 to 4.0 meteric tonnes per hectare. However, its application rate could be reduced to one tenth when applied in furrows to *kharif* crops (except lowland paddy). The lime application is required to be made till the pH is raised to about 6.0 (yearly monitoring of soil pH is essential).

Amelioration of 1 lakh ha of cultivable acidic soils in Himachal Pradesh promises additional 2 lakh tonnes of food grains and incremental monetary benefits of about Rs. 196 crore per annum. There is, however, need to operationalize technology by establishing effective marketing distribution network for supply of cheap liming materials to farmers.

Key words: Acid soils, amelioration, constraints, crop productivity

INTRODUCTION

Soil acidity is a crop production problem of increasing concern in most parts of India. The acid soils occupying over one fourth of total area in the country are found in high rainfall regions and hilly and mountainous ecosystems. These soils support livelihood and employment through important production systems including cereals, oilseeds, pulses, horticulture, plantation crops and forestry. The productivity of the resources is, however, very low due to acidic soil environment inducing deficiency as well as toxicity of certain plant nutrients and low biological activity. The limited fertilizer use is another factor for low yields in the areas.

The acid soils occupy about 90 million hectares, constituting over one fourth of total geographical area of the country. About half of the area is under cultivation and rest under forestry and other uses. However, about 25 million hectares of cultivated lands with pH value less than 5.5 are critically degraded with very poor physical, chemical, and biological characteristics (Sharma and Sarkar 2005). The state of Himachal Pradesh, in India, is a mountainous terrain receiving high precipitation (rainfall/snow) in its most parts. Soil acidity is one of the major constraints in crop production in agriculturally important districts of the state. Acid soils occupy around 17 lakh hectare of geographical area in parts of Kangra, Mandi, Chamba, Solan and Sirmour districts. But the soils having pH between 4.5 to 5.5 (moderately acid soils) are mainly confined to parts of district Chamba, Kangra, Kullu, Mandi and Sirmaur, representing an area of about 1.6 lakh ha of geographical area. The cultivated area under acid soils having pH below 5.5 is about one lakh hectare, which is about 16 per cent of the total cultivated area in the state. These areas henceforth have been designated as Acid Soil Regions (ASR) of Himachal Pradesh and need special attention for increased crop productivity *vis-à-vis* soil quality. The extent and distribution of acid soils in Himachal Pradesh are given in Table 13.1 and Fig. 13.1.

CHARACTERIZATION OF SOILS

Acid soils of Himachal Pradesh have taxonomically been classified in Alfisol, Mollisol, Spodosol and Inceptisol soil orders and occur primarily in areas receiving high rainfall (Mahajan *et al.* 1997). The texture of the soils varies from loamy sand to clay loam and organic carbon content low to very high. The soils had cation exchange capacity (CEC) 8.3 to 14.9 cmol (p+) kg^{-1}, base saturation 43.4 to 56.1 per

Table 13.1: *Extent of acid soils in Himachal Pradesh (000, ha)*

District	Strongly acidic (pH <4.5)	Moderately acidic (pH 4.5–5.5)	Slightly acidic (pH 5.5–6.5)	Total
Chamba	—	91.30	129.72	221.02
Lahaul and Spiti	—	0.00	0.00	0.00
Kangra	—	16.70	273.91	290.61
Kullu	—	8.35	247.45	255.80
Una	—	0.00	0.00	0.00
Hamirpur	—	0.00	2.23	2.23
Mandi	—	26.17	260.00	286.17
Kinnour	—	0.00	65.69	65.69
Bilaspur	—	0.00	15.59	15.59
Solan	—	0.00	37.30	37.30
Shimla	—	0.00	411.42	411.42
Sirmour	—	14.48	177.04	191.52
Total	—	157.00	1620.35	1777.35

Source: NBSS, LUP, Nagpur, India.

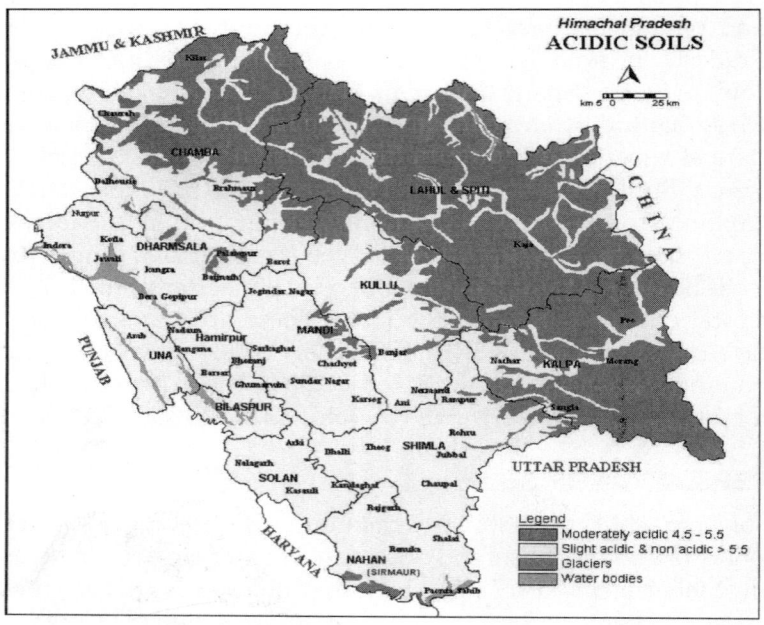

Fig. 13.1: Distribution of Acid soils in Himachal Pradesh

cent and exchangeable and extractable Al 0.01 to 1.03 and 1.2 to 4.8 cmol (p+) kg^{-1} respectively (Table 13.2).

Table 13.2: *General characteristics of acid soils of Himachal Pradesh*

Soil characteristics	Range	Average
Soil reaction (pH)	5.1–6.30	—
Organic matter (g kg^{-1})	6.20–30.30	1.30
Cation exchange capacity [cmol (p+) kg^{-1}]	8.3–14.9	9.5
Base saturation (%)	43.4–56.1	48.2
Exchangeable Al [cmol (p+) kg^{-1}]	0.01–1.03	0.5
Extractable Al [cmol (p+) kg^{-1}]	1.2–4.8	1.9

Source: Sharma, 1983.

FORMS OF ACIDITY

The total acidity in the soils of Himachal Pradesh range from 9.1 to 16.5 cmol (p+) kg^{-1} with average value of 12.7 cmol (p+) kg^{-1}. The exchangeable and pH dependent forms of acidity varied from 0.10 to 2.65 and 3.5 to 12.9 cmol (p+) kg^{-1} with mean values of 0.79 and 7.95 cmol (p+) kg^{-1} respectively. The dominance of pH dependent form of acidity in Acid Soil regions of the state is indicative of medium to high organic matter as one of the important factors contributing towards soil acidity. Besides, exchangeable and extractable Al^{3+} and exchangeable H$^+$ were the other important factors associated with soil acidity in the region.

PRODUCTION CONSTRAINTS

Problem acid soils have a pH of less than 5.5 and usually below pH 5.0. The low soil pH is associated with a number of soil chemical and biological characteristics that manifest themselves as the components of the problem acid soil syndrome. These components may adversely affect plant growth.

Acid soils have poor supply of calcium, magnesium and more concentrations of iron and aluminium. The soils therefore, suffer, due to deficiencies of phosphorus, calcium, magnesium, molybdenum and boron and toxicities of aluminium, mangenese and iron. The soils have low carbon and available nitrogen. The fertilizer use is also limited in these areas. The soils are prone to soil erosion due to their occurrence, generally, on hilly terrains. The crop production, therefore, suffers due to poor availability of nutrients, toxicities of aluminium and iron, poor biological activity of soils and frequent moisture stress.

The adverse effects of acid soils on plant growth are, therefore, mainly related to the presence of aluminum, manganese, and iron in toxic concentrations; low availability of bases, microbial and nutrient imbalances.

The following specific problems are associated with acid soils:

- Aluminium toxicity
- Manganese toxicity
- Calcium and magnesium deficiencies
- Molybdenum deficiency
- Legume nodulation failures
- Increase in plant disease
- Hydrogen ion toxicity
- Decreased phosphorous availability

Plants vary considerably in their tolerance to some of the components of the problem acid soil syndrome. The expression of some acid soil problems, therefore, is not merely one of soil chemical characteristics but rather the result of a complex interaction between the plant and the soil.

CROP PRODUCTION IN ACID SOIL REGIONS (ASR)

The main crops grown in the state of Himachal Pradesh are wheat, barley, gram and rabi pulses in rabi and maize, rice, ragi, millets and kharif pulses in *kharif* seasons. Maize and wheat, however, contribute about 42 per cent towards total food grain production and continued to be the main cropping system in acidic soil regions of the state. The average productivity of some of the important crops grown is still very low compared to the achievable yields on research farm of CSK HP Krishi Vishvavidyalaya, Palampur, with improved technology (Table 13.3).

Therefore, given the improved technology, there is vast scope to improve upon the productivity of acid soils of Himachal Pradesh.

Table 13.3: *Average yield of some crops grown in Acid Soil Regions (ASR) of Himachal Pradesh*

District	Average yield (q ha^{-1})			
	Maize	**Wheat**	**Pulses**	**Oilseeds**
Chamba	18.3	11.7	0.6	2.8
Kangra	11.5	13.3	4.3	6.1
Mandi	20.8	14.0	3.9	0.08
Kullu	9.6	15.1	1.5	2.98
Sirmour	23.3	13.5	3.4	2.60
CSK HPKV, research farm	45.0	37.0	18–20	10–12

Source: NBSS, LUP, Nagpur.

MANAGEMENT OPTIONS

The management of acid soils is aimed at realization of their production potential either by addition of the amendments to counteract the abnormalities of such soils or to manipulate the agricultural practices to obtain optimum crop yields under the acid conditions. In the latter case, the most important practice would be to grow acid tolerant plant species and varieties. But this approach seems to offer only a temporary solution, for the acid conditions may be aggravated by continuous cropping with tolerant crops. For this reason, liming has long been regarded by many as an essential component of good management of acid soils. During the last about 30 years, the volume of experimental data on liming has increased significantly. Commendable work on management of acid soils to increase their productivity has been done in Odisha, Northeastern region, Kerala, Karnataka, Maharashtra and Himachal Pradesh.

The first step in the management of acid soils is to identify the extent and severity of the problem. Poor yields of acid sensitive crops may indicate an acid soil condition, but soil tests are the only sure method of identifying an acidity problem. With careful sampling of fields, soil tests can determine the extent and severity of soil acidity, the rate of lime required, and provide an estimate of crop response to lime. An estimate of crop response along with the cost of lime provides a basis for assessing the economics of liming. Each field that is to be limed should be carefully sampled.

In some cases, growing crops that are more tolerant to acidity is an alternative to liming. But as soils gradually become more acid, the choice of crops becomes very limited. The long-term goal should be to lime soils to a pH value best suited to the crops being grown. After a desired soil pH has been achieved, the amount of lime required to maintain soils in a suitable pH range will depend on fertilizer rates, soil type and cropping practices.

There could be, therefore, two options for the management of acid soil:

Option I: Liming to correct soil acidity and to improve soil productivity.

Option II: Planting acid tolerant crops.

LIMING TO CORRECT SOIL ACIDITY AND TO IMPROVE SOIL PRODUCTIVITY

Lime Requirement

Among various lime requirement methods in vogue in various laboratories of the state, Shoemaker *et al.* (1961) buffer method, commonly known as SMP method, holds good for determining lime requirement of Acid Soils of Himachal Pradesh.

Liming Material

The marketable lime used normally for whitewashing of houses and other domestic purposes, is the only lime source available in the state of Himachal Pradesh which could be used for the amelioration of acid soils for increasing productivity. The average lime requirement of acid soils of the region determined by SMP buffer method varied from 3.0 to 4.0 meteric tonnes per hectare. However, its application rate could be reduced to one tenth when applied in furrows to *kharif* crops (except lowland paddy). The lime application is required to be made till the pH is raised to about 6.0 (yearly monitoring of soil pH is essential).

The marketable lime is available at the rate of about of Rs. 4,000/- (Rs. four thousand only) per tonne. So lime costing about Rs. 1,200/- to 1,600/- would be required in one hectare piece of land, which is somewhat beyond the reach of resource poor farmers of the state. For the operationalization of the technology, some other cheaper and effective sources of lime are required to be made available to the farmers in the fertilizer depots.

CROPS RESPONSE TO LIMING AND MINERAL FERTILIZERS

A series of experiments demonstrating the response of maize and wheat crops to lime either alone or in combination with mineral fertilizers were conducted on farmers' fields in some of the Acid Soil Regions of Himachal Pradesh. The field demonstrations were designed with a set of four treatments, *viz.* (1) Farmers' practice (FP); (2) Farmers' practice + lime (FP + lime); (3) 100% NPK* and (4) 100% NPK + lime. Lime was added at one tenth of lime requirement in furrows to maize crop only. N, P and K were applied as per their recommended levels for the respective crops.

The productivity of maize and wheat in a system under farmers' practice was around 39 q ha^{-1} which increased to 46 q ha^{-1} with lime application in furrows to maize crop (Fig. 13.2). The use of mineral fertilizers at their recommended level (100 per cent NPK); however, was the key factor in enhancing the system productivity by 56 per cent. Combining lime and mineral fertilizers further increased the system productivity by 11 per cent compared to the yield level with mineral fertilizers alone. The usefulness of lime application in combination with recommended levels of mineral fertilizers in enhancing crop productivity has also been established under long term fertilizer experiments being conducted at Palampur in Himachal Pradesh (Fig. 13.3) and Ranchi in Jharkhand (representing acid soil regions of the country) for the last about 35 years with productivity level of 68.5 q ha^{-1} at Palampur (HP). The crops performance under limed and unlimed situations both in the presence and absence of mineral fertilizers is shown in Plates 13.1 to 13.4.

Considering the state level average yields of 23 and 16 q ha^{-1} of maize and wheat, respectively, thus the system productivity of 39 q ha^{-1} in 2006–07, there is vast scope of increasing the system productivity to a level of about 70 q ha^{-1} following management practices of acid soils.

---

* 100% NPK corresponds to state level recommended dose of N, P and K for maize and wheat crops.

PLANTING ACID TOLERANT CROPS

A strategy to improve economic productivity of crops in the acidic soils is to identify acid-tolerant genotypes/cultivars. The popular released cultivars and elite genotypes of soybean and *Brassica napus* were screened at Palampur (HP) for their response to lime application. The experiments conducted provided information to identify cultivars/genotypes with inherent capacity to tolerate soil acidity as their yield was not affected by application of lime. At the same time, the genotypes which could partially overcome the adverse effects of soil acidity were also identified. Among soybean cultivars, 'Harasoya' being tolerant to acidic soil conditions could be recommended for its cultivation in acid soil regions of the state while 'Himsoya' performed well under limed conditions. Among *B. napus* genotypes, 'GSE 3A' and 'ONK 1' appeared to be tolerant to acidic soil conditions. Besides, 'GSE 1' and 'TERI 985' were more suitable for acid soil conditions if lime is applied. However, these results needed to be validated by further testing before making recommendations to the farmers.

ECONOMIC ADVANTAGE

The operationalization of technology in all the Acid Soil Regions of Himachal Pradesh will give an approximately 2 lakh tonnes additional food grain production with net returns of about 196 crore per annum to the state revenue.

CONCLUSION

The acid soils with pH less than 5.5 and need special attention are mainly confined to parts of district Chamba, Kangra, Kullu, Mandi and Sirmaur, representing an area of about 1.6 lakh ha of geographical area. The cultivated area under acid soils having pH below 5.5 is about one lakh hectare, which is about 16 per cent of the total cultivated area in the state and need special attention to improve upon productivity of these lands.

These soils support livelihood and employment through important production systems including cereals, oilseeds, pulses, horticulture, plantation crops and forestry. The productivity of the resources is, however, very low due to acidic soil environment inducing deficiency as well as toxicity of certain plant nutrients and low biological activity. The limited fertilizer use is another factor for low yields in the areas. Liming to ameliorate soil acidity or planting acid tolerant crops could be the viable technologies for improving productivity of acidic soils. Amelioration of 1 lakh ha of cultivable acidic soils in Himachal Pradesh promises additional 2 lakh tones of food grains and incremental monetary benefits of about Rs. 196 crore per annum. There is, however, need to operationalize technology by establishing effective marketing distribution network for supply of cheap liming materials to farmers.

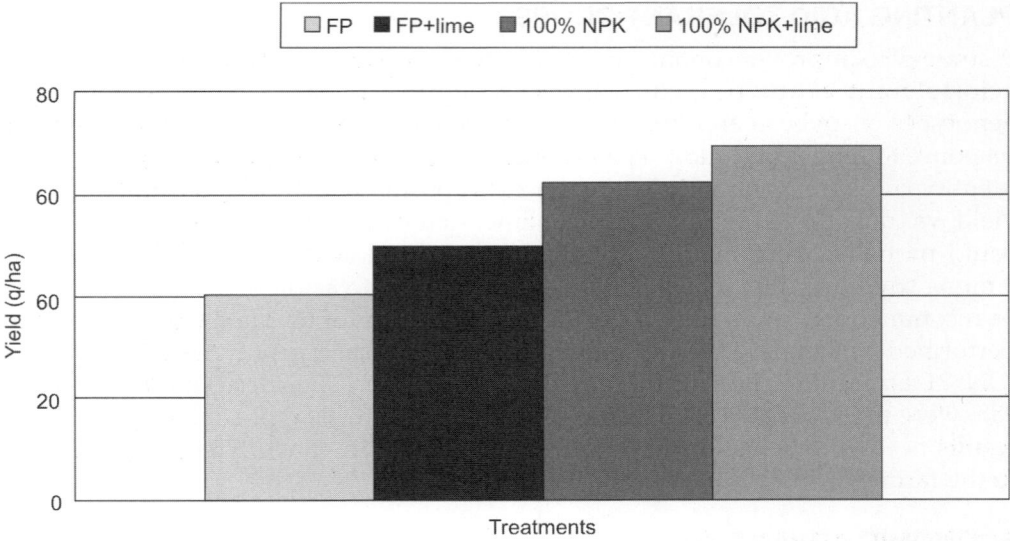

*Figures in bars are percent increases over farmer's practice.

Fig. 13.2: Effect of lime and mineral fertilizers on system (maize + wheat) productivity in district Kangra (ASR), Himachal Pradesh

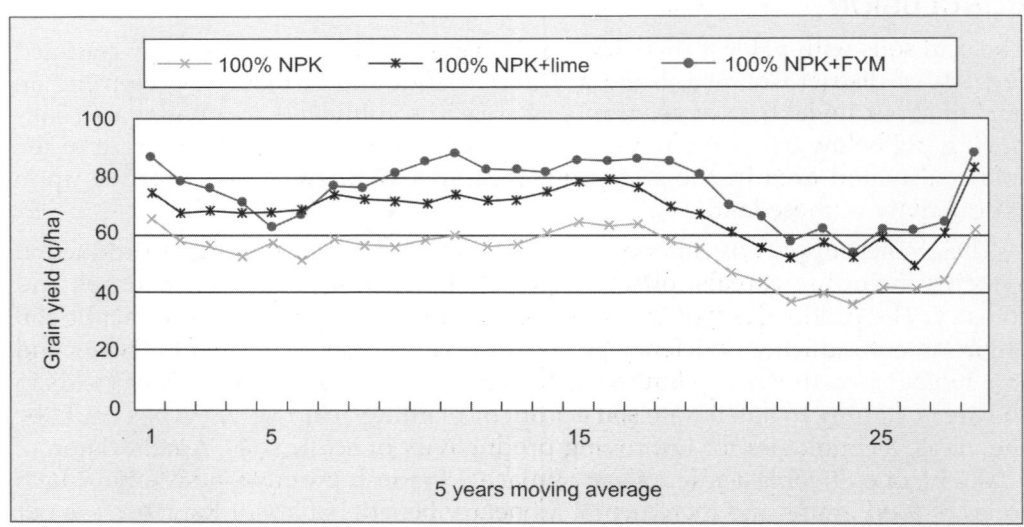

Fig. 13.3: Long-term effect of lime and mineral fertilizers on system production

Plate 13.1: Maize crop under farmer's practice and improved technology

Plate 13.2: Nutritionally starving local cultivars of maize

Plate 13.3: Maize crop under limed and unlimed situations

Plate 13.4: One of the farmers applying lime in furrows unlimed situations

REFERENCES

Mahajan KK, Sharma PK and Singh R. 1997. Amelioration of acid soils of Himachal Pradesh by liming for higher productivity, p33. Department of Soil science, HP Krishi Vishvavidyalaya, Palampur. Research Bulletin.

Sharma PD and Sarkar AK. 2005. Managing acid soils for enhancing productivity, p23. National Resource Management Division (ICAR), Krishi Anusandhan Bhavan-II, Pusa Campus, New Delhi. Technical Bulletin.

Shoemaker HE, McLean EO and Pratt PF. 1961. Buffer methods for determining lime requirement of soils with appreciable amounts of extractable Al. *Soil Sci. Soc. Am. Proc.* **25:** 274–277.

14

Soil Physical Management of Acidic Soils for Increasing Productivity

TC Baruah, NG Barua and DK Patgiri

ABSTRACT

Tillage is one of the important management practices by which physical properties of acid soils can be modified affecting crop growth and yield. The upland and lowland acid soils have distinct physical properties. Many tillage related soil constraints which have been identified for various upland and lowland soils, are also prevalent in acid soils. Therefore, like other upland soils, the acid upland soils can also be characterized by tillage related soil constraints namely, shallow soil depth, usually compact at soil surface, severe weed growth with distinct soil acidity. High infiltration rate, high permeability, low available water capacity, coarse soil texture, high bulk density and soil crusting are some of the basic features of these soils. Nutrient loss in these soils is considerably high except NH_4-N and P. This chapter discusses physical constraint in upland and low land in acid soil and problems of crop production arising from undesirable physical properties.

Key words: Acidic soils, physical management, tillage.

INTRODUCTION

Acid soils (pH < 6.5) in India occupy approximately 90 million hectares (m ha) of the geographical area (Sharma and Sarkar 2005). About 21 m ha of acid soils are distributed in northeastern region under arable and non-arable lands, with maximum area under Arunachal Pradesh followed by Assam, Meghalaya, Manipur and Mizoram. Besides north eastern states, acid soils are concentrated in Western Ghats, Jharkhand, Chhattisgarh, Uttarakhand with sporadic distribution in Himachal Pradesh, Odisha, West Bengal, etc. (Patiram 2007).

Lowland acid soils are medium to fine textured and have low content of organic matter. Low infiltration rate, high water retention capacity, moderate permeability, subsurface soil compaction, clodding, floppiness and low leaching loss of plant nutrients are some of the basic physical characteristics of these soils. Thus, the management of upland acidic soils differs distinctly from that of lowland acid soils so as to increase the crop productivity through amelioration of soil physical environment. Addition of organic matter or fine earth fraction, ridge and furrow tillage, conservation tillage, contour and strip cropping, intercropping of cereals with legumes, bench terracing, raising of field bunds for *in situ* rain water harvesting, life saving irrigation and increase in frequency of irrigation water are some of the suitable practices for raising crops in upland acid soils. Puddling for raising transplanted rice in medium textured soil, compaction of floppy soil, improvement of drainage of poorly drained soils and deep ploughing to overcome subsurface compaction and application of USG or slow release nitrogenous fertilizer are some of the effective methods for soil, water and nutrient management in lowland acid soils. Methods such as disc harrowing to break the soil clods and zero tillage or mulching for utilizing residual soil moisture could be effectively used to raise a second crop in lowland acid soils.

PHYSICAL CONSTRAINTS IN UPLAND ACID SOILS

Acid soils usually occur in high rainfall areas where leaching of bases, fine earth and organic matter is the predominant pedogenic process. As a result the organic matter content in the soil is usually low. Soils are usually coarser than loamy. The structure of soil is weak. High content of Fe and Al develops the acid soils to be usually granular or crumb structure. Due to coarse texture, the macropore content is very high leaving low content of storage pores in soil. Thus, the soils have high infiltration rates and high permeability of air and water, but a low water and nutrient retention capacity. Leaching of Fe and Al particularly after a heavy rainfall followed by a dry spell, leads to development of soil crust at a depth 2.0 to 3.0 cm below soil surface, which is peculiar characteristic for most of the upland acid soil. The bulk density of the soil rises to as high as 1.8 kg/m^3 and hampers germination of seeds and poor growth of the plant. Owing to low water retention, these acid soils become dry within 2 to 3 days of rainfall or irrigation. The zero soil water flux rapidly moves downward causing water deficit in soil surface zone. Thus, the cereals are affected by dry spells frequently as compared to non cereal crops. The water content at 15 atmosphere is low in these soils. It leaves the scope to raise a second crop in post monsoon season. The leaching loss of plant nutrients is also very high in these soils. The NO_3-N and NH_4-N are leached below the root zone of the crops within 24 hrs of its application. On the other hand, NH_4-N is retained within 2 to 5 cm of soil surface to a longer period for the availability of N to the crop. Phosphorous is not leached down the soil and is retained in soil with the sesquioxides. On the other hand, cations like Ca and K are leached down the soil due to the presence of predominantly 1:1 type of clay minerals. The extent of leaching loss may be as high as 30 per cent depending upon the frequency of rainfall or irrigation water. Therefore, these soils require soil application of nutrients like N, K and lime for their efficient use in crop production.

In general, water stable aggregates are found lower in cultivated soils than that of uncultivated soils. Shifting cultivation in hill soils causes marked decline of soil aggregate status in comparison to cultivated alluvial soils (Dutta 1968). Incorporation of organic matter can bring about improvement of soil aggregates by binding the individual soil particles into aggregates (Patgiri 1985, Borkakoty 1990). Incorporation of legume in the crop rotation followed by a fallow period improves aggregate status. Yield of rice is influenced by aggregate status and organic matter (Chutia 1975). The moisture retention properties are greatly influenced by the textural make-up. Hence, it is important to make up textural deficiencies in light textured soils with organic amendments (Patgiri 1985). Sarmah (1991) reported that increased electrolyte concentration beyond 250 ppm increases limitations in physical properties of soils. Hence, it is important to irrigate soils with water having low Fe and other soluble salts.

PHYSICAL CONSTRAINTS FOR LOWLAND ACID SOIL

Acid soils present in low lying areas are of two categories. Some soils are highly acidic and are present mostly in coastal areas; while, others are slightly acidic to neutral in reaction and are present in valley bottom lands of undulating terrain. Drainage is a major problem besides soil acidity in first kind of soils. In case of inland valley bottomland, run-off and elluviation from the upstream landslides enrich the fine earth fractions and base content in soils. The infiltration rate of the soil is low enough to cause surface stagnation or waterlogging in soil. The hydraulic conductivity of the soil is moderate to low which causes frequent rise of groundwater table and super saturation of the soil for prolonged period. Fine textured soil containing low organic matter promotes unfavourable soil structure. Angular blocky structure or prismatic structure is developed in super saturated soil. It also develops a reduced zone eliminating the possibility of growing non-rice crops even if the water holding capacity of the soil is high. When such soils are puddled to grow transplanted rice, a plow pan having bulk density as high as $1.8 \, kg/m^3$ is developed below the plough layer. This layer further intensifies reduced condition that affects growth and yield of rice. When such soils are dried during post monsoon season, surface cracking and clod formation become common features in these soils. Thus, fine texture, unfavourable soil structure, plow pan in wet season and development of clods in dry season are some of the soil constraints for crop production in wetland soils. High erosion ratio (>30 per cent) specially in the riverine soils is another aspect making these soils vulnerable to loss of fertile surface soils. These soils should be kept under vegetation throughout the year in order to reduce erodibility. Besides there are a number of other physical and chemical ways to reduce erodibility like use of soil stabilizers.

In lowland acid soils of Eastern India rice is often grown as a transplanted crop. Puddling is an important tillage operation required for growing transplanted rice as puddling facilitates transplanting, controls weeds and reduces percolation loss of water and nutrients (Ghildyal 1978). However, besides these advantages, puddling destroys the structural units and converts the soil into a massive plastic mud and creates soil physical condition detrimental to upland crop in a rice-based cropping system. Destruction of aggregates and excessive moisture in rice fields often hampers in seedbed preparation and delays growing of *rabi* crops and results in poor yield (Hobbs 1985).

Problems of crop production arising from undesirable physical properties:

- High percolation of water
- Nutrient loss in light textured red and lateritic soils
- Crust formation in red soils having >20% clay
- Quick drying of surface layer in shallow soils
- Hardening of soils
- Presence of compact layers and clay pans at shallow depths
- Puddled fields for non-rice crops
- Drainage problems in acid sulphate marshy soils
- Crop water stress due to low water retentivity
- Poor root growth in strongly acid soils
- Compaction of medium and light textured soils.

PHYSICAL MANAGEMENT OF ACID SOILS

The upland soils have diversified problems and need specific solutions for each type of problems. The following physical methods are useful to solve the problems:

Conservation Tillage

In order to check runoff and soil erosion, conservation tillage appears to be an effective method. It is found that once summer ploughing by MB plough followed by twice disc harrowing is effective in controlling the weed growth and increasing the yield of upland rice as compared to conventional tillage. Addition of organic matter @ 4 t ha^{-1} prior to adoption of conservation tillage helps to increase the mean weight diameter of soil aggregates and soil water storage besides increasing the yield of crops. However, conservation tillage is always associated with greater risk of weed infestation, disease and pest management problems.

Soil Compaction

Soils with relatively low percentage of fine fractions exhibit high permeability and compacting these soils near proctor moisture increases the yield. Soils that have very low clay respond more to clay addition followed by compaction.

In case of subsurface compaction, deep cultivation (chiseling/ploughing) has been found beneficial and generally found most economical if done at 50 to 60 cm interval. Besides, addition of organic matter also reduces the magnitude of compaction in soils (Sarmah 1991).

Soil Crusting

Soil crusting especially in case of vegetable crops is a serious problem during the seed germination period. Application of gypsum @ 1 tonne ha^{-1} along with FYM @ 5 tonne ha^{-1} has been found to alleviate soil crusting and increasing the grain yield of upland rice in lateritic soil. Addition of Fe_2O_3 for generating microaggregates enhances soil crusting. However, addition of $CaCO_3$ along with Fe_2O_3 and organic matter maintains a balance between soil crusting and aggregate formation (Borkakoty 1990).

Tillage for Rice Based Cropping System(s)

Puddling twice by tractor drawn cage wheel or power tiller operated rotavator reduces the permeability of soil and significantly increases the grain and straw yields of rice. Locally developed puddlers are also equally effective in increasing the puddling index, in decreasing the permeability and increasing the grain and straw yields of transplanted rice.

Barua *et al.* (2007) studied the effect of tillage on physical properties of lowland soils of Kakodonga watershed and yields of crop in rice-toria system. The puddling index values of lowland soils increased significantly over farmer's practice [MT1-summer ploughing (SP) with (1 pass) of country plough (CP) + puddling by 3 passes of CP + laddering] when puddling was done by power tiller operated cage wheel and rotovator (MT3) and by a helical blade puddler (MT2). Puddling index values were 82.44 per cent in MT2 and 81.54 per cent in MT3 treatments as compared to 78.16 per cent in MT1 treatment. Treatment MT3 resulted in more amount of water stable aggregates in lower size fractions (0.25 mm). Bulk density of surface soils (0.0–0.10 m) measured at harvesting of rice crop was highest in MT3 treatment (1.39 Mg m^{-3}). Saturated hydraulic conductivity (mm/hr) was found to be 3.76 times lower in MT2 treatment and 2.45 times lower in MT3 treatment as compared to MT1 treatment. The highest grain yield of rice *cv.* Basundhara (51.33 q ha^{-1}) was recorded in MT3 treatment with the highest B:C ratio of 2.19. Further, tillage of rice crop did not affect the yield of rabi crop (toria *cv.* TS-38). But, rabi tillage of twice MB ploughing + twice rototilling + line sowing of seed (ST2) increased the yield of rabi crop significantly over farmer's practice (ST 1–5 passes of CP+ broadcasting of seed). The yield of rabi crop increased from 1.89 q ha^{-1} in ST1 to 2.94 q ha^{-1} in ST2 treatment.

Shallow Depth

Construction of about 10 cm high ridge and furrow on shallow soils mitigate the depth related constraints; further addition of clay and organic matter improves the physical condition and crop growth. Under rolling topography, ridge plus live barriers has been effective; while, for desurfaced soil, deep cultivation has been beneficial.

Hill Soils

Adoption of modified land use system like agri-horti-silvi-pastoral system seems to be the most suitable for improving the soil hydrophysical conditions and conserving soil moisture as well in hilly agroecosystem of north eastern hills (Saha and Mishra 2007). This is because the mean weight diameter increases by 29.4 per cent and decreases the dispersion ratio decreases by 52.9 per cent over the shifting cultivation. With respect to available water content under modified system, it increases by 24.0–36.5 per cent over shifting cultivation.

REFERENCES

Barua NG, Borkakaty PK, Barua DC and Kalita J. 2007. Effect of tillage on physical properties of soil under lowland conditions and crop performance in rice-toria system. *Indian J. Dryland Agric. Res. Dev.* **22:** 52–56.

Borkakoty PK. 1990. Studies on micro-aggregation in some soils of Assam. Unpublished MSc. (Ag), Thesis, Assam Agricultural University, Jorhat, Assam.

Chutia R. 1975. Effect of crop rotations and fertilizer treatments on the physico-chemical properties of soil. Unpublished MSc (Ag) Thesis, Assam Agricultural University, Jorhat, Assam.

Dutta I. 1968. Studies on water stable aggregates in some soils of Assam. Unpublished MSc (Ag) Thesis, Assam Agricultural University, Jorhat, Assam.

Ghildyal BP. 1978. Effects of compaction and puddling on soil physical properties and rice growth. In Soil Physics and Rice, p32. IRRI, Los Banos, Philippines.

Hobbs PR. 1985. Agronomic practices and problems for wheat following cotton and rice. In Wheat for more tropical environments: Proc. Int. Sym., pp. 273–276.

Patgiri DK.1985. Studies on physical properties of some major soils of Assam. Unpublished MSc. (Ag), Thesis, Assam Agricultural University, Jorhat, Assam.

Patiram. 2007. Management and future research strategies for enhancing productivity of crops on the acid soils. *J. Indian Soc. Soil Sci.* **55:** 411–420.

Saha R and Mishra VK. 2007. Long term effect of various land use systems on physical properties of silty clay loam soil of NE Hills. *J. Indian Soc. Soil Sci.* **55:** 112–118.

Sarmah PK. 1991. Effect of synthesized microaggregates on maize (*Zea mays* L.). Unpublished MSc (Ag) Thesis, Assam Agricultural University, Jorhat, Assam.

Sharma PD and Sarkar AK. 2005. Managing acid soils for enhancing productivity. Indian Council of Agricultural Research, NRM Division, Krishi Anusandhan Bhavan II, New Delhi.

15 Characterization of Acid Soils and Evaluation of Different Lime Requirement Methods

TC Baruah, P Saharia and N Kalita

ABSTRACT

Soil acidity is one of the major problems in India. Such soils produce approximately 30 to 50 per cent of their potential capacity. The major focus is to get the optimum productivity of crops in the region through necessary intervention. This chapter discusses production constraints, management of acid soil, lime requirement, crop response to liming and scope of integrated nutrient management system for acid soil region.

Key words: Acidic soils, characterization, methods for lime requirement.

INTRODUCTION

In India, about 25 million hectares (m ha) of cultivated lands with pH < 5.5 are critically degraded. Such type of problematic soils in India are mainly concentrated in Northeastern region and Western Ghats, Jharkhand, Chhattisgarh, Uttaranchal with sporadic distribution in Himachal Pradesh, Odisha, West Bengal, etc. In northeastern region, the acid soils below pH 5.5 occupy 54 per cent of the total area of the country. Such soils suffering from severe nutrient deficiencies of P, Ca, Mg, Mo, B, toxicities of Fe and Al as well as high soil erosion rates have very low productivity of about 1 tonne ha^{-1}.

ACID SOIL INFERTILITY

Soil acidity plays a major role in determining the nutrient availability to plants and in many instances by specific mineral stress/toxicity problems. Acid soil infertility is the gamut of syndrome of problems that affect plant growth and development in soils of low pH. The most common chemical and biological problems in acid soils are, namely low pH, low CEC, nutrient imbalance, deficiency of bases (Ca, Mg, K) resulting in low level of base saturation, high level of Al, Fe and also Mn saturation percentage, high P fixing capacity, poor N_2 fixation by bacteria on root nodules of legumes, reduction of soil biological activities and low active clay fraction. Soil acidity *per se* poses no problem for growing rice in the wet season in the lowlands.

Phosphate fixation, high Fe concentration in soil solution of flooded rice soils and high Fe induces Zn deficiency may pose problem in some acid soils.

PRODUCTION CONSTRAINTS

In addition to infertility problems and low fertilizer use pattern, acid soils suffer from the following physical constraints:

- High percolation of water
- Nutrient loss in light textured red and lateritic soils
- Crust formation in red soils having > 20% clay
- Quick drying of surface layer in shallow soils
- Hardening of soils
- Presence of compact layers and clay pans at shallow depths
- Puddled fields for non-rice crops
- Drainage problems in acid sulphate marshy soils
- Crop water stress due to low water retentivity
- Poor root growth in strongly acid soils
- Compaction of medium and light textured soils
- Prone to soil erosion from undulating and sloppy topography.

MANAGEMENT OF ACID SOILS

Amelioration of acid soils by liming though accepted for raising productivity and ultimate food security, economics of liming is questionable. This is so, because lime requirement of acid soils of India are very high particularly in fine textured soils with high organic matter content. Moreover, the effect of liming does not stay long due to leaching losses of Ca and Mg. Instead of commercial limestone the resource poor farmers of the acid soil regions could use industrial waste(s), which are potential lime sources if available at an affordable transportable distance. Ecologically fragile and economically handicapped farmers of the acid soil region need to pursue an integrated system of nutrient management (discussed later) based on the four pillars of sustainability, *viz.* technical feasibility, economic viability, social acceptability and eco-friendliness.

LIME REQUIREMENT (LR)

The optimum soil pH range for optimum yield depends not only upon the type of crop grown, soil, but also goes with cultivars. Although, growing of acid tolerant plants species and varieties is suggested for acid soils, liming should be recognized as a standard management practice for increasing productivity of such soils. Lime requirement (LR) refers to the amount of lime required to neutralize the acidic components present in such soils and to improve the base saturation. While some chemical methods depend on measuring the buffering capacity of the acidic components found in the soil, others are based on determining the amount of exchangeable H^+ ions held by the soil particles using a titration procedure, and exchangeable Al^{3+} based for highly leached tropical soils. In addition to soil pH, the amount of lime to be used is affected by factors, *viz.* surface and subsurface texture and structure, clay content, organic matter, CEC, base saturation, crops to be grown, kind and mesh size of liming material and economic return from liming. The method(s) chosen for LR should be based on improvement of soil properties, accuracy and easiness to routine testing programme.

LIMING FACTOR

The methods available for LR include Shoemaker *et al.* method, Hunter method, Mendez and Kamprath-I & Mendez and Kamprath-II, etc. Many a times lime requirement determined in the laboratory by any one of the above mentioned methods fail to raise the pH to the desired level in the field condition due to the different losses, *viz.* leaching loss, solubility of liming materials, application loss, etc. To raise the pH to the desired level in the field, it requires liming materials more than the LR value to compensate these losses. So, to determine the amount of lime actually required in the field situation to raise the pH to a desired level, there is a need to evaluate Liming factor agroecological situationwise. Liming factor may be defined as the factor by which the actual amount of lime can be calculated from the estimated theoretical amount of lime. This factor varies from 1 to 3, depending on rate of limestone solution, plant uptake and leaching during the reaction period.

Data on lime requirement of soils in terms of pure $CaCO_3$ (Table 15.1) revealed that LR ranged from 0.28 to 2.35 t ha^{-1} in Buffer curve method, 0.44 to 4.70 t ha^{-1} in Hunter method, 0.28 to 0.84 t ha^{-1} in Mendez & Kamprath-I method, 0.28 to 1.12 t ha^{-1} in Mendez & Kamprath-II method, 7.56 to 15.71 t ha^{-1} in Woodruff method and 3.40 to 18.17 t ha^{-1} in SMP method. Both Mendez & Kamprath-I and -II methods reflected lower LR, as these methods aimed at neutralizing exchangeable Al^{3+} rather than adjusting soil pH to neutrality. Based on the degree of association with different soil properties, different LR methods could be rated as per their suitability in the following order:

Mendez & Kamprath-II >Hunter method > Mendez & Kamprath-I >Buffer curve> SMP>Woodruff method.

Stepwise multiple regression analysis (Table 15.2) indicates that soil properties jointly contributed about 42 per cent variation in lime requirement of soils and the partial contributions of different properties were; pH 3.56%, pH + CEC 25.30%, pH + CEC + Org.C 27.63 %, pH + CEC + Org.C + total potential acidity 42%. When clay was introduced into the regression, the predictability of LR of soils was not improved further.

CROP RESPONSE TO LIMING

The direct and indirect effects of liming generally lead to increased crop production, the magnitude of which varies widely under different soil conditions and cropping

Table 15.1: *Lime requirement (tonnes ha⁻¹) of soils from humid alluvial flood-free agro-ecological region of Assam*

Method	Range	Mean
Buffer curve	0.28–2.35	0.89
Hunter	0.44–4.70	1.85
Mendez & Kamprath-I	0.28–0.84	0.48
Mendez & Kamprath-II	0.28–1.12	0.84
Woodruff	7.56–15.71	9.22
SMP	3.40–18.17	4.85

Source: Final Report of ICAR sponsored project *Characterization and management of acid soils of UBVZ of Assam, 2000.*

Table 15.2: *Contribution of soil properties towards lime requirement of soils (M&K-II)*

$Y = 1.218 - 0.095\ X_1$	$R^2 = 0.0356$
$Y = 0.776 - 0.128\ X_1 + 0.098\ X_2$	$R^2 = 0.2530$
$Y = 0.544 - 0.084\ X_1 + 0.084\ X_2 + 0.169\ X_3$	$R^2 = 0.2763$
$Y = -0.223 - 0.020\ X_1 + 0.079\ X_2 + 0.195\ X_3 + 0.019\ X_4$	$R^2 = 0.4198$
$Y = -0.219 - 0.018\ X_1 + 0.075\ X_2 + 0.196\ X_3 + 0.019\ X_4 + 0.0005\ X_5$	$R^2 = 0.4198$

Note: Y = lime requirement; X_1 = pH; X_2 = CEC; X_3 = Org.C; X_4 = Total potential acidity (TPA); X_5 = Clay (%).

patterns. The beneficial effects of liming of acid soils may be attributed to amelioration of toxic effects of exchangeable Al, Fe and Mn, enhanced availability of plant nutrients and increased use efficiency of applied fertilizers. Based on the lime responsiveness the upland crops have been grouped into the following categories:

- High lime responsive—Pigeonpea, soybean and cotton.
- Medium lime responsive—Gram, lentil, pea, maize and sorghum.
- Low or no responsive—Rice and potato.

The existence of differential response of crops to liming suggests that the cropping pattern may be adjusted in limed soils to realize the maximum benefits from the investment of liming. Under rainfed conditions, it is suggested that lime responsive crops, *viz.* groundnut, cotton, soybean, pigeonpea, etc. may be grown in the first two years, followed by medium lime responsive crops, *viz.* maize, sorghum, blackgram, greengram, etc. while, rice, millets and potatoes may be grown in the last phase.

The benefits of liming acid soils are well known. The addition of lime to these soils neutralizes soil acidity and creates favourable environment for microbial activity, nutrient release and their availability to plants. Long-term fertilizer experiments conducted in acid soil regions for the last three to four decades have established the need of judicious integration of fertilizers, liming material, organic and/or green manures with biofertilizers and other limiting nutrients, *viz.* sulphur and boron to sustain high crop yields. In spite of these research results, the productivity of acid soil regions is still much below the potential. Almost doubling of yield of pulse and oilseed crops per hectare including those of vegetables is expected by integrated use of liming materials and balanced fertilizers. Therefore, the package developed on acid soil management has to be tested in different agro ecological situations for final recommendation to the farming community.

Liming has been found to be very effective in improving the base saturation, inactivating Fe, Al and Mn and thus reducing P fixation to a great extent, stimulating microbial activities leading to mineralization of organic nitrogen and atmospheric nitrogen fixation and thus increasing the yield of various upland crops in different parts of India (Mandal *et al.* 1966, Panda and Mishra 1970). Liming was found to effectively neutralize exchangeable Al in soils of Sikkim (Pradhan and Khera 1976), Meghalaya (Prasad *et al.* 1982) and Tripura (Laskar and Dadhwal, 1981), decrease significantly the water soluble and exchangeable Al and Mn content, increase Ca and available P content in Tropofluvent acid and Sulfaquept acid sulphate soils (Mongia *et al.* 1998). Increase in Ca and Mg in acid soils due to liming had also been reported by Mathur and Lal (1987).

Application of full dose of LR has not been beneficial as the leaching loss becomes very high, application of lime @ 25 per cent of LR in alternate year (in Odisha) and 10 per cent of LR (in Bihar) has been found effective in raising the yield. Mathur *et al.* (1991) compared the application of lime dose of 1/10, 1/15 and 1/20 LR at the time of sowing for six years with full lime dose applied once and found 1/10 LR application to be at par with 1 LR in crops like mungbean, groundnut, soybean, pea and gram. Furrow application of lime reduced the rate of liming without sacrificing crop yield in acid soils (Mathur *et al.* 1985). Liming @ of 1/10th of the LR every year in the furrows recorded yield of soybean, ground nut, etc. comparable to normal lime application schedule in Odisha (Mathur *et al.* 1985) while liming @ 0.25 LR effectively neutralized the toxic effect of exchangeable Al and increased the P and Ca uptake by crops (Prasad *et al.* 1983).

A number of experiments on farmers' fields were conducted under ICAR network project on acid soils to evaluate the effect of addition of lime, in the form of lime sludge and fertilizers on yields of important crops of Assam. Liming alone increased the yields of rapeseed and greengram by 18 and 14 per cent respectively over farmers' practice. Liming with recommended fertilizers increased the yields of rapeseed and greengram by 77 and 49 per cent respectively over farmers' practice. The increase in maize and mustard in Meghalaya were 189 and 391 per cent respectively. The yields with 50 per cent recommended NPK and lime were equal to or slightly higher than 100 per cent NPK. The practice of liming, therefore, pays dividend in terms of saving of chemical fertilizers by 50 per cent. Both liming and fertilization of soils proved to be economic in NEH region (Sharma *et al.* 2006).

INDUSTRIAL WASTE AS AMENDMENT

Several industrial wastes, *viz.* basic slag from steel industry, lime slug from paper mill, press mud from sugar mill, precipitated $CaCO_3$ from fertilizer factories, bone meal, and some low grade liming material from the natural deposits from North-East hill region have been tried as amendment from acid soils as they are cost-effective and eco-friendly. Lime sludge contains 65–84 per cent $CaCO_3$, 1 per cent free CaO and 1.5 per cent free alkali. Basic slag is the double silicate and phosphate of lime. On an average Indian slag contains 1–7 per cent P_2O_5, 24–50 per cent CaO, 2–10 per cent MgO (Panda and Das 1971). Sahu and Pal (1987) reported significant increase in crop yield with application of lime sludge. Barthakur (1990) reported use of rock phosphate in acid soils of Assam which releases P for a longer period of time.

Paradigms shift in liming technology (Sharma and Sarkar 2005, Sharma *et al.* 2006):

- Land situation
- Rainfed/irrigated uplands and medium lands with pH < 5.5.

RATE OF APPLICATION

Field experiments conducted on the basis of 100 per cent LR to reap the benefit of residual value of liming on the crops in sequence has led to the controversy on the cost effectiveness of the dose of liming. Besides, the use of 100 per cent lime on the soil nutrient environment is considered to be drastic. Further, the practice is not becoming popular with farmers because of initial heavy investment on liming.

The recent trend of liming is to use lime as a fertilizer rather than as an amendment so as not to disturb heavily the natural environment while ensuring sustained productivity. Generally, 2–4 q/ha in furrows (10 per cent of LR based on simple SMP method) is suggested. The rate may be somewhat higher for fine texture and organic matter rich soils. The exact rate may be calculated for such soils by multiplying the 1/10th LR value with the liming factor of the zone in question.

METHOD OF APPLICATION

Methodology

Liming material of 80 mesh size used to correct the rhizosphere soil acidity, should be applied in furrows at 25–30 cm apart with a thin soil cover to serve as a barrier to the fertilizer to be applied over it, followed by seeding over a thin layer of soil as a cover-up. Integrated use of lime and fertilizer may be done with the help of seed-cum-fertilizer drill. For very dry soil, water should be sprinkled to get the best use of lime. Seasonal application of lime should be preceded by a soil test to ensure if the pH is < 5.5.

Frequency of Application

For crops and cropping sequences—rapeseed, mustard, greengram, soybean, groundnut, lentil, pea, pigeonpea, maize, etc. Any prevalent cropping system may be followed as lime is to be added to every crop.

Scope of Integrated Nutrient Management System (INMS) for Acid Soil Region

Application of lime helps in correcting soil acidity, but for attaining high yield potential liming has to be accompanied with optimal dose of NPK and other limiting nutrients especially sulphur and boron. In order to maximize and sustain productivity without deteriorating soil health it is suggested that nutrient management practices in acid soils should be tailored to bridge differences in nutrient supply and crops demand by judicious integration of chemical fertilizers, liming material, organic and green manure, crop residues and biofertilizers with limiting nutrient(s). Therefore, eco-friendly IPNS and management strategies need to be developed, tested and practiced in acid soils to break the yield barrier and to ensure sustained production.

Application of liming material @ 1/10th of lime requirement (LR) of soil (based on SMP method) in furrows integrated with organic manure at least @ 2 tonnes ha^{-1} together with 50 per cent recommended dose of NPK is suggested for soils of pH < 5.5 under rainfed/irrigated upland and medium land. Sulphur and boron application may also be supplemented wherever necessary. The recommendation is meant for seasonal application of lime as a fertilizer, but not as an amendment for various pulse/oilseed/vegetable crops of the acid soil region. Lime is recommended for furrow application to detoxify Al^{3+} in the rhizosphere zone.

REFERENCES

Barthakur HP. 1990. Management of acid soil. In agronomic research towards sustainable agriculture, p119–130. Singh KN and Singh RP (Eds), Indian Soc. Agro, Indian Agricultural Research Institute, New Delhi.

Laskar A and Dadhwal RS. 1981. Annual Report, ICAR Research Complex for NEH Region, Agartola Centre, Tripura.

Mandal SC, Sinha H, Prasad CR and Ali MA. 1966. Effect of placement of lime on crop production in an acid soil. *Sci. Cult.* **32**: 149.

Mathur BS and Lal S. 1987. Response of rice to rock phosphate in an alfisol of Chotanagpur Plateau in Bihar. *J. Indian Soc. Soil Sci.* **35**: 249–252.

Mathur BS, Rana NK and Lal S. 1991. Effect of rhizosphere application of lime on crop yield, soil properties, nutrient uptake and economics. *J. Indian Soc. Soil Sci*. **39:** 523–529.

Mathur BS, Rana NK, Singh H and Lal S. 1985. Lime as an effective source of fertilizer in acid red loam soils of Bihar. *J. Indian Soc. Soil Sci*. **33:** 328–332.

Mongia A, Singh NT, Mandal LN and Guha A. 1998. Effect of lime and phosphorus application on nutrient transformation in acid and acid sulphate soils under submergence. *J. Indian Soc. Soil Sci*. **46:** 18–22.

Panda N and Das JC 1971. Evaluation of lime sludge from paper mills as an amendment for acid soils. *Proc. Int. Symp. Acid Soil Manag*., Bhubaneswar. p236–242.

Panda N and Mishra UK. 1970.Use of partially acidulated rock phosphate as a possible means of minimizing phosphate fixation in acid soils. *Plant Soil*. **33:** 225–234.

Pradhan HS and Khera MS. 1976. Acid soils of India: Their genesis, characterization and management. *Bull. Indian Soc. Soil Sci*. **11:** 291.

Prasad RN, Dadhwal RS and Munna R. 1982. Suitable lime requirement methods for acid of Meghalaya. *J. Res. Assam Agric. Univ*. **3:** 131–135.

Prasad RN, Patiram, Barooah RC and Munna R. 1983. Direct and residual effect of lime on yield of maize and uptake of nutrients in acid soils of Meghalaya. *J. Indian Soc. Soil Sci*. **31:** 233.

Sahu, S.K.and Pal SS. 1987. Direct and residual effect of paper mill sludge and lime stone on crop yield under three different crop rotations on an acidic red soil. *J. Indian Soc. Soil Sci*. **35:** 46–51.

Sharma PD, Baruah TC, Maji AK and Patiram. 2006. Management of acid soils in NEH Region, ICAR Technical Bulletin.

Sharma PD and Sarkar AK. 2005. Managing acid soils for enhancing productivity. Publ. Director NBSS and LUP, Amravati Road, Nagpur, 440 010, India.

Management of Phosphorus-deficient Acid Soils for Increasing Productivity

Patiram, VK Sharma and Rajendra Singh

ABSTRACT

Deficiency of phosphorus is the most limiting factor in acid soils for crop productivity. Iron and aluminum phosphates dominate in acidic soils and Fe-P is least soluble among the inorganic forms and tends to increase at the expense of more soluble Ca and Al phosphates in acid soils. The low available phosphorus in acidic soil is caused by high potential of P fixation due to high content of amorphous Fe and Al. Enhancing crop production on P-deficient acid soils requires the good management of P supplying power of soils and to improve the ability of crop plants to acquire nutrients from the soil to enhance efficiency of biomass production.

Key words: Acidic soil, crop productivity, phosphorus.

INTRODUCTION

Phosphorus (P) is an essential macronutrient element required relatively large amounts by plants. Phosphorus constitutes about 0.2 per cent of a plant's dry weight. It is a key component of nucleic acids, phospholipids, and ATP, so plants cannot grow without sufficient supply of phosphorus from the soil. Phosphorus is also involved in controlling key enzyme reactions and in the regulation of metabolic pathways. Organic compounds that contain P are used to transfer energy from one reaction to drive another reaction within cells. Globally after N, P is the most frequently limiting macronutrient for plant growth especially on acid soils after soil acidity. Adequate P availability for plants stimulates early plant growth and hastens maturity.

Plants obtain their needed phosphorus from their external environment in a soluble ionic form. This circumstance has metabolic consequences since the availability of phosphorus in soil is highly influenced by soil pH. Phosphorus is most readily available at pH around 6.0 to 7.0. Phosphorus is taken up by plants as inorganic ions ($H_2PO_4^-$ and HPO_4^{2-}), which are present in the soil solution. These inorganic phosphate ions will readily react with iron, aluminium and manganese. Phosphorus is particularly problematic; under low pH (pH < 5.5) and high aluminium concentration it is fixed as insoluble iron and aluminium phosphates. Thus, acid soils may have high total phosphorus but low available phosphorus. The more acid the soil, there is greater the reactivity of Al and Fe and the greater degree of phosphorus fixation.

PHOSPHORUS IN ACID SOILS

In soils P exists in organic and inorganic forms. The relative amounts of two forms of phosphorus vary greatly from soil to soil and organic form usually increases with increasing soil organic matter. Therefore, proportion of organic P is higher in surface soils as compared to subsurface soils. The organic P frequently varies from 20 to 80 per cent of the total P (Brady 1999). Of the organic P compounds identified so far, inositol $[C_6H_6(OH)_6]$ phosphate forms the major part (10–50 per cent of total) and nucleic acids and phospholipids can be present in lesser portion. Inositol phosphates are esters of phosphoric acid and inositol, a cyclic hex-carbon with an alcohol group at each C atom. The mineralization of organic P-compounds to inorganic forms is a necessary prerequisite for their availability to plants. Actual contribution of organic P to plant nutrition in practice is difficult, however, easily mineralizable organic P can contribute significantly to plant P nutrition. The mineralization of organic P is favoured in rhizosphere soil caused by exudation of certain enzymes by plant roots.

Almost all inorganic phosphorus is found in soils into two groups: (1) compounds of calcium and (2) those containing iron and aluminium. In calcareous and alkaline soils inorganic P exists as hydroxyapatite, chloroapatite, fluorapatite, carbonate apatite, wagnerite, wavellite and strengite. The native P in calcareous soils persists in all the inorganic forms with small fraction in organic form. Iron and aluminium phosphates dominate in acidic soils and calcium phosphate dominate in soils having pH 6.5 and above. Fe-P which is least soluble among the inorganic forms and tends to increase at the expense of more soluble Ca and Al phosphates in acid soils. The residual P fraction is made up of Fe and Al phosphates occluded in iron oxides coatings. Older and highly weathered acidic soils tend to contain more residual P depending on iron oxides present.

Most of the tropical and subtropical humid acid soils are low in available phosphorus caused by high potential of P fixation due to high content of amorphous Fe and Al. In acid soils, P is one of the least available nutrients. In some soils, the total content P may be as high as in productive soils having comparative low P fixation potential. When fertilizer P is added in acid soils, it reacts with Ca, Fe, and Al ions from the soil. Phosphate in acid soils reacts with Al and Fe in solution and form insoluble precipitate, and chemically bonded to the surface of Fe and Al oxides by specific chemical bonds. The high phosphorus fixation capacity of some tropical soils is related to the high affinity of the minerals surface for phosphorus. The reaction may be regarded as partly a displacement of water molecules and partly a displacement of hydroxyls, so that negative charge conveyed to the surface is usually lower than the charge on the anion (Barrow 1980). Soils with high amorphous oxides of Fe and Al adsorb the largest quantities of phosphorus (Patiram *et al.* 1990). The availability of soil P is negatively related to P adsorption capacity and P energy of adsorption (Patiram and Prasad 1991).

SYMPTOMS OF PHOSPHORUS-DEFICIENT PLANTS

Adequate supply of P allows the processes described above at optimum rates and growth and development of the plant to proceed at a normal rate. When P is limiting, most of the available P is concentrated in the roots, and top growth may be reduced. The most striking effect of limited supply of P is a reduction in leaf expansion and leaf surface area, as well as number of leaves. Inadequate supply of P slows the process of carbohydrate utilization and its production through photosynthesis. This results in a build up of carbohydrates, and development of a dark green leaf colour. In some plants (e.g. maize and tomato), P-deficient leaves develop a purple colour from the accumulation of unused sugar. Since P is highly mobilized in the plant and transported from the older part to active growing portion, resulting in foliar deficiency symptoms appearing on the older (lower) portion of the plant. Older leaves in P-deficient plants are often purple because of the accumulation of anthocyanins (purple pigments).

The influence of P on crop maturity has been observed in many crops. The deficiency of P delays the crop maturity. The early maturity of fruits and vegetables provide high price in the market. The inadequate supply of P to plants reduced the quality of forage, fruit, and vegetable and grain crops. The deficiency of P reduces the plant root activity and proliferation, thereby reduces the volume of soil from which root extract water and nutrient. Thus phosphorus increases water use efficiency (WUE) and drought tolerance of crops in moisture stress. Phosphorus improves the resistance and tolerance to diseases that can reduce the crop yield and quality.

MANAGEMENT OF PHOSPHORUS PROBLEMS IN ACID SOILS

In acidic soils, the production potential cannot be realized by simple application of irrigation water and other soil amendments. Enhancing crop production on P-deficient acid soils requires the good management of P supplying power of soils and to improve the ability of crop plants to acquire nutrients from the soil to enhance efficiency of biomass production. Some plants with superior ability to acquire nutrients to their maximum capacity under conditions of low nutrient availability due to their root traits. The problems of P fixation in acidic soils, high clay, and high sesquioxide (R_2O_3) soil can be reduced by a number of management practices.

USE OF PHOSPHORUS FERTILIZERS

It has been recognized that in P fertilization, only a small portion say, about 10–20% of the applied P is absorbed by crop and remainder is fixed in soil in different relatively insoluble forms. Most of the acidic soils respond to the addition of phosphate fertilizers and magnitude and rate depend on relative amount of available P present and P fixing capacity of soil. In most of annual crops, presence of adequate concentration of P in the rhizosphere is necessary for initial stages of growth and development of reproductive organs in later stages.

The use of low solubility P fertilizers reduces the inordinate amount of phosphorus fixed by tropical high P fixing acid soils. The direct application of phosphate rock (PR) in acid soils as a source of fertilizer P has been employed with varying degrees from twentieth century. However, relative effectiveness of PR markedly reduces when liming materials are applied to decrease soil acidity and increase soil calcium levels. High yield of crops cannot be obtained by applying PR, however, it is suitable for many acid soils where very high yields are not objective and sulphur is not deficient, because it is the cheapest source of P.

Over the years, soil acidity has been considered as the single most important agent responsible for enhanced availability of P in PR materials. The quality of PR is the most important for its direct application as a source P in acid soils. In acidic low soil pH, fracolite-type apatites are quite unstable, and they release P to react with Al and Fe in soil constituents. The formed Al and Fe-compounds are more stable than apatites at lower pH levels. The negative effect of excessive soil acidity on growth of certain crops may override its positive effect of PR dissolution. The soil's affinity for calcium promotes the dissolution of PR because it provides a sink for the Ca that is released by the congruous dissolution of apatite. This condition is met in acid soils which are low in base saturation. The pH of acid soils rises sharply after flooding and reaches levels that are mostly related to the bases released by the reducing condition, which involve CO_3^{2-}/HCO_3^- ions. However, the calcium saturation in waterlogged soil remains low even at elevated pH almost equal to initially acid soil.

As an effective P fertilizer, PR is limited to soils that are severely to moderately deficient in P. It has got almost nil value in soils of medium to high P status. The application of organic matter enhances the availability of PR related to provide effective sink for Ca. Inorganic P released from PR can be incorporated into the organic pool of P, which later on provide P to plants by mineralization.

LIMING OF ACID SOILS

Liming of acid soils is the common practice to increase the availability of soil phosphorus. It has been found that even without reducing the P fixation capacity of soils, liming increases the phosphorus uptake by plants caused by other corrective effects such as calcium deficiency, Al toxicity, and micronutrient imbalances.

Liming reduces the phosphorus fixation capacity of 2:1 clay minerals, in which acidity releases free Al. Applied P is then precipitated as Al-P, so that the application of lime eliminates the soluble Al, thereby has the direct and important effect on P-fixation. Liming increases P uptake, probably due to improved root growth, although increased mineralization and subsequent supply of P from organic matter may have also contribution.

PLACEMENT OF FERTILIZER

The advantage of banding phosphate fertilizers is well-known. Small amount of fertilizer placed in bands or rows is beneficial as compared to fertilizer is broadcasted in high P fixing soils. However, there may be no difference in low P fixing soils. Placement of P fertilizer is most important in soils low in available phosphorus that adsorbed or fixed high quantities of added fertilizer. The practical importance of band/row application of fertilizer is to maintain identical concentration of P in solution to the concentration that gives maximum yield in broadcast application. Placement is more important only at suboptimum levels of P application. On soils high phosphorus fixing capacity, it is more important to restrict the P adsorption in small volume of soil.

The importance of band application is that it gives the information if a farmer has a limited amount of P to be applied in acid soil. The knowledge of the concentration of P in soil solution necessary to obtain maximum yield of crop, the rate of P can be obtained from adsorption isotherm in order to achieve the highest yield possible for that amount of fertilizer. It requires full testing in the high P fixing capacity of soils from the view of farmers' perspectives.

APPLICATION OF ORGANIC MATTER

Negatively charged, high molecular weight, humic polymers can form strong bonds with metal hydrous oxides surfaces through both electrostatic bonding (anion exchange) and specific adsorption, i.e. ligand exchange (Stevenson 1994). Anion exchange is possible on the positive sites of amphoteric Fe and Al oxide surfaces and ligand exchange occurs through displacement of $OH_2^{0.5+}$ and $OH^{0.5-}$ groups on the humic molecules and results in strong bonding of the humic materials to hydrous oxides. Since humic molecules are specifically adsorbed onto oxide surfaces they have competitive effect on P adsorption.

The application of organic matter reduce the P adsorption and increase the P availability caused by release of inorganic P from organic residues, blockage of P adsorption sites by organic molecules released, rise in soil pH during decomposition and complexation of soluble Al and Fe by organic molecules. The use of farmyard manure and other forms of organic matter can also change plant available nutrients by changing both the physical and biological characteristics of the soil. In many circumstances, these changes improve soil physical structure and water holding capacity, resulting in more extensive root development and enhance soil microflora and fauna activity, all of which influence nutrient availability to plants.

Application of organic manures improves the solubility of sparingly P components in soils and enhances the utilization of P from fertilizers. Organic manures are also highly beneficial in acid soils and contribute the alleviation of adverse effects Al toxicity on crop production (Patiram 1996) and increase the concentration of soluble P.

INTRODUCTION OF MYCORRHIZAE FOR EFFICIENT PHOSPHORUS UPTAKE

In more than 90 per cent plants, symbiotic associations are formed with mycorrhizal fungi. The fungal hyphae play an important role in the acquisition of P for the plants (Smith and Read 1997). The mycorrhizal symbiosis is a mutuality exchange of C from plant in return for P and other mineral nutrients from the fungus. Influx of P in roots colonized by mycorrhizal fungi can be 3 to 5 times higher (rates of 10^{-11} mol m^{-1}s^{-1}) than in nonmycorrhizal roots (Smith and Read 1997). The extensive network of hyphae from the root, enables the plant to explore a greater volume of soil to overcome the limitations imposed by the slow diffusion of P in the soil. Cassava (*Manihot esculenta* Crantz) which grows well in acidic soils of deficient in phosphorus availability is highly dependent on it mycorrhizae on its roots. It may be of great benefit in cropping systems that include a perennial crop where a long time period for the development of symbiosis is possible. There is a great challenge in managing mycorrhizal for annual crops such that the soil is adequately inoculated, plant infection and mycorrhizal development occur in a timely fashion, and a highly functional symbiosis develops (Sinclair and Vandez 2002).

ADAPTATION OF PLANT TO PHOSPHORUS STRESS

The persistent low concentration of P in soil solution has led to numerous morphological, physiological, biochemical and molecular adaptations by plants to survive in the nature. Plants have evolved a number of adaptive mechanisms for growth on low P soils, and these include the exudation of several solutes from roots, including organic acids, phosphatases, and other compounds that may mobilize P from bound P pools in the soil (especially Fe-P, Al-P compounds, and organic phosphate esters) and thus contribute to P efficiency in plants. Plant species and genotypes of a given species develop diverse adaptive responses develop two major mechanisms: (i) P acquisition (root morphology, root exudation and P uptake mechanisms) and (ii) P utilization (internal mechanisms associated with better use of absorbed P at cellular level (Marschner 1995, Ragothama 1999).

ROOT CHARACTERISTICS

Plant root geometry and morphology are important for maximizing P uptake, a vigorous, highly branched root system with many growing points will more effectively explore a large volume soil to maximize P uptake (Lynch and Beebe 1995). Yan *et al.* (1996) reported that those common bean genotypes that performed well on low P available soils were those that produced the greatest root mass. Proteoid or cluster root formation is closely related to P deficiency in a number of plant species. Proteoid roots are highly efficient in synthesis and secretion of organic acids to the rhizosphere (Dinkelaker *et al.* 1995), which enhance the release of inorganic P (Pi) from calcium, iron and aluminium phosphates in the rhizosphere.

Root hairs greatly contribute to the ability of roots to take up mineral nutrients from the soil. Plants possessing a high root hair response to limited available soil P conditions are able to use in larger amounts than that have poor ability to proliferate root hairs. Therefore, increasing attention should be paid to the research aiming at developing to exploit the genetic variation in many crop species for root traits associated with high ability to acquire nutrients that are growth limiting under P-deficient soil conditions.

RELEASE OF PHOSPHATASE ENZYMES

In cultivated soils most of total exists in the form of organic P (Dalal 1977). Some plants, are able to activate extracellular enzymes including both acid phosphatases and phytases. Phosphatases under P stress are produced by root associated microbes or can be secreted into the rhizosphere by the root themselves in the absence of microbes. They can play important role in catalytic hydrolysis of organic P from phytate and subsequently acquisition of soil P by plants. Richardson *et al.* (2001) suggested that the phytase activity around plant roots is a significant factor in utilizing P from phytate in soils. Therefore, developing plants that over express extracellular phytases and other phosphatases is in an important challenge in future.

PRODUCTION OF ORGANIC ACID IN RHIZOSPHERE

Plants exude wide variety of organic and inorganic compounds into the rhizosphere to change the chemistry and biology of the rhizosphere and enhance adaptation to a particular environment (Ryan and Delhaize 2001) and has played a significant role in the distribution of plant species in various ecosystems. There is evidence that plant species which exude organic acids differ from other species in their ability to access various pools of soil P as a result of the changes in rhizosphere pH. The most important role of organic acid exudation to increase the availability of P in deficient soils may be the result of organic anions to complex with Al or Fe, resulting in increased solubilization of Al-P and Fe-P compounds. Citrate, malate and oxalate anions exudated by several acid tolerant grass and cereal genotypes, appear to be effective in forming complexes with Al (Jones 1998) and picric acid and its derivatives exuded from pigeonpea roots forming Fe complexes (Ae *et al.* 1990) enhance the P availability to roots.

GENETIC CONTROL OF PHOSPHORUS STRESS

There are number of reports on genetic variability for different traits associated with enhance P-acquisition ability. Phosphate deficiency results in distinct changes in gene expression (Raghothama 1999). Some of these altered gene products may serve as molecular determinants of plant adaptation to P deficiency. The genes coding for proteins under P-stress possess the distinct role. Use of markers in breeding programmes can range from facilitating appropriate choice for parent for crosses. Genetic improvement through biotechnology need conventional breeding for the selection of improved genotype parents and field testing across locations or cropping systems over the years caused by genotype-by-environment interaction. However, the P efficient lines of maize identified at Embrapa-Milhoe Sorgo are not tolerant to Al toxicity and the P inefficient lines are tolerant to Al toxicity. Thus, it is necessary to select Al tolerant cultivars with more efficient in P uptake with greater yield stability. Selections of crops and varieties that will grow well under conditions of low P availability constitute an important management strategy in acid soils.

CONCLUSION

Some plants with superior ability to acquire nutrients to their maximum capacity under conditions of low nutrient availability due to their root traits, root symbiotic associations with mycorrhizal fungi, production of organic acid in the rhizosphere, and genetical characteristics of the plants. These plant traits can be utilized to develop plants of superior ability to utilized the phosphorus in acid soils low in available P.

REFERENCES

Ae N, Arihara J, Okada K, Oshihara T and Johansen C. 1990. Phosphorus uptake by pigeonpea and its role in cropping systems of the Indian subcontinent. *Sci.* **248:** 477–480.

Barrow NJ. 1980. Evaluation and utilization of residual phosphorus in soils. In the Role of phosphorus in agriculture, p333–356. ASA-CSSA–SSSA, 667, South Segoe, Madson, WI, USA.

Brady NC. 1999. The nature and properties of soils. Tenth Edition. Mcmillan Publishing Comp., New York.

Dalal RC. 1977. Soil organic phosphorus. *Adv. Agron.* **29:** 85–117.

Dinkelaker B, Römheld V and Marschner H. 1995. Distribution and function of proteide roots and other root clusters. *Bot. Acta.* **108:** 183–200.

Jones DL. 1998. Organic acids in the rhizosphere- a critical review. *Plant Soil.* **205:** 25–44.

Lynch JP and Beebe SE 1995. Adaptation of beans (*Phaseolus vulgaris* L.) to low phosphorus availability. *Hort Sci.* **30:** 1165–1171.

Marschner H. 1995. Mineral nutrition of higher Plants. Academic Press, London.

Patiram. 1996. Effect of limestone and farmyard manure on crop yields and soil acidity on an inceptisols in Sikkim. *Trop. Agric* (Trinidad). **73:** 238–241.

Patiram and Prasad RN. 1991. Growth of maize and phosphorus uptake in relation to phosphate adsorption characteristics of acid soils. *J. Indian Soc. Soil Sci.* **39:** 302–307.

Patiram, Rai RN and Prasad RN. 1990. Phosphate adsorption by acid soils from different altitude. *J. Indian Soc. Soil Sci.* **38:** 602–608.

Ragothama KG. 1999. Phosphate acquisition. *Ann. Rev. Pl. Physiol. Pl. Mol. Biol.* **50:** 665–693.

Richardson AE, Hadobas PA and Hayes JE. 2001. Extracellular secretion of Aspergillus phytase from *Arabidopsis* roots enables plants to obtain phosphorus from phytate. *Plant J.* **25:** 641–649.

Ryan PR and Delhaize E. 2001. Function and mechanism of organic anio exudation from plant roots. *Ann. Rev. Pl. Physiol. Pl. Mol. Biol.* **52:** 527–560.

Sinclair TR and Vandez V. 2002. Physiological traits for crop yield improvement in N and P environments. *Plant Soil.* **245:** 1–15.

Smith SE and Read DJ. 1997. Mycorrhizal Symbiosis. Academic Press, London. 605 p.

Stevenson FJ. 1994. Humus chemistry: Genesis, composition, reaction. Wiley, New York.

Yan X, Lynch JP and Beebe SE. 1996. Utilization of phosphorus substrates by common bean genotypes. *Crop Sci.* **36:** 936–941.

Patiram

ABSTRACT

The strong acidic nature of acid sulphate soils induce aluminium (Al) and iron (Fe) toxicities and nutrient deficiencies, particularly of phosphate (P). So acid sulphate soils are frequently associated with unfavourable characteristics for agricultural production in most cases, the important crop is rice which is known to tolerate relatively high acidity. The acid sulphate soils can be productive by reducing harmful effects of toxic substance produce in soil, such as preventing the oxidation of pyrites contained in potentially acid sulfate sediments by ground water control; leaching harmful substances out of the rooting zone after allowing oxidation to occur; and inactivating aluminium and reducing the concentration of ferrous iron in the soil solution by raising the pH through liming.

Key words: Acid sulphate soils, nutrient deficiencies, productivity.

INTRODUCTION

Acid sulphate soils are found worldwide and mostly occur in tropical regions in coastal areas at low altitude developed from pyrite containing marine sediments (Pons 1973). It is estimated that acid sulphate soils occupy an area of 12.5 million hectares (FAO/UNESCO 1979). In India, acid sulphate soils occupy only a limited area of about 25,000 hectares in the state Kerala (Abrol 1990). However, Bandopadhyay and Sarkar (1987) reported 0. 5 million hectares potential acid saline sulphate soils in coastal area of Sundarbans of West Bengal. The land form in Kerala is nearly flat along the sea coast and soils are spread within width of about 25 km from the sea and 80 per cent soils are located in Ernakulam district only and called 'Kari' soil locally. The soils possess high salt content throughout the profile with dominance of chlorides and sulphates of Na, Mg and Ca with low pH (2.5 to 7.0) and a shallow saline water table. Nature of some acid sulphate soils in Sundarbans is given in Table 17.1.

In the coastal lowlands of Southeast Asia, it is found in two environments: (1) supports mangroves in a brackish water environment, and (2) swamp forest in a

Table 17.1: *Chemical characteristics of acid sulphate soils of Sundarbans area (Pal et al. 1991)*

Location	pH	ECE (dS/m)	CEC (me/100 g)	Org.C (%)	Soluble salts (me/kg)				
					Bases*	Al^{3+}	HCO_3^-	Cl^-	SO_4^{2-}
Nirdeshkhali-1	4.7	1.65	23.0	0.58	1.19	0.1	0.59	1.8	2.6
Nirdeshkhali-2	3.3	3.15	23.1	0.63	3.2	0.2	0.50	2.6	6.4
Nirdeshkhali-3	4.5	1.55	23.5	0.73	2.9	0.1	0.50	1.7	2.1
Nirdeshkhali-4	3.5	2.20	18.8	0.64	1.7	0.3	0.38	2.6	2.5
Nirdeshkhali-5	3.5	3.70	23.2	0.63	4.5	0.1	0.26	3.3	4.4
Nirdeshkhali-6	5.9	0.95	26.3	0.60	0.9	0.1	0.38	0.3	0.9
Nirdeshkhali-7	3.4	3.00	26.5	0.50	2.5	0.1	0.13	2.1	4.9
Nirdeshkhali-8	3.5	2.10	18.5	0.69	1.1	0.1	0.08	0.3	0.9
Shimultala-1	4.8	1.50	23.8	0.40	2.0	0.1	0.39	1.3	2.0
Shimultala-2	4.6	2.20	27.1	0.55	3.3	0.1	0.31	3.0	2.3
Shimultala-3	4.4	2.65	27.2	0.75	2.5	0.1	0.30	4.2	2.2
Shimultala-4	4.6	1.65	21.3	0.52	3.0	0.1	0.28	2.8	1.8
Malancha	4.4	3.00	25.2	1.06	3.7	0.1	0.51	4.8	2.7
Amjhara	4.8	2.55	23.9	0.52	2.3	0.1	0.42	5.5	1.8
Rajbari	4.4	3.20	26.9	0.67	2.9	0.1	0.39	4.6	4.0
Canning	3.6	6.25	25.9	0.59	7.5	0.2	0.20	7.5	5.7

*Sum of Ca, Mg and Na.

freshwater environment. As the mud is exposed to the air, either by natural land accretion or by artificial drainage, these sulfide materials undergo oxidation. As a result, sulphuric acid then forms, leading to strong soil acidity. Most of the areas are located in densely populated countries, where rice is the main diet, especially in the coastal areas of Southeast Asia and West Africa. The complex interaction between production of harmful substances affecting plant growth and alternate flooding and oxidation of soil is only left for rice cultivation. In Thailand, rice is cultivated around 1.5 million hectares in acid sulphate soils. It is not easy to get rid of these harmful oxidation products, whether by washing the sediments or by applying liming materials. As a result, very often the land is abandoned after a short period of utilization, reverting to brackish water swamps. The strong acidic nature of acid sulphate soils induce aluminium (Al) and iron (Fe) toxicities and nutrient deficiencies, particularly of phosphate (P).

FORMATION OF ACID SULPHATE SOILS

Acid sulphate soils are formed as a result of the oxidation of sulphide-containing sediments when exposed to the atmosphere, in the course of natural land accretion or in the process of artificial land reclamation. The land system suitable for the formation of potential acidity is saline and brackish swamps and marshes, saline and brackish lagoons and lakes, and sometimes poorly drained inland valleys receiving water high in sulphur. The general conditions that lead to the formation of sulphide-containing sediments are:

- The presence of marine or brackish water as the source of sulphate,
- Stagnation of water, as typically found in lagoons and bays and,
- A supply of decomposable organic matter.

The saline and brackish swamps and marshes, saline and brackish lagoons and lakes, support the highly productive herbaceous vegetation of mangrove swamps (*Rhizophora* sp. and *Avicennia* sp.) which provide the organic energy source needed for pyrite formation. Sediments and dissolved sulphate are produced by tidal cycles, which also serve to remove some soluble by-products of pyrite formation. The last condition is also favoured by the second. The stagnation of water facilitates the establishment of vegetation such as mangroves. The slow build-up of coastal land by silting may be counted as another condition that favours the formation of sulphide-containing sediments. Pyrite formation requires (Prasittikhet and Gambrell 1990):

- Sulphide derived from the reduction of S in anaerobic sediments by sulphate reducing bacteria (*Desulfovibrio desulfuricans*),
- Soluble ferrous iron from the reduction of insoluble ferric compounds in sediments,
- Organic matter to provide energy for bacteria, and
- An alternate aerobic-anaerobic soil or sediment environment during the pyrite formation process or at least some period of sediment oxidation during predominantly anaerobic conditions.

It is known that the greater part of these oxidizable sulfide compounds are present in the form of pyrite (FeS_2) and comparatively more stable than ferrous sulphide, (FeS). The pyrite is the basis of potential acid sulphate soils development varies from 2–10 per cent (Van Breemen 1982). Elemental sulphur may occur after the partial oxidation of sulphide to S. This process is mainly anaerobic, and limited to alternate aerobic process caused by zone of tidal fluctuation. According to Stumm and Morgan (1970) however, under acid conditions, elemental sulphur is formed as a result of the reduction of SO_4^{2-} as an intermediate product. Once formed, it may persist as a stable solid phase in recent marine sediments.

Upon exposure to the air, pyrite undergoes oxidation as follows:

$$FeS_2(s) + (7/2)O_2 + H_2O = Fe^{2+} + 2SO_4^{2-} + 2H^+ \qquad \qquad ...(1)$$

The ferrous iron is further oxidized to ferric iron and gets precipitated if the environmental pH is higher than about 3.

$$Fe^{2+} + (1/4)O_2 + H^+ = Fe^{3+} + (1/2)H_2O \qquad \qquad ...(2)$$

$$Fe^{3+} + 3H_2O = Fe(OH)_3(s) + 3H^+ \qquad \qquad ...(3)$$

The overall reaction is:

$$FeS_2(s) + (15/4)O_2 + (7/2)H_2O = Fe(OH)_3(s) + 2SO_4^{2-} + 4H^+ \qquad \qquad ...(4)$$

Thus, four equivalents of acidity are produced from the oxidation of one mole of pyrite.

It is known that the reaction (2) is a slow process if it proceeds in a purely chemical fashion. At a pH of 3.0, the half life of this reaction is around 1000 days (Stumm and Morgan 1970). In the soil, however, this reaction is mediated by autotrophic iron bacteria, *Thiobacillus ferrooxidans* and *Ferrobacillus ferrooxidans*, and proceeds much faster. The oxidation of pyrite also occurs by Fe^{3+},

$$FeS_2 + 14Fe^{3+} + 8H_2O = 15Fe^{2+} + 16H^+ + 2SO_4^{2-}$$

This produces even more acidity and reaction is quite rapid. The oxidation of sulphur in this reaction is mediated by another autotrophic bacterium, *Thiobacillus thiooxidans*.

$$S + (1/2)O_2 + H_2O = SO_4^{2-} + 2H^+$$

Jarosite is an intermediate oxidation product of ferrous sulphate in an acid medium:

$$Fe^{2+} + SO_4^{2-} + (1/4)O_2 + (3/2)H_2O + (1/3)K = (1/3)KFe_3(SO_4)2(OH)_6 + H^+ + (1/3)SO_4^{2-}$$

Jarosite appears in the pores and cracks of the soil as pale yellow (or straw yellow) mottles, and is an indicative of acid sulfate soils. Jarosite is further hydrolyzed in a less acidic medium, finally to precipitate iron as hydrated ferric oxides, releasing more acidity:

$$2KFe_3(SO_4)2(OH)_6 + 6H_2O = K_2SO_4 + 6Fe(OH)_3 + 3H_2SO_4$$

The acidity produced by pyrite oxidation may be neutralized if there is a large amount of lime ($CaCO_3$) contained in the sediment or brought in by water. In some coastal areas, plenty of fine gypsum crystals can be seen in the soil as the result of a neutralization reaction. However, in most of the humid tropics, the carbonate content is low or nil. Acidity remains in the soil to give a pH sometimes as low as 3.0.

FERTILITY STRESS IN ACID SULPHATE SOILS

Acid sulphate soils frequently associated with unfavourable characteristics for agricultural production in most cases, the important crop is rice which is known to tolerate relatively high acidity. The suitability of soils for rice production depends on the potential/actual acidity conditions and available management practices available to overcome the soil chemical problems. Aluminium toxicity in soils may

occur at pH levels below 5.0 for seedlings, but older plants do not show symptoms until the pH drops to near 4.0 and below. A number of processes, including precipitation of Al-P in the rhizosphere or impairing P utilization by the plant. Therefore, the low availability of P also favours the Al toxicity.

Under such a low pH, aluminum toxicity may be more important than the direct effect of hydrogen ion concentrations. A low pH and/or reducing environment favours the elevated level of reduced soluble ferrous iron and is an important factor affecting plant growth (Nhung and Ponnamperuma 1966). It is known that iron toxicity results from a complex nutrient imbalance (availability of iron relative to low available levels of Ca, Mg, K and P), but still the high ferrous ion concentration, coupled with high acidity and/or high salinity, may be an important element of the disorder frequently found in acid sulfate soils.

Of all the nutrient elements, probably phosphorus (P) is the most critical in acid sulphate soils. In addition to the inherent lack of P in these soils, the high activity of aluminum lowers the availability of P to rice. Phosphorus is so acutely deficient in some soils that no response, even to lime and nitrogen (N), can be expected, unless P is applied. The application of lime and phosphorus favours the increased supply of N by enhancing ammonification. Matsuguchi *et al.* (1970) found that applying lime and phosphate definitely increased the amount of biologically fixed N. Thus in many acid sulphate soils, P are the limiting factor for the increased growth and yield of rice.

The sulphides are produced under highly reduced condition from sulphate and inhibit respiration in rice caused by reduction of oxidizing power of roots. The concentration of sulphides tend to decrease with the production of high concentration of ferrous iron as FeS and high soil pH and organic matter content favour it. The elevated concentration of salts in saltwater tidal areas other than salinity problems, favour the plants to other toxic ions such as Fe and Al in solution by weakening the plant.

RECLAMATION OF ACID SULPHATE SOILS FOR RICE PRODUCTION

Potential acid sulphates soils do not get acidify where frequent tidal flooding occurs. Because it prevents the extended period of aeration required for pyrite oxidation. The effective management practices may include in reducing the harmful effects of toxic substances:

- Preventing the oxidation of pyrites contained in potentially acid sulphate sediments by ground water control,
- Leaching harmful substances out of the rooting zone after allowing oxidation to occur, and
- Inactivating aluminum and reducing the concentration of ferrous iron in the soil solution by raising the pH by liming.

However, the first measure, preventing the oxidation of pyrite, is not a positive solution to the acid sulphate soil problem. It suppresses the natural ripening process of the mud (potential acid sulphate sediments). The soil would still have strongly reducing conditions and be very difficult to work, the rice yield would be very low, and yet no positive measures for yield improvement could be taken.

The second measure, leaching out harmful substance, can be used only where there is good drainage. Most of the areas are low-lying, and natural drainage is severely restricted. During the rainy season, the entire land surface is submerged. During the dry season, however, the top 5–10 cm of soil become dry and upward movement of water cancels out this effect, bringing the toxic substances back to the surface. The minimum requirement for the reclamation of acid sulfate soils is to dig open ditches for drainage and prevent oxidation. The success of sea water leaching depends on soil permeability and groundwater hydrology with managed drainage to allow leaching, and fresh water must be available for a final leaching to reduce salinity to acceptable levels. This investment would certainly reinforce the washing effect during the rainy season, but it is not effective at all during the dry season unless there is an ample supply of fresh water. This is generally difficult to obtain in a monsoon climate zone.

In areas with a permanently humid climate of Sarawak, East Malaysia, leaching first with sea water or brackish water, followed by leaching with plenty of rainwater, could be an effective way of reclaiming acid sulfate soil. This method of soil amelioration has been adopted in Sierra Leone in West Africa, with some success. The *surjan* system in Indonesia, with broad ridges (*guludan*) and shallow furrows (*tabukan*), is a time-honored local practice for the utilization of acid sulfate soils.

The third measure, liming, is effective in raising the soil pH to precipitates the toxic aluminium. The lime requirement for the reclamation of soils is very high and also a recurring inputs beyond the capacity of the poor and marginal farmers. Van Breemen and Pons (1978) calculated that complete neutralization of the acidity generated in the uppermost 50 cm of soil containing 3 per cent pyrite would require 150 t ha^{-1} of lime, even when half the acidity is removed by leaching. Moreover, it must not be forgotten that acidity is generated only slowly upon exposure of pyritic mud to the air during the dry season. This means that the lime applications have to be repeated year after year for a long time.

Another point to be considered is that the oxidation of pyrite, the dominant form of oxidizable sulphur, is retarded if the pH is higher than 3.0. Therefore, if lime is applied at the beginning of reclamation, the time required to leach out the toxic products of oxidation would be prolonged. Thus, liming should be carried out only after oxidation and leaching are quite advanced. In Thailand, liming is recommended in amounts just high enough to inactivate aluminium (Komes 1973). When soil pH raised above 5.5 causes the reduction of sulphate in the rooting zone (van Breeman 1975). However, rice in acid sulphate soils usually do not suffer from the harmful effects of hydrogen sulphide because sulphate reduction is rather rare due to relatively higher enough to suppress sulphate reduction.

The application of phosphate fertilizers may be effective in suppressing Al toxicity in rice. Attanandana *et al.* (1982) demonstrated that in a high-phosphate plot, Al taken up by rice was concentrated in the epidermis of rice roots along with the P observing by an X-ray microanalyzer, They suggested that phosphates applied to the vicinity of rice roots could be effective in suppressing Al toxicity as compared with a homogeneous application of the same amount of phosphate. The use of ground phosphate rocks may be effective as the source of P.

OTHER OPTION

In Malaysia, oil palm is performing well under careful reclamation on soils where the toxic layers occur below 75 cm and water table is controlled to minimize oxidation of the sulphidic horizon. There is good prospect to utilize this land for aquaculture.

REFERENCES

Abrol IP. 1990. Problem soil in India. In Problem of soils in Asia and Pacific. Report of the Expert Consultation of the Asian Network on Problem soils, p153–165. Regional Office for Asia and Pacific (RAPA), FAO of United Nation, Bangkok.

Attanandana T, Vacharotayan S and Kyuma K. 1982. Fertility problems of acid sulphate soils of Thailand, pC1-1–C1-9. First Int. Symp. on soil, geology and landforms-impact on land use planning in developling countries, Bangkok.

Bandyopadhyay AK and Sarkar D. 1987. Occurrence of acid saline soils in coastal area in Sundarbans area of West Bengal. *J. Indian Soc. Soil Sci.* **35:** 542–544.

FAO/UNESCO. 1979. Soil map of the world, scale 1:5,000,000. Vols. I-X, UNESCO, Paris.

Komes A. 1973. The Reclamation of some problem soils in Thailand. Soils of the ASPAC Region; Part 5. Thailand. Tech. Bull. No. 14, Food and Fertilizer Technology Center, Taipei, Taiwan ROC.

Matsuguchi T, Tangcham B and Pakiyuth S. 1970. Nitrogen-fixing microflora and its activity in paddy soil of Thailand. Proc., 1st Asean Soil Conf. Bangkok, Thailand.

Nhung MM and Ponnampruma FN 1966. Effect of calcium carbonate, manganese dioxide, ferric hydroxide and prolonged flooding on chemical and electrochemical change and growth of rice in a flooded acid sulfate soil. *Soil Sci.* **102:** 29–41.

Pal S, Laskar BK, De GK and Debnath NC. 1991. Nature of some acid sulphate soils occurring in the coastal area of West Bengal. *J. Indian Soc. Soil Sci.* **39:** 56–62.

Pons LJ. 1973. Outline of genesis, classification and improvement of acid sulphate soils. In Acid Sulphate Soils, p3–17. Dost H (Ed), Proc. *Int. Symp.* ILRI Wageningen, The Netherlands.

Prasittikhet J and Gambrell RP. 1990. Acid sulphate soils. In Advances in Environmental Science, p35–82. Adriano DC and Salomons W (Eds), Spriger-Verlag, New York.

Stumm W and Morgan JJ. 1970. Aquatic Chemistry: An Introduction, Emphasizing Chemical Equilibria in Natural Waters. John Wiley and Sons, NY.

Van Breemen. N. 1975. Acidification and deacidification of coastal plain soils as a result of periodic flooding. *Soil Sci. Soc. Am. Proc.* **39**: 1153–1157.

Van Breemen N. 1982. Acidification and deacidification of coastal plant soils as a result of periodic flooding. In Acid Sulphate Weathering, p95–108. Kittrick JA, Fanning DS and Hossner LR (Eds). Sep. Pub. 10, SSSA, Madison, WI.

Van Breemen N and Pons LJ. 1978. Acid sulfate soils and rice. In Soils and Rice, p739–761 IRRI (Ed). IRRI, Los Banos, Philippines.